The Panorama
of the Renaissance

EDITED BY MARGARET ASTON

The Panorama

of the Renaissance

WITH OVER 1000 IMAGES

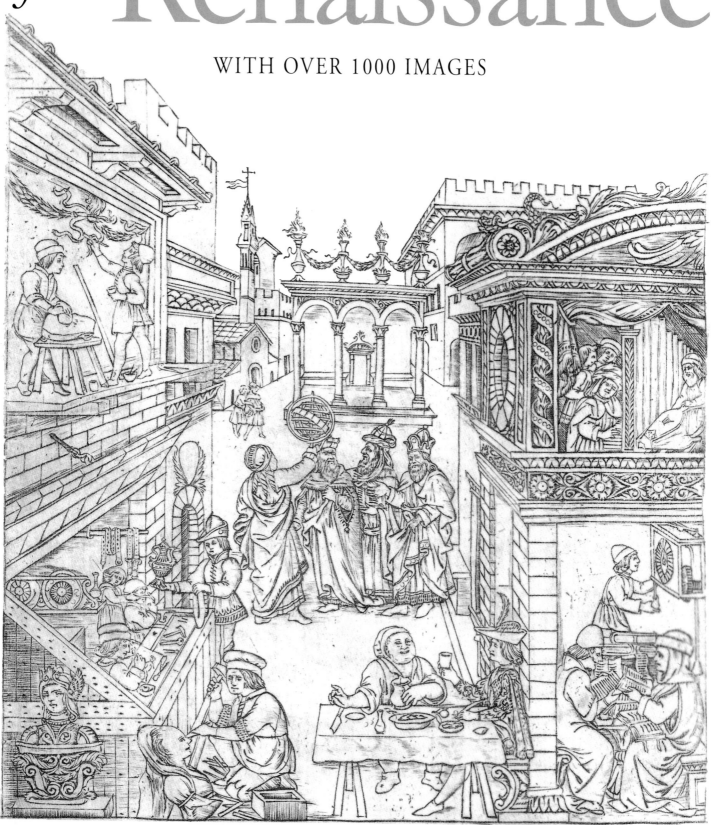

THAMES AND HUDSON

Contents

The Renaissance in the Perspective of History
MARGARET ASTON
9

A Renaissance Panorama

USING THIS BOOK

A number of special features allow the reader to move easily from one area of interest to another, assembling information in different combinations as needed.

The Introduction draws together the threads of all the sections of the book, showing us the complex pattern that was – and is – the Renaissance.

The Picture Pages form the main body of the book and are organized by theme. To find any particular topic turn to the **Index**. The double-page spreads are divided into eight chapters (see **Contents**, page 4), each of which is colour-coded: this colour is visible on the outside edge of the volume even when it is closed. At the bottom of each picture page a series of colour-indicators point to pages with subjects of related interest.

The Biographical Dictionary contains the names of *all* major figures who appear in the book, whether artist, writer or political or religious leader. It provides a short life of the man or woman concerned, plus a list of relevant pictures by or of him or her and reproduced in the book. Biographies of important families are also included. This section is cross-referenced by putting all names included in other entries in CAPITALS. Where appropriate, standard biographies are included, as well as family trees.

Timelines provide a visual overview of the whole period, decade by decade, organized in five categories: history, ideas, literature, art and architecture. A further visual diagram shows the geographical diffusion of humanist ideas through Europe over 250 years.

The Glossary gives simple definitions of specialized words that are used in the book.

The Gazetteer of museums and galleries serves as a guide to the location of particular pictures and as a general aid to further study of Renaissance art.

The Bibliography lists recommended books categorized according to topic. As noted above, biographies of individuals are given in the **Biographical Dictionary**.

The Index provides a comprehensive means of accessing the peoples, places and topics presented in the book.

The Renaissance in the Perspective of History

MARGARET ASTON

ELENA·RAPITA·DA·PARIS·

'No artifact is a work of art if it does not help to humanize us.' Bernard Berenson's words may be taken to heart today, half a century after they were written. The entire Renaissance movement was premised on a fresh awareness of the study of humanity, and what it meant to be fully human. The elevation of sight as the highest of the senses produced an enormous wealth of images whose full appreciation rests on some grasp of the philosophy that created them. Sculpting the human form and painting the human face reached new heights as a result of a fresh emphasis on all kinds of humane studies – studies which had their origin in the heritage of the ancient world and which came to influence literature, history, religious thought, political systems and social manners.

Every age has to make its own terms with the Renaissance. Our own age is so dominated by visual imagery that our iconographic vocabulary is in serious danger of getting out of step with the verbal. The problem facing anyone who offers a new survey of the Renaissance today is precisely how to use the pictorial resources open to us and at the same time ensure that the visual arts remain rooted in the literary and cultural soil from which they sprang.

The word 'Renaissance' began as a shorthand for the emancipation of Italian painting and sculpture from the stylized conventions of earlier Gothic and Byzantine forms, but gradually became descriptive of a wide cultural reorientation, and is now applied to an entire period of European history. Technology and historical methodology continue to change its meaning. We are already far removed from the world of Jacob Burckhardt, whose *Civilization of the Renaissance in Italy* of 1860 set so indelible a mark on the subject, let alone that of Giorgio Vasari, whose *Lives of the Most Excellent Painters, Sculptors and Architects,* first published in 1550, set lines for interpreting the artistic developments of the three previous centuries. Burckhardt was somewhat further removed in time from Vasari than Vasari was from Giotto, and it may seem that there are some ways in which we are now more distant from either than they were from each other.

Our perceptions of 'Renaissance', like those of our predecessors, are structured by word and image, but the relationship between these, and the learning they promote, is constantly in flux. Four or five generations ago, when the first edition of Burckhardt's book was published in Basle, European culture remained firmly rooted in the Greek and Latin learning established by Renaissance tradition. Knowledge of ancient languages and books held precedence over knowledge of the arts, and acquaintance with the latter depended as much on travel as on books and museums and libraries. Access to images through reproductions was still limited – to an extent barely conceivable to us now. It was more than puritanical prejudice that prevented Edmund Gosse from setting eyes on any representation of classical sculpture until he was thirteen and then at once was 'attracted violently', through some steel engravings of statues, to the beauties of Apollo, Venus, Diana and Jupiter. Thirty-six years after the publication of Burckhardt's work, Johan Huizinga, then aged twenty-four, was making arrangements for an illustrated lecture to be delivered in Groningen, based

Frontispiece of the 1550 edition of Giorgio Vasari's Lives.

Opposite

The men and women of the Renaissance, for whom remoteness in time did not entail remoteness of spirit, made the ancient world their own. In this Florentine illustration of the Homeric story of Helen of Troy (c. 1460), the setting is a classical tholos, *with an egg-and-dart cornice and a frieze of Roman putti lugging a huge garland. But Paris and Helen are dressed in the fashion of 15th-century Florence.*

In the 19th century the only available reproductions of Renaissance paintings were engravings. This plate showing a Pordenone altarpiece is from the standard history of Italian art of 1871 by Crowe and Cavalcaselle.

on a collection of photographs of Italian art which the lecturer had brought back from his travels. 'It is hard to imagine today', wrote Huizinga, recalling this event in 1943, 'how hard it was to get good reproductions of old masterpieces.'

Fifty years on, with Victorian prints of the Sistine Chapel long since banished even from backstairs walls, we are surrounded by reprographic riches that would have astounded, perhaps even appalled Huizinga. Important though the study of art had proved for his own counterpart to Burckhardt – *The Waning of the Middle Ages* – Huizinga lived long enough to regret the dominant influence of painting on views of the past. The arrival of mechanical means of reproducing works of art was not an unmixed blessing, witness the lament of Walter Benjamin in 1936. 'Even the most perfect reproduction of a work of art is lacking in one element; its presence in time and space, its unique existence at the place where it happens to be.' There was an inevitable severance of object from location, a loss of what Benjamin called the 'aura' of a work of art. Both he and Huizinga might well have deplored the position we have now reached in which the increasing founts of Renaissance imagery readily available to students are matched by decreasing knowledge of the classical languages and learning in which such imagery was rooted. It is paradoxical that unparalleled new opportunities for exploring the artistic achievements of the Renaissance without ever setting foot in Italy, have arrived at the very time when familiarity with the Latin and Greek sources that nourished these works is shrivelling into the confines of university study.

By organizing the present book not according to artist or to artistic school or to geographical region, but according to ideas or themes, it is our ambition to heal this breach, and to set the great works of painting, sculpture and architecture in the context for which they were created. Only one of the chapters is devoted to art for art's sake. The others define key areas of the period – the rediscovery of Antiquity, the political background, religion, urban development, daily life and science and discovery – presenting them in images drawn from a wide range of artistic and historical sources.

Fears of the ill effects of reproduction now belong to the past. Today the works of Botticelli, Leonardo and Dürer may be so familiar they can, like the music of Vivaldi, be subjected to the honour or indignity of popularity's final accolade: being fodder for advertising. Whether we recognize it or not, our world is full of objects whose form stems from enthusiasms kindled in 15th-century Italy. From the classical orders of Grand Central Station in New York to the allegorical carvings on the Paris Opera and the giant columns of Selfridges in London – let alone the new Mannerism of the Sainsbury Wing of London's National Gallery – we are surrounded by exercises in the architectural grammar relearnt with the renewed study of Vitruvius. It is as if the Renaissance had started an end game which is still being played out. Yet central commonplaces of Greek and Roman culture have vanished or are fading. The ancient gods have gone back to Olympus. In 1981, the advent of a Princess Diana failed to yield, through all the panoply of an English royal wedding, a single allusion to the virgin huntress who would once have been a conspicuous presence in such ceremonial. In some obvious ways our age is surely post-classical.

The 'rebirth' of Ancient Rome

We are in fact guilty of an initial distortion if our first thoughts of Renaissance are of the visual arts. The Renaissance was in its origins, and remained always at heart, a literary movement, concerned with the writings and teaching of classical Antiquity. It had begun generations before Brunelleschi's new dome took shape over the cathedral in Florence (p. 276), or Masaccio completed his frescoes in the churches of S. Maria del Carmine (p. 248) and S. Maria Novella (p. 246). There was no 1066 in this alteration of the mental and artistic climate, but we begin to breathe its heady atmosphere in the work of Petrarch. Whatever we make of Petrarch's reported climb up Mont Ventoux in Provence on 26 April 1336, the ceremony of the poet's coronation on the Capitoline in Rome on 8 April 1341 is an undeniable marker. Petrarch, faced with alternative invitations of honour from the University of Paris and the Roman Senate, chose to go south. His heart, his hopes and his ambitions lay in Rome. He anchored his longing for future fame to his Virgilian epic poem called *Africa*, for which, he wrote, if it should 'long outlive me, as my soul hopes and wishes, there is perhaps a better age in store; this slumber of forgetfulness will not last for ever. After the darkness has been dispelled, our grandsons will be able to walk back into the pure radiance of the past.'

The Paris Opera: an example of Roman architecture adapted to modern needs.

The idea of Renaissance was itself dualistic, implying sleep and awakening, going down as well as coming up, darkness before light, losing before finding. It was necessary to excavate before it was possible to build anew, and to see again in a new light implied new eyes, or at least better vision. There was a great sense of exhilaration, and at the same time a nervousness in the challenge of living up to the past. 'Now, indeed, may every thoughtful spirit thank God that it has been permitted to him to be born in this new age.' The words of the Florentine humanist, Matteo Palmieri, in his book *On Civic Life*, written in the 1430s, were echoed by many others, inside and outside Italy. 'Oh century! Oh letters! It is a joy to be alive!'; Ulrich von Hutten, newly crowned Poet Laureate of the German Empire, shared in 1518 with Willibald Pirckheimer, patrician scholar of Nuremberg, his delight in the studies and intellects of the time. There seemed no end to the possibilities of new work in literature, in the arts, in the whole scope of human endeavour. Humanists of the 15th century, unlike those of the twelfth, did not think of themselves as sitting on the shoulders of the giants of Antiquity. But was it possible to stand on the same ground as Virgil or Cicero, to speak and write with their words in their language? Emulating the past brought its own problems, and to claim equal (or greater) achievements implied new criteria of judgment. Metamorphosis proved to be inherent in rebirth.

The ultimate accolade: Botticelli's Venus used to advertise a fabric conditioner.

The spread of humanism

A variety of connections, personal and institutional, transmitted humanist enthusiasms from Italian soil to distant places. The role of the Church proved important. The papal curia – including the period when the popes were living 'in exile' at Avignon (1309–77) – was a nexus of patronage and influence for ecclesiastics and men of learning from all

Ulrich von Hutten (1488–1523), aristocrat, scholar and poet, is remembered chiefly for his scathing satires against the papacy.

BILIBALDI·PIRKEYMHERI·EFFIGIES
·AETATIS·SVAE·ANNO·L·III·
VIVITVR·INGENIO·CAETERA·MORTIS·
·ERVNT·
·M·D·XX·IV·

Willibald Pirckheimer of Nuremberg (1470–1530) was a scholar in his own right, as well as a generous friend and patron of Dürer, Erasmus and Hutten.

parts of Europe. It was while he was attached to this nerve centre (an Italian serving other Italians in the papal entourage) that Petrarch developed his passion for Antiquity and book collecting. Avignon provided Petrarch with the contacts that enabled him to make important advances in the textual study of his favourite Roman historian: Livy's history of Rome (*Ab urbe condita*). Thanks also to the presence in Avignon of the well-known Sienese painter, Simone Martini, Petrarch was able, in about 1340, to commission the frontispiece which adorns his most prized possession, the manuscript of Virgil which had been stolen and lost to him for twelve years (p. 34). The papal court served as a nourishing hive for many like Petrarch, who travelled to and fro across Europe, but the poet was among the first to undermine the content of the old adage 'where the Pope is, there is Rome'. If Rome was all things to all men, Petrarch, with his loyalty to both Cicero and St Augustine, solidly reaffirmed the eminence of pre-papal Rome.

After the papacy's return to Rome, meetings of the great church councils (which challenged papal authority, at the same time as working to end the scandal of rival popes who split church loyalties between 1378 and 1417) proved creative meeting places. At the Council of Constance (1414–17), Sigismund of Luxemburg, King of Hungary and German Emperor, persuaded Pier Paolo Vergerio to join the Hungarian court, where he remained until his death in 1444. Poggio Bracciolini's presence at Constance as apostolic secretary provided opportunities for hunting for manuscripts in neighbouring libraries. This proved wonderfully rewarding. During a lull in the council's proceedings in 1416, Poggio and his friends visited St Gallen, to inspect the large collection of books in the monastic library. They were ecstatic about the treasures they found there: a complete text of Quintilian; Vitruvius' *De architectura*, a commentary on Cicero's orations, and other works. The triumphant treasure-seekers saw themselves as liberators, freeing captives from imprisonment in which they had been left to languish in squalor by ignorant monastic warders. It was as if a rescue mission had occurred in the nick of time, and the work had to be continued. Poggio was persuaded by Henry Beaufort, Bishop of Winchester, whom he met at Constance, to visit England where he spent four years busily searching English libraries, though these yielded nothing like the excitements of Constance, and indeed it proved something of a literary exile for the humanist. Meanwhile Cosimo de' Medici, present at the council in his role as banker, caught the bibliophile's virus and began spending generously on the copying and search for books.

Subsequent church councils similarly helped to promote both humanists and book-collecting. Aeneas Sylvius Piccolomini (later Pope Pius II) was in his twenties and at the start of his career when Cardinal Capranica, passing through Siena on his way to the Council of Basle (1431–49), engaged him as secretary. Ten years and more travels later Aeneas Sylvius was at work in Germany, as secretary and Poet Laureate to the Emperor Frederick III. Franciscus Piccolpassus – who was a friend of Aeneas, Guarino da Verona and Poggio – was able to collect much of his library while attending the Council of Basle.

The council called by Eugenius IV, which met first at Ferrara and then at Florence from 1438 to 1439, and succeeded in effecting the union (albeit only temporary) of the Latin and Greek churches, gave a considerable spur to Greek studies. Indeed this event was probably of more importance for the fertilization of Greek in the west than the fall of Constantinople in 1453, which is so often regarded as seminal. Turkish pressure on the eastern empire had been bringing Greek scholars and Greek texts into Italy for years. Manuel Chrysoloras, a teacher of genius, who had come to Italy in the first instance to seek aid against the Turks, and was in 1397 given an official salary as instructor in Greek by the city of Florence, spent the last five years of his life at the papal court and died at Constance in 1415. It was one of Chrysoloras' probable pupils, Ambrogio Traversari (whose outstanding ability in Greek enabled him to do important work on the Greek church fathers), who played a leading role in bringing the two churches to agreement. The study of Greek, which meant direct encounters with Saints Athanasius, Basil and Chrysostom, as well as with Homer and Plato, remained an elusive goal for a number of leading humanists from Petrarch onwards. But many aspired and studied, and even in England in 1438, news of what was happening in Ferrara led Piero del Monte (the papal tax collector) to pick up the threads of the Greek he had learnt at school from Guarino.

Despite the hardships of contemporary travel, people crossed and recrossed the mountains and dangerous rivers and roads of the continent on private or public affairs, in the cause of business, diplomacy and official missions. Individuals like Piero del Monte, or Polydore Vergil, who also came to England as a papal collector seventy years later (and who was encouraged by Henry VII to write a history of England), played a substantial part in planting humanist interests outside Italy. Italians were in demand as teachers, especially when they could give instruction in Greek, as Gregorio Tifernate did in Paris in the late 1450s, and Stefano Surigone did soon after in Oxford, Cologne, Strasbourg and Louvain.

The recognition of new literary styles created its own demands. Leonardo Bruni obtained his post in the papal curia in 1405 by composing a more polished letter for Innocent VII to send to the duc de Berry than his rival applicant. Rulers who wanted to impress had to move with the fashion. They needed secretaries who could turn ordinary phrases into stylish Latin, and tutors to instruct their children in the courtly manners of a new generation. 'Master Enea,' the later pope was notified by the imperial chancellor, 'you may put this more elegantly so long as the sense is the same.' Another service Aeneas Sylvius rendered to Frederick III was to write a work on the education of children for the emperor's brother. The spread of Italian humanist culture in Poland owed much to the education which Sigismund I Jagellon had received from Filippo Buonaccorsi or Callimachus. He was a tutor who had much to offer, having started his career in Rome, and then lived in Greece, Cyprus and Constantinople, before reaching Cracow, where he spent the last part of his life, being buried there in the Dominican church.

Alongside the many Italians who left Italy, we must remember the numerous visitors from many places who went to Italy for sights and sounds, books and skills and buildings that seemed to exist there as nowhere else. In this age, though pilgrimage of the old kind still flourished, pilgrimages of various, more secular, kinds took place to shrines in which the arts might command as much devotion as the

Polydore Vergil of Urbino came to England in 1502 as a collector of papal taxes. Henry VII gave him various clerical preferments and commissioned him to write a history of England in Latin, which was eventually published in 1534, by which time he had lost royal favour. These marginal sketches (at the top, King Canute forbids the tide to rise) seem to have been added about 1540.

The Renaissance in the Perspective of History 13

Pope Sixtus IV inspects his library, a fresco by Melozzo da Forlì, c. 1475. The books are kept lying flat on desks. Sixtus, in the centre, is speaking to his nephew Cardinal Giuliano della Rovere (later Julius II). Behind him are another of his nephews, Cardinal Raffaello Riario, and his librarian Platina.

John Dee (1527–1608), England's foremost mathematician and Queen Elizabeth's astrologer. He was attracted to the court of Rudolf II and spent some time in Prague, claiming to be able to converse with angels.

God and saints they served. Florence, Rome and Venice were all Mecca in their turn. From England men like William Grey (later Bishop of Ely) in the 1440s, or John Colet (later dean of St Paul's) fifty years later, crossed the Alps in search of learning. Rudolf Agricola, who could be seen as virtually a Petrarch of Germany, spent the best part of ten years in Italy before putting his Greek and Hebrew and fully fledged humanist interests to inspiring use as a teacher in Heidelberg. And Conrad Celtis, who was crowned Poet Laureate by Frederick III and died in Vienna where he lectured on rhetoric and poetry, had been to Venice and then via Padua, Ferrara, Bologna and Florence to Rome in pursuit of the muses. By the time that Albrecht Dürer, in his thirties and already well-travelled north of the Alps, arrived in Venice on his second visit to Italy in 1505, much of the humanist expertise of the south was obtainable without setting foot in Italy.

Of course the channels of influence did not all flow one way. Dürer himself, through his graphic work, left his mark on Italian painting from which he had drawn inspiration. Leading composers and musicians were called from the Netherlands to serve in Italy. Guillaume Dufay, world renowned from his youth, travelled far and wide to compose music for court weddings, and wrote a motet for the consecration of Florence Cathedral in 1436 and a series of lamentations on the fall of Constantinople. He spent part of his life serving in the papal choir in Rome, as did the equally celebrated composer Josquin des Préz, who lived for many years in Italy making music for the choirs of Milan Cathedral, the Vatican and the court of Ferrara.

Great collections of books and the foundation of libraries are one way of plotting the advance of humanism during these formative years. The search for lost or incomplete texts of Antiquity, the laborious work of piecing together complete texts from scattered manuscripts, was in effect a co-operative enterprise, pushed ahead by infectious intellectual excitement. Its fruits appeared in the celebrated manuscript collections of individuals and later in the libraries of kings or universities in which the printed book held pride of place. Petrarch's unquenchable thirst for books resulted in his owning the largest collection of classical writings in existence in his day. In the later 15th century Florence owed its humanist library to Cosimo de' Medici, Buda in Hungary had that of Matthias Corvinus, while in England the library of Oxford University gained 280 books from the princely munificence of Humfrey, Duke of Gloucester. In Rome the manuscripts gathered by Nicholas V (over 1100 volumes, nearly a third of them in Greek) formed the core of the Vatican Library established by Sixtus IV in 1475. Leading humanist courts of the 16th century were rich in reading-matter, as in patronage. François I, having inherited a library at Blois that contained treasures won from the Visconti-Sforza family of Milan, started to build up a fine new library at Fontainebleau. Later in the century the multi-faceted interests of the Emperor Rudolf II ensured that Prague was an attractive centre for book-lovers, and able to hold even a great bibliophile like John Dee, who spent some time there in the 1580s.

'Magnificent buildings'

Books and libraries, however, are not, and were not, everything to everybody. For most people, buildings mattered more, and were naturally more noticeable. This self-evident truth was fully realized by the popes and cardinals, kings and princes who erected and displayed their magnificence in many temporary as well as permanent structures. Gianozzo Manetti, whose life of Nicholas V described the pope's grandiose plans for reconstructing the Borgo in the Vatican in the 1450s, also recorded the observations that he made about building in his deathbed speech. Those who studied texts could understand the great authority of the Roman Church:

> But the mass of the population is ignorant of literary matters and lacking in any culture. It still needs to be struck by grandiose spectacles because otherwise its faith, supported as it is on weak and unstable foundations, will end in due time by declining to nothing. With magnificent buildings, on the other hand, monuments in some sense perpetual that appear almost to testify to the hand of God himself, the popular conviction may be strengthened and confirmed in the same way as it is in the affirmations of the learned.

What a manifesto for the Renaissance papacy! And yet the argument itself could be seen as an adaptation of an ancient theory, already more than 800 years old, by which the church justified the visual arts as props for the faith of the non-reading populace.

When Nicholas V died in 1455, Rome – as he must have been all too aware – had nothing in the way of modern magnificence to match what was to be seen in Florence. There was certainly plenty to impress, but it was the grandeur of ancient ruins, not that of modern monuments. Another 50 years were to pass before Julius II embarked on perhaps the most breath-taking project of the age, a truly spectacular building, designed to win universal acclaim.

Clearly architects enjoyed a head start over sculptors and painters. The latter had no guide like Vitruvius' detailed advice on basic matters from building a temple or house to arranging water supply. The visible remains of ancient work available for study by sculptor or painter were not comparably documented, even though some identifiable sculpture (and much that was not) was visible in Donatello's day – including the colossal fragments which were moved from the Lateran to the Capital in 1489. More was to be recovered from the earth. The sculpture court in the Belvedere Courtyard (p. 157), which Bramante built for Julius II in the Vatican, enabled visitors to see some of the exciting recent finds, including the *Laocoön* and the *Apollo Belvedere*. Artists were naturally anxious to study such displays which came to include the sculpture courts of the Palazzo della Valle and Casa Sassi in Rome, François I's collection of casts of ancient statues at Fontainebleau, and Albrecht V's Antiquarium in Munich (p. 61), which housed Europe's first comprehensive collection of ancient portrait busts and statues.

Painters were obliged to study sculpture since, until the discovery of Pompeii in the 18th century, only fragmentary remains of ancient

The Laocoön *and* Apollo Belvedere *(above), two of the most admired works of classical sculpture, came to light during this period, the* Apollo *before 1500, the* Laocoön *in 1506.*

Piero della Francesca drew upon his knowledge of contemporary Roman fashion when he came to depict the ladies attending the Queen of Sheba: a detail from his fresco cycle of the Legend of the True Cross *at Arezzo (1452–57).*

painting were known. Findings of the 1480s of painted rooms in the buried remains of Nero's Golden House in Rome, provided inspiration for Pinturicchio and Raphael as well as promoting the fashion for decoration with grotesques (from these subterranean 'grottoes'). Lacking painted models, painters drew on other art forms. Extant drawings witness to the early spell cast by the *Apollo Belvedere*. Andrea Mantegna, whose *Triumphs of Caesar* (p. 57) were certainly based on knowledge of classical descriptions of triumphal processions (probably via Flavio Biondo's *Roma triumphans* of 1459) made drawings of reliefs and statues which informed these and others works.

True, there were ancient texts that offered some descriptions of ancient sculptors and painters and their work. Pliny the Elder's *Natural History* included chapters on statuary and painting and sculpture which provided quite a lot of information about Phidias, Zeuxis, Apelles and other great artists, naming some of their works. Like Petrarch and Poggio, Alberti and Ghiberti knew their Pliny, whose work was among the earliest classical texts to be printed in the 1460s. It is not surprising the discovery of the *Laocoön* in a Roman vineyard in January 1506 caused tremendous excitement, for this was a known work, representing an event in Virgil's *Aeneid*, which had been praised by Pliny as 'superior to all the pictures and bronzes in the world'. At the pope's request Giuliano da Sangallo (taking Michelangelo along with him) went to inspect this work while it was still in the ground, and pronounced the words of recognition, recalled in 1567 by his son Francisco who – as a boy of eleven – was present on this thrilling occasion. 'This is the Laocoön which Pliny mentions.'

A full description of Apelles' painting of *Calumny* – an incident of proverbial fame – was given by Lucian in one of his dialogues. The very rarity of this account helped to give it currency, and Lucian's dialogue *On Calumny* had by 1435 been translated from Greek into Latin by three Italians, one of them being Guarino da Verona, whose version was used by Alberti when he described the painting in his treatise *On Painting* (1435–36). Alberti advised painters to become conversant with poets, rhetoricians and men of letters in order to compose their subjects – almost an essential requirement for any painter anxious to rival the ancients. It was advice closely followed by both Mantegna and Botticelli when they set about respectively drawing and painting *The Calumny of Apelles* (p. 47). Painters breathed humanist air, even when they were not being guided towards specific texts. Piero della Francesca's *Legend of the True Cross* at Arezzo gained from his encounters at Pius II's court, just as Botticelli's *Primavera* (pp. 55 and 228) and *The Birth of Venus* (p. 53) have behind them the Neoplatonism of Marsilio Ficino's Florence, as well the most valuable ancient cameo in the Medici collection.

Alberti wrote his book on painting to provide painters with the theory that they lacked. Arriving in Florence in 1434 (his father had been banished from the city a generation earlier), Alberti was bowled over by what he saw. Brunelleschi's great dome over the crossing of the cathedral was nearing completion, and Masaccio's revolutionary frescoes were still fresh and new. Alberti prefaced his treatise with expressions of delight and amazement:

Who could ever be hard or envious enough to fail to praise Pippo the architect on seeing here such a large structure, rising above the skies, ample to cover with its shadow all the Tuscan people, and constructed without the aid of centering or great quantity of wood?

The greatness of this work was measured for Alberti by its having outdone Antiquity. The huge dome, which still dominates the city of Florence as it did in the 15th century, demonstrated that it was possible not only to rival the arts of the ancient world, but to surpass them. What models or instruction were there for this work? It was 'probably unknown and unthought of among the Ancients', and, Alberti thought, 'our fame ought to be much greater ... if we discover unheard-of and never-before-seen arts and sciences without teachers or without any model whatsoever.' His words could be read as a challenge as well as a triumphant claim for Renaissance skills. Antiquity was reborn not merely to be re-experienced or re-created; it was to be transcended. Brunelleschi's dome, based as it was both on the Pantheon in Rome and the Baptistery in Florence (a medieval building which the architect himself believed to be ancient), reveals the potential of a double inheritance.

The rebuilding of St Peter's in Rome gives us a measure to place beside Alberti's. Living as we do in a time of such respect for all monuments of the past, we cannot but be amazed by the heroic scale of confidence in the creative powers of the new age, which enabled Julius II to contemplate the destruction and replacement of the ancient church, in which the apostle's shrine had been venerated by generations of pilgrims. Fifty years earlier Nicholas V had begun some reconstruction around St Peter's tomb in the Basilica of St Constantine, one of the most sacred places in Christendom. Julius conceived of renovation of quite another kind. His was a vision of a new beginning of tremendous, stunning proportions. Magnificence, splendour, grandiosity, building on a scale not seen since Antiquity, were to transport the prince of the Apostles and his church into a new era. Dignity and display, not poverty and humility, were to convert the pilgrims of coming generations.

The huge crossing of Bramante's St Peter's dwarfs the old basilica, soon to be completely demolished. In the foreground, under a baldacchino, is the classical pinecone now in the Belvedere Courtyard (16th century).

Questioning and doubt

Julius had his critics, and some were greatly shocked. Was this vast new church really necessary? By the time of his death in 1514 Bramante had overseen the dismantling of the old basilica and in 1506 the foundations were laid and 2,500 workmen found employment on the new building, which started with the great piers of the crossing. Some contemporaries regarded the architect as a master of destruction (*maestro ruinante*), and indeed for a long time it was possible to consider this unfinished spectacle as itself little better than a ruin. Two years after his death a satirical dialogue had Bramante being called to task by St Peter, who reprimanded the architect for pulling down his old habitation, and condemned him to await entry into paradise until the new church was completed. It would have been a very long wait, despite (or thanks to) the endeavours of Antonio da Sangallo the Younger, Michelangelo, Giacomo della Porta, Carlo Maderno and all the other architects who became involved in continuing the construction and adapting the original plans.

INDEX AVCTORVM,
ET LIBRORVM, QVI

*tanquam hæretici, aut fufpecti, aut pernicio-
fi, ab officio. S. Ro. Inquifitionis re-
probantur, et in vniuerfa Chri-
ftiana republica inter-
dicuntur.*

ROMAE apud Antonium Bladum
Impreflorem Cameralem.
M. D. LVII.

*The Index of prohibited authors and books
('either heretical, or suspect or pernicious') was
inaugurated by the Catholic Church in 1557, in
an attempt to hold back the flood provoked by
the Reformation.*

*The cathedral of St Michael the Archangel in
the Moscow Kremlin, 1505–09, was built by
an Italian architect, Alevisio, a combination
of Renaissance ornament with traditional
Russian plan.*

Julius II's colossal aspirations for papal Rome looked to hebraic
as well as classical sources. The inheritance of this heir of St Peter,
who envisaged his Christian leadership as an imperial role, was that of
both Moses and Julius Caesar. The pope, like his architect, had trouble
at the gates of paradise. The style of this pontificate, and the new
sumptuousness of Rome in the palaces of cardinals as well as the Vatican
itself, was deeply provocative and had serious long-lasting results for the
future of Renaissance humanism. The horror which Erasmus felt at this
most unapostolic of belligerent popes was expressed in the anonymous
satire, *Julius exclusus*, which he wrote after Julius' death. Luther's
challenge, and the division of Christendom which ensued, originated
in opposition to the indulgence of 1517 being collected for the new St
Peter's. Ten years later the Sack of Rome, in which many libraries and
palaces were looted, proved devastating. 'The fall of Rome was not the
fall of the city, but of the world', as Erasmus put it. Yet for many of the
participants this was a just chastisement of the blatant opulence and
ostentatious pomp of the Renaissance papacy.

These events seem to mark the beginning of a great divide, a shifting
of values which produced marked variations in the course of humanistic
developments in different parts of Europe. Rome, seen from afar by those
who envisaged Italy with chastened eyes, became a place to shun, not a
storehouse of cultural riches. Instead of being regarded as the epitome
of civilization, letters and the arts, it was Babylon, the epitome of
corruption, irreligion and papal sensuality. Protestant iconoclasm
threatened the future of religious art. Many paintings and sculptures were
torn down, broken or burned in places where reforming Protestants
inaugurated their purifying regimes, and those whose spiritual life was
focused on scripture learned to suspect the role of the arts and aesthetic
pleasures when yoked to the service of God. Censorship began to affect
both intellectual and artistic processes. Printed books, part of the arsenal
of rival belief-systems, were subjected to controls and prohibitions, most
notoriously with the arrival of the Index of the Church of Rome in the
1550s. Works of art likewise came under scrutiny as scriptural criteria cut
into the easy assumptions of earlier generations of painters. The Council
of Trent, even while it reaffirmed the essential service of painting to
religion, set standards of propriety. The censuring eyes of puritans were
already putting loincloths on suspect nudes, and the tremors of moral
reappraisal and spiritual questioning reached even into the Sistine
Chapel's *Last Judgment* (p. 147) and Michelangelo's sonnets.

Humanism in eastern Europe

Though church building was to be adversely affected by the Reformation,
what has been called the architecture of humanism long continued to
find patrons throughout Europe. Thanks to Ivan III Italians were at work
in the late 15th century in Moscow, where the façade of the cathedral of
St Michael the Archangel bears witness to their influence. In Hungary
Matthias Corvinus sought works by leading Italian artists and invited
to Buda Benedetto da Maiano, Giovanni Dalmata and the architect
Chimenti Camicia, who produced work which could be compared with
that in Florence itself. Only fragments remain of the king's Italianate

castles at Buda and Visegrád above the Danube (which Sixtus IV's ambassador thought a veritable 'terrestrial paradise'), but the alabaster reliefs of Matthias and his wife Beatrix of Aragon, made by Giancristoforo Romano, are the most up-to-date beautiful *all' antica* profiles.

The court in Buda radiated stylistic innovations into other parts of eastern Europe, where they can still be seen today. Before he became King of Poland in 1506, Sigismund (or Zygmunt) I, who as we have seen had a humanist education, spent formative years in Buda, and attracted Italian masters from there to join his own court. But the architect who transformed his royal castle on the Wawel Hill in Cracow came from Florence. Franciscus Florentinus and his workshop built a new three-storied arcaded courtyard which is reminiscent of Bramante's recent S. Damaso Courtyard in the Vatican. The first surviving structure of its kind in transalpine Europe, this highly distinctive building proved extraordinarily influential. It set a pattern that was followed in many 16th-century castles throughout Poland, Hungary, Slovakia and Moravia which today boast the richest group of such Renaissance triple-storied courtyards outside Italy.

Matthias Corvinus' successor as King of Hungary was Sigismund's elder brother, Vladislav II Jagellon, who was King of Bohemia from 1471 to 1516. The huge new hall he added to the Hradcany Castle in Prague between 1493 and 1502 (p. 161) introduced new building styles to Bohemia. This imposing room served a wholly secular purpose, being built for tournaments and providing space for as many as a hundred horsemen. Its designer was a German, Benedikt Ried, who was knighted, as Giovanni Dalmata had been before him in Hungary, both of them bringing the new status of Renaissance artists into their world. The great hall in Prague, like the Wawel Castle in Cracow, displayed an inspired fusion of Renaissance classicism and traditional Gothic. Ried added new-style fenestration and portals to a Gothic hall whose vault is alive with writhing ribs. The interior of the Wawel Castle has a wonderfully inventive series of doorways which combine Renaissance and Gothic motifs. Both architects showed themselves uniquely qualified to work with dual forms, assured in their masterly ability to handle both old and new.

Northern Renaissance

Connections with Italy also introduced new tastes and buildings into Germany around the turn of the 15th century. The great Augsburg banking family of the Fugger, northern equivalents of the Medici, patronized new humanist styles. Jakob Fugger the Rich (who was closely involved in the financial management of Johann Tetzel's famous indulgence) was a princely patron of the arts with many lines of communication into Italy. They were centred in Venice, where the Fondaco dei Tedeschi was stylishly rebuilt in the early 16th century, and it was there that Jakob's younger brother Georg was painted by Giovanni Bellini in 1474. At home in Augsburg the family residence was remodelled with an arcaded court and other Italianate features, and the Fugger Chapel in the church of St Anne was also built at this time, with elegant classical arches and mouldings, making it an important

The Fondaco dei Tedeschi in Venice, the warehouse of the German merchants, was built in 1505 and originally adorned with frescoes by Giorgione. By the 19th century, it was in a sad state of decay and has since been drastically over-restored.

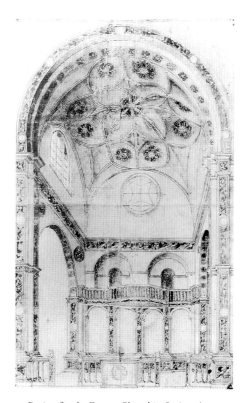

Design for the Fugger Chapel in St Anne's, Augsburg, by Sebastian Locher, 1509–10, one of the earliest examples of the Renaissance in Germany.

Part of Dürer's elaborate design for a triumphal arch for the Emperor Maximilian I, 1515–17. Inevitably, it remained on paper.

Two generations of designers epitomize the abrupt transition from Gothic to Renaissance in Germany: Peter Vischer's bronze shrine of St Sebald, Nuremberg, 1508–19 (above) and an alternative design by his son Hermann, 1516.

monument of the Renaissance style in Germany. Albrecht Dürer, who in 1510 designed some carved slabs for the east end, painted Jakob Fugger in the year the chapel was consecrated, 1518.

The huge triumphal arch which Dürer executed in 192 sheets of woodcut for the Emperor Maximilian I between 1515 and 1517, reflects features characteristic of this phase of northern Renaissance art. The classical elements have been fully learned through the artist's absorption of the Italy he knew well, but the whole is overlaid with a proliferation of decoration in multiple layers of ornament and symbolism. This was a triumph of technique – but it was a text more than a monument. Maximilian saved himself the expense of a more solid structure, but though Dürer's work did earn fame (and did endure), it is symptomatic that the emperor chose to be glorified in this arcane bookish structure.

In Dürer's own city of Nuremberg these years saw the completion of a new bronze shrine for the local patron, St Sebald (p. 50). This towering encrusted structure must strike anyone as a monument to the flowering of a late Gothic style which has borrowed a few Renaissance motifs. It was the work of a famous family of Nuremberg craftsmen, Peter Vischer and his two sons. The elder of these, Hermann, died before the shrine was completed but while it was under way he drew his own alternative design. Nothing could show more clearly the amazing divergence between two schools. Hermann had been to Italy and came home with a collection of the drawings he had made there, which reveal his interest in works of Bramante and Raphael, as well as in Roman buildings. He would himself have honoured St Sebald with a shrine of classical simplicity and purity, which could have come from the hand of Brunelleschi or Alberti. One wonders what he felt about the tapestry in bronze which he spent his last years working on.

In Portugal, where late Gothic ran riot in the encrusted Manueline style, with its nautical ropes and lacy vegetable ornament, purer forms made a relatively late arrival. John III was a lonely introvert with an ardent interest in architecture – characteristics that have led to his being compared with Philip II of Spain, though he has no Escorial to his credit. The king commissioned a large model of the Colosseum, and it was during his reign that the term *al Romano* began to make its appearance in building records. At this time João de Castilho was responsible for introducing some Renaissance forms into the cloister of the monastery church at Belém, and then, leaping into a completely different order, he built the hermitage chapel of the Immaculate Virgin at Tomar. If this was an architectural experiment it was supremely successful, a basilican church that recalls early Roman models, as well as the entrance hall of Antonio da Sangallo the Younger's Palazzo Farnese in Rome.

The rivalries of northern monarchs promoted art as well as letters. In England Henry VIII did his best to ape his contemporary, François I, whose court at Fontainebleau (p. 253) shone with the skills of Rosso Fiorentino and Primaticcio, while the royal collection included works by Raphael, Leonardo and Andrea del Sarto, as well as moulds of ancient statues (including the *Laocoön* and the *Apollo Belvedere*) from which bronzes were cast. The French king hosted Cellini, Serlio and Leonardo (who died near Amboise in 1519). Across the Channel, despite the patronage of Cardinal Wolsey (who was sensitive to the latest Italian fashions and did much to introduce new styles of sculpture into England), and despite Henry's lavish spending of monastic gains, England never had anything comparable to the 'School of Fontainebleau', and erected nothing in the whole 16th century to rival Philibert de l'Orme's Renaissance Château of Anet (pp. 111 and 281), built for François' successor Henri II between 1547 and 1552.

But there were some distinguished Italians in England, and Henry VIII did his best to build in new ways. King and cardinal employed the sculptors Pietro Torrigiano, Benedetto da Rovezzano and Giovanni da Maiano, and the former had the painter Girolamo da Treviso on his payroll for six years. Distinctive works by these men still remain to be seen at Westminster Abbey and Hampton Court Palace. Henry's most ambitious and unusual work, the lavish palace of Nonsuch, started in 1538 and still incomplete at the king's death, is no more, but certainly had Renaissance pretensions, with its plaster panels bearing classical motifs, its terracotta statues of Roman emperors and its finely carved slate. Thanks to the designs of Nicholas Modena, the decoration, but not the overall form of Nonsuch (whose elevation was most unclassical), showed something Italianate to English subjects.

By the time Henry VIII got to work on Nonsuch (building literally as well as figuratively on a despoiled church) François I had nearly twenty years of building behind him. The external galleries and free use of terracotta ornament – readily available in France after Girolamo della Robbia started making ceramics at Suresnes in 1528 – at the Château de Madrid in the Bois de Boulogne, as well as the excesses of Chambord, might well have aroused the English king's envy and emulation. François, like Henry, did not live to see the completion of his favourite palace, Fontainebleau. He knew enough of what was going on in England to criticize the use of gilding which both Henry VIII and Wolsey found essential to the glory of building, a taste which paraded to François a sure lack of Renaissance discretion. (The Field of Cloth of Gold was another matter.)

In northern lands classical models stood a better chance of adoption in secular than in ecclesiastical buildings. The Stadtresidenz in Landshut (1536–43) is a monument to the enthusiasm of Ludwig X of Bavaria for Giulio Romano's Palazzo del Tè (p. 269), which he saw when he visited Mantua in 1536. Ludwig, who imported Italian craftsmen to work under German direction, succeeded in creating his own small corner of Italy in Landshut, where his residence had a frescoed loggia, marble columns, work in stucco, and mythological paintings on the ceilings. A generation later in the 1560s another Duke of Bavaria, Albrecht V, planned the building of an Antiquarium in his Munich residence, to house his statue collection. This was to be a purpose-built structure on two floors, with the library installed over the sculpture gallery. It was also eminently fitting that it should have been designed by a man who was himself a great collector, Jacopo da Strada of Mantua. He was sent home to make drawings of the Palazzo del Tè, and produced for Albrecht a most accomplished Renaissance design.

As time went on, increasing knowledge and available publications reduced the need for direct exchanges with Italy. Vitruvius was brought out in a German translation by Walter Riff (Rivius) in 1548, and Strada,

The small chapel of the Immaculate Virgin at Tomar, in Portugal (above), built by João de Castilho, c. 1530–40, recalls Antonio da Sangallo the Younger's vestibule to the Palazzo Farnese in Rome (below) of 1515.

François I's Château de Madrid, built in the Bois de Boulogne, Paris, from 1528 onwards, made copious use of Renaissance features but survived only until 1793.

The Stadtresidenz, Landshut, in Bavaria, 1536–43: early Renaissance influence beyond the Alps.

An architectural allegory from the 1568 edition of Philibert de l'Orme's L'Architecture. The architect has four hands and winged feet. Note, in the upper storey, the 'French order' invented by Philibert (see p. 269).

who had a manuscript of Serlio with him in Munich, published in Frankfurt in 1575 the last of Serlio's seven architectural books. In France there was Philibert de l'Orme's *Architecture* (1567), and in England John Shute's *First and Chief Groundes of Architecture* (1563).

A new role for painting

Architects and books enabled new building styles to gain ground eventually in all parts of Europe. Other forms of art were themselves mobile. In the 15th century panels painted by Petrus Christus and Hans Memlinc found homes in Venice, while Venetian workshops were exporting altarpieces down the Adriatic to Bari, Apulia and Calabria. Paintings, though still in many places attached to the walls of churches and palaces – not only in Italy, the home of fresco – themselves travelled on panel and (increasingly) canvas at the whim of collectors. One of the greatest of these at the end of our period, who probably did more than any other individual to bring England belatedly into the orbit of Renaissance art, was the Earl of Arundel. His love of Dürer's works was such that when in 1636 the Bishop of Würzburg gave him a signed painting of the Virgin by this artist, he 'ever carried it in my own coach since I had it', adding (as he reported to the knowledgeable agent who collected for him), 'and how then do you think I should value things of Leonardo, Raphael, Correggio, and the like!'

There was a sense in which early Renaissance artists were themselves builders in paint even when they were not in fact working as architects. Throughout the period painters – even those of fame and distinction – were men of all trades, called on to make designs for court functions, jewels or ornaments, a whole range of objects not yet hived off into a separate category of 'decorative arts'. Florentine wedding chests (*cassoni*) were painted by Uccello and Botticelli; Holbein's work includes drawings for a clock (p. 230), dagger, jewelry and gold cups, as well as interior decorative schemes; Leonardo's inventions are proverbial. But the fact that early Renaissance pictures are so rich in architectural features is not simply the result of polymaths like Alberti, Raphael and Michelangelo having multi-media skills. For this was an important means to express what was probably the greatest leap forward in the contemporary artistic world: the discovery of perspective.

Painters made use of imagined classical buildings and paved courts to create the spaces calculated by linear perspective. But diminishing distance could also be represented by the effects of light, atmosphere and colour, subtle variations in depth of tone. Another generation of painters here carried further the discoveries that began in Florence, as the artistic focus shifted to Rome and Venice. The wonderfully suggestive recession of distance and light in the folds of hill and valley in Masaccio's *Tribute Money*, showed the possibilities of 'another kind of perspective which I call Aerial Perspective', in the words of Leonardo. He went on to explain how atmosphere enables us to distinguish distance, and how this affects the colour of objects – 'the more distant ones less defined and bluer', so the greater the distance proportionately the more intense the blue. Leonardo's own works (*The Virgin of the Rocks*, p. 169, and the *Mona Lisa*, p. 195) reflect the application of such observations, which characterize much that we prize in the painting of the high and late Renaissance. The clarity and cool planes of Masaccio, Piero della Francesca and Mantegna give way to the atmospheric colours, the play of light and shadow, and ultimately the sheer suggestiveness of paint, in works of Perugino, Raphael and Michelangelo, Giorgione, Titian, Veronese and Tintoretto. In verdant foliage, dark groves and distant shimmering hills, through the observed colours and contours of the human body, pictorial sensation was emerging as a source of pleasure in its own right. To know and understand naturally remained part of the spectator's role, but it was not the only source of delight for patrons and connoisseurs.

The most mobile form of Renaissance painting was also the most popular. This was the great age of the portrait which, in its many forms – from full-length and half-length figures on canvas, to miniature heads and medal profiles – could itself be a kind of ambassador for kings and courtiers, or messenger between intimates or relatives, as well as ancestral companion for aspiring gentry. Portraits might precede brides and grooms in the planning of marriage alliances. Holbein's 'very perfect' depiction of Christina of Denmark (p. 94), widowed duchess of Milan, proved very pleasing to Henry VIII in 1538 (though he could not catch this queen), and in 1561 Elizabeth I was said to be impressed by the looks of Erik XIV of Sweden, presented in paint as a potential husband.

The portrait too could borrow forms and features from Antiquity, thanks to fresh observation of Roman busts and the profile heads on coins and gems. The portrait's presence as speaking likeness (which was itself an ancient topos) is an immediate means by which we may feel we can communicate with men and women of the Renaissance, just as they in their turn opened converse with future as well as past. Leading artists, from Piero della Francesca and Desiderio da Settignano to Holbein and Titian, left much of their best work in portraiture, so that the period is truly humanist in being peopled with so many knowable faces and figures.

When the arts vied with each other, as well as with Antiquity, the lack of any ancient painted portraits enabled poets to score a point against painters. We now have the advantage, which Renaissance contemporaries did not enjoy, of being able to look at Roman faces, which stare at us with striking pictorial directness from their so-called 'mummy portraits' from Roman Egypt. Classical epigrams, reflecting on the ability of statue or painting to give life to the portrayed, compared the enduring fame bestowed by poetry and works of art. This dialogue, or contest, continued in the Renaissance. The speaking statue found a role in various places, and the battered ancient trunk known as the Pasquino to this day voices in anonymous verses Roman views on topical issues. Portraits also spoke – sometimes in the poetry they competed with. When Raphael painted his close friend the poet Antonio Tebaldeo, the picture was praised as being more like Tebaldeo than he was himself. The poet's sonnet eulogizing the portrait returned the compliment of artistic immortality with interest, pointing out that ancient writings had survived, but no paintings by Zeuxis or Apelles.

Detail from Masaccio's Tribute Money *at the Brancacci Chapel, Florence, a painting of the late 1420s which explored new techniques of conveying the physical body and recession into space.*

Pasquino was the nickname given to an antique torso to which it became the Roman custom to attach salacious and satirical epigrams.

The Renaissance in the Perspective of History   23

The town hall of Poznań in Poland was given an up-to-date arcaded loggia in the 1550s by an Italian architect, Giovanni Battista Quadro.

One of the most intriguing meetings of Gothic and Renaissance is to be found in the Vladislav Hall of Prague Castle (c. 1500), where the architect Benedikt Ried used a playful form of late Gothic vaulting for the hall itself but designed the doorways and windows in an equally playful Renaissance mode.

Hybrid styles

As new models in architecture, painting and humanist learning were translated from Italy into other parts of Europe, they were transmuted. Indigenous traditions affected the adoption of new styles, and even where Italians implanted pure new stock, strong varieties of mixed parentage were generated. The very diversity and vitality of these hybrid forms is at the heart of the movement we know as the Renaissance. European culture was itself of mixed inheritance, and the renewed understanding of classical forms, literary and artistic, in a profoundly Christian world, increased contemporaries' consciousness of their inherited Christian ambivalence towards the this-worldliness of paganism. They were well aware of the impossibility either of stepping back into a lost past, or of re-creating Antiquity in their own time. Petrarch and Alberti alike aspired to model their work on ancient patterns but at the same time to transcend those patterns. Imitation was not the same as copying.

There are different kinds of hybrids, some of them capable of excelling pure breeds. We have exciting examples of classical forms being ingeniously adapted to transform existing buildings. An early example is S. Francesco in Rimini (p. 281), on which Alberti started an experiment in about 1450, modifying a Roman triumphal arch to make a church façade. A hundred or so years later a similar exercise was carried out in Poland, when Giovanni Battista Quadro wrapped a Renaissance coat, which included an arcaded loggia, round the late Gothic town hall of Poznań. In London St Paul's Cathedral was encased in a stylish classical skin in the 1630s by Inigo Jones, its most conspicuous feature being the colonnaded portico at the west front. Such remodelling taxed the inventiveness of designers, perhaps with benefit. But the best buildings are always unities, complete harmonies, and those that please most from the Renaissance period, are not only the ones that speak most purely in the relearnt Vitruvian vocabulary, but those that harmonize old and new grammars. With the advantage of half a millennium of additional seeing, the buildings we can now take to heart are not only Brunelleschi's Pazzi Chapel in Florence (p. 276), Bramante's Tempietto in Rome (p. 275), and Palladio's Redentore in Venice, but the mixed styles of cross-breeds such as the cloister at Belém in Portugal, the S. Gregorio Courtyard at Valladolid in Spain, or the great hall already mentioned in Prague.

Pure imitation, archaic purity for its own sake or for display, could be sterile, and the juxtaposition of new and old ran the risk of provocation or disapproval. There were humanists who believed that Christian formulas could be presented to the world in the pure diction of Antiquity, just as old churches could be made more fit and beautiful for the new age by being classicized into temples, like Sigismondo Malatesta's pagan presences in S. Francesco – the 'Tempio Malatestiano' – in Rimini (which even Pius II thought had gone over the top). Paolo Pompilio went so far as to put the Nicene Creed into classical phraseology and imagery, and in the early 16th century Leo X thought that liturgical hymns should conform with humanistic standards. The *New Ecclesiastical Hymns* produced by Zaccaria Ferreri in 1525, which were intended to replace existing Breviary hymns, were classical not only in diction and metre, but in the naming of gods and goddesses – Venus, Bacchus, Circe. There seemed nothing strange to those who had immersed themselves in classical writings about speaking of Christian saints as *divus* or *diva*. This could be seen as a matter of form, not a change of substance.

The pagan world baptized

Reinstating or making play with ancient words and names did not imply any change of belief. There was nothing unusual or shocking about borrowing antique models for Christian art. In Pollaiuolo's tomb for Sixtus IV (p. 100) Diana, as a sparsely draped reclining nude, stands for theology. Gods and goddesses of the ancient past, who had always jostled with other kinds of holy presences in the Christian world, lent their features with varying degrees of recognition to the sometimes studiously allusive holy arts of the high Renaissance. The limp dead body of the ancient hero, Meleager, shown tenderly carried on a Roman sarcophagus, was transmuted by Raphael into the dead Christ of his *Entombment*. The Virgin Mary, 'that true Diana' to Erasmus, is implicitly present in Michelangelo's *Pietà* (p. 143), in which the Virgin wears across the crumpled folds on her breast the quiver strap of the huntress goddess. Popes were happy to associate themselves with the great of ancient history and mythology – Alexander VI with Alexander the Great, Paul III with Jupiter, while Julius II (that new Julius Caesar) could be addressed as Mars or Hercules. Perhaps the greater the familiarity with Antiquity, the less the sense of incongruity. New Rome could be built out of, as well as over, ancient Rome.

Yet there were always fears, of the kind which gave St Jerome such a bad dream, that full service to Cicero conflicted with serving Christ. Deep immersion in classical philosophy, living with an ancient author on terms of familiar converse could undermine Christian belief. Self-knowledge might result in introspection which had little or nothing to do with confession. 'What use is it', Petrarch rhetorically chided Cicero, 'to teach others, what use is it to orate about virtue if you fail to listen to yourself?' Study and imitation of ancient values could change attitudes – some thought dangerously.

Both Reformers and counter-Reformers helped to put up shutters of censorship against the breezy classicizing of early humanist generations. The secular and the pagan, as much as theological misrepresentation and doctrinal error had to be guarded against. It was as improper for Michelangelo to put Charon into the *Last Judgment* as for Veronese to include unscriptural dogs in his *Feast in the House of Levi* (p. 199). Sculpting a drunken Bacchus or Danae in a shower of gold might seem to endanger souls, and Sixtus V prudently decided that Moses would do better than Neptune in the Fontana dell'Acqua Felice in Rome.

The Renaissance ensured that Latin was the lingua franca of European learning, yet ironically the neo-classical Latin writings which the humanists themselves most valued are now the least read. Petrarch rested his posthumous fame on his Virgilian epic, *Africa*, his Livy-inspired history, *De viris illustribus* (*On Famous Men*), and his Ciceronian *De remediis utriusque fortune* (*Remedies for Both Kinds of Fortune*). But it is his Italian poetry, the *Trionfi* and *Canzoniere*, which has above all earned him the lasting laurels he so much desired. To

Agostino di Duccio's exquisite reliefs in the church of S. Francesco at Rimini (1450–57) are more often pagan than Christian in content (here, Diana, the moon, governing her zodiac sign), and the church itself came to be known as the Malatesta Temple, 'Tempio Malatestiano'.

Title page of Pietro Bembo's Prose della volgar lingua *(1538), a defence of the Italian vernacular as a literary language.*

Title page of Fernando de Rojas' tragicomedy of Calisto and Melibea (edition of 1526), better known by the name of its chief character, the procuress La Celestina, was one of the formative works of literature in Spanish.

humanists of the 15th century – and long after – the superiority of Latin as the medium of enduring literature seemed obvious. It needed a bold spirit to argue, as Leonardo Bruni, Chancellor of Florence, did in a humanist debate in 1435, that vernacular Italian was an independent language in its own right, as old as Latin, a popular equivalent of a learned tongue. Yet the Italian vernacular was advanced even in the 15th century by humanist writings. Alberti, who defended the Italian language in his *Della famiglia*, and made his book on painting popular in the 15th century by translating it into the vernacular, also composed the first Italian grammar. In the 16th century Machiavelli wrote his *Discourses on Livy* as well as his plays in Italian, despite their following of Roman models.

As national identities became more conscious and recognized across the whole of 16th-century Europe, vernacular writings rose to new heights, enriched by injections from classical learning. Familiarity with Latin (and to a lesser degree Greek) and training in Ciceronian diction fed back new styles and new words and new forms of writing, and it came to be seen that the vernaculars could claim equal rights with the classical languages. Pietro Bembo in his *Prose della volgar lingua* (1525) did for Italian what Joachim du Bellay did for French in his *Défense et illustration de la langue françoyse* (1549); modern languages, subject to the rules that ennobled Cicero's Latin, could yield illustrious works. The standard of comparison died hard in a world Erasmus did so much to educate. Through the conversational verve of Erasmus' *Colloquies* and the readable pools of classical references in his *Adagia* (themselves examples of rich new hybrid forms), generations were introduced to the commonplaces of Renaissance learning. Plautus and Terence, studied and staged anew, transmitted the heritage of Roman comedy to Machiavelli's *Mandragola*, to Fernando de Rojas' *La Celestina* and to Shakespeare. If there was a sense in which Valla gave birth to Erasmus, and Petrarch to Montaigne, we can also say that without the humanists and without Erasmus, we would not have had Shakespeare.

Changing perspectives

Human nature may not change over millennia, but ways of thinking and perceiving do. Our mental processes owe much to the Renaissance. It was a movement that was both born from and gave birth to an awareness of style – in literature, architecture, sculpture and painting – and though our understanding of the concept may differ, it has descended to us from that period. Style, *maniera*, was central to the thesis of Vasari's *Lives*, which played so important a role in forming the idea of rebirth and renewal in the arts. Discernment of style was a necessity for artistic creation, which itself was progressive, being the process of becoming ever more competent in representing the most beautiful things in nature. Perfection was the goal, ultimately attainable – and attained by Michelangelo. In Vasari's eyes he surpassed all artists, living and dead 'even those most celebrated ancient artists themselves, who beyond all doubt surpassed Nature'. We may no longer subscribe to this thesis, but we cannot help being affected by it. We have ingrained in us the analytical eye that relates art to period and periods to each other, just as

Vasari looked at the phases of development away from 'the old Greek style'. Our judgment is incurably time oriented and historical.

Renaissance refashioning helped to alter the consciousness of time. Temporal dimensions became more defined. There was a clearer understanding of how words and objects belong to their period and are dislocated by being misplaced in time, 'against time'. The concept of anachronism was growing long before the word arrived in the middle of the 17th century. Lorenzo Valla's consciousness of linguistic change enabled him to see that the Donation of Constantine contained words that proved it could not date from the 4th century. Stylistic judgment of another kind made it possible, a generation or so later, to identify the statue long honoured as Constantine at the Lateran Palace in Rome as that of the Emperor Marcus Aurelius. The young Michelangelo brought off a coup early in his career by carving a *Sleeping Cupid* which was sold in Rome in 1496 as an ancient work. When the buyer found out he refused to accept it, but the sculptor gained in repute. Expert judgment as well as expert skill was here on display, for implicit in the making and unmasking of fakes is a grasp of period and style.

Time, and the consciousness of its units – hours, half-hours and minutes – became more noticeable in literature, as it must have been in many lives. 'What time of day is it lad?' Falstaff himself was not immune to the tick of time, even though his might seem to be measured in sack, capons and the exchange of the bawdy house. To the ancient theme of *Carpe diem* (harvest the day) was added the precept 'do not waste time' – God's time. If every humanist's study should (as one thought) ideally be furnished with a clock, the time computed in reading, writing, sleeping and eating was rendered to God's account, since it was he who dispensed the years, months, days, hours and the shorter moments which were only just beginning to be measurable. Vespasiano da Bisticci wrote of a contemporary that 'he placed great store by time and never lost an hour', and Rabelais' Gargantua 'was instructed by Ponocrates, and in such sort disciplined, that he lost not one hour of the day'. Improved time-keeping honed the economy of time – itself attached to self-improvement.

It was not only men of learning who kept a close eye on the passage of hours. The movement of time, more tangibly measured in the pointing hand on the dial of the clock than it was in the drip of the water clock or the hour-glass slide of sand, through the shadow on the sundial or the sound of the bell, promoted time-watching. The clock (an analogy for the universe in the wonderful co-ordination of its moving parts) was watched to keep account of the spendthrift conscience, and for Protestants that meant a solitary personal book-keeper, unaided by any external confessional teller.

Even a portrait could measure personal time. Dürer's series of self-portraits marked his artistic passage through time, as did his careful dating of his works. In England the Tudor musician Thomas Whythorne had himself painted four times. His third likeness showed him time's toll 'by the long [*sic*] and fullness of my beard, the wrinkles on my face, and the hollowness of mine eyes, and also that as my face was altered so were the delights of my mind changed'. As well as being a traditional kind of *memento mori*, Whythorne's portraits served the same introspective purpose as the autobiography in which he recorded

Dürer (1471–1528) portrayed himself over many years, recording the process of ageing from youth to maturity. These two paintings show him at 22 and 28.

The Renaissance in the Perspective of History

The English musician Thomas Whythorne had his portrait painted four times. This is the third from 1569, when he was 41 and already considered himself an old man. He lived to be 67.

these reflections. The pictorial assessment was part of an exercise in self-knowledge.

The pursuit of excellence through imitation, learning to follow ancient models of expression, promoted habits of comparison and self-awareness. Once the rules of the old grammar had been learnt and mastered (absorbed both by those using them and by the connoisseurs who appreciated and commissioned or bought the results), it became possible to break or bend them. Classical orders and Vitruvian proprieties could be adapted and twisted. The proportions of the human body, just as much as the constructions of linear perspective, could be manipulated for deliberate effect. Bramante's spiral staircase in the Belvedere Courtyard in the Vatican, and the vestibule staircase in the Laurentian Library in Florence (p. 288) showed that shock tactics as well as new skills formed part of stylistic development. The elements of licence and distortion that became evident in the paintings of Parmigianino and El Greco, the pursuit of inventiveness, as well as the quality of 'grace' so prized by Vasari, reveal mannerism as a logical development of *maniera*. Art was feeding on itself – as Vasari had shown it must. But that meant that the post-Michelangesque had to arrive, and if, as John Hale has put it 'Mannerism offered a holiday from the *School of Athens*', in the end it was ultimately the same process that produced pre-Raphaelites. The Renaissance established ways of seeing, as well as conventions of painting. The illusions of Escher are premised on Alberti.

There was a kind of end-process for the Renaissance self. After so much refashioning, or self-fashioning, through the imitation of classical models, it was eventually possible to discover more about both the world and the ancient past by turning inwards, taking the self as the object of study. 'I study myself more than any other subject. That is my metaphysics, that is my physics.' It was Montaigne, trying (assaying) himself in his *Essais*, who established this new department of knowledge. Here was an inescapable book to illuminate every library, 'the only book in the world of its kind'. The ancient Delphic instruction 'know thyself' now meant something further: self-ownership. 'The greatest thing in the world is to know how to belong to oneself.' It reads like Montaigne's message to posterity. And Petrarch, continuously revolving around and redefining his literary identity for transmission to his successors, had long before pointed the way.

Europe in 1600 was very different from what it had been in 1300, and it still seems fair to summarize the change by the term Renaissance. It is a period which we need to return to, since our world is rooted in it, to the extent that visiting it may involve a sense of recognition. Just as Petrarch, Machiavelli and Montaigne felt at home talking familiarly with their ancient authors, so we can feel an intimate proximity to these great figures of the Renaissance past. Distant as they are, their voices sound not unlike our own. We can recognize some of our own features in them. We can find delight in surveying their world as one that gave birth to to our own, doubtful though we may be of our present's ability to live up to this inheritance. We may share their sense of the greatness of the past, even if we lack their confidence in the mission to re-create it.

A Renaissance Panorama

Rediscovering Antiquity
Rulers of the World · God and Man
The Image of the World · Living and Dying
Science, Invention and Discovery · The Power of Art
Rebuilding Antiquity

REDISCOVERING ANTIQUITY

F ROM the day in 1345 when Petrarch discovered Cicero's letters in a library in Verona, to the appearance in 1528 of Erasmus' *Ciceronianus*, satirizing pedantic imitations of Cicero, and further on still to the time two generations after that when Montaigne decided, 'I would rather be an authority on myself than on Cicero', it was the ability to read, consort with and talk to, live and have being through the great writers of the classical – especially Roman – past that fired the enthusiasm of scholars, writers and teachers. By means of recovered texts they could establish new links with a seemingly neglected world of supreme accomplishments in literature, building and the arts, which might yet be renewed in the work of a new generation. The world so eagerly sought for was lost and distant, and yet simultaneously close enough to converse with and re-create. The city of Rome, with its crumbling ruins, was both a reproach and a summons.

Italy, with its spread of cities and urban schools and surviving visible Roman buildings – all more evident than those in northern Europe – was the home of this revival. It was however, in Florence, not Rome, that the new movement first took shape. 'There is no place in the world', Leonardo Bruni wrote home from Viterbo in 1405, 'to compare with the splendour of Florence or the urbanity of the Florentines'.

Thanks to its university being a quite recent and weak foundation, and to a relative lack of tight guild restrictions, Florence enjoyed circumstances in which it was easier than in many other places for intellectual and artistic talent to explore new paths. Above all, there was the great wealth of this city of cloth workers, centred in the Medici banking house, on which 15th-century popes depended, especially after Martin V appointed this firm to be the papal bankers in 1421. The scale of patronage that accompanied such business is vividly illustrated by the ability of Cosimo de' Medici – in the days when books were costly handwritten works – to order two hundred volumes at once. 'As there was no lack of money', the famous Florentine bookseller, Vespasiano da Bisticci, was able to arrange for 45 scribes to complete the necessary copying in less than two years, all the daily costs being settled at the bank. From Florence, which became a magnetic source attracting the wonder of visitors from other parts of Italy and elsewhere, new initiatives in both learning and the arts fanned out, initially to other parts of Italy, and then further afield throughout Europe.

In the 15th century many people travelled in search of books, teachers and education. Of course this was not a new phenomenon. The fame of Peter Abelard in the 12th century had drawn many students to Paris. What made the travels of this period distinctive was the concentrated search for the texts of ancient authors and for new kinds of teaching and learning. The 'humanists' were those engaged in *studia humanitatis*, the studies that concerned humanity, the condition and qualities of man and human nature (as opposed to Abelard's divinity, or theology, the study of matters belonging to God). The humanists' work necessarily centred on the record of the page, and from the 1460s it was increasingly possible for that page to be printed: Cicero's *De oratore* was

St Jerome (c. 331–420) *spent his life partly in the Syrian desert meditating, learning Hebrew and mortifying the flesh (and, as legend has it, making friends with a lion, from whose paw he removed a thorn), and partly in Rome, where he was secretary to Pope Damasus, translated the Bible into the Latin (the Vulgate) and wrote the works that place him among the Fathers of the Church. He was often shown as a hermit striking his breast with a stone, but Renaissance artists preferred to see him as a scholar in his study. In Dürer's engraving of 1514, the lion, who has here lain down with a small dog, rests peacefully in the foreground; at the back hangs his cardinal's hat (an anachronism indicating his status as a theologian). Jerome himself is intent upon his text, an image with which any humanist could identify.*

The tomb of Leonardo Bruni (died 1444), scholar, historian and Chancellor of Florence. 'The Muses, Greek and Latin alike', runs the inscription, 'cannot restrain their tears'.

Federigo da Montefeltro, Duke of Urbino, on the left, with the humanist writer Cristoforo Landino. Landino's most famous work, Disputationes camaldulenses *(c. 1472), records philosophical conversations between Lorenzo de' Medici, Alberti and Marsilio Ficino.*

printed at Subiaco in 1465 and Quintilian's *Institutio oratoria* at Rome twice in 1470. Humanist educators trained their pupils not for the church, or the scholar's study, or university lecture hall, but for active participation in the life of city and court. Grammar was the basis, leading on to rhetoric (the art of persuasion), ethics, poetry (audible painting) and history, topics through which individuals learned the arts of social interaction, and were prepared for their full, committed and accomplished say in the affairs of the world.

Poggio Bracciolini (p. 35) expressed this understanding of the priority of the well-phrased spoken word in a letter written in 1416 – when he was in his mid-thirties – at a time of great excitement. It was addressed to Guarino da Verona, six years his senior and a man who (unlike Poggio himself) had considerable knowledge of Greek. Guarino owed this proficiency to the years he spent in Greece, where he pursued his studies in Constantinople in the entourage of Manuel Chrysoloras, returning in 1408 with a small library of 54 Greek manuscripts. Poggio's words would have been music in the ears of a man who was to become one of the most famous teachers of his day. Speech, wrote Poggio, 'is the greatest gift of all'.

> For it is speech alone which we use to express the power of our mind and which separates us from the other beings. And so we must be deeply grateful to the pioneers in the other liberal arts and especially to those who by their concern and efforts have given us rules for speaking and a pattern of perfection.

Guarino's celebrated school at Ferrara (1429–36), like that of his own teacher, Vittorino da Feltre at Mantua, was of courtly origin and educated the children of the Este family as Vittorino had those of the Gonzaga, though others were also admitted (and Vittorino himself supported his poorest charges). Through philosophy and eloquence, both mental and physical schooling, these aristocratic heirs were to learn 'the life of social duty'. The influence of these two dedicated teachers proved to be far-reaching. One of Vittorino's pupils who made full use of his learning at Mantua's 'Casa Gioiosa' was Federigo da Montefeltro (p. 73), whose court at Urbino became a centre of Renaissance lustre. A distinguished pupil of Guarino was Janus Pannonius, who helped to transplant humanist thought into Hungary, while in the next generation the discriminating artistic patronage of Isabella d'Este, Marchioness of Mantua, perhaps owed something to her classical studies with Guarino's son, Battista.

The manuscripts assembled by early humanists, on which advances in knowledge so greatly depended, always ran the risk of dispersal at the deaths of their owners. Like Petrarch (pp. 34, 35), Coluccio Salutati and Niccolò Niccoli were both fervent bibliophiles who made important collections of classical texts during their lives. Salutati, Chancellor of Florence, acquired some of Petrarch's books at his death in 1374 and gathered 600 or so volumes, making a library about three times the size of the poet's, which he was generous in allowing fellow scholars to borrow from and use much like a public library. But when Salutati died in 1405, this collection too was dispersed. Only later in the 15th century was one of these libraries kept together, as its owner had wished. Niccoli had an unrivalled collection of classical texts – built up through energetic correspondence and the copying of his own hand, which become a magnet for all visitors to Florence. He wanted his books to be available to 'all studious citizens', and four years after he died, in 1437, they passed into the library of the Dominican house of S. Marco, thanks to the generosity of Cosimo de' Medici, who shouldered Niccoli's burden of debt. Although this was not the same as a public library, the idea of such an institution had been seeded. Even in far off, less urbane London the wealth of a leading citizen was dedicated early in the 15th century to the creation of a public library in the Guildhall.

Much could be learnt from books – but creative work depended on patrons – and scholars and connoisseurs congregated in the places where they could find the best collections of works of art, antiquities and 'curiosities', as well as books. Individual collectors could play a very influential role in educating the taste of their contemporaries – monarchs included. Jacopo da Strada, with his many contacts inside and outside Italy, was such a man. By the time he went to the court of Albrecht V of Bavaria he had published an illustrated work on ancient coins, which he had worked on while in the service of Hans Jakob Fugger (p. 232) in Augsburg. He kept his own great numismatic collection in Vienna, where he became court antiquary and artistic adviser successively to the Emperors Ferdinand I and Maximilian II. Strada spent the last years of his life in Prague, and died in 1588 in the service of Rudolf II. Titian's portrait (p. 60) seems a true memorial to this 'Civis Romanus' and 'Antiquarius', who is shown in the act of displaying an antique sculpture, with coins on the table before him, and books on the cornice above his head.

Late 16th-century Europe had nothing to compare with the court of the Emperor Rudolf, who ruled over Bohemia from 1575 to 1612. He was the greatest collector of his day, and his collections reflected his encyclopaedic interests, including plants, animals and minerals, as well as books, paintings and engravings. Visitors to his court could find there men of science and occult learning, as well as humanist scholars like Strada. Tycho Brahe (p. 215) and then Johann Kepler held the post of imperial astronomer; the English mathematician John Dee pursued his occult studies in Prague; and the artists who worked for the court included Bartholomeus Spranger (pp. 51, 53), the engraver Aegidius Sadeler, and Giuseppe Arcimboldi (p. 259), a close associate of the king. Rudolf, who seemed to some another Hermes Trismegistus, had made Prague the cynosure of the art world by 1604, when Karel van Mander, the Vasari of northern artists, wrote in his *Het Schilderboeck* (*The Painter's Book*), 'whoever so desires nowadays has only to go to Prague ... to the greatest art patron in the world at the present time.'

The library of S. Marco, Florence (after 1438), where Niccolò Niccoli's books found a final home. Financed by Cosimo de' Medici, the building was designed by Michelozzo Michelozzi.

A cabinet of natural curiosities, similar to that maintained by the Emperor Rudolf II. It belonged to Ferrante Imperati in the late 17th century.

1. Manuscript of Livy copied and annotated by Petrarch (*c.* 1330).

2. Pietro Bembo, poet, scholar and later cardinal, by Raphael (*c.* 1500).

3. Daniele Barbaro, philosopher, writer and patron, by Veronese, detail (*c.* 1555).

4. Petrarch in his study, miniature, detail (mid-14th century).

5. Tomb of Lorenzo Valla, scholar, teacher and papal secretary (1460).

Humanist beginnings

THE curtain rises on the Renaissance not amid the splendour of courts or the colourful activity of artists' workshops, but in the quiet studies of scholars. Many Latin authors, of course, had been neither lost nor forgotten, but they were read in medieval (that is Christian) terms. The first achievement of the humanists, of whom the pioneer was characteristically a poet, Petrarch (1, 4), was, by an effort of the imagination, to grasp the classical world in its own terms (7). Appreciating the literary quality of their authors, they tried to emulate them, at the same time purging them of textual corruption (5) and searching out hitherto unknown manuscripts (6). The second achievement was the mastery of Greek, which opened up whole new intellectual horizons, but had initially to be translated with Latin (9). All this needed leisure, and all scholars depended upon patrons (3, 8) to give them that leisure, a debt repaid by a new breed of scholar-diplomats and scholar-churchmen (2, 5). The result has been called 'a perturbed mental stocktaking', an openness to classical values at every level, including the ethical.

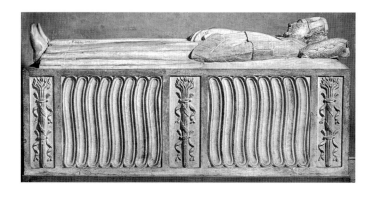

8. Lorenzo de' Medici with philosophers and scholars by Vasari (1559).

6. Poggio Bracciolini, scholar and arch-discoverer of classical manuscripts, detail (1455).

7. Frontispiece to Petrarch's copy of Virgil by Simone Martini (mid-14th century).

9. Dedication of Marsilio Ficino's *Life and Works of Plotinus* (late 15th century).

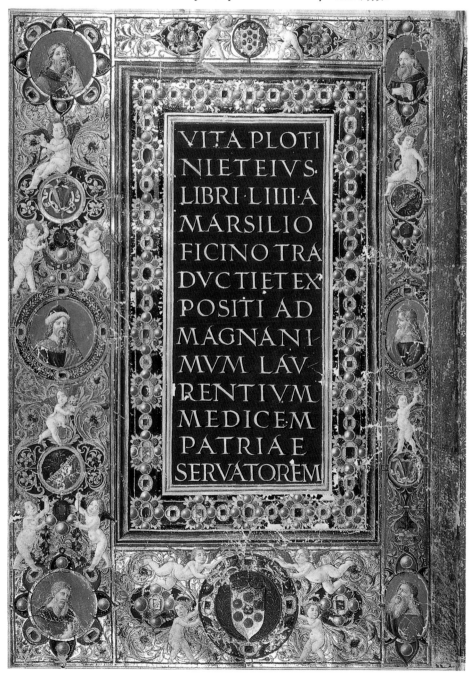

VITA PLOTI
NIETEIVS.
LIBRI·LIIII·A
MARSILIO
FICINO TRA
DVCTI ET EX
POSITI AD
MAGNANI
MVM LAV
RENTIVM
MEDICEM
PATRIAE
SERVATOREM

1. Title page of Erasmus' *Adagia*, 1523, with portraits of Greek and Latin authors.

2. Sir Thomas More, author of *Utopia* and Lord Chancellor; executed 1535. Portrait by Holbein, detail (1527).

3. John Colet, scholar, teacher, Dean of St Paul's; died 1519. Portrait by Holbein (1530s).

4. Guillaume Budé, scholar, adviser to François I; died 1540. Portrait by François Clouet (*c.* 1536).

The northern humanists

THE first wave of humanist scholarship was Italian. The second belonged to the north. But no sooner had it got under way than it was engulfed by the Reformation and men who, like Melanchthon (**6**), would have been happy to spend their lives quietly teaching Hebrew and Greek were forced to take up a position in the religious conflict. Some – Colet (**3**), Celtis (**9**) – died before the choice became necessary. More's choice, to refuse assent to Henry VIII's oath of supremacy, cost him his life in 1535 (**2**). Budé (**4**) and Vivès (**10**) also held to the old religion, though the latter chose not to live in his native Spain. Pierre Gilles (**8**), Amerbach (**7**) and – greatest of them all – Erasmus (**5**) remained loyal to Catholicism though with many reservations, and hoping always for reconciliation. All these men were scholars first and polemicists second. The work by Erasmus which probably made the most impact on European culture was the *Adagia* (**1**), a selection of sayings from classical authors, with his own lengthy commentaries, moral, philosophical and personal.

Old and new learning, 42–43

The Bible, 118–19

The printed page, 208–09

6. Philip Melanchthon, scholar, teacher, Reformer, main author of the Confession of Augsburg; died 1560. Portrait by Lucas Cranach the Elder, detail.

5. Desiderius Erasmus, scholar, editor of classical, patristic and biblical texts, author of *The Praise of Folly*; died 1536. Portrait by Holbein, detail (1523).

7. Bonifacio Amerbach, friend and heir of Erasmus. Portrait by Holbein (1519).

8. Pierre Gilles, town clerk of Antwerp, friend of More and Erasmus, appears in person in *Utopia*; died 1533. Portrait by Massys (1517).

9. Conrad Celtis, scholar and editor of classical texts; died 1508 (1508).

10. Juan Luis Vivès, Spanish scholar who spent most of his life in the Netherlands; died 1540.

Rediscovering Antiquity   37

1. *Ariosto* presumed portrait by Palma Vecchio, detail (1515).

2. Niccolò Machiavelli by Santi di Tito, detail (16th century).

3. Baldassare Castiglione by Raphael, detail (1513).

4. Michel de Montaigne (late 15th century).

5. William Shakespeare from the First Folio (1623).

6. Miguel de Cervantes by Juan de Jauregui (1600).

Classical models and new literature

THE extraordinary literary flowering of the Renaissance was the product of a medieval tradition fertilized by the rediscovered classics. The legacy of the Middle Ages was not immediately discarded. Dante (11), though long dead, was still being read and illustrated; the old tales of chivalry (10) were read, if only to be mocked by Cervantes (6), and Rabelais' grotesquely learned farce of Gargantua and Pantagruel (9) rests solidly on scholastic philosophy. Boccaccio (12) gathered his stories from every century. Other new forms reflect classical models – though often so distantly that they are virtually unrecognizable. Seneca, Plautus and Terence are the remote ancestors of popular drama in England (5) and Spain. The romantic epics of Tasso and Ariosto (1, 13, 14) descend ultimately from the *Odyssey* and the *Aeneid*; humanist political satire, from Machiavelli (2) and Aretino (7) to More (8) learnt much from Lucian, as well as Latin moralists such as Cicero and Juvenal; while the social and psychological insights of Castiglione (3) and Montaigne (4) spring from minds thoroughly at home in the world of Horace. Yet what is most striking in this whole panorama of genius is the number of its innovations; almost every literary form has Renaissance roots.

7. Pietro Aretino by Titian, detail (1545).

Old and new learning, 42–43

The printed page, 208–09

The theatre, 282–83

8. Woodcut of More's *Utopia* (1518).

11. Illustration from Dante's *Paradiso* (Dante exiled from Florence) by Giovanni di Paolo (1445).

9. Woodcut of Pantagruel arriving in Paris from Rabelais, *Pantagruel*, Book II (1547).

12. Illustration of the story of Nastagio degli Onesti from Boccaccio's *Decameron* by Botticelli (1482–83).

10. Title page of the tale of *Amadis de Gaula* (1531).

13. Title page of Tasso's *Gerusalemme liberata* (1590).

14. Title page of Ariosto's *Orlando furioso* (1542).

The world of humanism

RAPHAEL'S great painting *The School of Athens* (1509–10) in the Vatican is a pictorial expression of all that the Renaissance stood for in the secular sphere (its religious equivalent, *The Disputà*, faces it on the opposite wall). In the centre of this detail stand Plato and Aristotle, Plato, holding his *Timaeus*, pointing upwards (his philosophy being transcendental and mystical), Aristotle, who holds a copy of his *Ethics*, downwards (concerned

Rediscovering Antiquity

with earthly reality). Bringing together ancient and modern, Raphael represents the writers and thinkers of Antiquity in the guise of men of his own day. Plato, for instance, is Leonardo da Vinci; Heraclitus, in the foreground, writing on a block of stone, is Michelangelo; Euclid, on the right, bending down with compasses in his hand, is Bramante. The setting for the assembly is Bramante's then unfinished basilica of St Peter's.

Old and new learning

IN the schools and universities of the Renaissance, humanist learning was grafted onto an educational system inherited from the Middle Ages, the aims of which were essentially vocational. The Hill of Knowledge (1) began with the gate of Grammar, ascending through the other Liberal Arts – Arithmetic, Logic, Music, Astronomy, Geometry and Rhetoric – to the summit of Theology. But if this was the theory, the practice was more pragmatic, with the old universities of Europe from Poland (2) to Spain (3) specializing in rhetoric, law or medicine according to the student's needs. Up to the mid-16th century books were scarce; teaching was face-to-face through lectures and readings (4, 5, 6, 7). Libraries were to be found in universities, monastic schools and privately endowed institutions (8). Innovative teaching like that of Vittorino da Feltre and Guarino da Verona and some of their pupils had an important influence on contemporaries.

1. *The Hill of Knowledge*, Florentine miniature (late 15th century).

3. Entrance to Salamanca University (founded 1242).

2. Courtyard of the Jagellonian University, Cracow (founded 1364).

Allegory, 46–47

The Ages of Man, 176–77

The printed page, 208–09

4. Teachers and students (Grammar), terracotta plaque by Luca della Robbia (1431–38).

5. Lecture at Salamanca University (16th century).

6. Notes taken by a student at a lecture by William Sellynge (late 15th century).

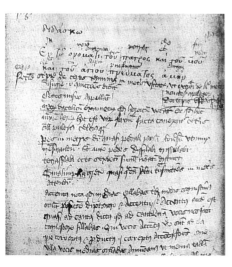

7. A lecture in law (*St Augustine Teaching in Rome*) by Benozzo Gozzoli (15th century).

8. Laurentian Library, Florence, by Michelangelo (begun 1523).

Rediscovering Antiquity   43

1. The Neoplatonic scholars Pico della Mirandola, Marsilio Ficino and Angelo Poliziano in a fresco by Cosimo Rosselli (1486).

2. Ficino, Cristoforo Landino, Poliziano and Giovanni de' Becchi in a fresco by Ghirlandaio (1485–90).

Plato and Hermes

THE single most important task for Renaissance thinkers was to reconcile classical philosophy (which they revered) with Christianity (in which they believed). The allegorization of myth was one means of doing this. In the strictly philosophical field, it was Plato who seemed to come closest to Christian values – or rather the later Platonic philosopher Plotinus, who lived in the 3rd century AD. Plotinus made Plato into a mystic whose concept of 'the Good' could be equated with God (4, 6). At the same time, the west discovered another collection of late Greek writings attributed to an Egyptian sage, Hermes Trismegistus ('Thrice-Great Hermes') who was believed to be a contemporary of Moses (7, 8) and was valued as highly as Plato. Marsilio Ficino (1, 2), at the request of Lorenzo de' Medici, translated both into Latin (1463–69). A host of other, now little read, texts were scoured for non-Christian parallels to Christian doctrine, from the Jewish Cabbala to the Roman cult of Isis and Osiris. In the painting below (3), we see, at the bottom, the marriage of Isis and Osiris and, going in a clockwise direction, Osiris teaching fruit gathering, the cultivation of the vine and the use of the plough. (The ox was the Borgia heraldic animal.)

3. The myth of Isis and Osiris, ceiling fresco in the Borgia Apartment in the Vatican, by Pinturicchio (1492–95).

Allegory, 46–47

The uses of myth, 48–49

Alchemy and astrology, 216–17

4. Reverse of a medal of Marsilio Ficino, 'Platone', by Niccolò Fiorentino (before 1500).

7. Hermes Trismegistus, Isis and Moses, detail of a fresco in the Borgia Apartment in the Vatican, by Pinturicchio (1492–95).

5. Reverse of a medal of Angelo Poliziano, 'Studia', by Niccolò Fiorentino (before 1500).

6. Detail of a bust by Donatello showing the platonic image of the soul, the charioteer, drawn to God by the two horses of will and reason (mid-15th century).

8. Hermes Trismegistus from the mosaic floor of Siena Cathedral (1488).

Allegory

THE Renaissance loved allegory – loved it too much, sometimes, for modern art historians' peace of mind. Like so much else, Antiquity set the precedent. Lucian describes a painting by Apelles representing *Calumny* (Calumny is the young woman in the centre, dragging a man by the hair; Rumour going before; Truth and Remorse to the left), and several painters, including Botticelli (5), reconstructed it. Without this knowledge, the painting would be incomprehensible. More straightforward are other allegories by Botticelli (9) whose point is that humanist learning conquers barbarism, and by Baldung Grien (10) with its conventional symbolism of death. Others yield to intelligent guesswork. Tura's female figure (4) is probably one of the seasons, either spring or summer. Eworth's *Sir John Luttrell* (8) celebrates a peace treaty after a sea battle. Dürer's *Melancholia* (7) is a complex exercise in reference and allusion – too many meanings rather than too few. But Titian's *Sacred and Profane Love* (6), so called only in the 17th century, keeps its secret: is it a Neoplatonic image of the Terrestrial and Celestial Venuses, an episode from the *Hypnerotomachia*, or a wedding portrait of a Venetian nobleman's wife at the Fountain of Venus?

3. Giovanni Bellini: *Allegory of Inconstancy* (*c.* 1490–1500).

1. Giovanni Bellini: *Sacred Allegory* (*c.* 1490–1500).

2. Leonardo da Vinci: *Allegory* (*c.* 1510).

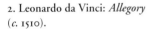

4. Cosimo Tura: *Allegorical Figure* (1480s).

The uses of myth, 48–49

Alchemy and astrology, 216–17

5. Botticelli: *The Calumny of Apelles* (*c.* 1494–95).

6. Titian: *Sacred and Profane Love* (1515).

9. Botticelli: *Pallas Athene and the Centaur* (*c.* 1482–83).

10. Hans Baldung Grien: *Vanity* (1509–11).

7. Dürer: *Melancholia* (1514).

8. Hans Eworth: *Sir John Luttrell* (1550). It has recently been suggested that this is an allegory of the Treaty of Boulogne between England and France. Peace holds an olive branch while behind her Venus bridles a war-horse.

1. Raphael: *Venus, Ceres and Juno* in the loggia of the Villa Farnesina (1569).

2. Bronzino: *Andrea Doria as Neptune*, detail (*c.* 1540–50).

3. School of Fontainebleau: *Diana the Huntress* (*c.* 1550).

The uses of myth

CLASSICAL mythology became so familiar to educated men and women of the Renaissance that it could be used as an allegorical language conveying meanings not always obvious to modern eyes. Sometimes these meanings are political: Queen Elizabeth's beauty confounds the three goddesses who competed for the Golden Apple (7); Doge Andrea Doria celebrates his fame as an admiral by assuming the character of Neptune, ruler of the sea (2); Diane de Poitiers, mistress of Henri II, appears as Diana the huntress (3); while François I has himself portrayed, rather absurdly, with the combined attributes of Mars (war), Minerva (wisdom), Diana (the chase), Mercury (eloquence) and Cupid (love) (4). Other paintings would have been given more general applications: the sad tale of Psyche as told by Apuleius in *The Golden Ass* (recently translated by a friend of Raphael's patron, Agostino Chigi) – here the jealous Venus seeks the aid of Ceres and Juno to find Psyche, but they refuse (1); love conquering war for the studiolo of Isabella d'Este, with Mars and Venus at the top, and Vulcan, Mercury, Apollo and nine dancing muses (5); and Apollo and the Muses again, signalling harmony for Henry VIII's wedding to Anne Boleyn (6).

4. Niccolò dell' Abbate: *Mythological Portrait of François I*, detail (*c.* 1545).

5. Mantegna: *Parnassus* (1497).

6. Hans Holbein: *Parnassus* (1533).

7. Hans Eworth: *Queen Elizabeth and the Three Goddesses* (c. 1516).

1. Piero della Francesca: *Hercules* (late 15th century).

2. Peter Vischer the Elder: detail of Hercules from the shrine of St Sebald, Nuremberg (1508–19).

3. Baccio Bandinelli: *Hercules and Cacus* (c. 1530).

Hercules

HERCULES was a popular figure in Renaissance poetry and art, partly because he could stand for such a wide range of meanings beside the conventional one of heroic valour (1). Erasmus considered the stories about him to be beneficial fables; his Twelve Labours were sometimes represented in churches as a parallel with the punishment of Adam. Peter Vischer the Elder included him, along with other figures from classical legend, on his shrine of St Sebald at Nuremberg (2). For Florentines he was a particular favourite as their mythical protector – he even appears on seals of the Signoria – and his conquests over Cacus (3), Antaeus (6) and the Hydra (4) – are images of Florentine victories over their enemies. Other aspects of his eventful life also had their appeal, such as his marriage with Dejinira whom he saved from the centaur Nessus (7).

The uses of myth, 48–49

The human form, 248–49

Sculpture: a new dimension, 262–63

4. Antonio Pollaiuolo: *Hercules and the Hydra* (*c.* 1470).

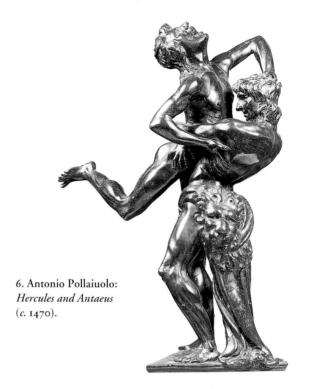

6. Antonio Pollaiuolo:
Hercules and Antaeus
(*c.* 1470).

7. Bartholomeus Spranger: *Hercules, Dejinira and the Dead Nessus*
(1580).

5. Dürer: *Hercules* (1498).

1. Francesco del Cossa: *The Month of April*, detail (1470).

3. Annibale Carracci: *Venus and Anchises*, detail (1595–1600).

Venus

VENUS in the Renaissance stood for sexual love; but, laden with meanings from the ancient world, from the Middle Ages, astrology and occult philosophy, she stood for much more. As a planet, she ruled the season of Spring, presiding over Nature's fecundity (1). Botticelli shows her new born from the sea, in a picture that has been interpreted as an expression of Neoplatonic ideas (6). As the lover of Mars, she represents peace opposed to war – Cossa shows him kneeling before her in chains (1) and Giulio Romano brings them into more intimate harmony (8). In her role as goddess of love (2), she completely loses the hostile overtones of the Middle Ages, which associated her with lust; with her mischievous son Cupid she spreads happiness and mocks prudence and reason (7, 9). Her many love affairs gave Venus a particular appeal to the humanist courts of Italy. Aeneas, the hero of Virgil's epic and the founder of Rome, was the offspring of her union with Anchises (3), but her passion for Adonis could not save him from his fatal love of the chase (4, 5).

4. Veronese: *Venus and Adonis* (c. 1580).

5. Titian: *Venus and Adonis*, detail (1554).

2. Titian: *Venus of Urbino* (1538).

A new eroticism,
192–93

Sex and gender,
196–97

The human form,
248–49

7. Lucas Cranach the Elder: *Venus and Cupid* (1508–09).

6. Botticelli: *The Birth of Venus*, detail (*c.* 1485).

8. Giulio Romano: *The Bath of Mars and Venus*, detail (1528).

9. Bartholomeus Spranger: *Venus, Mercury and Cupid*, detail (1580s).

Rediscovering Antiquity 53

1. The Three Graces (Hellenistic period).

2. Francesco del Cossa: detail from *The Triumph of Venus* (1470).

The spell of the Antique

SINCE virtually no classical painting survived, it was sculptured images that haunted the Renaissance. Some of them (like the Belvedere Torso) turn up in disguised and unexpected ways. Others go through a series of metamorphoses, but are instantly recognizable. The Three Graces, attendants on Venus, were known from a famous Roman group in Siena (1). The first artist to revive the pose – two seen from the front and one from the back – seems to have been Cossa (2). In Niccolò Fiorentino's

medal (5) they are given allegorical qualities – Chastity, Beauty and Love. They appear again, attending upon Flora, in Botticelli's *Primavera* (6) and yet again, more enigmatically, in the monument made by Germain Pilon supporting the urn that contained the heart of Henri II (7). Another classical figure, once called 'Cleopatra' but now identified as the sleeping Ariadne (3), was copied many times, most voluptuously by Titian in his *Bacchanal* (4).

3. Sleeping Ariadne (Roman).

4. Titian: detail from *Bacchanal* (c. 1518).

The uses of myth, 48–49

The human form, 248–49

Sculpture: a new dimension, 262–63

5. Niccolò Fiorentino: medal of Giovanna Tornabuoni, reverse (1486).

6. Botticelli: detail from *Primavera* (*c.* 1478).

7. Germain Pilon: monument for the heart of Henri II (1559).

1. View of Rome, fresco in the Palazzo Ducale, Mantua (15th century).

2. The Colosseum by Silvestro da Ravenna (c. 1480).

3. Reconstruction of the Temple at Palestrina, near Rome, by an unknown artist (first half of the 17th century).

4. Part of a Roman calendar copied by Jean Matal (late 16th century).

The ruins of Rome

THE city of Rome was itself the most cogent sign and symbol of classical civilization. Every Roman or visitor to Rome was aware that here he was among the ruins of greatness. They inspired Cola di Rienzi in the early 14th century to revive the republic. Petrarch was crowned Poet Laureate on the Capitol in 1341. Artists and architects from Masaccio and Donatello to Giuliano da Sangallo (8), Heemskerck (6) and Silvestro da Ravenna (2) measured and drew Roman buildings and inscriptions (4), and in their imagination reconstructed what they had once been (3). This vision of a vanished past was perhaps realized most completely by painters. Mantegna, a man deeply versed in Antiquity, re-created the stern world of the Caesars (5, 7) for the Gonzaga court of Mantua, as Antoine Caron did, rather less seriously, for the Valois in Paris (see p. 264). Views of the city, such as that painted for the Mantuan Palazzo Ducale (1) dwell particularly on the ancient structures that remained – the wall, the aqueduct, the Colosseum, the Pantheon, the Arch of Septimius Severus and the Columns of Trajan and Marcus Aurelius.

7. Part of Mantegna's *Triumphs of Caesar* (1486–94).

5. Mantegna: detail from the *Martyrdom of St Christopher* (1459).

8. Roman Architecture and Sculpture drawn after Giuliano da Sangallo (late 15th century).

6. Roman sarcophagus and sphinxes by Maerten van Heemskerck (c. 1532).

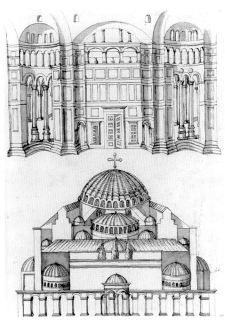

1. Interior and exterior of Hagia Sophia, Constantinople, after Giuliano da Sangallo from Ciriaco d'Ancona's original (early 17th century).

3. Oldest known map of Constantinople (1420).

2. Gentile Bellini: *Cardinal Bessarion presenting a Reliquary of the True Cross*, detail (*c.* 1472).

4. Opening of Aristotle's *Historia animalium* printed in Venice in 1497 (it was owned by Pirckheimer, for whom Dürer added the two cupids at the bottom).

5. Manuel Chrysoloras (1408).

Humanist beginnings, 34–35

Classical models and new literature, 38–39

Old and new learning, 42–43

6. Gentile Bellini: *St Mark Preaching in Alexandria*, detail (*c.* 1507).

Constantinople and Greek learning

C ONTACTS between Italy and the Byzantine Empire were close – Ciriaco d'Ancona made architectural sketches in Constantinople (1) and Athens in 1418. And as the Turkish threat grew more serious they became closer. Visits to the west by emperors and churchmen brought scholars who often stayed to teach Greek to a public hungry for such expertise – Chrysoloras in 1397 (5), Gemistus Pletho and Bessarion in 1438. The latter settled in Rome, became a cardinal, presented a reliquary to the church of the Carità in Venice (2), lived long enough to see the beginning of printing there (4) and left his library of Greek books to the Venetian republic. After the fall of Constantinople to the Turks, this interchange ceased, but links were not entirely broken. Gentile Bellini went there from 1478 to 1481 and painted Sultan Mehmet II's portrait (7). His picture of St Mark preaching at Alexandria (6) is a strange mixture of Istanbul and Venice, whose basilica of St Mark is itself a Byzantine building on Italian soil, adorned by the bronze horses from Constantinople – gains from the Fourth Crusade in 1204.

7. Gentile Bellini: portrait of Sultan Mehmet II (1480).

1. Jacopo da Strada by Titian (1567–68).

Collectors and collections

SCHOLARS collected books and manuscripts. Antiquarians collected sculptures (1, 3), coins (2), gems and inscriptions. Only later did the idea of collecting contemporary art by famous artists arise, but by the late 16th century a library and an art gallery had become necessary items of cultural prestige, from bankers (5) to popes. In the north, collecting was less discriminating in its range, and a typical 'cabinet of curiosities' might contain anything from oil paintings to sea shells (7). Sometimes special rooms were built to house the collections. The Earl of Arundel's sculpture gallery in London (4) was unique in England. Most splendid of all was the Antiquarium (6) built in the Munich Residenz to house the collection of Albrecht V of Bavaria.

2. Coin cabinet made for the Emperor Frederick III (1590).

3. Andrea Odoni by Lorenzo Lotto (1527).

6. The Antiquarium of the Munich Residenz designed for Albrecht V of Bavaria by Jacopo da Strada (1570).

4. The Earl of Arundel in his sculpture gallery in London designed by Inigo Jones, by Daniel Mytens (*c.* 1618).

5. The banker Lorenzo Galli's garden of antiquities in Rome, which included Michelangelo's *Bacchus* (*c.* 1535).

7. *Cabinet of Curiosities* by Franz Francken the Younger (1636).

RULERS OF THE WORLD

UNLIKE today's world, fashion in Renaissance Europe was part of politics. The great powers of the day ruled through magnetic splendour; authority was ostentatious and centred in courts, princely, royal and imperial. Patrons and place-seekers congregated where service was needed, where benefits might flow and new talents be discovered. Courts were hubs, not only of government and administration, but also of manners and etiquette, of the latest styles of writing, composing and dressing, and increasingly, of building and painting.

Naturally the scene shifted with changes on the international stage. In the course of the 15th century Rome was transformed from being a no-man's land, without the papal court, into a world power, capable of literally dividing the globe between Spain and Portugal when, in 1494, the Treaty of Tordesillas and Alexander VI's papal bull arbitrated the rival claims over the newly discovered lands, and drew a line which determined the future of central and south America and claims to the Spice Islands in the eastern hemisphere. In the 15th century, when the city states of Italy, especially Florence and Venice, were becoming standard bearers of culture over the Alps, the late-Gothic refinement of the duchy of Burgundy, with its control over much of the Low Countries, still dominated western Europe. In the 16th century, when imperium was the name of the regnal game, the kings of France and England envisaged their rule in terms of such supremacy, though that did not prevent either Henry VIII or François I from aiming at the imperial title in 1519. The increasing strength and cohesion of the French and English monarchies made the courts of Fontainebleau and London desirable centres, while the territorial power of the Habsburgs brought distinction in turn to Brussels, Antwerp, Prague and Madrid.

War could bring booty and renown as well as territorial acquisition. The contests in which Florence, Milan and Venice established themselves as powerful city states made lasting heroes of several condottieri careerists. France became a new entity as the result of the long struggle with England and the eventual expulsion of the English from all French soil except Calais (which was not French until 1558). Italy became the theatre of northern ambition when Charles VIII of France invaded in 1494 and proceeded to conquer Naples, followed by François I's campaign of 1515 (when the French king defeated the Sforza duke of Milan at Marignano), and culminating in the crushing defeat of the French by the forces of Charles V at Pavia in 1525, and the shock of the Sack of Rome by the unpaid imperial troops two years later.

Dynastic rule and the future of whole regions might switch as the result of the fortunes of war. Richard III's death in the fighting at Bosworth in 1485 put Tudors in place of Plantagenets on the English throne. The death of Charles, Duke of Burgundy, at the battle of Nancy in 1477 split the Burgundian inheritance, with the lion's share of these lands passing into Habsburg control through the marriage of Charles' daughter Maria to Maximilian I. Yet given prevailing chivalric conventions, the great were as likely to die in a hunt or tournament as they were in the field of battle. François I was taken prisoner at Pavia, but

*'The **Emperor** led his troops in person, mounted on a Spanish horse, dressed in a sumptuous habit and carrying a lance in his hand.' Titian's portrait of Charles V at the Battle of Mühlberg became the standard model for equestrian portraits of Baroque monarchs. It shows Charles at the peak of his power as the champion of Catholic Europe. In 1547 Luther's Church was dominant in most of the German states. Charles tried first compromise and then force, and at Mühlberg on the upper Elbe he defeated the Protestant army of the Elector of Saxony. Titian came to Augsburg in the summer of 1548 to paint the picture. Mühlberg in fact solved nothing. Eight years later, in 1555, the Treaty of Augsburg accepted the status quo and the two factions concluded an uneasy peace that lasted until the outbreak of the Thirty Years War in 1618.*

An elaborate entertainment organized for Queen Elizabeth in 1591: a pond was specially dug, a fort built on an island, nereids swam, cannons fired and tritons blew their horns.

The Valois Tapestries, made probably in the 1580s, celebrate various festivities presided over by Catherine de Médicis during her regency. This one took place in Bayonne in 1565, when the Spanish and French royal families met. In the background knights are running at the quintain, a dragon whose tail swings round to hit the unwary contestant in the back. In the foreground stands the future Henri III in Roman costume.

his son Henri II – known as a man who took terrible risks in the hunting field – died in 1559 after a bout of exhibitionism at the tournament, held to celebrate the peace of Cateau-Cambrésis, in which he received a wound in the eye from which he died ten days afterwards (p. 200).

Courts and rulers could communicate through diplomatic contacts (pp. 82–83). Resident ambassadors, whose job it was to convey the official line ('sent to lie abroad for the good of their country', as Sir Henry Wotton put it) sent home interesting gossip in addition to matters of state. The arts as well as politics formed part of ambassadors' news flashes. In 1494 the French envoy in Venice, Philippe de Commynes, reported the deep impression the city's appearance made on him. 'I marvelled greatly to see the placement of this city and to see so many church towers and monasteries, and such large buildings, and all in the water.'

The rulers of the day assumed as axiomatic that dignity involved display, and conspicuous expenditure went on the ephemeral as well as the durable. The rites of passage that marked their lives were occasions of public concern, often reported for posterity visually as well as verbally, and carrying their name and fame far afield in their own time. In the 17th century Europe's three most impressive sights were deemed the crowning of the German emperor at Frankfurt, the coronation of the French king at Rheims, and the burial of the Duke of Lorraine at Nancy.

Royal coronations, weddings and funerals alike involved immense preparation and ceremony. The magnificent festivities put on at the French court for the wedding in 1581 of Marguerite de Lorraine and Anne, duc de Joyeuse, included the performance of a *Ballet comique* which was commemorated by being depicted both in print (p. 98) and in the so-called Valois tapestries. At royal funerals, in which the deceased monarch, having lain in state, was present in effigy for the final rite, vast numbers of mourners, carefully ordered by social rank, participated in processions. About 9,000 people received mourning clothes to take part in the ceremony for James I in 1625, and clearing the way through the London streets made work for 150 men. In France the belief that 'the king never dies' was embodied in the presence at the funeral rite of a life-sized effigy of the deceased monarch, attended and served – even at a banquet – as the living king had been.

The demands of courts and patrons called for a wide range of works, many of which were never intended to outlast the occasion. Ceremonial statues, arches and entire palatial structures were erected for royal entries into cities and diplomatic gatherings. Charles V's entry into Bruges (p. 90) and François I's into Lyon (both in 1515), Philip II's entry into Lisbon in 1581 and various English state entries into the city of London (p. 281) have left behind records of the elaborate works that were never intended to survive the event. Nor, likewise, were the costly buildings put up near Calais in 1520 at the sumptuous meeting of monarchs at the Field of Cloth of Gold (p. 83). Court artists, from Alberti to Holbein and Inigo Jones, were expected to turn their talents to creations whose glory was that of insubstantial pageants. Enormous skills might be called for. Antoine Caron's painting of a night festival, showing a mock combat surrounding a castle on which stands an elephant, shows what could be involved.

The more public the display, the wider the political impact. For, of course, only a small minority of subjects would ever make suit to a royal court, belong to a legislative assembly, understand the workings of power or set eyes on their rulers. The nearest they would ever get to the seat of authority might be a face on a coin, or the gruesome proof of the arm of the law in the bodies of malefactors swinging on gallows, or painted in public effigy (p. 76), as they were in Florence. Monarchs knew the importance of making themselves as omnipresent as possible. Queen Elizabeth I (who was portrayed in print as well as paint) controlled her own image, and the ubiquity of the royal portrait in her reign was a matter of policy as well as vanity (p. 95). Royal mobility was both tactical and practical. The movements of Charles V across his wide domains, like the summer progresses of the English queen, kept subjects, as well as royal servants, on their toes. Processions of all kinds, religious and civic as well as royal, were displays of unity and order, which served the end of social cohesion as well as the the immediate occasion, be it a Corpus Christi commemoration (pp. 88–89) or a doge wedding the sea or the admission of a distinguished person to a knightly order.

It was impossible to be courtly without being properly dressed. Dress was more a matter of social display than personal expression, but if courtliness was also seemliness, over-dressing was as much out of place as being under-dressed – witness Machiavelli, changing out of his country clothes to put on 'robes of court and palace' for an evening's bookish converse with the ancients. People were supposed to dress according to rank (pp. 92–93). The sumptuary laws that were repeatedly issued and revised throughout the period attempted to prevent the most costly fabrics (cloth of gold and silver, silks and furs) being worn by the wrong people. It was socially confusing, and false, for a burgher to look like a count. It was also foolish, if not dangerous, for a king to look like a peasant. Even Queen Elizabeth, who was not prepared to splash out on any palatial building (unlike her father), knew the value of spending lavishly on clothes.

Yet in the 16th century reaction against sartorial extravagance itself became a fashion. Sobriety and restraint became the order of the day. Montaigne, commenting on how Frenchmen were accustomed to wearing varied colours, confessed that he, like his father, seldom wore anything but black or white. Castiglione indicated that the best dress for courtiers was 'sober and restrained rather than foppish; so it seems to me that the most agreeable colour is black, and if not black, then at least something fairly dark.' The many contemporary portraits of those who followed this advice include both Charles V (who usually wore brown or black, except for special occasions), and his son Philip II (p. 93), who was described by a papal emissary visiting Madrid in 1594 as being dressed in black, seated in a chair of black velvet beside a table covered in black velvet. Outside a funeral one could not ask for a better model of gravity. By the 17th century, when the collector Earl of Arundel (p. 61) adopted this style, it had become known as 'Spanish garb'.

Corpses of criminals were left to hang in public as a deterrent. A drawing of Bandini de' Baroncelli after execution (1479/80) is attributed to Leonardo.

Costume design drew on the talents of the most eminent artists. These sketches for court dress (15th century) are by Antonio Pisanello.

1. Pinturicchio: *Arrival of Pope Pius II Piccolomini at Ancona*, detail (1502).

The Papacy

THE second half of the 15th century marked the spectacular recovery of the Papacy from two of the most serious threats it had ever faced – the exile in Avignon (1309–77) and the Great Schism (1378–1417). Re-established in Rome and unchallenged in authority, the popes embarked on a vigorous programme of political reorganization and artistic patronage. Pius II (1) finally repudiated the conciliar theory which would have limited his powers. Sixtus IV (3) defended the Papal States against Florence and Venice, as well as building the Sistine Chapel. Alexander VI (2), venal and unscrupulous as he was, at least provided strong leadership. Julius II (4), superb administrator and patron of Bramante, Michelangelo and Raphael, demolished the ancient basilica of St Peter's and began a new one. Leo X (5) spent equally lavishly but must be held partly responsible for Luther's defection. Clement VII (6) had to endure the horror of the Sack of Rome. Paul III (7) restored prosperity to Rome, encouraged learning and the arts and reformed the Church. All these men were cultivated and intellectually gifted, with tastes and interests far beyond their priestly office. They created Renaissance Rome.

2. Pinturicchio: *Pope Alexander VI Borgia*, detail (1492–95).

3. Melozzo da Forlì: *Pope Sixtus IV Della Rovere Appointing Platina as Papal Librarian*, detail (1477).

4. Raphael: *Pope Julius II Della Rovere* (*c.* 1503–13).

6. Giorgio Vasari: *Pope Clement VII Medici with the Emperor Charles V* (*c.* 1560).

7. Titian: *Pope Paul III Farnese with his Nephews*, detail (1545).

5. Raphael: *Pope Leo X Medici, with Cardinals Luigi de' Rossi and Giulio de' Medici* (*c.* 1517–19).

The Holy Roman Empire

THE emperor, appointed by an electoral college of three archbishops and four German princes, was the secular equivalent of the pope. Most of Germany owed him allegiance (4), and so in theory did many states in northern and southern Italy. But the gap between prestige and power was wide and growing wider. By the 15th century imperial authority hardly existed in Italy, and in the north, undermined by the secession of the Lutheran princes, it rested only on the vast territorial possessions of the Habsburg family, who were regularly elected emperors (1): Maximilian I (2) in 1493; his grandson Charles V (5) in 1519; Charles' brother Ferdinand I in 1558; Ferdinand's son Maximilian II in 1564; and Maximilian's son Rudolf II (3) in 1576. All these were outstanding men, culturally as well as politically – Maximilian I a generous patron of the new learning, Rudolf one of the great collectors of his age. Between emperor and pope, there was constant rivalry, and it was reluctantly that Clement VII agreed to crown Charles V (6) in 1530, only three years after the Sack of Rome.

2. The Emperor Maximilian I by Dürer (1519).

1. Thirteen Habsburg emperors with Charles V and Ferdinand I at the top, followed by Maximilian II, Rudolf II, Matthias and Ferdinand II; bowl of a goblet made in Augsburg (1645).

3. The Emperor Rudolf II by Adrian de Vries (1609).

The northern monarchies, 70–71

Government, 74–75

Cities of central Europe, 160–61

4. Symbolic eagle of the Empire, with arms of the component states (1510).

5. The Emperor Charles V by Titian, detail (1547–48).

6. Charles V crowned by Pope Clement VII by Vasari, detail (c. 1560).

7. The Emperor Charles V enthroned between the Pillars of Hercules, holding the orb and the sword, and attended by his defeated foes – the Sultan Suleiman, Pope Clement VII, François I of France, the Duke of Cleves, the Duke of Saxony and the Landgrave of Hesse: an illuminated manuscript by Giulio Clovio (mid-16th century).

1. Jean Clouet: François I, King of France (*c*. 1520).

2. Lucas Cranach the Elder: Christian II, King of Denmark, detail (1523).

3. Anonymous: Zygmunt III Vasa of Poland, detail (copy of 16th-century portrait).

4. Lucas Cranach the Younger: Joachim II, Elector of Brandenburg, detail (1571).

The northern monarchies

THE Renaissance was the time when Europe crystallized into the collection of nation states that it basically is today. England (**5, 6**) had been one country since the 11th century and in 1603 united with Scotland. France (**1**) had gradually come together under one ruler throughout the Middle Ages, and by the early 16th century it comprised most of modern France. Spain (**8**) was united by the marriage of Ferdinand and Isabella in 1469, though Portugal (**7**) remained independent. Denmark (**2**) was an ancient kingdom, often in uneasy conjunction with Norway and Sweden. Poland (**3**) declared itself an elective monarchy in 1572, usually choosing members of foreign nobility as kings. But Germany (**4**) remained, like Italy, divided into a host of small states.

The Holy Roman Empire, 68–69

Renaissance diplomacy, 82–83

The secret code of dress, 92–93

5. Pietro Torrigiano: Henry VII, King of England, detail (*c.* 1512).

6. After Lucas de Heere and Hans Eworth: *Allegory of the Tudor Succession*, showing Philip II, Mary I, Henry VIII, Edward VI, Elizabeth I (*c.* 1589–95).

7. Nuño Gonçalves: *Alfonso V, King of Portugal, Kneeling before St Vincent*, with Henry the Navigator behind him (*c.* 1460).

8. Titian: Philip II, King of Spain (1551).

1. Botticelli: *Adoration of the Magi* showing members of the Medici family (*c.* 1475).

2. Giorgio Vasari: *Duke Cosimo I of Florence Studying Plans for the Conquest of Siena* (*c.* 1559).

The rulers of Italy

IF the nation state was a feature of the Renaissance, Italy was still living politically in the Middle Ages. Only southern Italy (the Two Sicilies) was a kingdom, and a very unstable one. The Papacy, which ruled central Italy, was an elective monarchy. Venice and Genoa were republics, but with the franchise confined to a tiny minority. Florence (1) was a truer democracy, but was dominated by a party permanently headed by the Medici, who eventually became dukes (2). Milan (3), Ferrara (4), Mantua (6) and Rimini (7) were controlled by autocrats who attempted to transmit power within their families. Their strength depended on their wealth, since armies were not citizens but mercenaries serving for pay. Some princes built up their power at home by leading mercenary armies elsewhere, notably in Urbino (5).

3. Pisanello: Filippo Maria Visconti, Duke of Milan (1441).

6. Mantegna: Lodovico Gonzaga, Duke of Mantua, with his family (1474).

4. Pisanello: Leonello d'Este, Duke of Ferrara (c. 1445).

7. Piero della Francesca: *Sigismondo Malatesta, Duke of Rimini, Kneeling before St Sigismund* (1451).

5. Piero della Francesca: Federigo da Montefeltro, Duke of Urbino (1474).

1. Sano di Pietro: *Allegory of Good Government*, detail (1474).

2. *Polish Diet* from A. Guagninus, *Sarmatiae descriptio*, Cracow, 1590.

Government

'**G**OOD GOVERNMENT' was a subject much debated by the humanists in philosophical terms, and often illustrated in allegories such as the Sienese example (1), in which Liberty, holding a staff and an orb of the world, presides over officers of the state. The reality was somewhat different. In many northern countries the theory of the divine right of kings still held sway, but the sovereign was normally advised by a privy council and his decisions (particularly financial) endorsed by an assembly that in some sense represented his subjects, at least the privileged among them. England (3, 4) had its two houses of parliament, the Lords and the Commons, whose powers steadily increased from the time of Henry III onwards. France (5) had its Estates-General, though long periods passed during which they were not summoned (the meeting shown here was the last for 150 years). Poland's monarchy (2) was elective and its Diet retained very large powers. But only in the Swiss cantons and some city states of Italy did any popular assembly have final authority. Venice (6) was governed by a committee of the Great Council, the Council of Ten.

Law and punishment, 76–77

Renaissance diplomacy, 82–83

A new world of finance, 232–33

3. Session of English Parliament under Henry VIII (1523).

5. The French Estates-General of 1614.

4. State opening of English Parliament under Charles I (1628).

6. Giacomo Franco: *The Grand Council of Venice* (c. 1600).

Law and punishment

IN Renaissance political theory, the ruler's will was law (3), limited only by ancient custom (such as the Salic Law) and the law of God. The philosophy of law, therefore, could only take the form of advising the prince how he ought to act, as Erasmus did seriously and Machiavelli cynically. (Such studies were more fruitful in the north than in Italy, leading to a great age of jurisprudence in the 17th century.) In day-to-day practice, however, criminal law was uncomfortably arbitrary, detection erratic and punishment harsh (2, 8). The Church had its own law and law enforcement, punishing witchcraft and heresy; the Spanish Inquisition was founded in 1478, the Roman Holy Office in 1542. Almost everywhere, torture was a legitimate means of discovering the truth (4, 5, 6, 7). Civil law was another matter, and most lawyers would have been employed in private litigation based on precedent and custom.

1. Marble tondo showing column with the figure of Justice (mid-16th century).

2. Pisanello: detail of hanged men from *St George and the Princess* (1437–38).

3. Charles VII of France at a 'lit de justice' (1458).

7. Page showing torture and punishments from *De sphaera* (*c.* 1450–60).

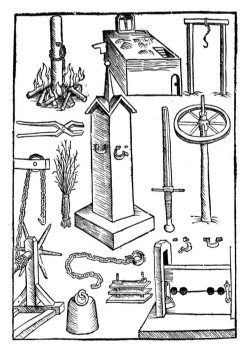

4, 5, 6. Pages showing tortures and executions from the *Bamberger Halsgerichtsordnung* (1508).

8. Executions in Brussels, from *De leone belgico* (1588).

1. Palazzo Medici-Riccardi, Florence, by Michelozzo with alterations by Michelangelo (begun 1446).

2. Cancellaria, Rome, the papal chancellery (begun 1486).

3. Courtyard of the Palazzo Ducale, Urbino (begun 1444).

4. Palazzo Vendramin, Venice (begun 1481).

5. Palazzo Chiericati, Vicenza, by Palladio (begun 1550).

Palaces and palazzi

WHAT is a palace? Before the 15th century it was merely a disparate collection of buildings, some pretentious, some humble, where the business of a ruler or great man was carried out. The old palaces of Westminster and Whitehall were like this. (The Kremlin in Moscow and the Topkapi in Istanbul are surviving examples.) In the Renaissance the idea arose that a palace should be a symbol of the ruler's authority: prominent, unified and architecturally impressive. It was an Italian idea, deriving from the palazzi of rich merchants and noblemen in Florence (**1**), Rome (**2**) and the Veneto (**4**, **5**). François I of France led the way with a series of palaces including Chambord (**9**) and the Louvre (**10**). Henry VIII attempted to rival him with Nonsuch (**7**). Rulers in Germany (**6**) and Poland (**8**) modernized parts of their palaces in the new style. But all were outshone by Philip II of Spain, whose vast Escorial (**11**), palace, cathedral and monastery in one, based on biblical as well as Vitruvian models, aped the Temple of Solomon itself.

Inside the palace, 80–81

Rome, 156–57

Venice, 158–59

6. The Ottheinrichsbau, Heidelberg Castle (begun 1556).

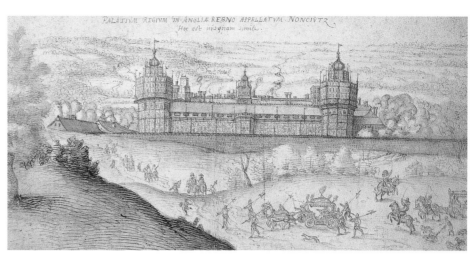

7. Nonsuch Palace, Surrey (begun 1538).

8. Courtyard of the Wawel Palace, Cracow (begun 1502).

9. Château of Chambord, on the Loire (begun 1519).

10. Earliest wing of the Louvre, Paris, by Pierre Lescot (begun 1546).

11. The Escorial, Spain, by Juan Bautista de Toledo and Juan de Herrera (begun 1559).

1. Palazzo Davanzati, Florence; bedroom (15th century).

2. Villa Farnesina, Rome; salone (1510–20).

3. Palazzo Vecchio, Florence, Sala dei Gigli (1481–85).

Inside the palace

INTERIOR decoration followed the Italian example, with compromises dictated by cost, climate and available expertise. In Italy the essential elements are fairly constant, whether in a relatively unpretentious house like the Palazzo Davanzati, Florence (1), with its frieze of scenes from a medieval romance along the top, or the immensely rich Villa Farnesina (2), owned by Agostino Chigi, who employed Peruzzi to design the building and paint the *trompe-l'oeil* perspective, the frieze of mythological scenes and the Forge of Vulcan over the fireplace. In Florence, the Palazzo Vecchio's Sala dei Gigli – Room of the Lilies – (3) was frescoed by Ghirlandaio with Roman heroes above the windows. Federigo da Montefeltro's study at Urbino (4) is small in scale but richly lined with marquetry pictures – the scholar's books, the soldier's arms. Two of the most splendid rooms in Denmark (5) and France (6) reflect the Italianate ambitions of, respectively, Christian IV and François I. In England, neither Elizabeth I nor James I built palaces, and the closest parallel is Bess of Hardwick's Hardwick Hall (7), with its charmingly naive frieze of rustic scenes and animals in stucco.

Palaces and palazzi, 78–79

Italy: the language of decoration, 252–53

The interior as work of art, 254–55

5. Frederiksborg, Denmark; ballroom (1606–20).

4. Palazzo Ducale, Urbino; studiolo (1476).

6. Fontainebleau, France; ballroom (1540–52).

7. Hardwick Hall, Derbyshire, England; presence chamber (1590–97).

1. Conclusion of the papal league against the Turks, detail (1571).

2. The betrothal of Emperor Frederick III and Eleanor of Portugal, part of a series of frescoes illustrating the life of Pius II by Pinturicchio (begun 1502).

3. Boyar ambassadors from Russia arriving at the court of Maximilian I by Hans Burgkmair (1516).

Renaissance diplomacy

DURING the Middle Ages it was common practice for states to negotiate through special embassies with clearly defined powers. Only on exceptional occasions, such as the Field of Cloth of Gold (6) did sovereigns meet. Special missions remained important ceremonial events (3, 5, 7), but the innovation of Renaissance diplomacy was the establishment of resident ambassadors. The demand rose for men with a fluent command of Latin, and many leading humanists attained high positions. Aeneas Sylvius Piccolomini, later Pope Pius II, acted as private secretary to the Emperor Frederick III and negotiated his betrothal (2). Through such channels alliances were arranged and treaties drawn up. In 1571, the papal league against the Turks (1) united (on paper) Spain, Venice, Savoy, Parma, Urbino, Tuscany, Malta and Genoa. Charles VIII's invasion of Italy, the beginning of so much misery, was the result of a diplomatic initiative on the part of Lodovico Sforza, who encouraged the king's claims on Naples in order to avail himself of French aid. Charles' entry into Florence (4), a by-product of the invasion, led to the expulsion of the Medici. But increasingly high-level conferences were being called to resolve international problems, such as that held in London in 1604 (8), when peace was signed with Spain.

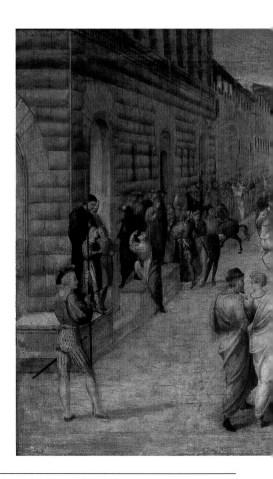

5. An embassy from Tsar Ivan IV to Maximilian II by Michael Peterle (1576).

6. Detail from the Field of Cloth of Gold (*c.* 1522).

7. Queen Elizabeth greeting Dutch ambassadors (*c.* 1585).

8. The Somerset House Conference, detail (1604).

4. The entry of Charles VIII into Florence by Francesco Granacci (1494).

1. Piero della Francesca: *Defeat of Chosroes by Heraclius* (1452–59).

2. Jan Bruegel the Elder: *Battle of the Issus*, detail (1602).

4. Albrecht Altdorfer: *Battle of the Issus*, detail (1529).

Faces of battle

3. Michelangelo: *Battle of Cascina*, copy (1506).

LARGE battle pictures were virtually a Renaissance invention, but there are interesting differences in the way they are handled. Sometimes they are painted with all the realism that the artist can command, for instance in the two pictures of Alexander the Great's *Battle of the Issus* by Altdorfer (4) and Jan Bruegel (2); at other times they are reduced to stately ceremonies of slaughter, such as Piero's *Defeat of Chosroes* (1) and Uccello's *Rout of San Romano* (5). Curiously, some of the most distant and legendary battles are given realistic treatment and contemporary ones treated ritualistically. San Romano was a small scuffle between the Florentines and Sienese in 1432, glorified by Uccello in three large panels that make it look almost like a tournament. Cascina was a similarly minor victory of Florence over the Pisans in 1364, celebrated in frescoes by Michelangelo (3) and Leonardo in the Palazzo Vecchio. Michelangelo characteristically chose a moment before the battle when soldiers were surprised while bathing. Parma (6), Orsha (7) and above all Lepanto (8) were major military engagements affecting European history.

Defensible spaces, 164–65

Landscapes of fantasy, 168–69

The art of war, 222–23

5. Paolo Uccello: *Rout of San Romano* (1454).

6. Tintoretto: *The Taking of Parma*, detail (1579).

7. Anonymous: *Battle of Orsha*, detail (1514).

8. Anonymous: *Battle of Lepanto* (1571).

1. *Marcus Aurelius*, Roman bronze equestrian statue (2nd century AD).

2. Jean Clouet: François I (*c.* 1525).

3. Paolo Uccello: equestrian portrait of Sir John Hawkwood, Florence (1436).

Equestrian monuments

ONE bronze equestrian monument survived from ancient Rome, that of *Marcus Aurelius* (1), formerly outside the Lateran, later incorporated by Michelangelo in his new scheme for the Campidoglio. It was a model for the whole Renaissance and subsequent centuries, though technically very difficult to imitate. In paint or in relief there was no problem – Jean Clouet's François I (2), Uccello's Hawkwood (3) and the anonymous Roberto Malatesta from Rimini (6). Some Renaissance sculptors made ambitious designs – Pollaiuolo for Francesco Sforza (4) and Leonardo for Trivulzio (5). But only two succeeded in actually casting them: the sternly Roman Gattamelata of Donatello (8) and the fiercely dynamic Colleoni of Verrocchio (7). Both men were condottieri in the service of Venice.

4. Antonio Pollaiuolo: design for equestrian monument to Francesco Sforza (1489).

5. Leonardo da Vinci: sketch of monument to Gian Giacomo Trivulzio (c. 1511).

6. Marble relief of Roberto Malatesta (1484).

7. Verrocchio: bronze equestrian monument to Bartolomeo Colleoni, Venice (1479–88).

8. Donatello: bronze equestrian monument to Gattamelata, Padua (1444).

Rulers of the World 87

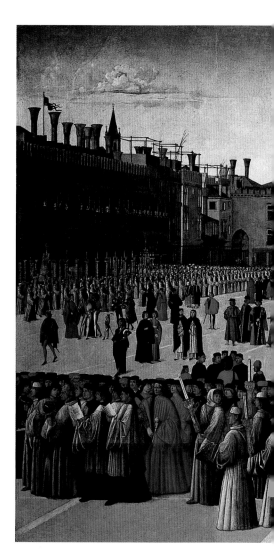

1. School of Vasari: *Procession in the Piazza S. Giovanni (c. 1556–61).*

gelifte, orate pro nobis
Omnes fancti difcipuli domini,
orate pro nobis
Omnes fancti Innocentes, orate

Civic processions,
90–91

Rome,
156–57

Venice,
158–59

2. Gentile Bellini: *Procession of the Reliquary of the True Cross* (1496).

Religious processions

MOST great religious festivals were marked by processions, a way of including the whole population of a city in a celebration. Since the civic powers too took part, there was often a strong element of local patriotism as well. In the Florentine example (1) the procession is entering the Baptistery, with the unfinished façade of the Cathedral to the left. In Venice (2) the city's relic of the True Cross (under the canopy in the centre) is carried round St Mark's Square accompanied by members of the main *scuole*, or charitable institutions. The procession in Rome (3) is one of the most important of the year, Corpus Christi. Paul III makes his way from the Castel S. Angelo to St Peter's in 1546; neither Maderna's façade to the church nor Bernini's Piazza yet exists.

3. Giulio Clovio: *Corpus Christi Procession* from *The Hours of Cardinal Alessandro Farnese* (1546).

Civic processions

STATE occasions were the excuse for pageantry on a large scale, often with the most elaborate and recherché symbolism. In Charles V's entry into Bruges (1) a man is entirely dressed in candles. Chivalric orders (4), coronations (3) and the entry of ambassadors (5) all required a procession. But the most spectacular of all must have been the Triumph of the Regent Isabella in Brussels in 1615 (2). It contained over a dozen picturesque carts bearing allegorical figures – one of which (at the back, far right), a ship pulled by sea horses passing the Pillars of Hercules, had been used in the mourning procession of Charles V in 1558. Others include Apollo and the Muses and Diana with her nymphs.

1. Entry of Charles V into Bruges (1515).

2. Denis van Alsloot: *The Ommeganck Procession* (1615).

3. Edward VI's coronation procession, watercolour copy (1785) of 1547 original, detail.

5. Stefano della Bella: *Entry of the Polish Ambassadors into Rome* (1633).

Government, 74–75

Religious processions, 88–89

Court entertainment, 98–99

4. Marcus Gheeraerts the Elder: *Procession of Knights of the Garter* (1576).

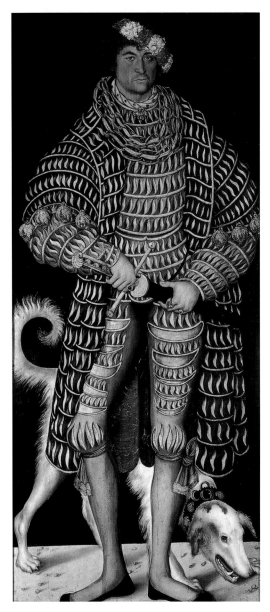

1. Lucas Cranach the Elder: Henry the Pious, Duke of Saxony (1514).

3. Nicholas Hilliard: *Young Man amid Roses* (*c.* 1587).

2. Holbein: Henry VIII (*c.* 1537).

4. Domenico di Bartolo: *Gentleman*, detail from a fresco (early 15th century).

5. Giovanni Battista Moroni: *Portrait of a Gentleman* (16th century).

6. François Clouet: Charles IX of France, detail (mid-16th century).

7. Sanchez Coello: Philip II of Spain (1582).

The secret code of dress

THERE was no 'Renaissance costume'. Dress varied from decade to decade, from country to country, and from class to class. It was conditioned by wealth, fashion, rank and government decree. In most European countries sumptuary laws dictated what could be worn by whom. They covered materials (with the aim of encouraging national industries) and the display of jewelry and colour (with the aim of preventing the lower classes from aping their betters). The northern courts were the most lavish. One striking innovation was 'slashing', where the garment seemed to have been ripped apart and the lining pulled through (1, 2). In England under Elizabeth I, the male cloak almost lost its function and was worn negligently over one shoulder, with sleeves that were frequently sham (3). Before the middle of the 16th century, however, the mood had darkened. Charles V always dressed in black and so did his son Philip II (7). Soon Spanish sobriety had almost extinguished northern extravagance (5), though wealth and status could still be signalled in other ways. Charles IX of France (6) is luxuriously sombre in silver-embellished black.

1. Titian: Isabella of Portugal (1548).

2. Bronzino: Lucrezia Panciatichi (*c.* 1540).

3. Holbein: Christina of Denmark, Duchess of Milan, detail (1538).

The glass of fashion

WOMEN's dress, like men's, conveyed covert social messages, though they are not always easy for us to read. Italy was the centre of fashion. Sleeves became fuller, often using the technique of slashing (1). Décolleté, which had been popular before the 16th century, gave way to the ruff, which was to increase in size and complexity until it dominated both male and female costume in the 17th. Ingeniously, however, the ruff could be combined with décolleté, the intervening area being covered by a transparent fabric (5). Tall head-dresses, which had reached unbelievable heights in the north, subsided under Italian influence (4). The favourite colour was red: Lucrezia Panciatichi (2), painted by Bronzino about 1540, is as modern in her dress as in her jewels. Christina of Denmark (3) owes the rich dignity of her black attire to the fact that she was technically in mourning (for Francesco Maria Sforza; Henry VIII was considering her as a possible fourth bride). Outshining them all was Queen Elizabeth (6), for whom dress was a proclamation of royalty, often loaded with symbolic and allegorical content.

4. Bernhard Striegel: Sibylla von Freyberg (*c.* 1520–23).

6. Workshop of Nicholas Hilliard: Queen Elizabeth I (the Hardwick Portrait) (*c.* 1599).

5, 7. Elizabeth of Austria painted by François Clouet as Queen of France, mid-16th century (above) and by Jacob Seisenegger aged four, 1530, detail (right).

1. Mantegna: *Hunters and Dogs of the Gonzaga Court*, detail (1470).

The gentry at play

Hunting and fighting: these were the two primordial occupations which the ruling classes made into their sports. Both signalled status and rank and had long been topics of art. Hunting had been the privilege of kings and courtiers since the dawn of history. In the Renaissance it seems to have been pursued more single-mindedly in the north (2, 3) than in Italy (1). Ceremonial fights – jousting – were equally popular in both (5, 7) and were among the purposes served by the great city squares (6, 8). Even the popes enjoyed them (9) and they were, up to a point, a way of training for war.

2. Lucas Cranach the Elder: *Deer Hunt of the Elector Frederick the Wise*, detail (1529).

3. Hans Holbein the Younger: *Portrait of the Falconer Robert Cheseman* (1533).

4. Lucas van Valkenborch: *Spring*, detail of a picnic scene (1587).

5. Tapestry of Catherine de Médicis: *Jousting 'alla sbarra'*, detail (mid-16th century).

7. Vasari: *Joust in the Piazza S. Croce* (*c.* 1555–65).

6. *Celebrating St John's Eve with Fireworks in the Piazza della Signoria,* detail (*c.* 1560).

8. Vicenzo Rustici: *Bullfighting and other Games in the Piazza del Campo, Siena* (*c.* 1600).

9. *Joust in the Belvedere Courtyard, Vatican* (16th century).

Court entertainment

RENAISSANCE guides to social conduct, like those of Castiglione and Della Casa, pay much attention to table manners and one has the impression that codes of behaviour were becoming more refined. In the Italian banquet scene (1) distinguished guests are at the upper table, being entertained with music, the rest lower down, waited on by pages. Note the plate displayed on the dresser, right. New to 15th-century Europe was the polite pastime of playing cards – the Tarot (6) seems to have been native to Italy. The masque including traditional rustic figures (3, 7) has its roots in folklore, but by the 16th century had developed into a sophisticated medium, the ancestor of modern opera and ballet (4), claiming the talents of such men as Ben Jonson and Inigo Jones (5). A spectacle like the sea battle staged in the flooded courtyard of the Palazzo Pitti (2) – part tournament, part political statement, part pantomime – must always have been highly exceptional requiring considerable technical expertise.

1. *The Banquet of Dido and Aeneas*, attributed to Apollonio di Giovanni, detail (15th century).

4. *Ballet comique de la Reine*, performed in honour of Queen Louise de Lorraine (1582).

2. Sea battle in the courtyard of the Palazzo Pitti by Orazio Scarabelli (16th century).

6. *The Game of Tarot* by Niccolò dell' Abbate (mid-16th century).

3. Entertainment provided for Charles V and Philip during their visit to the Netherlands in 1548.

5. Costume design for Queen Henrietta Maria as 'Divine Beauty' in the masque *Tempe Restored* by Inigo Jones (1632).

7. Detail from the memorial painting of Sir Henry Unton showing a banquet with musicians and a masque (1596).

Italian funerary monuments

To be remembered after death by a magnificent tomb was an ambition as typical of the Middle Ages as of the ancient world. Italian tombs of the Renaissance recall elements of both and finally achieve effects that go beyond either. These extraordinary monuments, lodged immovably in (sometimes obscure) churches and cathedrals all over Italy, constitute the greatest body of masterpieces in the history of sculpture. Pollaiuolo's Sixtus IV (1), surrounded by reliefs of the cardinal and theological virtues, and Donatello and Michelozzo's John XXIII (3), the Anti-Pope, subsequently deposed, derive from medieval floor- and wall-monuments. Lamberti's Onofrio Strozzi (2), Rossellino's Cardinal of Portugal (4) and Lombardo's Andrea Vendramin (7) are variants on classical themes. Jacopo della Quercia's Ilaria del Carretto (8), without the slightest sense of incongruity, places a medieval effigy on a classical sarcophagus. But Michelangelo's Medici tombs (5, 6) are entirely without precedent, uncompromising statements of purely Renaissance power.

2. Niccolò Lamberti: tomb of Onofrio Strozzi in S. Trinita, Florence (1421).

3. Donatello and Michelozzo: tomb of Anti-Pope John XXIII (died 1419) in the Baptistery, Florence.

1. Antonio Pollaiuolo: tomb of Pope Sixtus IV (died 1484) in St Peter's, Rome.

4. Antonio and Bernardo Rossellino: tomb of the Cardinal of Portugal in S. Miniato al Monte, Florence (1466).

The Papacy, 66–67

The heroic, 250–51

Sculpture: a new dimension, 262–63

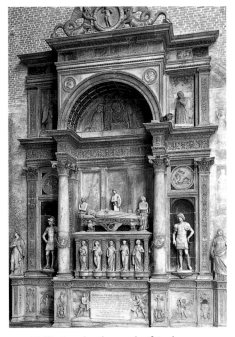

5, 6. Michelangelo: tombs of Giuliano de' Medici, Duke of Nemours, and Lorenzo de' Medici, Duke of Urbino (1520–34) in the New Sacristy, S. Lorenzo, Florence.

7. Tullio Lombardo: tomb of Andrea Vendramin in S. Giovanni e Paolo, Venice (1492–95).

9. Tullio Lombardo: tomb of Guidarello Guidarelli (1525).

8. Jacopo della Quercia: tomb of Ilaria del Carretto in Lucca Cathedral (1406).

1. Tomb of Bishop Alonso Tostado, by Vasca de la Zarza, in Avila Cathedral (1518).

2. Tomb of Charles V and his family, by Pompeo Leoni, in the Escorial (1598).

Funerary monuments of the north

THE normal convention for funerary sculpture throughout medieval Europe was a recumbent effigy on a tomb. Additional small-scale figures might stand in niches along the sides of the tomb chest. These conventions did not disappear (8, 9), but a host of new ideas came flooding in from Italy, stemming ultimately from the Antique. Gradually the sleepers awoke (5), and were shown alive in all their power and glory (1, 2). Tombs acquired elaborate architectural settings (10), with trophies (7), allegorical virtues (3) and legendary heroes (6), or – a clear allusion to Michelangelo's Medici – stepped from the very world of ancient Rome (4).

3. Figure of a virtue from the tomb of Philibert le Beau of Savoy in the abbey church of Brou (c. 1530).

4. Monument of Francis Holles, by Nicholas Stone, in Westminster Abbey (1622).

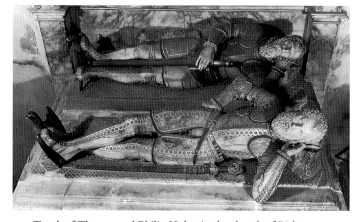

5. Tomb of Thomas and Philip Hoby, in the church of Bisham, Berkshire (c. 1570).

Illness and death, 200–01

The Renaissance medal, 244–45

Sculpture: a new dimension, 262–63

6. King Arthur and King Ferdinand of Portugal, by the workshop of Peter Vischer the Elder, from the tomb of Emperor Maximilian I in the Hofkirche, Innsbruck (1513).

7. Tomb of Admiral Van Tromp in the Oude Kerk, Delft (1653).

9. Tomb of Philip the Bold, Dijon, by Claus Sluter and Claus de Werve (*c.* 1400).

10. Tomb of François I and Claude de France, by Philibert de l'Orme and Pierre Bontemps, in the Basilica of St Denis (1548).

8. Tomb of Henry VII and Queen Elizabeth, by Pietro Torrigiano, in Westminster Abbey (1512–18).

Rulers of the World   103

GOD AND MAN

South of the Alps churches began to look different in the 15th and 16th centuries; what went on inside them continued much as before. North of the Alps church exteriors changed more slowly, but in many places what went on within was revolutionized. A transformation of the patterns of belief and worship produced drastic alterations to church interiors, and in the course of Reformation and the conflicts it generated ecclesiastical buildings were damaged or destroyed in many northern cities. The traditional Church could never be the same again.

The art of the Renaissance was largely religious, and it can be assumed that the religious thoughts of contemporaries were infused with images. To think of Christ was to envisage the crucified figure hanging on the cross (pp. 140–41); to think of God the Father was to summon up a white-bearded ancient, leaning down from celestial clouds in the act of Creation, or as the mainstay of the Trinity, holding the crucified Son beneath the hovering dove of the Holy Spirit (pp. 128–29). Paintings of the Last Judgment (pp. 146–47) might stand over judges who ministered secular justice, as well as over the heads of congregations in church. The scene of the Apostles seated round the table at the Last Supper, painted in refectories, reminded those who sat down to dinner of the sacramental aspect of daily bread (pp. 138–39). Daily life was filled with spiritual analogies, and so imbued were such mental processes that they seemed as natural as thought itself. 'Whether I will or not,' wrote Luther, 'when I hear of Christ, an image of a man hanging on a cross takes form in my heart, just as the reflection of my face naturally appears in the water when I look into it' (p. 117).

For most believers a nearer presence was the Blessed Virgin Mary, intercessor supreme for sinful mortals who looked to her, along with the rest of the company of saints, to help them in times of need, to provide the comfort of her protection, and to put a helping hand on the scales when souls were weighed at the Last Judgment. There were many sermon stories describing miracles in which the Virgin came to the rescue of sinners or set things to rights by putting in a good word with her Son. The Virgin is as omnipresent in different art forms as she was present with the immediacy of a reflex action at times of personal crisis, springing to lips in cries of help. In her many roles, as mother with the young Child (pp. 132–33), as the *pietà* mourning over the dead Christ (pp. 142–43), and as the Madonna of Mercy protecting devotees under her mantle, the Virgin represented the accessible nourishing (feminine) face of the faith.

Other holy helpers were also sources of power, cultivated for their special qualities. Unlike the Virgin, who was bodily assumed into heaven leaving no mortal remains accessible to postulants on earth (apart from those who believed in her grave-clothes, or relics of her milk or tears), the bodies of saints, acting as spiritual conduits, seemed to concentrate their energy in particular places. But one did not have to pilgrimage to seek the aid of these specialist helpers, men and women of superhuman courage and virtue, whose resolution in overcoming great sufferings rendered them capable of easing similar pains of ordinary Christians. Saints were sought by prayer. The Roman martyr St Sebastian, p. 249

Dürer's great Adoration of the Trinity sums up a world-picture that had not changed substantially since St Augustine wrote The City of God. *He completed it in 1511, well before the words of Luther began to be heard in Germany. By 1528, when he died, Dürer had swung decisively to the side of Reform, and his estimate of the papacy would no doubt have been different. The painting shows the Trinity in the centre – the Dove of the Holy Ghost, Father and crucified Son. To the left are the Virgin and female saints (including St Catherine with her wheel and St Agnes with her lamb), on the right John the Baptist with male saints and Old Testament figures (Moses with the Tablets of the Law, David with his harp). At the lowest level are the earthly powers of Church and State, pope and emperor (the pope possibly a portrait of Julius II). On the left, amid cardinals, monks and friars is the donor of the painting, Matthias Landauer, and on the right members of his family, including his son-in-law, dressed as a knight. At the very bottom the tiny figure of Dürer points to a plaque bearing his name and the date.*

Piero della Francesca's Madonna della Misericordia *(1445), 'Madonna of Mercy' – the protectress of suffering mankind: a timeless image of Christian consolation.*

Before the Reformation, Christian doctrine was taught through words and images, but unauthorized translations of the Scriptures were discouraged by the Church, because only the Church was qualified to interpret it correctly. The Biblia pauperum *(here of c. 1480) was a learned construction of image and texts, probably for meditation – not for the poor.*

(sentenced to be shot with arrows, though martyred by other means) was joined by the 14th-century hermit St Roch (who all but died of plague) as miracle-curers of plague victims; St Erasmus (allegedly martyred by the extraction of his intestine) was the helper for stomach troubles; St Apollonia (said to have had her teeth pulled out before she was burned) was looked to by sufferers from toothache.

Spiritual companions-in-aid of this kind seemed to Luther, Zwingli and Calvin to be trespassing terribly in God's domain. They had been worshipped, prayed to, and believed in as only God should be. They stood in God's light. Sainthood had nothing to do with golden crowns and the granting of passports to spiritual or material benefits; the true communion of saints was the fellowship of all devout believers, sharing blessings and sufferings in common. Accordingly Protestants did away with shrines and pilgrimages, and the sculptures, altarpieces and paintings of the saints were destroyed (pp. 122–23) or removed from places of worship (though Luther here showed himself more tolerant than the fathers of Zurich, Geneva and England).

Luther's great insight, centred on words of St Paul, rocked the Church with sensational effect. Release into the joyful security of justifying faith set the Word firmly at the heart of Protestant faith, and swept into irrelevancy a vast apparatus of devotional works. Salvation was not won by external deeds but by the inner process of turning to Christ and trusting his promise. If purgatory did not exist it was no use praying for souls. Monasteries and confraternities and chantries dedicated to the service of the dead and the care of funeral rites, lost much of their *raison d'être*. The dead ceased to be a daily responsibility of the living; they were transferred into a zone where they had to look after themselves until the last trump sounded. They could be remembered and praised and emulated – but not helped. Likewise many charitable activities, which had been linked with such intercessory prayers, moved among Protestants into the care of secular institutions.

Scripture honed away a great deal of traditional religion. If Old Testament law authoritatively condemned the religious use of images, the New Testament was the canon prescribing the Christian ritual. So the sacraments themselves were reduced in number (pp. 112–13), since for the Reformed, only two, those of baptism and communion, had biblical authority. The remaining five were not essential to salvation.

The Bible (pp. 118–19) and its preaching lies at the heart of Protestant religious experience. The strength of commitment to the written source of the faith – fed by humanist textual studies – is conspicuous in many places, in the arduous labours of editors and in the dedication of translators. The freshly translated Latin of Erasmus' New Testament seemed like a revelation to some readers who were familiar with the old words of Jerome's Vulgate. The great polyglot produced at Alcalá opened the way to new scholarly study of the texts of both Testaments in their original languages. But it was the vernacular versions that formed the backbone of the Reformation.

Scripture had to be in the hands of all Christians if the faith were truly to live. It was essential both that the Bible should be faithfully translated from the original languages and that it should be comprehensible to all. Luther and Tyndale both worked on these premises, and their respective German and English versions, products of linguistic knowledge and stylistic skills, proved highly successful. Luther's translation – which replaced a German Bible translated from the Vulgate that had been in print for over 50 years – found immediate and widespread readership. Tyndale had to convince the English regime that Bible-reading in the vernacular would not undermine church and state. He was executed before Henry VIII changed his mind on this score – to sponsor an English Bible in which Tyndale's words remained influential.

Scriptural enthusiasm, spreading like wildfire thanks to printing, provoked reaction. The Council of Trent ordained that the Vulgate (in a revised version) should be the authoritative Bible for the Roman Catholic Church. Not until the 18th century was the Holy See ready to endorse a vernacular Bible for Italian Catholics. The Emperor Charles V himself (who in 1529 had placed controls on vernacular scripture) obtained permission from the Inquisition in his retirement at S. Jerónimo de Yuste to read a French translation of the Bible.

The Reformation undoubtedly dented the Renaissance process. Literature and art were both subjected to the restraints of censorship as the Council of Trent drew up its list of proscribed books and its directions on the excesses that religious painting must avoid. Bishops had to ensure that new art did not introduce erroneous belief; saints must not be painted in ways that provoked lascivious thoughts; scriptural scenes should not depart too far from the words of Scripture; nor should church music include profane tunes or be so thick with counterpoint and polyphony that the words became inaudible. Nudity itself came to seem indecent so that Michelangelo's *Last Judgment* (p. 147) was threatened with destruction and Paul IV and Pius IV both had loincloths and draperies painted over genitals. Protestant scrutiny started the definition of a dividing line separating the secular from the sacred.

But the response of the Church to the Protestant challenge was also constructive and resulted in positive developments. The value of the arts in Christian religion was forcefully reaffirmed, and religious instruction was promoted in new ways. There were new church buildings with rich decorative schemes; new religious orders, like the Jesuits and the Theatines, dedicated to teaching, missionary work, and the reform of abuses; new attention to catechetical instruction and the texts it needed.

By the 17th century Protestants and Catholics had come to serve God in such different ways that their divisions could – as the Thirty Years War demonstrated – tear them apart. But there was still sharing as well as separation, and some paradoxical consonances. When Zwingli rejoiced in the beautiful light and brightness of Zurich's churches, purged of their accumulated imagery, he was unwittingly echoing Alberti who years before had recommended whitewashing churches since 'purity and simplicity of colour, as of life, must be pleasing to the divine being'. The Renaissance inheritance crossed confessional boundaries.

St Roch, pointing to his plague sore, and St Sebastian, shot with arrows, were among those who would intercede on behalf of the sick: detail from an altarpiece by Titian (c. 1511).

The Society of Jesus bred a new kind of saint. Francis Xavier (here in 1542), one of the first to pledge himself to Ignatius Loyola, spent his life leading missions to India and the Far East.

1. Alberti: S. Maria Novella, Florence (1456–70).

Christian classicism: Renaissance church design

CHURCH façades gave Renaissance architects the opportunity to use the classical vocabulary with considerable freedom. Alberti solved the problem of linking high nave with lower aisles by inventing scroll-buttresses (1), an idea taken up eagerly by later architects (2) and becoming a cliché of the Baroque. The pedimented façade based on the Roman temple front was also widely popular (4), combined by Alberti with the triumphal arch motif (3). Finally Palladio suggested the presence of two overlapping temple fronts – one corresponding to the nave, the other to the aisles (8). Outside Italy, the new style was not long in reaching Poland (5), Spain (6), England (10) and France. The French solutions offer an interesting contrast: De Brosse's (7) an orthodox superimposition of the three orders, Le Mercier's (9) a naive application of classical ornament to Gothic structure.

2. Giacomo del Duca: the Gesù, Rome (begun 1568).

3. Alberti: S. Andrea, Mantua (begun 1470).

4. Giuliano da Sangallo: S. Maria delle Carceri, Prato (1485–95).

The classical orders, 268–69

The central-space church, 274–75

Triumphal arches, 280–81

5. Bartolommeo Berrecci: St Sigismund Chapel, Cracow (1519–33).

6. Alonso Cano: Granada Cathedral (remodelled 1528).

7. Solomon de Brosse: St Gervais, Paris (1616–21).

8. Palladio: S. Giorgio Maggiore, Venice (designed 1565).

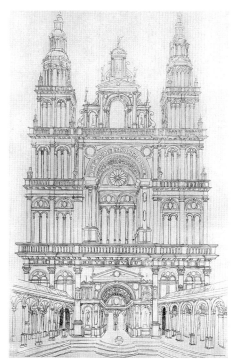

10. Inigo Jones: St Paul's, Covent Garden, London (1631).

9. Pierre Le Mercier: design for façade of St Eustache, Paris (c. 1530).

God and Man 109

1. Brunelleschi: S. Lorenzo, Florence (designed 1418).

2. Bramante: false perspective chancel of S. Maria presso S. Satiro, Milan (*c.* 1480).

3. Alberti: S. Andrea, Mantua (begun 1470).

4. Bramante: S. Maria delle Grazie, Milan (begun 1492).

5. Brunelleschi: S. Spirito, Florence, (designed 1436).

Inside the churches

LIKE nearly all Renaissance architecture, churches in the new style were an adaptation of the classical language to wholly unclassical functions. The architects' models were the churches of the Early Christians and the halls of Roman lawcourts. Brunelleschi (1, 5) went to the first, Alberti (3) and Bramante (2, 4) to the second, but all three had to retain the traditional medieval arrangement of an aisled nave and a chancel for the altar, since the liturgy, of course, remained the same. A century later, Palladio (6) and Vignola (7) could play sophisticated games with these elements. By the time the Renaissance was taken up in France (8), Germany (9) and eastern Europe (10), often under Italian supervision, it had evolved a stable tradition of its own.

6. Palladio: S. Giorgio Maggiore, Venice (designed 1565).

8. Philibert de l'Orme: chapel of the Château of Anet (1547–52).

9. W. Miller and F. Sustris: St Michael, Munich (1582–97).

10. Bartolommeo Berrecci: St Sigismund Chapel, Cracow (1519–33).

7. Vignola: the Gesù, Rome (1575–84).

The sacraments

IN Catholic doctrine there are seven crucial events in human life that require the mediation of a priest: baptism, confirmation, confession, holy communion, ordination, marriage and extreme unction. Luther, whose aim it was to purge the Church of later accretions and return to the purity of the Early Christians, held that only two had actually been sanctioned by Jesus: baptism, to which he had submitted at the hands of John the Baptist, and holy communion, which he had instituted by blessing the bread and wine at the Last Supper – from which Luther also drew the conclusion that the laity should 'partake in both kinds', i.e., both eat the bread and drink the wine, traditionally the prerogative of the priest only.

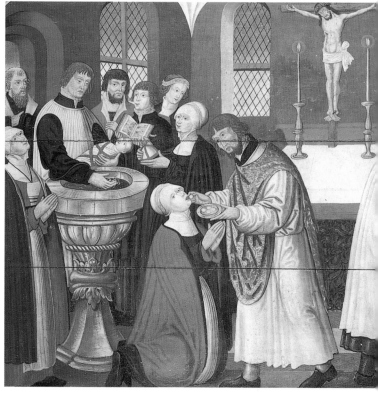

The Catholic Sacraments, three details from an altarpiece by Rogier van der Weyden (*c.* 1453–55).

1. Far left: baptism, confirmation and confession.

2. Left: holy communion, or the Eucharist, the priest at the altar raising the consecrated wafer which becomes the body of Christ.

4. Right: ordination, marriage and extreme unction – the last rites of the dying.

The Lutheran Sacraments, an altar painting from Thorslunde Church, Denmark (1561).

3. Below: baptism and communion in both kinds. Note the emphasis also given to preaching the word of God.

1. Luther writes his theses on the church door – an allegorical painting with the other reformers taking feathers from his quill (16th century).

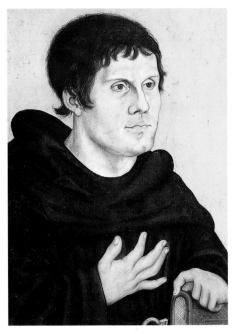

4. Martin Luther as a young man by Lucas Cranach the Elder, detail (c. 1520).

2. The selling of indulgences in church (1520).

3. Caricature of Johann Tetzel, the indulgence salesman (16th century).

5. Huldreich Zwingli by Hans Asper, detail (1531).

6. Jean Calvin, detail (c. 1536).

Reformation history

THE movement known as the Reformation began as a limited critique of some practices of the Church and of the doctrines that justified those practices. Its starting-point is conventionally dated to 1517, when Martin Luther (4) is said to have nailed his 95 theses to the door of the castle church at Wittenberg (1). What offended Luther above all was the open sale of indulgences – documents that officially guaranteed the forgiveness of sins even for the dead (2, 3). But if Luther was a reformer, Zwingli (5) and Calvin (6) were revolutionaries: the first rejected the authority of any Church, the second rejected man's responsibility for his own salvation. The religious quarrel immediately became a political quarrel, as the princes of Europe took sides – populations invariably followed their rulers. The Confession of Augsburg (7), presented to Charles V in 1530, was an attempt to heal the rift. It failed. The Council of Trent (8), which met over a prolonged period between 1545 and 1563, had to face the fact that half of Europe was outside the Catholic fold.

The Papacy, 66–67

The Bible, 118–19

The Reformation: a battle of images, 120–21

7. The presentation of the Confession of Augsburg in 1530. The Emperor Charles V is enthroned on the left. In the foreground sit the princes of German courts who supported Reform, and at the back the German bishops.

8. The final session of the Council of Trent (1563) attributed to Titian. Pope Pius IV presides; the body of the cathedral is filled with the mitres of bishops.

2. The outdoor pulpit of Prato Cathedral (1428–38).

3. Woodcut by Hans Baldung Grien on the title page of Geiler of Kaisersberg's *Das Buch Granatapfel* (1516), showing the author preaching.

Preaching the word

BEFORE the 16th century books were not a medium for influencing public opinion, and the key works of religious controversy were in Latin. In a world where books and literacy were rare, Christian teaching reached most people by the spoken word. Preaching was an activity in which the mendicant orders particularly excelled, and great preachers such as S. Bernardino of Siena (1) and Savonarola exercised great influence. The Reformers' scriptural belief that faith comes through hearing made sermon and pulpit central (4, 6), and printed sermons, which might be published from auditors' notes like Geiler of Kaisersberg's (3), made it possible to study preached words. Churches could be too small to hold the audience (2). St Paul's Cross in London (5) was even used by the government for official announcements.

5. Preacher at St Paul's Cross, London (*c.* 1616).

4. Ferdinand I listening to the papal nuncio in the Augustinerkirche, Vienna, by Jacob Seisenegger (1560).

6. Luther preaching in the parish church of Wittenberg by Lucas Cranach the Elder (mid-16th century).

1. Part of *Ecclesiastes* from the Complutensian Polyglot: Greek, with Latin gloss; Vulgate version; Hebrew (1514).

2. Title page of the second volume of the Bible in French, Lyon (1521).

3. The beginning of Chapter I of *Genesis* from Luther's Bible (1534).

4. Part of the *Gospel of St Matthew* from a Bohemian Bible (1489).

5. The opening of the *Book of Kings* from a Danish Bible (1550).

The Bible

WHATEVER the esteem given to the Greek and Roman classics, nothing could diminish the authority of the Bible, which was as central to Renaissance culture as to that of the Middle Ages. It was inevitable that the first book printed by Gutenberg should have been the Bible. Two factors, however, were causing it to be read in a new way. One was the application of humanist learning to the Latin Vulgate. First Valla and then Erasmus cast doubt on Jerome's infallibility as a translator. Both, however, remained Catholic and in terms of linguistic expertise the Catholic countries were at least equal to the Protestant. The greatest feat of pure biblical scholarship was the Complutensian Polyglot (1), published by the University of Alcalá, giving the text in Greek, Latin and (for the Old Testament) Hebrew. The other factor was the claim by Reformers to interpret the sacred text for themselves independently of the Church's authority. Proto-Reformers like the English Lollards and the Bohemian Hussites (4) both possessed vernacular versions of the New Testament. This made the Church suspicious of some translations and in England – though vernacular versions were already in print elsewhere in Europe – Tyndale's translation (6, 7) was banned. Tyndale paid for it with his life, though a few years later it was to form the basis for Henry VIII's 'Great Bible' (9). But Luther's version (3) made the Bible a German classic, and before long there were translations into every European vernacular (2, 5).

6. William Tyndale (after 1536).

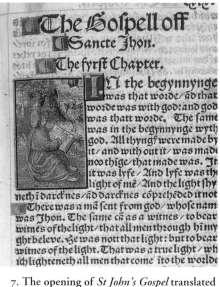

7. The opening of *St John's Gospel* translated by William Tyndale (1526).

9. Title page of Henry VIII's 'Great Bible' showing the king handing the 'Word of God' to his bishops and so, via the clergy, to a grateful populace (1539).

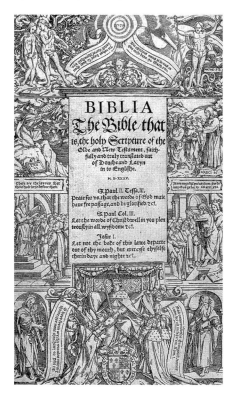

8. Title page of Coverdale's Bible (1535). Coverdale translated not from the original languages but from Jerome's Latin and Luther's German.

The Reformation: a battle of images

THE Reformation was a war waged by pamphlets, some of which have survived as classics of religious polemic. But it was also a war of pictures, and here the Protestant side must be judged the more effective. In the most elaborate of them (4) Lucas Cranach the Elder showed, as the caption tells us, 'the difference between the true religion of Christ and the false idolatrous teaching of Antichrist'. On the left Luther, inspired by God, preaches true Christianity, with baptism and communion conducted in the foreground; on the right a friar (Tetzel?) sells indulgences, while the pope counts his money and God and St Francis look down in horror. The younger Cranach could even depict the Reformers as Apostles at the Last Supper (1); Luther is at the left-hand corner on the far side, Melanchthon on the right next to Christ. Other common targets were the contrast between Christ's poverty and the pope's wealth (6), the Church's veneration of relics (2) and the pope as Satan or Antichrist (5). At another level Foxe's *Book of Martyrs* (3) commemorated the Protestants who had died in England under Queen Mary I.

2. Title page of Calvin's *Der Heilige Brotkorb* (1584).

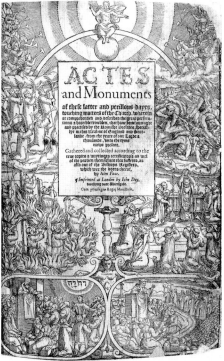

3. Title page of Foxe's *Book of Martyrs* (1563).

1. Lucas Cranach the Younger: *The Last Supper* (1565).

Reformation history, 114–15

Preaching the word, 116–17

The Bible, 118–19

4. Lucas Cranach the Elder: coloured woodcut contrasting Protestant and Catholic Christianity (*c.* 1545).

5. The pope as Satan or Antichrist (1545).

6. Coloured woodcut contrasting the poverty of Christ with the wealth of the pope (*c.* 1540).

1. The Calvinist Temple at Lyon (1564).

2. A member of Zwingli's congregation at Zurich, Jode Snider, making his public confession (1572).

Iconoclasm: the Puritan backlash

As part of their return to apostolic – even Hebraic – purity, all the Protestant Churches were in some measure hostile to the representation of God in human form (which was blasphemous), to the use of images in worship (forbidden in the Old Testament), to praying to saints (only God was holy) and to the mediating role of the priesthood (which came between the worshipper and God), though they differed in their degrees of hostility. A French Protestant church (1) is bare of images,

the only decoration being texts and heraldry; instead of an altar, the pulpit is the focus of the service. In Zwingli's Zurich, confession and penance were public acts (2), not a secret between priest and sinner. In books, the bodily representation of God was replaced by abstract symbols (3, 4), while in churches all over northern Europe, statues and altarpieces were thrown down and destroyed (6, 7). Even frivolities like jewelry and games (5) were cast into the fire.

3. *The Creation of Eve* from a Dutch Bible printed in Cologne in 1565.

4. The same scene from an English Bible of 1568 in which God the Father has been replaced by the Hebrew *Yahweh*, the Tetragrammaton.

5. A bonfire of vanities from a Swiss chronicle (1548).

6. Clearance of church 'idols' in Zurich (1524).

7. Destruction of religious images in an Antwerp church (1566).

1. Detail from Veronese's *The Wife of Zebedee Interceding with Christ* showing angels adoring the Eucharist (late 16th century).

Counter-Reformation

THE attacks of Luther and his allies forced the Catholic Church to look afresh at its practices and beliefs. When the Council of Trent assembled in 1545 it had two main aims – the reform of abuses and the redefinition of doctrine. The first went some way towards meeting the Reformers' criticisms, but the second served only to separate the two sides more firmly than ever. New emphasis was laid on the miraculous nature of the sacraments (1), the cult of the Virgin (6), the intercession of saints, the use of images and the veneration of relics – all things which the Protestants rejected. New monastic orders were formed (2) with the special mission of defeating heresy, and the Church reiterated its claims to be the sole means of salvation (3). Under Philip II Spain assumed the leadership of Catholic Europe (4, 5). Christendom was now permanently divided, political rivalry made more bitter by the difference of creed.

2. St Ignatius Loyola, founder of the Society of Jesus, the Jesuits, by Juan de Roelas (*c.* 1622).

3. Detail from *The Ship of the Church* by an anonymous Spanish artist (16th century). In this elaborate allegory, the Ship, with its three decks – the vows of Poverty, Chastity and Obedience – is manned by ecclesiastical virtues and its souls filled with the winds of Counsel, Fear, Wisdom, Intellect, Piety and Fortitude, which all emanate from the dove of the Holy Spirit. Angels occupy the crow's nest. The saved are dragged from the water, the damned swallowed by the giant fish of Hell.

The Papacy, 66–67

The Reformation: a battle of images, 120–21

The Last Judgment, 146–47

4. *Religion Succoured by Spain* by Titian (*c.* 1575). Spain, symbolized by the figures of the Church Militant and Triumphant, rescues Faith fallen through Sin, symbolized by Mary Magdalene.

6. *The Assumption of the Virgin* by Titian (1516). The doctrine of the Virgin's bodily assumption into Heaven, though never a dogma, was believed by all Catholics but rejected by Protestants.

5. *The Dream of Philip II* by El Greco (1578). The king sees a vision of the holy monogram of Christ, IHS, adored by angels. With Philip are St Paul, the Pope and the Doge of Venice. On the right, the jaws of Hell.

The relief of poverty

Dᴜʀɪɴɢ the Middle Ages the upkeep of hospitals and the relief of poverty were religious duties (1). In the 16th century the situation changed – in the north because the dissolution of the monasteries threw the burden of relief on the secular authorities or private charity (5, 6), in Italy because the rise in population created problems too large for the Church alone to solve. Many cities built hospitals, foundling homes and almshouses of architectural grandeur (4). Charitable bodies with religious affiliations, such as the confraternities, dedicated themselves to one or all of the traditional Seven Works of Mercy: feeding the hungry (3), clothing the naked, visiting the sick (2), befriending the prisoner, succouring the pilgrim (7), comforting the afflicted, and burying the dead – themes often illustrated in art.

1. *St Lawrence Distributing Alms* by Fra Angelico (1447–49).

2. Visiting the sick, from the frieze of the Ospedale del Ceppo, Pistoia, by the Della Robbia workshop (1514).

3. Feeding the hungry, from the frieze of the Ospedale del Ceppo, Pistoia, by the Della Robbia workshop (1514).

The Ages of Man, 176–77

Illness and death, 200–01

Sculpture in relief, 260–61

4. Scenes showing the work of the Foundling Hospital of S. Maria della Scala, Siena: nursing, educating, baptising and finally marrying the foundlings by Domenico di Bartolo, detail (15th century).

5. Feeding the lame and the poor in Augsburg (1537).

6. Master of Alkmaar: feeding the hungry, detail (1490–1510).

7. Succouring the pilgrim, from the frieze of the Ospedale del Ceppo, Pistoia, by the Della Robbia workshop (1514).

God and Man　127

1. Andrea del Castagno: detail of *The Trinity with St Jerome* (1451–56).

2. Michael Pacher: detail of *The Coronation of the Virgin* (begun 1471).

3. Jan van Eyck: *God the Father* from the *Ghent Altarpiece* (*c.* 1432).

The Last Judgment,
146–47

The heroic,
250–51

The Sistine ceiling,
256–57

God the Father

I N representing God the Father, painters had to imagine something which was strictly unimaginable, but the Renaissance inherited an iconographical convention from the Middle Ages. Most convincing were those images where the Father was shown alone in glory (3) or as the first person of the Trinity (2), something for which the northern artists had an

4. Michelangelo: *The Creation of Adam* (1508–12).

instinctive feeling. Castagno's *Trinity* (1), seeking a modern approach, placed the Father, Holy Ghost and crucified Son in unusually dynamic foreshortening. God as Creator was in some ways even more demanding. Michelangelo (4) succeeded in his tremendous image on the Sistine Chapel ceiling. Tintoretto's relatively mundane composition (5) illustrates all too well what a challenge such a subject could be.

5. Tintoretto: *The Creation of the Animals* (c. 1550).

1. Piero della Francesca: *The Nativity*
(1475–80).

2. Hans Baldung Grien: *The Nativity*, detail
(1520).

3. Hugo van der Goes: *The Nativity* from the
Portinari Altarpiece (*c.* 1475).

4. Dürer: *The Nativity,* detail from the
Paumgartner Altarpiece (1503).

5. Botticelli: *The Mystic Nativity* (1500).

6. Ghirlandaio: *The Nativity* (1485).

The Nativity

THE Gospels give only the barest account of the birth of Christ
(not even mentioning the stable), so that artists were free to
compose a wide range of variations on the theme. It was usual to
include Mary and Joseph kneeling in adoration of their new-born
son, plus the visit of the shepherds and sometimes the Magi. Piero
(1) underlines the miraculous nature of the event by a prominent
choir of angels. Dürer (4) too includes angelic putti, together with
miniature figures of the donors. Hugo van der Goes (3) introduces
a note of rustic realism with his unkempt shepherds. When this
Flemish picture arrived in Florence it caused a sensation, as is
evident in Ghirlandaio's version of the scene (6) where virtually
the same group of shepherds appears, this time against the ruins
of the classical world (the manger is a disused sarcophagus and
the Magi arrive through a triumphal arch). The dramatic night-
Nativity by Hans Baldung Grien (2) is lit only by the radiance
of the holy Child, while Botticelli (5), in a picture painted near
the end of his life, when he was under the influence of Savonarola,
unfolds the whole theology of the incarnation, with a circle of
dancing angels in the sky and on earth the promise of redemption,
Satan defeated and more angels embracing saved mankind.

1. Masaccio: *Madonna and Child* (1426).

2. Andrea del Sarto: *Madonna of the Harpies* (1517).

3. Petrus Christus: *Madonna and Child* (late 15th century).

4. Giovanni Bellini: *Madonna of the Pomegranate* (c. 1489).

Marriage and the family, 190–91

Renaissance women, 194–95

Sex and gender, 196–97

Virgin and Child

No image is more universal than the mother and child, a subject that occurs in the symbolism of many religions. Christian doctrine presented the artist with two special problems: to convey Mary's virgin purity as well as her motherhood, and to show clearly that this is no ordinary child but the incarnation of the deity. Earlier centuries had given the pair a hieratic solemnity, but by the late Middle Ages the emphasis was already on tenderness and beauty. How to carry this further without sacrificing the aura of divinity was the task facing the Renaissance painter. Mary customarily sits on a throne, attended by angels, and the Child is usually shown as an infant at least one year old with an intelligence beyond babyhood. Masaccio (1) makes him suck his fingers, but there is no mistaking the group's supernatural charge. The same equation holds in varying degrees for other artists, each finding his own solution, from almost literal domesticity (4) to the monumentality of a living statue (7). Raphael's *Sistine Madonna* (6) is one of those supreme masterpieces whose appeal crosses every barrier of education and taste, while Parmigianino's Madonna (5), full of strange juxtapositions of scale, makes the Child so large that it is hard to exclude the thought of the dead Christ of the *pietà*.

6. Raphael: *Sistine Madonna*, Madonna and Child with Pope Sixtus IV and St Barbara (*c.* 1513–16).

7. Jan Gossaert, called Mabuse: *Virgin of Louvain*, detail (1516).

5. Parmigianino: *Madonna with the Long Neck* (*c.* 1535).

God and Man   133

2. Gerard David: *Baptism of Christ*, detail (1502).

1. Piero della Francesca: *The Baptism of Christ* (c. 1440).

3. Sansovino: *Baptism of Christ* (1502).

The sacraments, 112–13

The human form, 248–49

The heroic, 250–51

4. Giovanni Bellini: *Baptism of Christ* (*c.* 1500).

The baptism of Christ

BAPTISM was the least controversial of Christian doctrines, being retained by even the most extreme Protestant sects. The only serious question was when it should be performed. In the early centuries baptism was only for adults, but since, according to St Augustine, it washed away original sin, the sooner it was done the better. The child became part of the community ('body') of Christ. Jesus' own baptism by St John was obviously different from this, and unique, but however problematic theologically, it was popular as a subject simply as symbolizing the sacrament's redemptive power. Piero (1) and Sansovino (3) signal its sacred nature by the presence of angels. More normally God the Father is included blessing his son (4) – Piero shows the Dove only. El Greco (5) gives us the whole panoply of Heaven – a cosmic event and a mystical revelation.

5. El Greco: *Baptism of Christ* (1596–1600).

2. Rogier van der Weyden: *The Virgin and Child*, with Saints Peter, John the Baptist, Cosmas and Damian (*c.* 1450).

1. Pietro Lorenzetti: *Polyptych,* the Virgin and Child with Saints Donatus, John the Evangelist, John the Baptist and Matthew (early 14th century).

3. Mantegna: *The S. Zeno Altarpiece,* the Virgin and Child with Saints Peter, Paul, John the Evangelist and Zeno (left) and Saints Benedict, Lawrence, Gregory and John the Baptist (right), *c.* 1456–59.

Virgin and Child, 132–33

The mastery of space, 246–47

The human form, 248–49

4. Giovanni Bellini: *S. Giobbe Altarpiece*, the Virgin and Child with Saints Francis, John the Baptist, Job (counted as a saint in Italy), Dominic, Sebastian and Augustine (*c.* 1480–90).

5. Fra Angelico: *Bosco ai Frari Altarpiece*, the Virgin and Child with Saints Anthony, Zenobius, Francis, Cosmas, Damian and Peter Martyr (*c.* 1438–40).

6. Raphael: *Madonna of the Baldacchino*, the Virgin and Child with Saints Peter, Bruno, James and Augustine (*c.* 1505–09).

Conversing saints

THROUGHOUT the Middle Ages, one of the most popular subjects for an altarpiece was what came to be called the *sacra conversazione*, 'holy conversation' – a central figure (usually the Madonna and Child) flanked by saints. In early examples (1) each saint has his or her self-contained space in a niche or canopy. By the early Renaissance, in both north (2) and south (3, 5) they occupy the same pictorial space and form a convincing social group. By the High Renaissance, the opportunity is taken to dramatize the scene by making the saints converse, gesticulate and sometimes apparently argue with each other (4, 6), pointing the way to the almost theatrical tableaux of the Baroque.

The Last Supper

THE Last Supper was commonly painted on the walls of refectories, since that was where communal meals took place. But it had two levels of much deeper meaning: it was the occasion when Christ foretold his betrayal by Judas and when he initiated the Eucharist, or Holy Communion. Painters could stress one or the other aspect, as the situation demanded. Dieric Bouts in an altar-picture (1), makes it very clearly a depiction of the Eucharist, with Jesus blessing the wafer and the chalice exactly as the priest would in the Mass; all the details are meticulously taken from Flemish 15th-century life. Ghirlandaio's fresco (2), which continues the architecture of the refectory in which it was painted, shows Christ handing the bread to Judas, signifying that he would be the one to betray him. Leonardo (3) chooses a moment just before, when Jesus has said, 'One of you will betray me', and the disciples look at one another 'uncertain of whom he was speaking'. Tintoretto (4) returns to the Eucharistic theme, showing Christ personally administering communion to one of the disciples amid a blaze of angelic glory.

1. Dieric Bouts: *The Last Supper* (1464–67).

2. Ghirlandaio: *The Last Supper* (late 15th century).

The sacraments, 112–13

Conversing saints, 136–37

Italy: the language of decoration, 252–53

3. Leonardo da Vinci: *The Last Supper* (1497).

4. Tintoretto: *The Last Supper* (1592–94).

1. Perugino: *Crucifixion* (1496).

2. Masaccio: *Crucifixion* (1426–27).

The Crucifixion

FOR Christians, the Crucifixion is more than the painful death of a man on the cross – it is a turning-point in world history, the moment when Christ's sacrifice redeemed mankind from eternal punishment. The painter's task, therefore, was to convey a profound ambiguity – suffering and thanksgiving in one. The Renaissance, with its new-found mastery of perspective, anatomy and other techniques of realism, tended to move away from the medieval religious icon towards a more naturalistic rendering of the scene, but at the same time to preserve a sense of cosmic significance. Perugino (1) sets the scene in an idyllic landscape, the figures in calm contemplation. Masaccio (2) makes Christ's body physically convincing but gives it a ritualistic gold background. Michelangelo (3), as always, expresses the spirit through the flesh, while Grünewald (4) follows the northern convention of dwelling almost sadistically on Christ's tortured body against a black sky; but on the right John the Baptist, with the sacrificial Lamb of God, points to the theological meaning: 'He must increase but I must decrease' (John, III, 30). Both Tintoretto (5) and El Greco (6) fill the scene with figures in violent motion, conveying its supernatural quality through drama.

3. Michelangelo: *Crucifixion* (*c.* 1550–55).

4. Grünewald: *Crucifixion* (*c.* 1515).

6. El Greco: *Crucifixion* (1584–94).

5. Tintoretto: *Crucifixion*, detail (*c.* 1588).

God and Man   141

1. Rogier van der Weyden: *The Descent from the Cross* (*c.* 1435).

2. Hans Holbein: *Dead Christ* (1521).

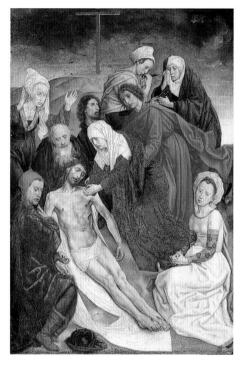

4. Hugo van der Goes: *Lamentation over the Dead Christ* (*c.* 1470).

3. Botticelli: *Lamentation over the Dead Christ* (*c.* 1490–92).

5. Ercole de' Roberti: *Pietà* (*c.* 1485).

6. Michelangelo: *Pietà* (*c.* 1500).

7. Titian: *Pietà*, detail (1573–76).

8. Sebastiano del Piombo: *Pietà* (*c.* 1517).

Lamentation

I N the Passion story, the Descent from the Cross and the Lamentation over the dead Christ (known as the *pietà* when Mary alone is present with her son) marks in human terms the lowest point: a moment of utter despair after the Crucifixion and before any hint of the Resurrection. It challenged Renaissance artists both in the realistic depiction of the nude body and in the expression of profound emotion. The northern painters (1, 4) combine astonishing realism in the details with highly stylized compositions. Roberti (5) and Botticelli (3) both turn to a classical model (the dead Meleager) but transform it by their

concentration on the frenzy of grief. In Titian (7) and Sebastiano (8) there is a desolation that seems to include the whole world. This is a theme that stirs deep feelings and yet can evoke totally opposite responses. Holbein's *Dead Christ* (2) is an uncompromising image of mortality, the eyes open, the discoloured flesh tensed in rigor mortis. Michelangelo (6) ignores realism – Christ's body is unblemished, the mother is no older than her son – and through the open gesture of Mary's left hand conveys the redeeming nature of Christ's sacrifice and the promise of new life.

The Resurrection

THE last act of the Passion story breaks free from the need to convince at a mundane level. The Resurrection is the supreme miracle, when Jesus triumphs over death. The only parallel episode in the Gospels is the Transfiguration, where Jesus is seen in his glorified state by Peter, James and John with Moses and Elias at his side. In both scenes, the challenge for painters was to reveal Christ as divine, transcending the limits of ordinary humanity. Some chose to do this by the intensity of facial expression (1) or sublimity of gesture, in Piero's case (4) achieving what has been called 'the best picture in the world'. Others attempt to follow the words of the evangelist: 'The appearance of his countenance was changed and his raiment became radiant white'. Grünewald (2) creates a 'night scene' in the northern tradition. Fra Angelico (3) even prefigures the Crucifixion. Raphael (5) somewhat confusingly combines the Transfiguration with an episode that happened the next day when Jesus cast out a devil from a paralytic boy. Only Giovanni Bellini (6) conveys a sense of the miraculous without compromising fidelity to the real world of grass and sky and distant hills.

2. Grünewald: *The Resurrection* from the *Isenheim Altarpiece* (1512–15).

3. Fra Angelico: *The Transfiguration*, detail (*c*. 1440).

1. Hans Pleydenwurff: *The Resurrection* from the Hofer Altar (*c*. 1485).

4. Piero della Francesca: *The Resurrection* (c. 1460).

5. Raphael: *The Transfiguration* (1517).

6. Giovanni Bellini: *The Transfiguration* (c. 1480).

1. Rogier van der Weyden: *The Last Judgment* (c. 1450).

The Last Judgment

THE iconography of the Last Judgment was fixed by Early Christian times and remained virtually unchanged. Rogier van der Weyden's altarpiece (1) is a clear diagram of the traditional scheme. At the top sits Christ the Judge, flanked by angels bearing the instruments of the Passion, and beside him the Virgin and St John interceding for mankind. Beneath him, surrounded by the saints, St Michael weighs souls. At the bottom the dead rise from their graves (note the way limbs are emerging from the cracking earth) and are taken up to heaven, on the left, or cast down to hell, on the right. The naked bodies of the damned, racked by violent emotions, appealed to painters, such

as Signorelli (2), who had made a special study of anatomy. Michelangelo's vast fresco in the Sistine Chapel (3) retains the conventional arrangement. Here too angels bear the instruments of the Passion, top right and left. But there is no St Michael. Christ himself, with the Virgin cowering almost in terror at his side, condemns the wicked to eternal punishment. At the bottom, the dead rise – one dragged by an angel from the clutches of a fiend – and Charon loads his boat to transport them to hell, bottom right. In between are the ranks of the saints – in Rogier decorously clothed, in Michelangelo (originally) naked.

2. Signorelli: *The Damned Consigned to Hell*, detail (1499).

God the Father,
128–29

Illness and death,
200–01

The human form,
248–49

3. Michelangelo: *The Last Judgment* (1536–41).

ROMA

PER SACRAM B.PETRI SEDEM CAPVT ORBIS EFFECTA. S.LEC

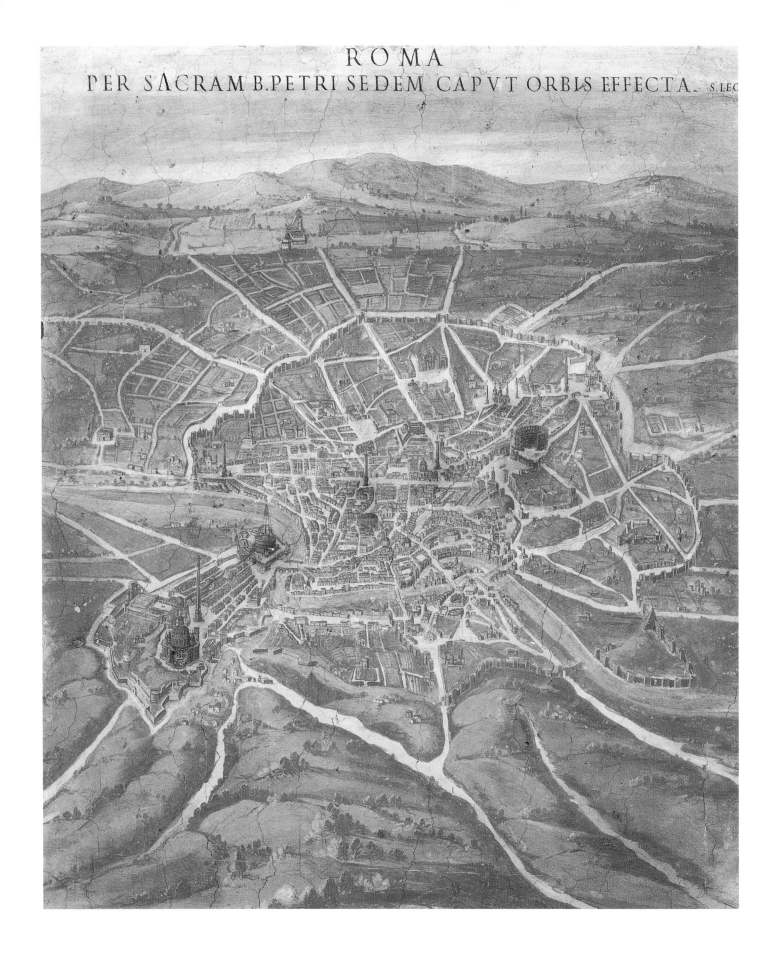

THE IMAGE OF THE WORLD

During the Renaissance the appearance of the world changed both outwardly and inwardly. Not only were the great cities and palaces of the time transformed by new buildings and new architectural styles, but also the area of the known world and knowledge of it was revolutionized. Geographical space became understood as never before and the opportunities for vicarious travel, for visiting distant places and seeing them in the mind's eye through depictions and descriptions, increased enormously. Even though physical travel was arduous and expensive, the expanding world was contracted intellectually by the medium of print.

Throughout Europe cities were altered by developments in the art of war. The inventions of gunpowder and artillery introduced new elements into military architecture, and in place of the towered defences of the past, city walls were constructed with angle bastions for the emplacement of heavy guns. These great, often star-shaped constructions, many of which are still to be seen, became features of the landscape in all areas where Europeans were engaged in defence, from the Diu in India to Mombasa in Africa and Berwick-upon-Tweed, the northernmost town in England. Artists and architect-engineers from Giotto to Michelangelo undertook the design of fortifications (p. 164), and though the military buildings of the Renaissance went far beyond Vitruvius, it was still possible to compare impressive new structures with great ancient buildings. Vasari so admired the S. Andrea fortress in Venice (designed by Michele Sanmicheli in 1535) that he described it as representing 'the grandeur and majesty of the most famous buildings of Roman greatness'.

With the discovery of new lands maps became more accurate and realistic (pp. 152–53), and thanks to printing more commonly available. It was not only military campaigners or statesmen like Lord Burghley who realized the value of maps; they also formed part of art collections, and both globes and the maps printed to hang on walls helped to make many a metaphor before John Donne apostrophized his mistress as 'my America, my new found land'. From the detailed plotting of coastal outlines to the global depiction of continents and seas, Portuguese and Spanish voyages to reach the east by rounding Africa or by a westward sea route resulted in the making of new and clearer terrestrial images. The Atlantic arrived, firmly in place as *Oceanus Atlanticus* in Mercator's world map of 1569. Gerard Mercator, who helped to give currency to the name, made it easier through the terrestrial globe he produced in 1541 and the great atlas (the first collection of its kind) which was completed after his death, to take in at a glance the position of Europe between the old lands in the east and the new continent to the west.

Although, as Walter Raleigh remarked, maps continued to perpetuate fictions and false hopes, they also helped to inculcate new and truer views of the world, and globes, becoming commoner in the later 16th century, made it easier to visualize the planet, floating in space like the moon. Others besides Michael Drayton, a poet who wrote a topographical description of Great Britain in verse, could imagine 'The earth in perfect roundness of a ball / Exceeding globes most artificiall!'

In the mid-16th century *the technique of the bird's-eye view was relatively new, and enabled town layouts to be represented with hitherto unknown clarity. Ignazio Danti's fresco of Rome – Caput orbis, 'The head of the world' – was painted for the Vatican Library. The inhabited part of the city filled only part of the area enclosed by the Aurelian Wall (3rd century AD). Prominent, bottom left, are the unfinished basilica of St Peter's and the Castel S. Angelo. Other landmarks such as the Colosseum, centre right, are portrayed with meticulous precision.*

Detail from Martin Waldseemüller's world map of 1507 showing Amerigo Vespucci and the New World to which he had just given his name.

The most distant city illustrated in Braun and Hogenburg's great work on the cities of the world (1574) was Goa, in India.

The world began to be lodged in minds in the shapes it still has.

The new might be named in terms of Antiquity, witness atlas and Atlantic, or the River Amazon, called after some Indian women of the 1540s, who fought the Spaniards so fiercely they seemed like the legendary Amazons. But the *Novus Mundus* itself, in becoming America, immortalized a contemporary whose printed account of his voyages impressed the map-maker, Martin Waldseemüller. His huge world map of 1507 – one of the first to be separately printed – in summarizing the astonishing transformation of geography, also epitomized the conjunction of old and new. At the top Ptolemy, beside the old world, is placed opposite Amerigo Vespucci, next to the new western hemisphere. Waldseemüller was still using the Ptolemaic model, though he extended it, and the word AMERICA stands clearly on the large new continent, whose eastern seaboard, detailed with rivers and names, contrasts with the schematic *terra incognita* of its western side.

By the late 16th century contemporaries were becoming aware of having stepped out of ancient bounds, and that their horizons were not those of Ptolemy, or Homer, or Cicero. They could not but be struck by the fact that 'our classical authors had no knowledge of all this America, which we call New Lands', and the invention of the printing press, together with the discovery of the new world, seemed to deserve comparison 'not only to Antiquity, but to immortality'.

Maps, besides being informers, became objects of art, a means of display or satisfying pride. Pius II sent to his new city of Pienza a *mappa mundi* of the 1460s, painted on canvas by Girolamo Bellavista, and Gregory XIII had the walls of a huge gallery in the Vatican decorated in the 1580s by Antonio and Ignazio Danti with maps of all the regions of Italy (pp. 156–57). Printing helped to extend cartographic literacy and to satisfy the curiosity to know about the appearance of distant places. Fifteenth-century Italian painters had accustomed people to seeing historical or biblical events taking place in towns they knew, and the 16th century developed a market for accurate topographical prints of European cities. Views of Antwerp, Augsburg and Nuremberg, Venice and Rome, could both please local pride and serve distant interests.

Sense of place as well as sense of the past was producing increasing numbers of books devoted to towns, regions, or nations: works such as Johann Cuspinian's *Austriae regionis descriptio* and Conrad Celtis' *Norimberga* (part of a planned *Germania illustrata*) or, later in the 16th century, Hadrianus Junius' *Batavia*. In England William Lambarde's *Perambulation of Kent* was followed by William Camden's *Britannia* and John Stow's *Survey of London*. The pleasure of armchair travel to different parts of the earth, to look at landscape, rivers and towns, to comprehend 'the form of the whole Earth in which we live' was offered to readers of the large series of city views published from the 1570s by Georg Braun and Franz Hogenberg (p. 165). Travel of the new age could be pleasure for itself; it did not have to be pilgrimage.

Though it was a long time before education made geographical mental imagery a widespread possession, the start of this process was important. It applied to the knowledge of one's own country or region, as well as to the globe. Christopher Saxton, who followed Mercator in producing a wall map of the British Isles, also published in 1579 the first atlas of England and Wales, an unequalled cartographic survey, the only precedent for which was one made in Austria in 1561. The inhabitant of Italy, France, or England, who nowadays can summon without effort into his mind's eye the outline of his homeland, automatically does so with a north–south orientation. We owe this global assumption to Renaissance explorers and map-makers, who by extending the known world with the aid of the compass ended the orientation of the old *mappa mundi*, which placed east at the top. They established a scientific norm for something that had previously been a matter of religious convention.

There were also new ways of seeing towns and landscape. Bird's-eye views of cities, like those of Florence (p. 154) and Rome, produced in the late 15th century by the engraver and printseller Francesco Rosselli, or the enormous six-part woodcut of Venice in 1500, made by Jacopo de' Barbari and Anton Kolb, or Anton van den Wyngaerde's 1553 etching of Genoa, offered completely new topographical images. It was a novel experience to hang in space over a city depicted in exact and realistic detail (perhaps to spot your own house, or church, or workplace) with the free detachment of an aerial observer. What we may now take for granted as virtually mundane was in 1500 akin to gaining godly vision – flying being the province of gods and birds. Indeed in Jacopo de' Barbari's woodcut the viewer shares his lofty viewpoint with Mercury and the puffing Winds, and looks down on Neptune, stationed in Venetian waters far below. Such a celestial view of the world was also used in painting. Albrecht Altdorfer's wonderful panoramic *Battle of Issus* (pp. 84, 169) sets the vast military mêlée of Alexander the Great's defeat of Darius and the Persians in a magnificent panorama of hanging castles and buildings, with distant lakes and mountains disappearing over the curved horizon in swirls of cloud. We look on the scene as mile-high travellers who have left the terrestrial globe.

While artists continued to construct imaginary landscapes as the idealized settings for the Holy Family and saints, they also began more frequently to transcribe the details of personally observed places, towns as well as countryside, specific plants and trees. They might do so for themselves, like Dürer's remarkable watercolours, some made on his first journey across the Alps (p. 167), of the walls of Trent, or a grove of pine trees in the sunset. Such topographical observations might also be commissioned by a patron, like the vivid drawings in which Wenceslaus Hollar recorded the progress of the Earl of Arundel's barge along the Rhine and Danube in 1636.

Habits of observation were growing, and it came to seem a virtue in an artist to put down the realities of the world as seen. The fertility of art could reflect the fertility of nature, by 'depicting so attractively the lie of valleys and farms, the course of rivers and narrows, vessels under sail, people going to town by mule or cart, or walking about in broad-brimmed hats against the sun'. Thus a famous Dutch humanist praised a painter friend, with patriotic pride.

Detail from Jacopo de' Barbari's bird's-eye view of Venice (1500), showing St Mark's and the Palazzo Ducale in the background and S. Giorgio Maggiore in the foreground. In the middle sits Neptune on a dophin.

In 1636 Wenceslaus Hollar sailed down the Danube in a barge with the Earl of Arundel, making coloured drawings on the way. This is Wüntzen, now Winzer, in Germany.

1. Catalan *mappa mundi* (*c.* 1450–60).

2. Fra Mauro: world map (1459).

Mapping the world

THE Renaissance saw the birth of geography as we know it. Before the 15th century maps were either diagrams of received dogma or charts detailing the route from one point to the next. By 1450, Europe, North Africa and East Asia were sufficiently understood to make a reasonably accurate map, though the Catalan example shown here (1) retains many traditional conventions (e.g., the Red Sea in red and Jerusalem the centre of the world). Fra Mauro's map of 1459 (2) incorporates some new information (south is at the top, so everything looks upside-down). But with the great voyages of discovery which began in the 1480s, the known world expanded in an unprecedented way. The 'Cantino' world map (3), made in Lisbon about 1502 and named after the patron who commissioned it, was the first to include the discoveries of Columbus: it shows the Caribbean islands, part of Brazil and part of Florida. In the Old World, the shape of Africa, after Vasco da Gama, is now virtually complete. (But note that the Red Sea is still red and Jerusalem still prominent in the centre.)

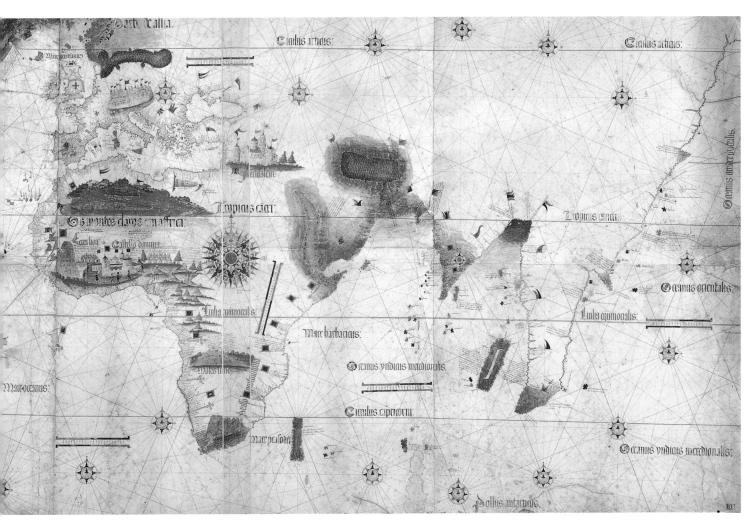

3. 'Cantino' world map (c. 1502).

1. Florence Cathedral and Baptistery, detail (mid-15th century).

2. Ghirlandaio: detail from a *Miracle of St Francis* showing the Via Tornabuoni and the old Ponte S. Trinita (1483–86).

3. Bird's-eye view of Florence, copy of the Carta della Catena (c. 1480).

Florence

WHY did the Renaissance begin in Florence and why were so many of its leading personalities Florentine? Several circumstances combined auspiciously. Economically, Florence was prosperous, more prosperous than any other city in Italy. Politically, it was ruled by those responsible for its prosperity – merchants, manufacturers and bankers, free from both outside interference and native aristocracy. This ruling class was proud, competitive, intellectually curious and culturally discerning. Four of Florence's Chancellors (Salutati, Bruni, Marsuppini and Poggio) were outstanding humanists. By the mid-15th century, the walled city on the Arno (3) controlled most of Tuscany. Brunelleschi's vast dome of the cathedral (1) dominated its skyline, surrounded by public buildings (5, 6) and the palaces of rich families (4) – families which vied with each other in the patronage of scholarship and the arts.

4. Palazzo Strozzi by Giuliano da Sangallo, Benedetto da Maiano and Il Cronaca (1489–1501).

Humanist beginnings, 34–35

The rulers of Italy, 72–73

A new world of finance, 232–33

5. Palazzo Vecchio and Loggia dei Lanzi, detail from a painting of the execution of Savonarola (1498).

6. School of Vasari: *Ceremony of the Candles* in the Piazza della Signoria (c. 1550).

Rome

THE revival of classical architecture coincided with the establishment of firm papal rule. Under a series of dynamic popes, Rome soon outshone Florence as the Renaissance city *par excellence*. The Cancellaria (**6**) was the first building in the new style of Bramante, though apparently begun before he arrived in the city. Julius II, however, employed him for the new St Peter's (**3**) and the Belvedere Courtyard (**5**) and he also designed private palaces (**2**), while Raphael worked on the Villa Madama (**7**), incorporating antique decorative motifs recently discovered by excavation. Grandest of all were the projects of Sixtus V, who not only commissioned a range of public buildings (**1**), but also drove three new streets through the medieval city fanning out from the Piazza del Popolo (**4**).

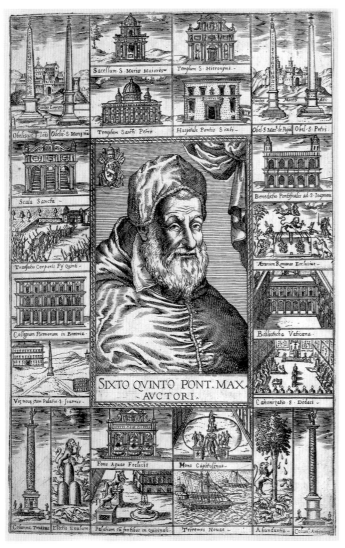

1. Pope Sixtus V and the achievements of his pontificate (1589).

2. Bramante: House of Raphael (*c.* 1512).

3. Maerten van Heemskerck: new St Peter's under construction (*c.* 1510).

The Papacy,
66–67

Palaces and palazzi,
78–79

Planned urban space,
270–71

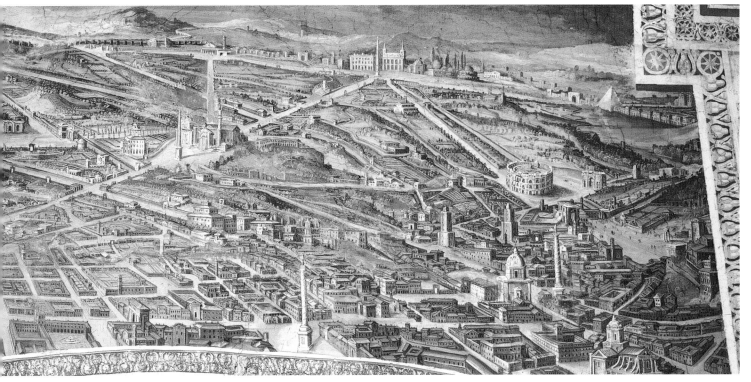

4. Fresco showing Sixtus V's street plan for Rome, detail (*c.* 1590).

5. Bramante: Belvedere Courtyard, Vatican, Rome (*c.* 1510).

6. Courtyard of the Cancellaria, Rome (*c.* 1490).

7. Raphael: loggia of the Villa Madama, Rome (begun 1516).

The Image of the World   157

1. Bird's-eye view of Venice in about 1600; note the Doge's ceremonial barge, the *Bucintoro*, foreground right.

3. Palazzo Corner by Sansovino (begun *c.* 1545).

2. St Mark's Library (Biblioteca Marciana) and to the left the Mint (Zecca), both by Jacopo Sansovino (begun *c.* 1540).

Venice

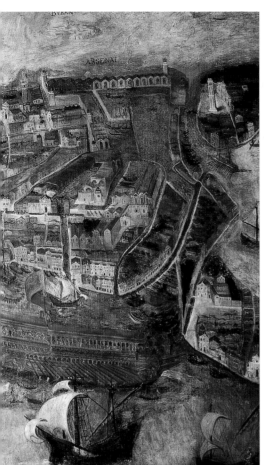

VENICE was the only Italian state to have an overseas empire, stretching down the eastern Adriatic coast and including the islands of Crete and Cyprus. Venice also ruled a large area of mainland Italy, the Veneto. Its remarkably stable government rested on an oligarchy drawn from about two hundred top families. Politically it was inflexible and conservative, but culturally fairly free, a leading centre of printing and home of a distinctive school of painting that included Bellini, Giorgione, Titian, Tintoretto and Veronese. Architecturally it was less adventurous, drawing architects from outside – Sanmicheli from Verona, Sansovino from Florence (2, 3, 6), Palladio from Vicenza – and adapting its own traditional building types only minimally to the new style – the palaces on the Grand Canal never lost their symmetrical façades with the central three bays opening onto a hall (3, 5).

4. Vittore Carpaccio: the Lion of St Mark with the Palazzo Ducale in the background (1514).

5. Palazzo Loredan (early 16th century).

6. Loggia of the Campanile of St Mark's by Sansovino (begun 1538).

7. The Arsenal of Venice in the late 16th century.

1. Elias Holl: Augsburg Town Hall (1614–20).

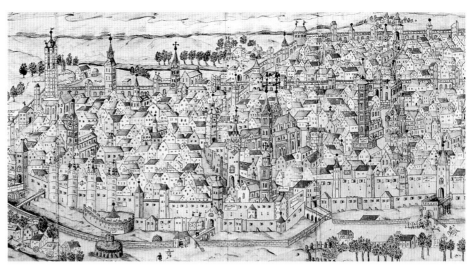

2. Panorama of Augsburg (*c.* 1530).

3. Harbour and town of Antwerp (*c.* 1540).

4. Cornelis Floris: Antwerp Town Hall (1561–65).

5. Panorama of Nuremberg (*c.* 1520).

The Holy Roman Empire, 68–69

A new world of finance, 232–33

Gothic survival, 272–73

6. Detail of the Schwarzenberg Palace, Prague (1545–63).

7. Paolo della Stella: portico of the Summer Palace, Prague (1535–41).

8. Benedict Ried: porch added to the church of St George, Prague (c. 1500).

9. Benedict Ried: Vladislav Hall, Prague Castle, detail (built c. 1500; painting 1607).

10. *Pietra dura* mosaic of the city of Prague by Giovanni Castrucci (c. 1600).

Cities of central Europe

No northern city was visually transformed by the Renaissance. Nonetheless, Augsburg, Antwerp, Nuremberg and Prague were centres of cultural and intellectual activity that made them more than figuratively the heirs of Florence, Venice and Rome. In Augsburg (1, 2) the Fuggers vied with the Medici as patrons as well as financiers; Antwerp (3, 4) flourished on its commerce and led Europe in its printing; Nuremberg (5) was the enlightened home town of Dürer. Prague (6–10), chosen by the Emperor Rudolf II as his capital in preference to Vienna, was the most intriguing of them all, though its legacy of classicizing buildings is not large. The hall of Prague Castle (9) is an amazing mixture of playful late Gothic (the vault) and strict Renaissance (the doors and windows).

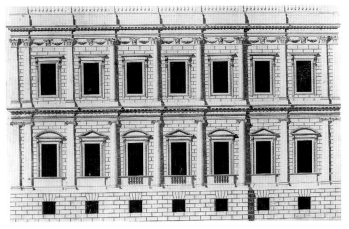

1. Inigo Jones: Banqueting House, Whitehall (1619–22).

London

HUMANIST scholars were no strangers to England, and Italian sculptors introduced the new style as early as the accession of Henry VIII. Architecture was slower to respond, and London remained a basically medieval city until the Fire of 1666. The Royal Exchange (4) was an early exercise in classicism, based on Flemish rather than Italian precedent. It was not until the reign of James I that England produced in Inigo Jones an architect thoroughly trained in the Renaissance manner. His portico to Old St Paul's (3), Banqueting House, Whitehall (1) and the gallery attributed to him at Somerset House (2, centre) showed him to be a master not merely of the detail, but also of the underlying principles of Palladianism.

2. Old Somerset House, with portico in the centre associated with Inigo Jones (built 1661–62).

4. Royal Exchange, London (1566–71).

3. Inigo Jones: portico added to Old St Paul's (1633–40).

The domestic setting, 188–89

The classical orders, 268–69

Planned urban space, 270–71

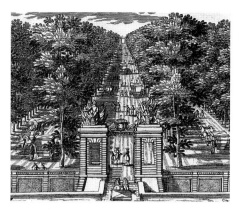

1. View of the Cours de la Reine, Paris (laid out 1616). Engraving by Aveline.

2. Place Dauphine, Paris (laid out 1607). Engraving from Claude Châtillon, *Topographie française*, 1641.

3. Place des Vosges, Paris (laid out 1605). Anonymous 17th-century painting.

Paris

Pₐₐᵣᵢₛ welcomed the Renaissance more readily than London, although there was no one of Jones' generation who could match his Italianate purity. The ambitious Place Dauphine (2) and Place des Vosges (3) showed urban planning of an advanced order. Both were part of Henri IV's improvements to the city, the first associated with the Pont Neuf, the second, on reclaimed ground, was the first 'square' north of the Alps. Parisian architecture, however, never gave up its steep roofs and tall chimneys (4). Another planning feature, destined to be part of the French grand manner, was the *cours* (1), a formal area intended for the parade of carriages.

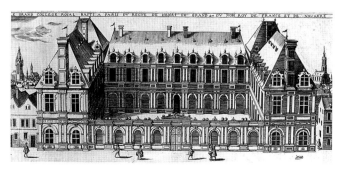

4. Collège Royale, Paris (began 1610 but never finished). Engraving from Claude Châtillon, *Topographie française*, 1641.

1. Francesco di Giorgio Martini: catapult used against a walled town (late 15th century).

2. Siena under siege in 1526.

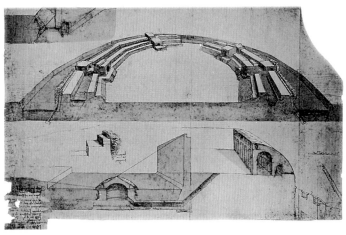

3. Leonardo da Vinci: plan for a fortress (c. 1500–05).

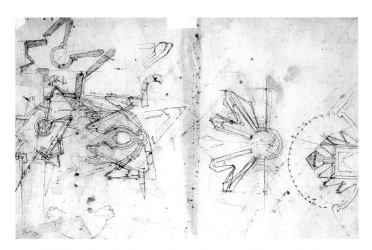

4. Michelangelo: sketches for the fortification of Florence (1528–29).

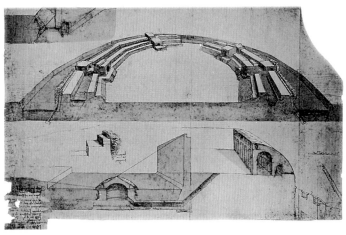

6. Planned city of Palmanova, based on the star-bastion system (1598).

5. Aerial view of Lucca, surrounded by star-bastions built in the 16th century.

Faces of battle, 84–85

The art of war, 222–23

Planned urban space, 270–71

Defensible spaces

THE introduction of artillery in the mid-15th century made every fortification in Europe out of date. The old castellated walls (1, 2) had to be replaced by a new system invented in Italy, the star-bastion. Here the defended area was ringed by pointed bastions made of earth faced with stone (5, 7), the re-entrant angles of which concealed guns able to command the whole space between one bastion and the next, but impregnable from outside. The result, though governed entirely by military science, had a geometrical beauty that appealed strongly to architects (3, 4), producing almost abstract patterns (6).

7. Aerial view of Berwick-on-Tweed (defences built *c.* 1600).

8. Design for an entrance to a French fortress (1600–22).

9. Calais in 1597.

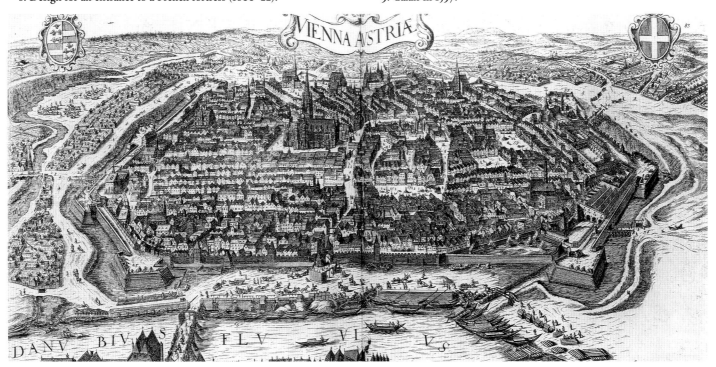

10. Vienna *c.* 1600.

1. Pinturicchio: *Aeneas Sylvius Piccolomini (Pius II) Sets Out for the Council of Basle*, detail (1503–08).

2. Giorgione: *La Tempesta*, detail (*c.* 1500).

3. Joachim Patenier: *The Rest on the Flight to Egypt*, detail (*c.* 1520).

4. Piero della Francesca: *The Nativity*, detail (*c.* 1445).

5. Giovanni Bellini: *Madonna of the Meadow*, detail (*c.* 1500–16).

6. Mantegna: *Death of the Virgin*, detail (*c.* 1492).

In the countryside, 184–85

Botany: medicine and art, 228–29

The mastery of space, 246–47

7. Konrad Witz: *The Miraculous Draught of Fishes*, detail (1444).

The landscape of reality

Pure landscape painting was rare in the Renaissance, and unknown south of the Alps. But artists were clearly fascinated by its potential and used the scenery they knew as backgrounds for sacred subjects. Pinturicchio's rainstorm as Pius II leaves for the Council of Basle (1) is observed from nature, as are the rustic buildings of Giorgione (2), Patenier (3) and Bellini (5). In some cases we can actually identify the place: the strange white hills near Siena in Piero's painting (4), Lake Constance in Konrad Witz's (7), Arco, near Lake Garda, which Dürer painted on his Italian journey (8) and the Danube near Regensburg by Altdorfer (9). Two townscapes are faithful to reality: Mantegna's view of Mantua seen through the Virgin's window (6) and the vignette of a Flemish city in Jan van Eyck's portrait of Chancellor Rolin (10).

8. Dürer: *View of Arco*, detail (1500–10).

9. Altdorfer: *Landscape of the Danube near Regensburg*, detail (1520–25).

10. Jan van Eyck: *Madonna with Chancellor Rolin*, detail (c. 1435).

1. Leonardo da Vinci: *The Virgin of the Rocks* (*c.* 1483).

2. Mantegna: *Agony in the Garden*, detail (*c.* 1459).

3. Niccolò dell' Abbate: *The Rape of Proserpine*, detail (mid-16th century).

4. Altdorfer: *St George and the Dragon* (1510).

Landscapes of fantasy

THE imaginary landscape is, paradoxically, older than the real. In religious and mythological painting, it was customary to construct the settings for the sake of dramatic or atmospheric effect. The fiery sunset behind Altdorfer's battle (5) or the cool serenity of Patenier's River Styx (6) are main elements in the stories, while the dark clouds that gather over Niccolò dell' Abbate's Proserpine (3) express more eloquently than words her sad change from sunlight to shade. Sometimes quasi-scientific interests threaten to take over the picture. Altdorfer's St George (4) almost disappears in the vast forest around him. Leonardo's geological and botanical observations are meticulously recorded (1), and Mantegna's strange, stratified rocks (2) look even more studied.

5. Altdorfer: *Battle of the Issus*, detail (1528–29).

6. Joachim Patenier: *Crossing the Styx* (1520–24).

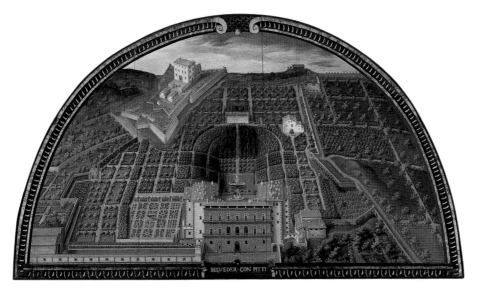

1. The Boboli Gardens, Florence, at the time of the Medici, by Giusto Utens (1599).

3. Woodcut from Colonna's *Hypnerotomachia Poliphili* (1499).

The art of the garden

GARDENING in the Renaissance was not the poor relation of architecture that it is today, but a major art form in its own right. Gardens were 'composed' like poems and were read as poems (6). One of the most influential literary works of the 15th century, the *Hypnerotomachia Poliphili* (3), a strange mixture of history, allegory and romance, took the garden as its central symbol. Real Renaissance gardens (1, 2, 4), frail combinations of artifice and nature, have only rarely survived, but some have been re-created (7, 8) and their complex geometric landscapes can once again be experienced. Mazes, a popular feature of Renaissance gardens, have a long history beginning in ancient Greece. In both literature and gardens they featured as allegories of human life. Daedelus of Crete was counted as the first architect, and the labyrinth thus became the architect's symbol too.

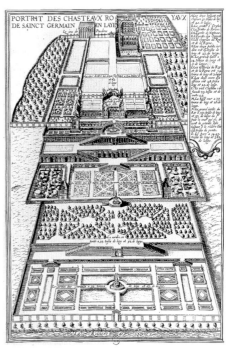

4. The great terrace garden of St Germain-en-Laye, near Paris (1614).

2. The Hortus Palatinus at Heidelberg by J. Fouquières (1620).

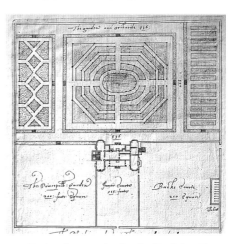

5. Design for a garden by the English 16th-century architect Robert Smythson.

The landscape of reality, 166–67

Landscapes of fantasy, 168–69

In the countryside, 184–85

6. Tintoretto's allegorical garden, *The Labyrinth of Love* (*c.* 1550–60).

7, 8. The gardens of the Villa Lante, Bagnaia, Italy, as they are today.

THE vast majority of the population in the Renaissance period, perhaps 80 or 90 per cent, were peasants and labourers living in extreme poverty, who were quite untouched by cultural change (pp. 184–85). What we know about them comes from estate records or reports of mortality rather than any visual witness. They may appear with sudden reality, like the English harvesters who dropped dead in the fields in the excessively hot summer of 1473. The poorest, most numerous strata of society, living on the margins of existence in hovels or perishable dwellings and dying in unmarked graves whence their bones would pass into charnel houses, were fated to belong to archaeology more than history. Yet their worth was recognized, even in the traditional theory of the deeply divided society to which they belonged. For according to the tripartite conception of mutually interdependent estates, those who laboured for the sustenance of praying clergy and militant secular rulers were equally part of a divinely ordained order. If the body politic was comparable to the human body, toiling feet were as necessary as heart or head.

But of course the situation was far from stable. The labouring classes on whom others depended included increasing numbers of skilled workers, who were among those gaining from educational advances and access to the printed page. If plague and war took the heaviest toll from those least able to bear it, there may also have been enlarging awareness of social discontents. Peasant revolts played their part. The English rising of 1381, with its famous question, 'When Adam delved and Eve span, who was then a gentleman?', and the German Peasants' War (1524–25), which was helped by the ability to air grievances through print, both made deep and long-lasting impressions.

Contemporaries were aware not only of the potential threat of resentful workers, but also of their needs. Across the whole of Europe there were religious confraternities, associations which both enabled individuals to make provision for their own funeral expenses and prayers, and which also functioned as charitable foundations (pp. 126–27). The confraternity of S. Maria della Pietà, founded in Florence in 1410, drew its members from all classes of society except the very lowest, which its activities were aimed to help, by means of distributions of bread and wine, alms and the release of prisoners. The Foundling Hospital for abandoned babies, designed by Brunelleschi for the commune and the silk guild, finally opened in 1445 and became a model for hospitals elsewhere. The *scuole* in Venice, supported by gifts and bequests of the faithful, performed a variety of charitable works. And in London, after the Reformation had swept away parish fraternities and, in the absence of a foundling hospital, the destitute were forced to leave unwanted babies on the doorsteps of the rich, testators were encouraged to remember the needs of the poor. Those disfigured by 'great pocks ... or great sores or maladies tedious, loathsome or horrible to be looked upon' were an obligation that in reformed countries and cities had to be shouldered by secular authority or the almshouses established by individual benefactors.

Artists and craftsmen *born under the planet Mercury are illustrated in a manuscript of* De sphaera *('Of the Sphere'), an astrological text deriving ultimately from Antiquity, painted in Milan about 1450–60. In the centre is a banquet with, beneath it, two cooks at an oven preparing the food. On the left, from top to bottom: a scribe, clock-makers and armourers. On the right: painter, sculptor and organ-maker.*

The Foundling Hospital in Florence, designed by Brunelleschi and opened in 1445, was one of a growing number of charitable institutions in 15th-century Italy.

Detail from Titian's Diana and Actaeon (1556–59): the goddess Diana, like any fashionable Venetian lady, has a black slave to attend her.

In the illuminations of Books of Hours the peasants who plough, sow, reap and harvest are not usually shoeless or emaciated by famine, and their clothes, even if torn, are brightly coloured. Reality was different, and some contemporary observations bring it closer. Montaigne who pondered on the great gulf between his own way of dressing and that of unbuttoned labourers around him, reported an exchange with a beggar, as full of cheer in the depths of winter, despite being clad only in his shirt, as a man of means muffled up to his ears in sable. Euricius Cordus, a contemporary of Luther, wrote a poem on the wretchedness of peasants, scarcely able to recoup a living from the fields which they cultivated for the benefit of others, freezing and sweating like slaves.

There were plenty of actual slaves who might well have been better off than peasants bound to the land. By the end of the 15th century, when Portuguese voyaging down the African coast introduced black slaves, and people of various races (Tartars, Greeks and others) were bought from Turks, Italy's slave markets had made exotic faces familiar in domestic service. 'I shall need a female slave or two, and a little slave-boy, as you prefer', the Prato merchant Francesco di Marco Datini told his wife in 1385. Pius II related how in the festive ceremonies at Pienza in 1462 the winner of the boys' race was a small slave, disqualified for cheating on his age. Though Petrarch used the term 'domestic enemies' for such servants, they may have added a certain cachet to noble courts and gentry households throughout the period. We catch glimpses of them, peering down in a striking turban from the ceiling of Mantegna's Camera degli Sposi at Mantua (pp. 254, 279), or glistening in a striped dress in Titian's *Diana and Actaeon*. In England Queen Elizabeth took steps to deport a number of 'blackamoors' who were competing in the labour market.

Blackness, like nakedness, was subject to ambiguous attitudes. Both were affected by ingrained theological assumptions. The widening acceptance of nudity that extended from studies of classical statuary was a pivotal achievement of Renaissance art. Freedoms existed that may seem surprising, such as the bath-house for both sexes at Basle (where a visiting Castilian amused himself throwing coins for girls to dive for). Erasmus commented on carters and seamen who frequented public baths, and both Leonardo and Dürer visited them in order to observe naked bodies. Observations of the nude also tipped over into blatant eroticism in the prints of Marcantonio Raimondi, which were suppressed by Clement VII. The shame of original sin continued to influence views of nudity, and Columbus' report of the inhabitants he found on his first landfall in the West Indies was tinged with Genesis and its fig leaf.

Events across the world widened consciousness of the diversity of the human race (pp. 210–11). The Turkish threat to Vienna in the siege of 1529 began to make more familiar (through paint and print) the figures of turbaned orientals. Increasingly it became possible to observe the strange features of peoples in far-off lands. In 1590 Theodor de Bry, who had acquired drawings made by John White in Virginia, and some others of Florida, started the publication of a great illustrated work on contemporary travel and discovery in east and west (p. 199).

The discoveries of the New World added new dimensions to the familiar terrors of disease and death. Ordinary ailments of the old world proved catastrophic in lands where the inhabitants lacked biological defences. The Carib population of the West Indies was almost completely wiped out after the arrival of Europeans; the native inhabitants of both Peru and Mexico were decimated by illness. In Europe itself plague, endemic since its arrival in the mid-14th century, continued to carry off men and women of all classes in recurring outbreaks throughout the period, though the poorest were likely to be worst hit, since they lacked the means to take themselves away from crowded, rat- and flea-infested conditions, in which the contagion flourished (pp. 200–01). The new disease of the age (believed to have come from the New World) which spread with alarming rapidity from the armies at the siege of Naples in 1494, was syphilis, named from a Latin poem of that name by Girolamo Fracastoro, a physician of Verona, in which the symptoms are described.

Death was an ever-present reality, women's death in childbirth and infant mortality part of the painful expectations of life. Significantly, we are more likely to know the date of an individual's death than when he or she was born. Birthdays were not matters of importance, and most people were hazy about their exact age. The phases of life were stereotyped, and the Ages of Man (or Woman) became a popular topic for printmakers, depicting the several stages of being (varying from three to seven or fourteen) from infancy, childhood and adolescence, to youth and maturity, into old age and senility (pp. 176–77). Given the shortness of life expectancy, it is not surprising that there were more early than late divisions of the human span. Yet there were stalwart individuals – not all cardinals and aristocrats – who reached the ripeness of an eighth or ninth decade. But the conventionalized patterning of man's ages affected as well as reflected the expectations of the time. To arrive at forty was to reach the threshold of old age, to prompt thoughts of last things. Erasmus, having completed his fiftieth year, recorded his relief at having come to terms with death; 'as so few out of so many reach this age, I cannot rightly complain that I have not lived long enough'.

Few contemporaries could console themselves, like Erasmus, that their posterity was secured in famous works. Most lives, circumscribed by local fields and streets, and the tools of daily work, began and ended in anonymity. Distant travel was the luxury of the great, and even for them it remained dangerous and uncomfortable, despite the invention of the coach (with its body suspended on leather straps), and the improved speed that came with post-changing (pp. 178–79). For the female half of the human race, condemned to subordination by the prevailing belief that they were effectively a subspecies, Creation's botched men, recognition was an unlikely goal. Accidents of birth and opportunities of education brought fame to a few and there were some consolations in widowhood, for women who outlived and perhaps outmanoeuvred men and managed their lands or business (pp. 194–95). But a female Erasmus remained as unthinkable as visiting the moon. Nannina Tornabuoni put it in a nutshell. 'It's no use being born a woman if you wish to do what you want.' But the very expression of such frustration was itself a sign of change.

Bath-houses shared by both sexes were notorious for their relaxed moral standards. This establishment shown in 1597 at Liège combines bathing with drinking (at a partially submerged table), music and social diversions.

Illustrations of the newly discovered lands were usually made by artists who had never been to them. This is Theodor de Bry's idea of the inhabitants of Madagascar (1599).

1. Raphael: *La Gravida* (*c.* 1506).

2. *Children's Games* from *Splendor solis* (16th century).

3. Giorgione: *La Vecchia*, detail (1506–08).

4. Giorgione: *The Three Ages of Man*, detail (early 16th century).

Work and trade, 186–87

Marriage and the family, 190–91

Illness and death, 200–01

5. Master of the Housebook: *Lovers* (late 15th century).

6. Tobias Stimmer: *The Ages of Man: Maturity* (16th century).

7. Tobias Stimmer: *The Ages of Man: Old Age* (16th century).

8. Domenico Ghirlandaio: *Old Man and Boy* (1480s).

The Ages of Man

THE convention of the Three (or frequently Seven) Ages of Man reflects the stereotyped patterning by which contemporaries viewed their own development from infancy to childhood, adolescence, maturity and old age. Manuals on childhood (Ascham's *The Schoolmaster*) and adulthood (Castiglione's *The Courtier*) were widely read. Popular books of woodcuts took men – and women – from lover (**5**), soldier and householder (**6**) to grandparent (**7**). Infancy was carefree (**2**), but education began early and soon the child was a miniature adult. Painters enjoyed placing the generations next to each other, looking forward and backward in time. In Giorgione's painting (**4**), youth and maturity are absorbed in their task while old age looks out sadly at the spectator. Most charming of all is Ghirlandaio's portrait of an old man with a boy (**8**), their happiness unmarred by his disfiguring ailment.

1. Carpaccio: *The Arrival of St Ursula and her Virgins at Cologne*, detail (1490s).

2. A Venetian carrack (late 15th century).

3. Raft on the Vistula, Poland (1597).

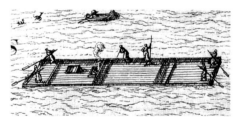

4. Venetian gondola (1609).

5. Travelling carriage near Copenhagen (1597).

Travel and transport

TRAVEL was slow, uncomfortable and frequently dangerous, yet Renaissance men and women did not shirk long journeys. River transport was the least hazardous. Carpaccio represents St Ursula and her companions arriving in Cologne (1) in what look like large sea-going ships. It was here that technical advances had made the greatest change, making possible the great voyages of discovery (2). Large rivers were highways where heavy materials could be moved on barges or rafts (3), while the gondola (4) was cleverly adapted to the narrow canals of Venice. On horseback, a fast courier could cover 50 miles a day, with changes of mount, but travellers in carriages – 'farm waggons with seats', as they have been described (5, 7) – were lucky to do half that, though luxury coaches (9) were becoming status symbols. Of particular interest in the context of humanism is the *ex voto* of Tommaso Inghirammi, a papal librarian, giving thanks for escaping unhurt from a traffic accident near the Arch of Titus in Rome (8).

Exploration and discovery, 210–11

Ships and shipbuilding, 212–13

6. Italian horse-drawn waggon near Rome (1617).

7. Jan Bruegel the Elder: *Landscape with Flooded Road and Windmill*, detail (early 17th century).

9. Model of a coach presented by Queen Elizabeth I to Tsar Boris Godunov of Russia (1600).

8. *Ex voto* of Tommaso Inghirammi, detail (early 16th century).

1. Apollonio di Giovanni: *Acrobat and Wrestlers,* detail (mid-15th century).

2. Jan Mostaert: *The Egg Dance* (early 16th century).

Pleasures and pastimes

THE amusements and off-duty diversions of all classes are more often described in literature than represented in art, but a cross-section is assembled here, from the courtly display of acrobatics and wrestling – to musical accompaniment – in 15th-century Florence (1) to the rustic wedding depicted by Bruegel, where behaviour is far from courtly (3). In Jan Mostaert's painting (2) the aim is to dance round the egg without breaking it. The royal sport of cock-fighting (4) was observed by a Dutch visitor to London in 1614, when James I was among the spectators. The banquet of the Archers' Guild of Amsterdam (5) is interesting not only for the participants (who are enjoying themselves somewhat sadly), but also for the detailed depiction of the food, glasses and plate; their badge (on the sleeve) is a crossbow, two of which are being held up at the back.

3. Pieter Bruegel the Younger: *Village Wedding*, detail (early 17th century).

4. Michael van Meer: *A Cockpit* (1614).

5. C. Anthonisz: *Banquet of the Archers' Guild* (1533).

1. Page from the Bergamo sketchbook, showing a black-winged kite, a goldfinch and a green parrot (*c.* 1400).

2. Detail from Leonardo da Vinci's *Lady with the Ermine* (*c.* 1485).

3. Jan Bruegel the Elder: *Earthly Paradise* (early 17th century).

4. Detail from Bassano's *Earthly Paradise* (late 16th century).

5. Dürer: *Study of a Hare* (1502).

6. Detail of a fresco in the Palazzo del Tè, Mantua (1527).

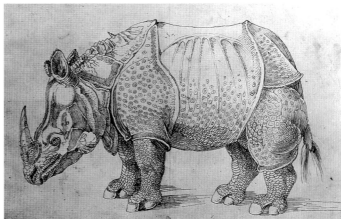

7. Dürer: *Rhinoceros* (1515).

8. Detail from Piero della Francesca's portrait of Sigismondo Malatesta before St Sigismund (1451).

The animal kingdom

IF animals were objects of beauty and part of God's creation, few would have denied that nevertheless they existed only to be exploited by man. Kings collected them, scholars studied them and artists depicted them with interest but without sentimentality. The animal kingdom as a whole was an image of innocence, as in Bassano's peaceable domestic group (4) or Jan Bruegel's panoramic paradise (3) about to be shattered by man's Fall. Many animals carried symbolic or heraldic messages: dogs (8) stood for fidelity, ermine (2) for chastity. In art, exact definition may not be all it seems. Artists kept sketchbooks (1) – not always their own – of a stock repertoire that could easily be incorporated into larger paintings. The splendid Gonzaga horses in the Palazzo del Tè (6) are faithful portraits, and Dürer, endlessly curious about the external world, surely studied his hare (5) first hand; but he is known to have drawn his rhinoceros (7) from a description.

In the countryside

Pictures of peasants at work were not painted for peasants. They were made for rich patrons, either as fresco decoration in country houses (2), oil paintings (3) or manuscript illuminations (4, 7). Like pastoral poetry, they tended to follow artificial conventions, of which the commonest was the schematized sequence of the Labours of the Months, from winter feasting and spring sowing to summer harvest and autumn vintage. Rarely is there any hint of hardship (9), yet this was a period of disturbing social change in many countries from a feudal to a capitalist economy (5), leading to some of the worst peasants' revolts in the history of Europe.

1. Giovanni Pisano: *July – Threshing and Winnowing* (1277). Fonte Maggiore, Perugia, Italy.

2. Bartholomäus Dill Riemenschneider: *Autumn – the Grape Harvest* (1530). Fresco in the Castle of Buonconsiglio, Italy.

4. Simon Bening: *July – Haymaking*, detail (mid-16th century).

3. Francesco Bassano: *Autumn – the Grape Harvest* (late 16th century).

5. Hans Wertinger: *August – Overseer Selling Corn* (1530).

6. Hans Wertinger: *September – Fruit Picking, Ploughing, Harrowing* (1530).

7. Spanish manuscript of Virgil's *Georgics – Ploughing* (15th century).

8. Conrad Meyer: *Autumn* ('Fifty Years Old') from the *Ages of Man* (16th century).

9. Pieter Bruegel the Elder: detail from *The Census at Bethlehem* (1566).

1. An Italian tailor's shop (*c.* 1500).

Work and trade

INCREASED population, the growth of towns, technical advances, improved transport, a fluid money supply – all these helped to make the Renaissance an age of manufacture and trade, and in that sense the cradle of the modern world. Local markets (8) were the venues for buying and selling not only food and drink, but also goods from further afield. A view of the market at Antwerp (6) in the 16th century shows a wide variety of activities, including a meeting of wealthy merchants engaged in some business transaction. Manufacturing industries – clothes-making (1), or metalwork (4, 5), or sculpture (3) – might use imported materials and export the finished product. One factor that complicated economic life was the diversity of weights, measures and currencies all over Europe. Crossing the frontier between even one Italian city and another meant long sessions with the money-changer (7). Only rarely was the coinage of a single state (e.g., the Florentine florin) strong enough to be current in others.

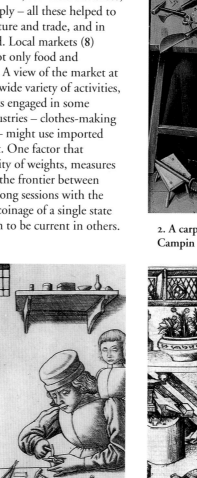

2. A carpenter's shop (St Joseph) by Robert Campin (*c.* 1425–30).

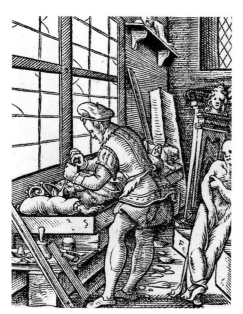

3. A sculptor's workshop by Jost Amman (1568).

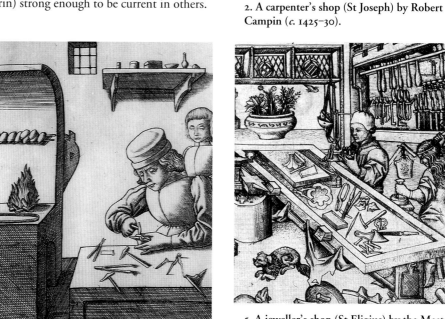

4. A metalworker (15th century).

5. A jeweller's shop (St Eligius) by the Master of Bileam (15th century).

Cities of central Europe, 160–61

Travel and transport, 178–79

A new world of finance, 232–33

6. The market at Antwerp (late 16th century).

7. The money-changer from *De sphaera* (15th century).

8. Mercato Vecchio in Florence by Vasari (mid-16th century).

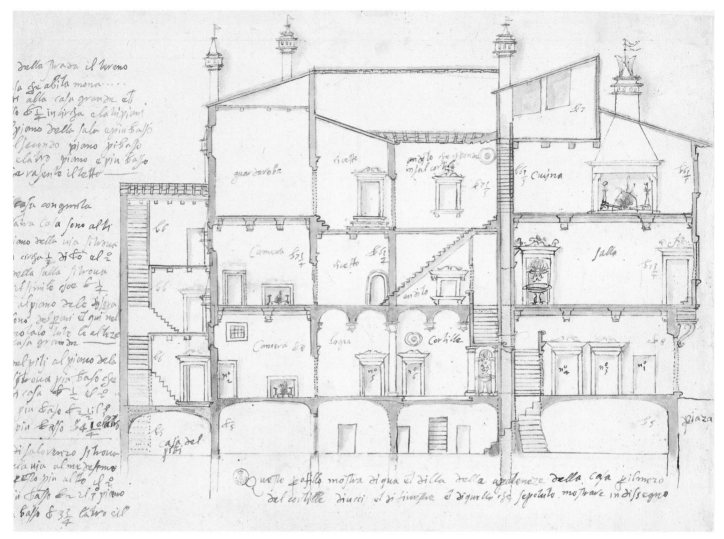

1. Aristotile da Sangallo: section through
a house for the Gaddi family, Florence.
The lowest storey is a basement. The
house is entered from the right under an
overhanging bay on a bracket. A vestibule
leads through into an open courtyard
(*cortile* – note the projecting tiled roof at
second-floor level), with a doorway, stairs
and a fountain, beyond which is an open
loggia behind columns. Upstairs, the main
room (*sala*) is in the front, with the kitchen
(*cucina*) above it. The bedrooms (*camere*)
are at the back. Several details, such as
door-surrounds and fire places, are also
carefully included (16th century).

2. Detail from Giorgio Vasari's *Giostra
del Saracino in Via Largo*, showing
traditional houses in Florence (mid-
16th century).

Cities of central
Europe, 160–61

Marriage and the
family, 190–91

Planned urban space,
270–71

3. Zamosc, Poland: houses in the central square (late 16th century).

4. Segovia, Spain: Casa de los Picos (16th century).

6. Erfurt, Germany: 'Zum Breiten Herd' (1584).

7. Schaffhausen, Germany: 'Goldener Ochs' (1608).

The domestic setting

THE Renaissance brought no fundamental changes to the way ordinary houses were built and used by the family (2), but it did affect their outward appearance. In every country traditional structures were re-styled to give them an up-to-date look. The arcaded street in Poland (3) has a classical frieze; the forbidding Spanish house (4) is given fashionable diamond rustication; even the French spiral staircase (5) is furnished with classical windows. In Germany the stepped gable (6) and the *erke*, or projecting oriel (7), neither of which had the remotest precedent in ancient Rome, receive the same treatment. Significantly, too, houses now came to be designed by professional architects, not by builders, which meant that for the first time plans, elevations and sections had to be drawn in advance. Aristotile da Sangallo's design for the Casa Gaddi (1) is a rare survival, showing that the architect was concerning himself not merely with structure, but also with the way the building would work in practical terms as a family home.

5. Lyon, France: Hôtel Bulliond by Philibert de l'Orme (1536).

1. School of Giulio Romano: *The Holy Family with St Anne* (mid-16th century).

3. Jan Van Eyck: betrothal portrait of Giovanni Arnolfini and his wife (1434).

4. Lorenzo Lotto: *Messer Marsilio and his Wife* (1523).

2. Bernhard Striegel: *The Family of Maximilian I* (1515).

5. Hans Holbein: *The Painter's Wife and Children* (1528).

Virgin and Child,
132–33

Renaissance women,
194–95

Sex and gender,
196–97

6. Titian: *The Vendramin Family before a Relic of the True Cross* (1520–22).

Marriage and the family

FAMILY life during the Renaissance has been the subject of much research but little agreement. Undoubtedly, wealth, power and privilege depended almost entirely on family relationships (2, 6) – hence the aristocratic obsession with genealogy and heraldry. But what of the ordinary middle-class citizen? Some historians have found in this period an increased emphasis on privacy and a shift from the 'extended' family to the 'nuclear' family – parents and children living together in a closed unit (5, 7). Marriage, already a Christian sacrament, with the Holy Family (1) as its perfect exemplum, becomes a personal commitment (3), with sexual love as an essential component (4) and infidelity not just a sin but a betrayal. At the same time, literature reflects a new willingness to open up the whole subject to radical debate: More's *Utopia*, Bacon's *New Atlantis*, Doni's *The Worlds* and Campanella's *City of the Sun*.

7. Baldassare Estense: *Family of Umberto de' Sacrati* (15th century).

Living and Dying **191**

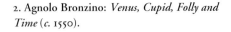

1. Plate from the alchemical treatise *Splendor solis* showing the union of two chemical elements (16th century).

2. Agnolo Bronzino: *Venus, Cupid, Folly and Time* (c. 1550).

3. After Michelangelo: *Leda and the Swan* (mid-16th century).

A new eroticism

THE writers and artists of the Middle Ages had not shut their eyes to sex. They either laughed at it or condemned it, and ecclesiastical teaching imposed certain restrictions. Renaissance sexuality was different. The naked human body could now be admired without inhibition. Humanist reading of the classics, particularly Ovid and Catullus, opened up fresh perspectives on human relationships. Religious taboos were losing some of their force and naturalism in art encouraged explicit representation. Pagan mythology could be explored with new emotional freedom (2, 3, 6). The erotic even crept into alchemy (1). More straightforwardly, contemporary sexuality began to be portrayed with tolerance and even with a certain relish (4). In literature, this tendency went much further, and illustrations to Boccaccio's *Decameron*, for instance, were generally more decent than the text (5).

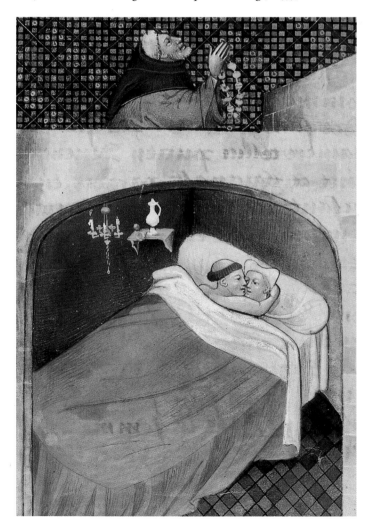

4. Altdorfer: fresco fragment of *Couple Embracing* (*c.* 1535).

6. Correggio: *Jupiter and Io* (1530).

5. Illustration to one of Boccaccio's tales in the *Decameron*. A monk, having designs on a married woman, gives the husband a prolonged penance (top) while he goes to bed with the wife (1430–40).

1. Lambert Sustris: *Scene of a Birth* (16th century).

Renaissance women

WOMEN did not lack recognition in Renaissance Europe, but it was recognition by men. Talented, intellectual, courageous and fascinating as they obviously were, we see them almost always through men's eyes, judged by men's standards. The accident of genealogy sometimes put a woman at the head of a duchy or a nation, and in these cases few doubted that they were fully men's equals. Marguerite d'Angoulême, Queen of Navarre (8), the sister of François I, wrote the *Heptameron*, a collection of stories modelled on Boccaccio. In Italy (and to a lesser extent in northern Europe) women began to achieve success in the arts and professions, though they needed to be not only very gifted, but also very lucky. Laura Battiferri (3) was a noted poet; Tintoretto's daughter Marietta (6) painted herself as a musician; while Sofonisba Anguissola (2) represented herself – an interesting statement on gender roles – *being painted by a man*. Otherwise, unless they entered the religious life, women were either condemned to menial work (4, 7) or spent their lives as the wives (5), mothers (1) or mistresses (9) – of men.

2. Sofonisba Anguissola: *Bernardino Campi Painting Sofonisba Anguissola* (late 1550s).

3. Bronzino: Laura Battiferri (c. 1555–60).

5. Leonardo da Vinci: *Mona Lisa* (c. 1502).

8. Marguerite of Navarre (c. 1540).

4. *Washerwomen* from a German manuscript, *Splendor solis* (16th century).

6. Marietta Robusti: self-portrait (1580–90).

9. Carpaccio: *Courtesans on a Balcony* (1510–15).

7. Peasant women returning from hay-making. A detail from a painting by Pieter Bruegel the Elder (mid-16th century).

1. Titian: *Tarquin and Lucretia* (c. 1571).

2. Lucas Cranach the Younger: *Judith with the Head of Holofernes* (1530).

3. Properzia de' Rossi: *Joseph and Potiphar's Wife* (c. 1520).

Sex and gender

THE Renaissance has recently been subjected to a new kind of criticism, loosely called 'the new art history', which tries to look beneath the overt intentions of the artist into the unconscious motives, values and prejudices that are part of his age. One of its successes has been the exploration of sexuality. Explicit representations of sexual subjects during this period are rare, but we can learn much from the choice of subject-matter and the tacit assumptions that are revealed. Renaissance art was, with very few exceptions, male art. What can it tell us about male attitudes? Is there significance in the fact that favourite classical and biblical subjects so often included scenes of rape (1) and voyeurism (6)? How much did women feel threatened by the display of such paintings? Conversely, can we detect in other works an unspoken fear of female sexuality – the strangely

popular Salome with John the Baptist's head (4) and Judith and Holofernes (2), where the woman has beheaded – symbolically castrated – her lover? And what of homosexuality? It is known that many of the greatest Renaissance artists, including Leonardo and Michelangelo, were homosexual, but that could not be expressed openly. Sodomy was a crime, punishable in some countries by death. But stories like that of Ganymede, the beautiful boy taken up to Olympus by Jupiter in the form of an eagle (5), gave scope for expressing fairly plain homoerotic feelings. Finally, a curiosity. One of the few familiar stories in which the woman took an actively sexual role, though conventionally condemned for it – the attempted seduction of Joseph by Potiphar's wife – was actually sculpted by a female artist (3).

A new eroticism, 192–93

The human form, 248–49

4. Bernardino Luini: *Salome* (early 16th century).

5. *Ganymede*, copy after an original by Michelangelo (1532).

6. Tintoretto: *Susanna and the Elders* (1560s).

Race and colour

JEWS in the Renaissance were alternately tolerated and persecuted, as they had been for a thousand years. In Spain, the Moors, infidels and age-old enemies, were banished in 1502. The Turks, who had conquered Constantinople in 1453, were hated and feared. In all these cases the hostility was motivated by religion and politics and was not primarily racial in origin. Black Africans were few in number and were seen as exotic strangers (2, 5, 6). One of the three Magi was conventionally shown as black (7). On the stage, Shakespeare's Othello is an admired professional soldier, flawed by emotional naiveté and violence, though his Aaron in *Titus Andronicus* (3) is presented as an unmitigated villain. Only the newly colonized lands of America provided fuel for a serious debate on the moral question of attitudes to other races. Throughout the 16th century the Spaniards mercilessly enslaved and exploited the native peoples of Mexico and Peru, provoking heated controversy at home between those for whom they were by nature inferior (4) and those who saw them as human beings with souls to be saved (1).

1. A Dominican friar with two Aztec converts in Mexico (mid-16th century).

3. Contemporary drawing of Shakespeare's *Titus Andronicus* (1595).

2. Detail showing a black gondolier from Carpaccio's *Miracle of the Reliquary of the Cross* (completed by 1494).

Constantinople and Greek learning, 58–59   Exploration and discovery, 210–11

4. The Aztecs as seen by the west, by Giulio Clovio (*c.* 1550).

5. Detail from an altarpiece by Fra Angelico showing Saints Cosmas and Damian curing a man who had lost a leg by replacing it with one from a black man (1450–55).

7. Balthazar from Dürer's *Adoration of the Magi* (1504).

6. Detail showing a young black servant from Veronese's *Feast in the House of Levi* (1571–73).

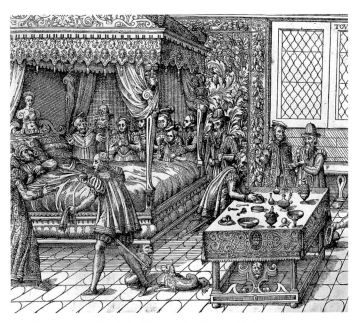

1. The death of Henri II of France, fatally wounded in a jousting accident (1559).

3. *The Triumph of Death*, engraving illustrating Petrarch's *Trionfi* (c. 1470).

2. Burial of Sir Henry Unton from his memorial painting (1596).

4. *Ex voto* showing a sick man being carried to hospital by members of a charitable confraternity (16th century).

The Last Judgment, 146–47

Medicine: theory and practice, 224–25

Anatomy: the body's structure, 226–27

Illness and death

CARE of the sick was a religious duty (4, 5), as it had been in the Middle Ages, but even in the hospitals (6) there was little that medicine could do. Disease was still seen as God's punishment, the best remedy being prayer and repentance. Such fatalistic attitudes had produced a whole startling iconography featuring Death's Triumph (3) or the morbidly popular theme of Death carrying off young girls (7). The rituals of the death-bed (1) and the funeral (2) gave consolation, at least to the living, but for those left crippled by disease (8) there was only charity or the miracles that were still sought at the shrines of saints. To the familiar terror of plague there was added the new sexual infection of syphilis (uniquely named after a poem), probably imported from America, while European illnesses caused high mortality in newly discovered lands (see pp. 224–25).

5. Domenico Ghirlandaio: *Visiting the Sick*, one of the Seven Works of Mercy (late 15th century).

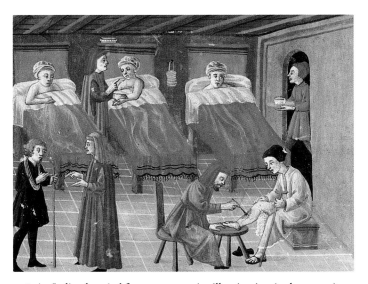

6. An Italian hospital from a manuscript illumination (15th century).

7. Hans Baldung Grien: *The Knight, the Maiden and Death* (1545).

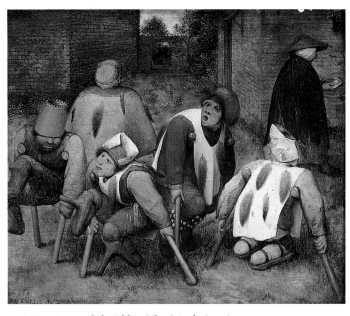

8. Pieter Bruegel the Elder: *The Cripples* (1569).

Holbein's painting The Ambassadors *is almost a visual compendium of Renaissance ideas. The two men are Jean de Dinteville, French ambassador to England, and Georges de Selve, Bishop of Lavaur and French ambassador to the Imperial Court, Venice and the Holy See. The time is April 1533. International diplomacy is therefore one theme. Others are music, science and mortality. Music: a lute, a case of flutes, a Lutheran hymn-book. Science: terrestrial and celestial globes, a book of arithmetic, dividers, a sundial, a quadrant, and a polyhedron. Mortality: a giant skull seen in extreme foreshortening cutting across the foreground, so that it has to be looked at obliquely from the far right. The mosaic pavement is copied from one in Westminster Abbey. On the shelf at the back is a Persian rug. Many of these objects must have a symbolic meaning that can now only be guessed at.*

6

SCIENCE, INVENTION AND DISCOVERY

Science as we know it, and technology (as opposed to method), did not exist in the Renaissance, but humanist textual interests fed habits of thought that we may now see as scientific. The legacy of recovered texts and the newly established understanding of Greek provided the essential base for more investigative, questioning, observational attitudes of mind.

The invention of printing was critical for this process. 'The printing press sowing knowledge', along with the invention of the compass and the making of gunpowder, were commonly acclaimed as the three revolutionary discoveries by which the age was altered. The compass (known since the 13th century) helped the discovery of new lands; gunpowder transformed warfare; printing made known rescued texts and much more besides. Without the invention of movable type the Renaissance might have been just another renaissance.

Printing in its various forms permeated and perpetuated the Renaissance (pp. 206–07). Texts recovered from classical Antiquity and freshly edited or translated, could cross frontiers of space and time as never before. Nor was it only words that could be sped from the printer's workshop to affect the eyes and ears of readers and hearers from one end of Europe to the other. Every kind of learning and accomplishment was affected by the ability to multiply fixity on the page. The work of painters and musicians could reach new viewers and audiences through engraved reproductions and printed music. Knowledge of the globe itself, from local regions to distantly discovered lands, became accessible to more people.

Ptolemy's *Geography*, a 2nd-century repertory of Greek geographical learning, had been lost to the west until it reached Italy about 1397. Niccolò Niccoli owned a copy in Greek and by 1406 the text had been translated into Latin. A number of Latin editions were in print by 1500 and many more editions appeared thereafter, including Erasmus' Greek edition of 1533 and others in the vernacular. Celsus, unknown for 500 years, was discovered in 1426 and in 1478 became the first work of classical medicine to be printed. Together with improved knowledge of Galen (printed by the Aldine Press in the 1520s, and translated into Latin by Thomas Linacre), the way was open to new beginnings in empirical medicine, anatomical research and dissection (pp. 224–27).

New work grew out of improved understanding of ancient authorities and was grafted onto them at the same time as overreaching them. Ptolemy's *Geography* had originally included maps, as well as rules for how to make them. Renaissance geographers, who inherited Ptolemy without his maps and with a keen interest in his methods for making them, made good their lack by not only redrawing Ptolemy's world but also adding maps of their own – with places and continents unknown to Ptolemy – in editions of his work from 1513 on. In the same way Pliny's *Natural History*, the authority on zoology, botany (pp. 228–29) and minerals, received in its various editions growing accretions of new knowledge. In the end – witness the works of Vesalius, Conrad Gesner, Sebastian Münster and Ortelius – new discoveries eroded old learning and began to elbow out classical authorities.

The Ptolemaic universe (1559): the earth at the centre, then the seven planetary spheres, and at the edge the crystalline firmament and the primum mobile, the fixed stars, ordered into their Zodiac signs. Atlas supports the whole.

Printing was probably the most important single invention of the whole Renaissance. In this 16th-century miniature the master-printer stands on the left, an assistant works the press, and on the right three scholars are proof-reading – an occupation that called for educated men.

Vesalius, who deplored the feebleness with which men 'have laboured in the field of anatomy from the time of Galen to the present day', was able to see his book *On the Structure of the Human Body* (p. 227) as a first real step on from Galen. Gesner, whose wide-ranging knowledge enabled him to be regarded as Germany's own Pliny, published his *History of Animals* (1551–58) at a time when herbals and botanical works in both Latin and the vernacular were enjoying quite a vogue, with Pliny's reputation already dented by fresh observations as well as corrections. Münster and Ortelius did for cosmography what Agricola did for metallurgy, showing 16th-century students how far studies had travelled since Ptolemy and Pliny.

In all this work the illustrative opportunities opened by print were critical. Accurate and repeatable drawings of the human body, of plants and animals, mining processes and pumps (p. 236), maps and surveying techniques, could reach and teach readers with profound effect. In herbals the role of illustrations was an essential means of identification, given the lack of a precise vocabulary for scientific description. Significantly Otto Brunfels called his 1530 book *Living Portraits of Plants*. The corpus of botanical knowledge, increased by work like that of Leonard Fuchs (whose 1542 *History of Plants* was arranged alphabetically) grew far beyond Dioscorides, the Greek authority on plants and their medical uses. By 1623 his list of about 600 known plants had increased tenfold.

Mathematics was the key to many advances, both practical and theoretical (pp. 218–19). It was as necessary for working out the foreshortening and vanishing points in perspective, as it was for mapping, surveying, or the calculations of astronomy (pp. 214–15). The double entry book-keeping expounded by Luca Pacioli in 1494, and the extending use of arabic numerals both helped the world of business and finance. When Galileo, after more than twenty years teaching mathematics at the universities of Pisa and Padua, sought a position at the court of the Duke of Tuscany in Florence, he was concerned with the application of this branch of learning to the physical laws, or (as he later put it) philosophy, 'written in that grand book of nature that stands forever open to our eyes'.

Numbers could be interesting in themselves. In 1555 Sir William Cecil did something utterly unusual: he had himself, his wife, his son and household servants weighed, and listed the results. It was an action highly suggestive of the enquiring habits and increasingly numerical thinking of the time. The idea might have been seeded by Sir Nicholas Bacon, in whose house Cecil had been weighed two years before. Bacon was himself a learned man, who decorated his house with his own Latin verse in praise of arithmetic, geometry, music, and other subjects of study. His youngest son, Francis, whose *Novum organum* did so much to promote the advance of empirical knowledge, died of bronchitis in 1626 as a result of collecting snow to investigate its capacity to preserve a bird.

Yet despite the seeming modernity of such actions, the arcane and mysterious and unreachable still dominated much thinking. Mathematics could seem the best method of explaining (as Nicholas of Cusa did) how the infinity of the universe is an expression of the unity and ubiquity of God. At the heart of knowledge lay mystery, and at the centre of mystical experience is the unknowable being of God. To reach up into theories of the universe, or down into matter through laboratory experiments in chemistry, or the study of metals, precious stones and plants; to attempt to synthesize the wisdom of east and west, Hebrew, Greek and Latin, was to probe beyond common reach. Mythological learning was secretive, a means of veiling expression through allegory, which might retain elements of mystery even for initiates. Pico della Mirandola, who envisaged God telling Adam 'we have set you at the world's centre that you may more easily observe from there whatever is in the world', published his 900 theses in the 'holy ambition' of increasing spiritual understanding by plumbing this well of occult divinity.

Belief in astrology, which Pico attacked, flourished (pp. 216–17). The influence of the stars on world events and individual lives was an accepted part of the mental landscape, the meat of many prognostications and popular almanacs. Extraordinary effects were predicted from the appearance of a new star in 1572 and a comet in 1577, while the conjunction of the planets Jupiter and Saturn in 1583 was widely feared to presage a major occurrence in world history. Influential people took care to consult an astrologer before taking important actions, and horoscopes were cast for weddings and at births. Tycho Brahe cast horoscopes for Frederick II of Denmark and his children; Kepler was involved in this activity throughout his career; and John Dee was in deep trouble and suspected of treason in 1555 for having cast several royal horoscopes.

The stars might (according to orthodox teaching) incline although not compel, but many assumed it risky to leave them out of account. The planets controlled different parts of the body and physicians needed to bear them in mind in prescribing medical treatment. The timing of blood-letting depended on astrology as well as the four humours. Not for nothing did doctors become known as leeches, given the lasting acceptance of this practice.

In spite of the continuation of old assumptions and archaic methods, the Renaissance was inventive. Hydraulic devices made possible deeper mining and better town water supplies, as well as the fun and games of fountains and surprise water splashes (pp. 234–35). New kinds of ships and rigging facilitated voyaging in the open seas and improved the manoeuvrability of vessels (pp. 212–13). Daily time, like historical time, was more accurately measured (pp. 230–31). More people came to be within range of clocks, or even watches, and grew accustomed to having their days regulated by other means than sun and season. Both clocks and (still more) watches long continued to be luxuries, prestige objects that might be ornaments or jewels for display more than practical timekeepers – though that did not prevent them serving both purposes. François I owned two tiny watches that fitted into the hilt of a dagger, and Rudolf II's elaborate copper-gilt ship-clock could entertain his guests at banquets, sailing along the table while various small figures processed and bowed, and men in the crows' nests struck the hours and quarters.

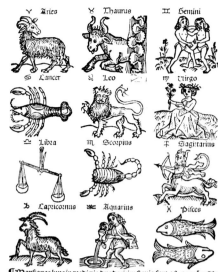

The signs of the Zodiac, a woodcut of 1489. Belief that the stars governed (or at least 'inclined') human life was a legacy from the ancient world and was not discarded until the late 17th century, if then.

A luxury clock in the form of a ship, attributed to Hans Schlottheim of Augsburg and made for the Emperor Rudolf II about 1580.

1. Page from Gutenberg's 42-line Bible, printed between 1452 and 1455. The letters closely imitate script and the decoration is added by hand.

2. Emblem of Aldus Manutius, c. 1500, anchor and dolphin symbolizing his motto *festina lente*, 'make haste slowly'.

3. Caxton's colophon, London, c. 1487.

4. Emblem of Simon Vostre, Paris, early 16th century.

The printing revolution

THE invention of printing changed the whole intellectual world for ever. Without it classical learning would have been confined to a small coterie of scholars; the Reformation would have been a quarrel between theologians; popular literature would have been impossible; scientific discoveries would have languished unread. Inevitably, the first printed books were imitation manuscripts (1). But within 20 years printing had evolved its own conventions and had conquered Europe. Gutenberg's first Bible appeared in Mainz in 1455 (1). The technique was rapidly taken up in the Netherlands (8), France (4) and England (3). Two Germans installed a press near Rome in 1465, and by the end of the century Italy was the most important source of printed books (2).

5. Casting type in hot metal, 1568.

6. Typesetting and inking, 1568.

7. Cutting a woodblock, 1568.

8. Printing press in the Netherlands, 1628: inking, printing, typesetting.

9. Bookbinding, 1568.

10. Paper making, 1568.

1. Cicero's *De oratore*, the first book printed in Italy, printed by Sweynheym and Pannartz at Subiaco, 1465. Painted initial added.

2. Page from Caxton's first printed edition of Chaucer's *Canterbury Tales*, London, c. 1478.

3. Page from Gratian's *Decretium* (written 12th century), printed in Venice by Nicolaus Jensen in 1477: text in the centre, commentary round the edge. Painted decoration by Girolamo da Cremona; the miniature shows Gratian presenting his book to the pope.

The printed page

ONCE printing had been established, what books were published? Those that attract most attention today are the Greek and Latin classics (1). But religious books (7) outnumbered them, while many more were devoted to practical information, education and entertainment (5, 6), and yet others described events of the day (8). Letter forms in the north followed 'Gothic' or 'black-letter' script (2); in the south, the humanists had perfected 'Roman' script (1, 5) based on Carolingian writing, normally the oldest version of classical texts they could find, and this became the basis for modern typography. Very soon, Greek (4), Hebrew and other scripts were being printed. Illustrations were usually woodcuts but there was a brief phase when, in luxury books, the whole page might be represented as if it were a manuscript, the decoration painted and the printed part disguised as torn or fragmentary sheets illusionistically superimposed (3).

4. Page from Constantine Lascaris' *Epitome*, printed in Venice by Aldus Manutius, 1494.

cum religiofo tripudio plaudendo & iubilando, Quale erano le Nymphe Amadryade, & agli redolenti fiori le Hymenide, riuirente, faliendo iocunde dinanti & da qualúq; lato del floreo Vertunno ftricto nella fronte de purpurante & meline rofe, cum el gremio pieno de odoriferi & fpectatiffimi fiori, amanti la ftagione del lanofo Ariete, Sedendo ouante fopra una ueterrima Veha, da quatro cornigeri Fauni tirata, Inuinculati de ftrophie de nouelle fronde, Cum la fua amata & belliffima moglie Pomona coronata de fructi cum ornato defluo degli biōdiffimi capigli, parea ello fedéte, & a gli pedi dellaquale una coctilia Clepfydria iaceua, nel le mane tenente una ftipata copia de fiori & maturati fructi cum imixta fogliatura. Præcedéte la Veha agli trahenti Fauni propinqi due formofe Nymphe affignane, Vna cū uno haftile Trophæo gerula, de Ligoni. Bidenti. farculi. & falcionetti, cū una fpendéte tabella abaca cū tale titulo.

INTEGERRIMAM CORPOR. VALITVDINEM, ET STABILE ROBVR, CASTASQVE MEMSAR. DELITIAS, ET BEATAM ANIMI SECVRITATEM CVLTORIB. M. OFFERO.

m iiii

Au dedans de ces prez fe trouuoit vne multitude infinie de peuple champeftre, tel que ie n'auoie iamais accouftumé de veoir. Il me fembla veftu rufiquement, de peaux de Dains, Cheureulz, Onces, & Leopardz. Certains autres eftoient accouftrez de feuilles de Bardane, Philopate, Mixe, ou Sebeften, enfemble de la grand Farfuge. Leurs brodequins eftoient de Parelle, & d'Ozeille, bordez de fleurs, pourautant qu'ilz folennifoient vne fefte auec les Nymphes Hamadryades, a l'entour de Vertumnus, qui eftoit vn chapeau de Rofes, & fon giron plein de fleurettes. Aupres de luy eftoit fa Pomona, coronnée de fruictage, les cheueux pendans fur fes efpaules : tous deux affiz en vn chariot de triumphe, tiré à tractz de rameaux & feuillages, par quatre grans Faunes cornuz. A leurs piedz y auoit vne Châtepleure : & Pomona tenoit en fa main vne corne d'abondance, pleine de feuilles & de fruictz. Au deuant du chariot alloient deux belles Nymphes port'enfeignes, l'vne aiant en fa deuife des fers de charue, marres, hoyaulx, faulx, faucilles, fleaux, pelles, & autres inftrumés de labeur, tous pendás au bout d'vne lace. En l'autre y auoit ne fçay quelz greffes ou reiettons, auec vne petite ferpe, & vn tableau ou eftoit efcript ce qui s'enfuyt:

INTEGERRIMAM CORPORVM VALETVDINEM, ET STABILE ROBVR, CASTASQVE MENSARVM DELICIAS, ET BEATAM ANIMI SECVRITATEM CVLTORIBVS MEIS OFFERO.

M

5, 6. The same passage from Colonna's *Hypnerotomachia Poliphili* in the first edition, printed by Aldus Manutius in Venice in 1499; and in the French edition, printed in Paris in 1546, with new woodcut and typeface.

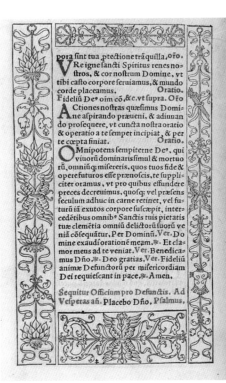

7. Double-page from a *Book of Hours* printed in Paris in 1525 with woodcut borders and illustration.

9. Initial letters designed by the French typographer Geoffroy Tory, 1521.

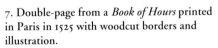

8. German announcement of two newssheets describing an earthquake in Italy, and a town in Turkey that sank beneath the sea, 1542.

Science, Invention and Discovery   209

1. Taking a reading on a star from a manual of navigation (1563).

2. 'How sailors observe the elevation of the north star' from Theret's *Cosmographie* (1575).

3, 4. The astrolabe measured the altitude of the sun and the stars and hence allowed mariners to calculate time and latitude. The dial indicated the changes in the sun's position throughout the year (1565).

5. Marine compass (*c.* 1580).

Mapping the world, 152–53

Ships and shipbuilding, 212–13

Astronomy, 214–15

6. Vasco da Gama, Portuguese navigator, c. 1460–1524.

7. Ferdinand Magellan, c. 1480–1521, died attempting to sail round the world.

8. Francis Drake, English circumnavigator, c. 1545–96.

Exploration and discovery

DURING the last decade of the 15th century the horizons of knowledge rolled back dramatically. Columbus (9) reached the Caribbean Islands in 1492; Cabot landed in North America in 1497; Vasco da Gama (6) found the sea-route to India in 1498. By the 1520s men had been round the world: Ferdinand Magellan (7) died in the attempt, but one of his ships reached home. Drake (8), intent on conquest and plunder rather than discovery, repeated the exploit between 1577 and 1580. Such voyages were only possible with accurate navigation, a technique that was turning into a science (1–5). There was intense curiosity about the newly discovered lands (11), though it was at first difficult to see them in any but European terms (10). This thirst for new knowledge paralleled the thirst for old knowledge which was humanism. The French historian Michelet summed it up when he characterized the Renaissance as 'the discovery of the world and of man'.

9. Christopher Columbus, c. 1446–1506, by Ridolfo Ghirlandaio.

10. How a Netherlandish artist saw the conquest of America: Jan Mostaert's *West Indian Landscape* (1545).

11. Eskimos, as seen by Martin Frobisher in 1577.

Ships and shipbuilding

WITH the development of navigational instruments went improvements in the design of ships. The Mediterranean ports (1), especially Venice (5), lost their predominance to the new maritime nations, England (2, 3), the Netherlands (7), Spain and Portugal. The improved sea-worthiness of the Portuguese caravel in the 15th century resulted from the adoption of the Arab lateen sail, which was successfully combined with European square rig. Late in the 15th century, sails increased from three to five, the main topsail and the spritsail, under the bowsprit (4), joining the traditional mainsail, foresail and mizzensail. The 'carrack' had a triangular overhanging forecastle, the slightly later galleon (3) increased the height and length of the hull to incorporate two or three gun decks. Henry VIII's *Henry Grace à Dieu* (6) combined both features.

1. Ships off the port of Naples, 1481.

2. Woodcut from John Dee's *Perfect Art of Navigation*, 1577, showing Queen Elizabeth ruling the waves.

4. Drawing by Holbein illustrating the ship (including main, topsail and spritsail, furled) and the varied activities of those on board, 1530s.

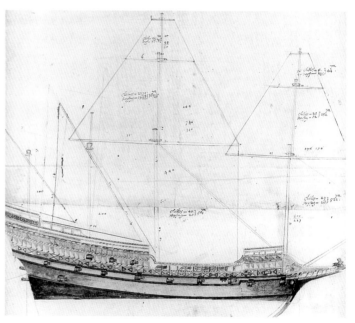

3. English galleon, *c.* 1585.

Race and colour, 198–99

Exploration and discovery, 210–11

Astronomy, 214–15

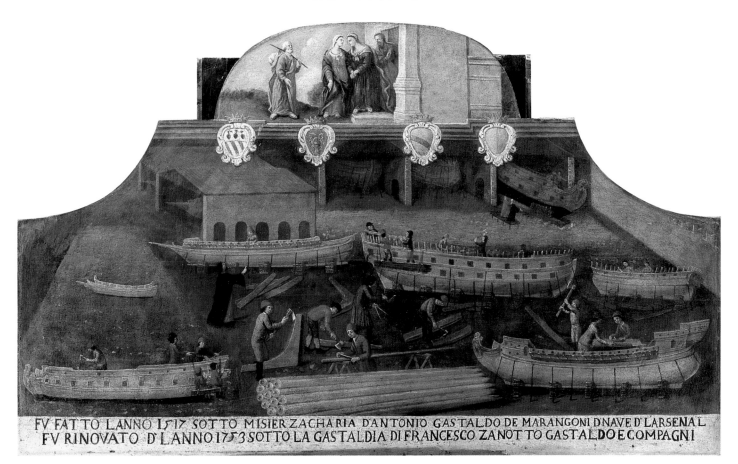

FV FATTO LANNO 1517 SOTTO MISIER ZACHARIA DANTONIO GASTALDO DE MARANGONI DNAVE D LARSENAL
FV RINOVATO D LANNO 1753 SOTTO LA GASTALDIA DI FRANCESCO ZANOTTO GASTALDOE COMPAGNI

5. Shipbuilding in the Arsenal of Venice, 1517 (partly repainted in the 18th century).

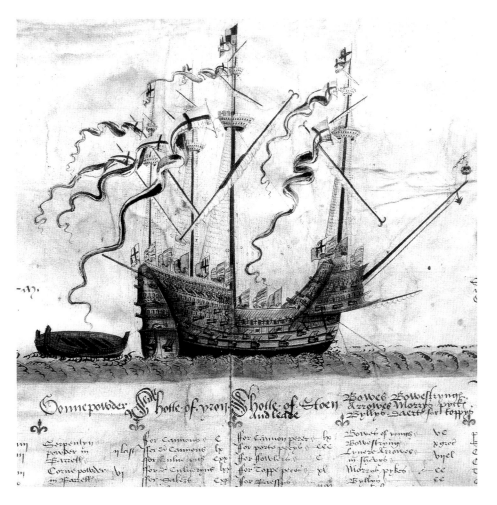

7. Ship under construction in Amsterdam, 17th century.

6. Henry VIII's warship *Henry Grace à Dieu*, 1546.

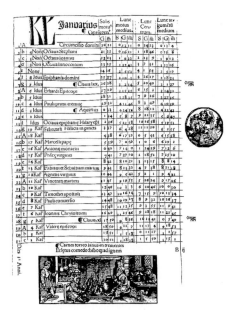

1. Page from the calendar of Johannes Stöffler, 1518, showing the positions of the sun and moon in the zodiac.

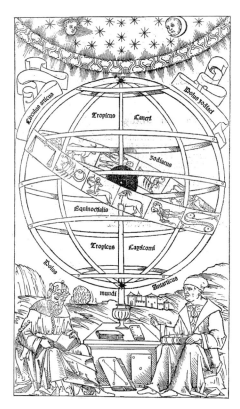

2. The Ptolemaic globe from Johannes de Montregis' *Epitoma*, Venice, 1496.

4. Celestial globe by Georg Roll and Johannes Reinhold, Augsburg, 1584.

3. Hans Holbein: *Nicolas Kratzer, Astronomer to Henry VIII*, 1528.

5. Tobias Stimmer: *Copernicus* from the astronomical clock in Strasbourg Cathedral (16th century).

Astronomy

THROUGHOUT the 16th century the classical, or Ptolemaic, model of the universe (2), with the earth in the centre, was the one most commonly accepted. It did not prevent a vast amount of authentic data from being collected (1), nor celestial globes of great beauty being created (4). In 1543 Copernicus (5) published his heliocentric theory as a mathematical hypothesis, not a physical fact. Using the newly invented telescope (7), Galileo was able to prove its reality by observation (8), though he still believed that planets revolved in circular orbits. Kepler, using the immensely detailed records compiled by the Danish astronomer Tycho Brahe (6), showed in the early 17th century that they were ellipses.

6. Tycho Brahe's quadrant and observatory, 1602.

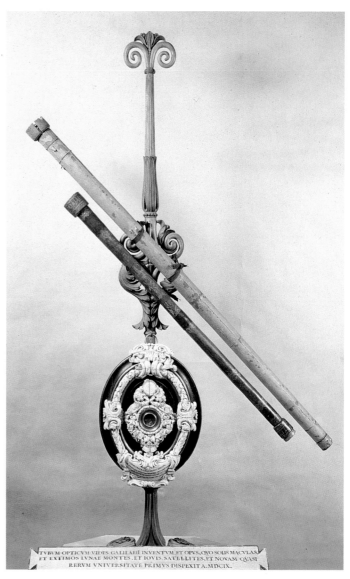

7. Galileo's telescopes, *c.* 1610.

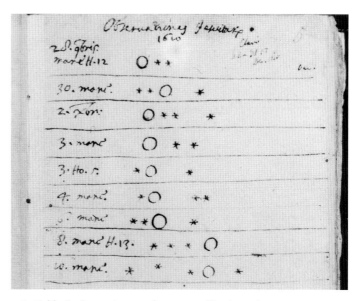

8. Galileo's observations on the moons of Jupiter, 1610.

Alchemy and astrology

THE Renaissance was a pre-scientific age. Until the 17th century ideas were more powerful than observation and experiment, especially since those ideas received the support of the ancients and were not denied by the Church. Dominant among them was the idea of 'correspondence', the ability to find patterns and meanings in what are, to us, quite unrelated areas of enquiry – four elements (2), four humours (6), four directions, four Gospels; seven planets, seven notes in the scale, seven deadly sins, seven days of creation. None of these correspondences was an accident, and mastery of the whole system of cosmic harmonies was the key to power. What we call magic was real. The planets and signs of the Zodiac through which they passed, each with its own sphere of influence (the very phrase is astrological), presided over our activities and coloured all our passions (4, 5, 7, 8). Few doubted that the motions of the heavenly bodies meshed with the motions of human choice. Even the distinction between the physical and the moral was blurred. The fusion of chemical elements was a marriage (3). And just as the spirit could be purged and purified of sin, so could base metals be purged into the purity and perfection of gold (1).

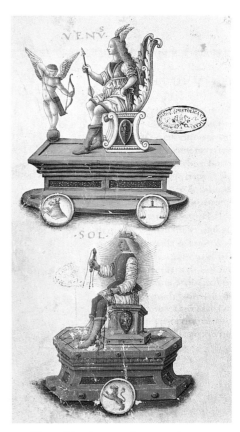

2. Venus (the element of copper, the volatile, mercurial female principle) and Sol (the element of sulphur, the principle of dominion over animal, mineral and vegetable realms) (1480).

3. The male principle, the 'seed', called 'The Old Man', weds the female principle in the bowels of the earth. At the top, the angel in the red castle unites the volatile and the fixed (1480).

1. Giovanni Stradano: *The Alchemist*, detail (16th century).

4. The planet Jupiter, passive in Pisces, active in Sagittarius, ruler over trade and exchange (15th century).

5. The planets focusing on Mercury, the mutable and transforming principle, symbolized by the two-headed bird (16th century).

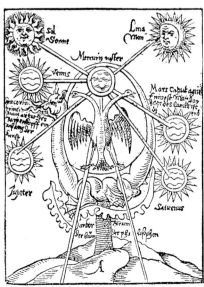

6. The four humours that go to make up the human personality, from a German text book of 1574.

7. The Astrologer, calculating propitious weather for a voyage (16th century).

8. Cancer, the Crab, ruler over the sea and ports, by Agostino di Duccio in the Tempio Malatestiano, Rimini (1450–57).

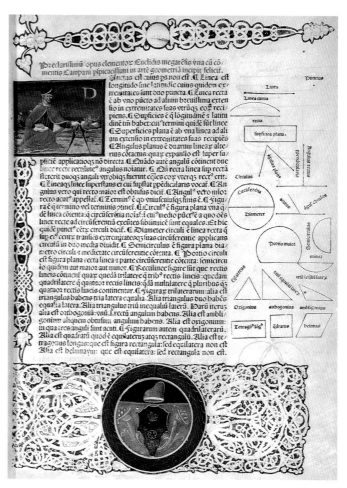

Mathematics: the power of number

THERE were two sides to Renaissance mathematics. On the one hand, the rediscovery or wider availability of Euclid (1, 3), Archimedes, Apollonius (on conic sections) and others led to advances in both pure and applied mathematics (5), especially geometry. Luca Pacioli (8) was one of those who mastered this new knowledge and passed it on to, among others, Leonardo da Vinci. 'Arabic' numerals, using the zero sign as we do today and expressing fractions as decimals (6), replaced Roman numerals as early as the 13th century. An illustration of 1503 (4) contrasts this system (associated with the 6th-century philosopher Boethius, who could actually never have used it, though it was through him that classical mathematics survived in the Middle Ages) with the abacus (associated with Pythagoras). The other side of Renaissance mathematics was not scientific but mystical. Plato had found in number an image of eternal truth. Number systems were central to Neoplatonic thought, and it is probably in this light that we should see Raphael's portrait of Euclid in the *School of Athens* (2), tracing a geometrical figure in the ground, and Pinturicchio's figure of *Arithmetica* (7) surrounded by the sages of Antiquity. When a translation of Euclid was published in England in 1570 (1) it had a preface by the magus John Dee stressing the occult power of numbers, even to command spirits, and quoting Pico della Mirandola: 'By number a way is had to be searching out and understanding of everything able to be known.'

1. Title page of H. Billingsley's translation of Euclid's *Elements*, 1570, with preface by John Dee.

2. Detail of Euclid from Raphael's *School of Athens* (1509–11).

3. Page from Euclid's *Elements* printed in Venice in 1482.

Exploration and discovery, 210–11

Astronomy, 214–15

Time and the hour, 230–31

4. Woodcut from Gregorius Reisch's *Margarita philosphica* (1503).

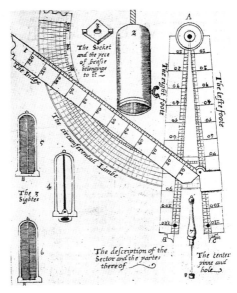

5. The sector, an engraving from T. Hood: *Making and Use of ... the Sector* (1598).

DISME:
The Art of Tenths,
OR,
Decimall Arithmetike,

Teaching how to performe all Computations
whatfoever, by whole Numbers without
Fractions, by the foure Principles of
Common *Arithmeticke*: namely, Addition, Subftraction, Multiplication,
and Diuifion.

Inuented by the excellent Mathematician,
Simon Steuin.

Publifhed in Englifh with fome additions
by *Robert Norton*, Gent.

Imprinted at London by *S. S.* for *Hugh*
Afley, and are to be fold at his fhop at
Saint Magnus corner. 1 6 o 8,

7. Pinturicchio: *Arithmetica* (1492–95).

8. Jacopo de' Barbari: *Portrait of Luca Pacioli* (1495).

6. Title page of Simon Stevin's *Disme: The Art of Tenths* (1608).

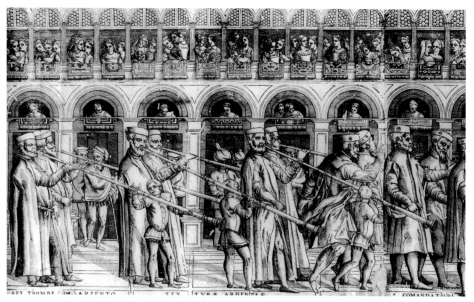

2. Henry VIII's 'musick', a drawing attributed to Hans Holbein the Younger (*c.* 1520).

1. Musicians in the Palm Sunday procession at St Mark's, Venice (16th century).

3. Detail from *The Sense of Hearing* by Jan Bruegel the Elder (*c.* 1617).

The measure of music

WESTERN music as we know it – a blend of instruments and/or voices arranged in formal polyphonic structures – begins with the Renaissance. Since no Greek or Roman music survives, there were no classical models to follow. Music, with arithmetic, geometry and astronomy, was traditionally one of the higher branches of learning, and was associated with ancient theories of the harmony and proportion governing the universe (5, 9). The design of instruments, especially keyboards and strings (3, 4), was improved (violins reached perfection in the late 17th century and have never changed since), and a galaxy of composers, such as Orlando Lassus (8) and Josquin des Préz, equally at home on both sides of the Alps, exploited these resources to make music more complex, personal and passionate. Most music was private (7), but ensembles of musicians at court were beginning to constitute a recognizably modern orchestra (4). No solemn occasion, sacred or secular, was complete without a musical element (1) and the Council of Trent gave considerable attention to drawing up rules for the setting of religious texts, a discipline in which Palestrina (6) became the ideal exponent.

4. Detail from *The Marriage at Cana* by Paolo Veronese (c. 1562–63).

5. Franchino Gaffurio lecturing, from his *Practica musica* (1512).

7. Title page of *Parthenia*, London (1611).

6. Autograph music by Palestrina (late 16th century).

9. Diagram of the modes from Franchino Gaffurio, *De harmonia musicorum* (1512).

8. Page from a book of madrigals by Orlando Lassus (1557).

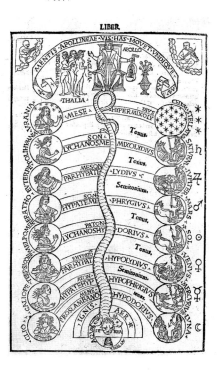

1. Suit of English ceremonial armour given to the Duke of Brunswick by Prince Henry in 1613.

2. Giorgione: *Armed Warrior with his Squire* (*c.* 1500).

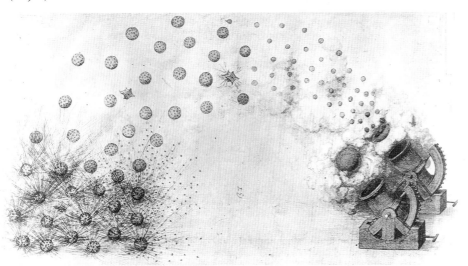

3. Leonardo da Vinci: mortars discharging shells that explode on impact (*c.* 1485–88).

4. Leonardo da Vinci: a warrior dressed in fantastic armour (*c.* 1480).

Faces of battle, 84–85

The gentry at play, 96–97

Defensible spaces, 164–65

5. Charles V's parade helmet (1541).

The art of war

THE Renaissance must be the last period of world history when war could be seen as an aesthetic spectacle. Artists since then have made great art out of the horror of war, but Renaissance artists are able to enjoy it almost as theatre. Weapons and armour become objects of beauty (1), and were represented in art like still-lifes (2, 6, 8). In jousts, tournaments and parades, the paraphernalia of war is often no more than a form of fancy-dress (5, 7). Cannon balls fall in elegant trajectories (3). Leonardo da Vinci, who knew that 'war is a bestial madness' and who invented the most gruesome war machines, could nevertheless turn it into a pageant of fantastic chivalry (4).

7. Nicholas Hilliard: *George Clifford, Earl of Cumberland, Master of the Queen's Horse* (c. 1590).

8. A cuirassier and his armour (1611).

6. Marquetry panel from the Duke of Urbino's studiolo (1474–82).

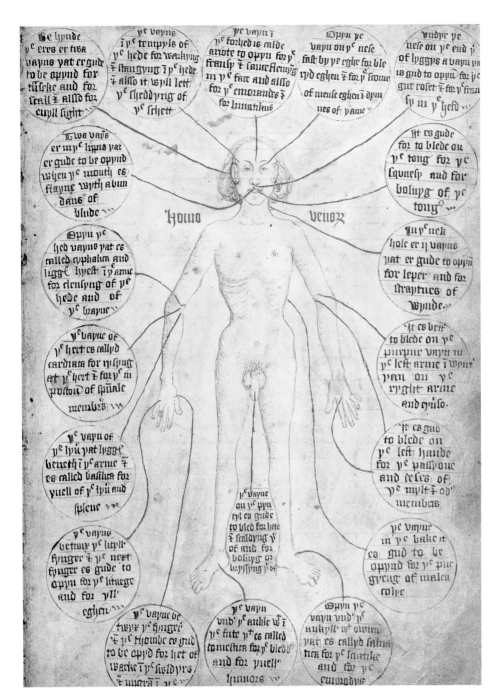

1. Anatomical figure showing parts of the body from which blood could be let; from a manuscript of the barber surgeons of York (15th century).

2, 3. Diagrams showing treatment of head and leg injuries, from a treatise by the 2nd-century AD Greek physician Soranus of Ephesus.

Medicine: theory and practice

DURING the Renaissance, the gap between the theory of medicine and what doctors actually did was wider than at almost any other period of history. The theory, derived from Aristotelian philosophy, enshrined in textbooks and taught at universities, was that the body, like everything else, consisted of four elements (fire, air, water, earth), manifested in four 'humours' (hot, cold, wet, dry), determined by four bodily fluids (blood, yellow bile, phlegm, black bile) which in turn produced four temperaments (sanguine, choleric, phlegmatic, melancholic). Health was a matter of maintaining a balance of these humours. Illness was caused by one coming to dominate the rest. Cure consisted in restoring the balance – hence, for instance, the efficacy of bleeding (1). Unchallenged throughout the Middle Ages, and only partially modified by improved texts of Galen, Hippocrates and later Greek writers (2, 3), this theory was in fact useless as a way of treating disease. In practice, doctors worked by trial and error. Urine examination was the commonest diagnostic procedure (6). A vast repertory of natural drugs at least alleviated symptoms (5, 9), and operations like trephining were often safely carried out (8). It seems to have been Paracelsus, in the early 16th century, who first openly rejected the theory of humours and taught that specific diseases called for specific remedies, though he also held other quite irrational beliefs. From about 1500 Europe had to face a new and terrible scourge – syphilis. Widely seen as a punishment from God, it haunted the imagination of writers and artists, among them Dürer (7).

4. A consultation of physicians from an Italian textbook (1495).

5. Physicians in an apothecary's shop from a German treatise (1496).

6. Examining a urine sample (1491).

7. Woodcut by Dürer showing a syphilitic. It illustrated a poem by the town physician of Nuremberg, Dietrich Uelzen, who described syphilis for the first time. The astrological globe above his head points to the year 1484 when a conjunction of planets and Zodiac signs were thought to have inaugurated the new plague (1496).

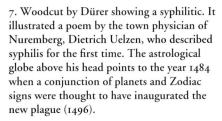

8. A trephining operation (1573).

9. Mixing drugs and administering them to the patient (1488–93).

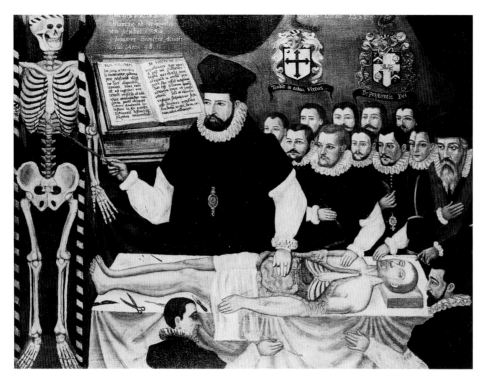

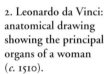

1. The English anatomist John Banister lecturing in London (1581).

2. Leonardo da Vinci: anatomical drawing showing the principal organs of a woman (c. 1510).

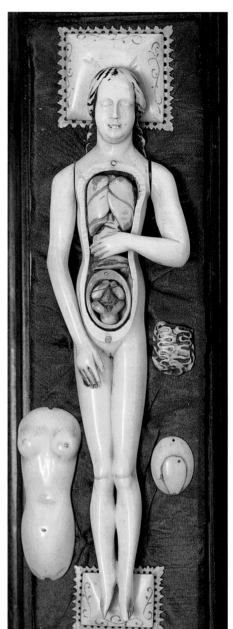

3. Italian ivory anatomical figure (late 16th century).

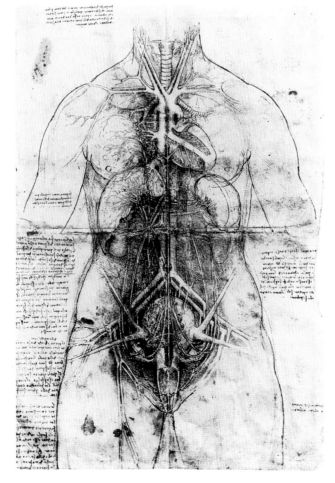

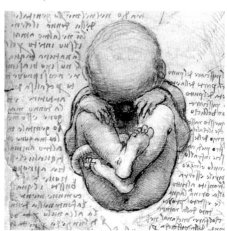

4. Leonardo da Vinci: drawing of a foetus (c. 1510–12).

Illness and death, 200–01

Medicine: theory and practice, 224–25

The human form, 248–49

7. Anatomical lecture from Realdus Columbus, *De re anatomica* (1559).

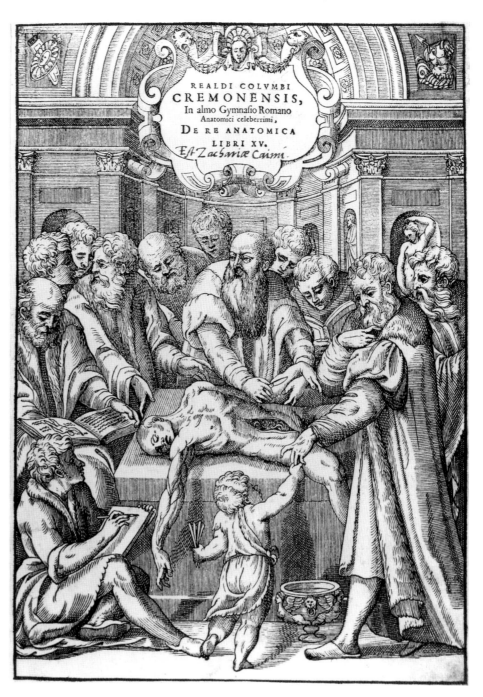

5. Portrait of Andreas Vesalius (1543).

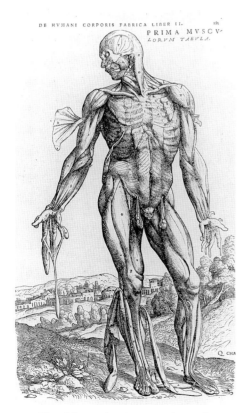

6. Flayed figure showing musculature from Vesalius' *De humani corporis fabrica libri septem* (1547).

KNOWLEDGE of how the body was made, as distinct from how it worked, made crucial advances in the Renaissance. The old prejudice, which had made the dissection of dead bodies a rare event even in university faculties of medicine, was gradually reduced. First in Italy and then in the north the study of anatomy became an essential part of a doctor's training (1, 7) and also – interestingly – of an artist's. Leonardo's interest went beyond the understanding of bone and muscle, and his wonderfully rendered drawings (2, 4) are those of a research biologist. Equally concerned to be aesthetic is the little Italian figure in ivory (3); the front of the torso is removeable, revealing the organs underneath. Later in the 16th century, Andreas Vesalius (5), from Brabant but working in Italy, published the most famous anatomical treatise of the age with flayed and dissected bodies standing in the elegant poses of classical sculpture (6).

Anatomy: the body's structure

Botany: medicine and art

IT used to be said that the Renaissance 'discovered the
natural world', which the austere Middle Ages had wilfully
ignored. This is now seen to be absurd, but it remains true that
Renaissance artists did study plants and flowers with particular
intensity. Foremost among them was Leonardo da Vinci (1, 2),
whose interest can genuinely be called scientific. Botticelli, too,
must have closely examined dozens of plant species, which appear
prominently in his paintings and which in the *Primavera* (4) are
mythologized in the person of Flora, bringer of fertility. But it
was in the north, where landscape had become an art form in
its own right, that the loving depiction of nature in all its detail
reached a climax: no one ever looked at grass with a finer perception than Dürer (6). For a more practical purpose, systematic
catalogues of medicinally useful plants – 'herbals' – began to
be compiled in the 16th century and by the 17th had become
scientific works of reference (5, 7, 8, 9). Clouet's portrait of a
famous French pharmacist, Pierre Quthe, shows him with an
open book in which pressed specimens are preserved (3).

1, 2. Leonardo da Vinci: oak leaves and acorns (*c.* 1505–08), and lily
(*c.* 1480–83).

3. François Clouet: detail from *The Pharmacist Pierre Quthe* (1562).

4. Botticelli: detail of *Primavera* (*c.* 1478).

The landscape of
reality, 166–67

In the countryside,
184–85

Medicine: theory and
practice, 224–25

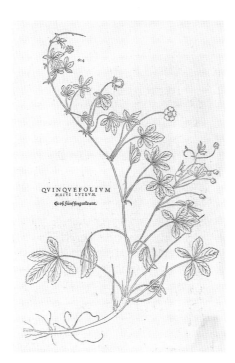

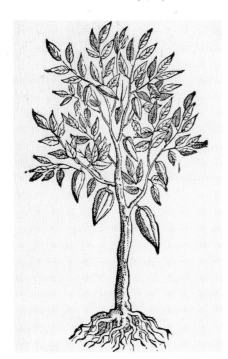

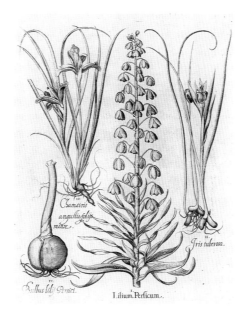

5. Cinquefoil from L. Fuchs, *De Historia Stirpium* (1547).

6. Dürer: *The Great Piece of Turf* (1503).

7. Cacao plant from the Herbal of Francisco Hernandes (1649).

8. Three plants from Basil Besler, *Hortus Eystettensis* (1613).

9. Holly from Gerard, *Herball* (1636).

1. Ring incorporating a watch, made in Germany (1580).

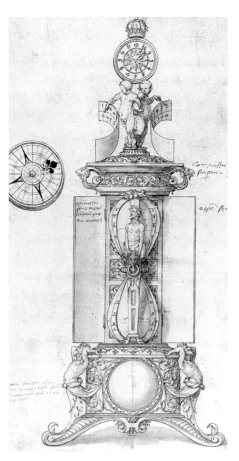

2. Hans Holbein: design for a clock (1530s).

4. Torre dell' Orologio, Venice, by Mauro Coducci (1496).

3. Astronomical clock at Hampton Court by Nicholas Oursian (1540).

5. Silver-gilt clock, made in Augsburg (17th century).

6. Clock on the Town Hall of Prague (originally 1410).

Time and the hour

CHANGES in our perception of time are subtle and hard to trace. Before the 13th century there were only sun-dials and hour-glasses, both of limited use; time-keeping had to be approximate. In the Middle Ages there were large mechanical clocks in some churches and cathedrals (those of Wells and Strasbourg survive). During the Renaissance clocks became a feature of important public buildings (3, 4, 6). By the 15th century technology could produce small clocks for the houses of the rich (5, 7), and portable watches appeared about 1500 (1). Time, one could say, passed from being ecclesiastical to being public and official, then domestic and finally private and personal. The religious affinity, however, was slow to fade. One of the oldest secular public clocks, on Prague Town Hall (6), not only tells the hour, the day, the phases of the moon and the signs of the Zodiac, but also incorporates, each hour, a moving procession of Apostles. Similarly, the clock tower of Venice of 1496 (4) includes an angel blowing a trumpet and the three kings paying homage to Mary. The highly elaborate clock erected by Cardinal Wolsey at Hampton Court in 1540 (3) is purely secular: it tells the hour, the day of the month, the phases of the moon and – a novel touch – the time of high water at London Bridge. By the 17th century clocks had become marvels of ingenuity, both mechanically and artistically, occasions for the display of superfluous wealth (5, 7). Every technical advance served to sharpen the sense of time and divide it into smaller and smaller units. Holbein made a design (2) in which man himself is the sand trickling through an hour-glass.

7. Table clock of gilt brass, silver and enamel made by David Ramsay (1610).

Science, Invention and Discovery   **231**

1. Banking scene, Italy (late 14th century).

2. Florentine money-changer (1493).

3. Payment of state salaries in Siena (1430).

4, 5. Jakob Fugger in *c.* 1519 with his clerk, surrounded by ledgers (above), and a later member of the family, Christoph Fugger in 1541, detail (below).

7. Florentine currency. The internationally used florin.

8. A Venetian ducat.

Travel and transport, 178–79

Work and trade, 186–87

Mathematics: the power of number, 218–19

6. Jost Amman: Allegory of Commerce (late 16th century).

A new world of finance

CAPITALISM is curiously involved with humanism. Both trace their origins to 15th-century Florence, where the great patrons of scholarship were bankers and businessmen. The world of credit and exchange, which benefited from the adoption of arabic numerals, the introduction of double-entry book-keeping and business insurance, still had its arcane side. Jost Amman's panorama of trade in 16th-century Germany (6) is filled with allegorical figures – 'obligation', 'freedom', 'knowledge of languages', 'silence', 'integrity' – and at the very centre, like a shrine on an altar, is 'The Book of Secrets', the ledger containing inventory and accounts. Elsewhere we see bales and barrels being packed, coins collected and exchanged, entries made in books. That all this expertise should have begun in Italy was not surprising, since every state and almost every city had its own fiscal arrangements (1, 3, 9) and currency (7, 8), giving plenty of work to the money-changers (2). A northern equivalent of the Medici were the Fuggers of Augsburg (4, 5); the portrait of Jakob Fugger in his office vividly illustrates the extent of his contacts, with ledgers bearing the names of cities all over Europe.

9. Sienese finances in peace and war; on the right mercenary soldiers receive their pay (1468).

Water for recreation and work

THE hot dry climate of Italy gave water an obvious appeal, and in most Italian towns the communal drinking fountain was the occasion for some special display, often employing the talents of a leading sculptor. For the humanists there was the added attraction of classical precedent, and the possibility of matching Hadrian's garden at Tivoli or Pliny's description of his Tuscan villa. At Pratolino (7), laid out in 1569 for the Grand Dukes of Tuscany, there was an amazing series of pools descending the hillside, while at Tivoli (2) Cardinal Ippolito d'Este built from 1560 to 1575 a water garden as spectacular as any of the later Baroque. Nothing in northern Europe would equal this for over a century, but France (4), England (3) and the imperial court (1) followed Italianate fashions as far as they could. Pumping machinery kept pace with these demanding devices (5, 6) and would soon be used for industrial power, while Leonardo already understood how the invention of the pound lock could improve water transport.

1. The 'Singing Fountain', in the Belvedere Garden at Prague, made by Tomás Jaros from designs by Francesco Terzio (1564).

2. Part of the gardens of the Villa d'Este at Tivoli by Pirro Ligorio, painted by Giovanni Muziano (1568–69).

3. Fountain in the inner court of Nonsuch Palace (1590).

4. The Tiber Fountain at Fontainebleau by Alexandre Francini (late 16th century).

The art of the garden, 170–71

In the countryside, 184–85

Villa life, 284–85

5. Mill for raising water to work a fountain (*c.* 1580).

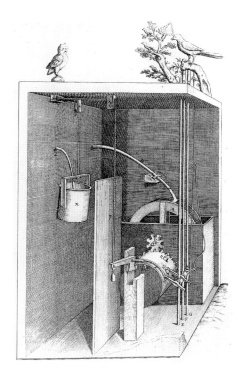

6. Hydraulic machine by Salomon de Caus working mechanical singing birds (early 17th century).

7. Part of the garden of the Villa at Pratolino, near Florence; detail from a painting by Giusto Utens (1598).

1, 2. Construction of a mineshaft and a furnace for smelting tin from Georgius Agricola's *De re metallica* (1556).

3. Detail from Jan Bruegel the Elder's *Forge in the Mountain* (early 17th century).

Treasures in metalwork

WORKS in metal – gold, silver, bronze – were the luxury artefacts of the Renaissance, as they had been for the Middle Ages. In the north, it was primarily this medieval tradition that was continued, the workshops of Germany (7) and the Netherlands (5) producing marvels of intricate artistry in the form of table ornaments and objects of devotion. Something of the magical richness associated with these treasures is conveyed in Bruegel's painting (3). In Italy classical motifs were giving new life to the old forms, in such semi-utilitarian objects as plate and

candelabra (6). Benvenuto Cellini used the figures of Venus and Neptune to represent land and sea in the famous salt-cellar (9) that he made for François I. Fairly large-scale sculpture in bronze took its place as a major art form (8), all the more popular because it could be reproduced in smaller versions. Processes of mining and smelting, meanwhile, were made widely accessible in such books as Georgius Agricola's *De re metallica* (1, 2), which described the various pumping mechanisms developing in this period.

4. Detail from Giulio Romano's *Marriage of Cupid and Psyche* (1528).

5. Charles the Bold holding a reliquary of St Lambert (1498).

6. Andrea Riccio's bronze candelabrum
(early 16th century).

7. Silver 'nef' made in Nuremberg (1503).

8. Giambologna's *Mercury* (1564).

9. Benvenuto Cellini's salt-cellar (*c.* 1540).

THE POWER
OF ART

RULERS competed among themselves for the accolade that art could bring. The Marquis of Mantua, Lodovico Gonzaga, was particularly pleased with an architectural drawing made by Mantegna, since 'frequently ambassadors and lords come, and to honour them one seeks to show them stupendous works, and I will now have this marvellous drawing to show'. At the Field of Cloth of Gold near Calais in 1520, where Henry VIII strove to impress his sophisticated contemporary, François I, the elaborate and hugely expensive temporary palace built by thousands of workers for the occasion, of brick, timber and canvas, complete with glass windows and carvings, included images of classical figures holding the armorial bearings of royal ancestors.

Association with Antiquity was the order of the day. It was indeed a matter of etiquette almost as much as of display. The good courtier, like the good pupil, must 'make a constant effort to imitate', as a spokesman in Castiglione's *Courtier* put it, and there was no doubt about the desirable models. Even in England where to 'hunt cunningly, neatly train and use a hawk' once seemed the be-all and end-all of gentility, the study of literature ceased to be regarded as the preserve of peasants' sons and paupers. To be unable to sing a madrigal or play the lute could seem a social disqualification, and by the 17th century a gentleman needed sufficient knowledge of classical poetry and mythology to be able to appreciate contemporary collections of statuary and coins. He might even learn to paint or carve himself, as did some princes like Alfonso d'Este at Ferrara, Erik XIV of Sweden and the Emperor Rudolf II with their various abilities in potting, painting and drawing.

The study of Antiquity had widened the scope of the arts, producing forms and topics that were effectively new. The extraordinary shallow reliefs in which Donatello demonstrated the capacity of sculpture to come close to painting in the subtle manipulation of receding planes broke new ground. Portrait medals, painted miniatures and the small bronzes, which could ornament domestic interiors, all developed out of ancient forms (coins, cameos and sculpture) but were made into something new. The science of perspective allowed painters fresh power to translate three dimensions into two. And if luminosity and depth of colours were enhanced by the medium of oil paint, the use of canvas instead of panels made the creation and mobility of large pictures easier. Perhaps most momentous of all, renewed knowledge of the art of Antiquity opened European eyes to appreciation of the human form. Viewing classical carving and talking about classical mythology facilitated the re-entry of the nude (pp. 248–49), so central to classical art.

The power of paint was extended by the currency of print. Woodcuts, engravings and etchings enabled painters and their works to become known far from home. Some painters, such as Dürer, Maerten van Heemskerck and Hendrik Goltzius, made graphic work an important part of their *œuvre*. Marcantonio Raimondi, whose prints did much to spread knowledge of Renaissance painting, was praised by Vasari for 'the benefit that northerners have had from seeing, by way of prints, the styles of Italian art'. By this means works of Raphael, Giulio Romano and

Of Greek painting *little was known except for a few anecdotes in Lucian and Cicero. The former describes the allegory of* Calumny *painted by Apelles (see p. 46). The latter tells the story of Zeuxis commissioned to paint a picture of Helen, the most beautiful woman in the world. No real woman could come up to this ideal, but Zeuxis sought out five of the most beautiful and combined the best features of each to create perfect beauty, an idea that for the Renaissance had intriguing echoes of Neoplatonism. Vasari's version of the scene shows one model posing, another preparing to pose and a third getting dressed (1560s). The subject of Zeuxis' painting, however, seems to be the goddess Diana, not Helen.*

239

Donatello's relief of St George and the Dragon *(1415–17) was the first work to make use of the science of perspective in the receding arcade behind the princess.*

Italy excelled in maiolica ware. In this pleasing piece of self-reference, a painted plate bears the image of an artist painting a plate; the centre will perhaps be a portrait of the betrothed couple who sit and watch him (late 15th century).

Michelangelo became known across Europe, and the print collections of individuals or workshops enabled Renaissance images and motifs to appear in many media, from the grotesques of carved ornament and painted interior designs to the classical themes of tapestries, *cassoni* and maiolica dishes, all variously contributing to the visual vocabulary and commonplaces of coming generations.

In the days when Michelangelo was 'Il Divino', and Titian – himself ennobled by Charles V – could be introduced as 'the first man in Christendom', the arts themselves seemed canonized into a new sphere. The creations of man more nearly matched those of the Creator himself. They glorified man as well as God. Artists (in our general sense of the word, which itself came into being as a result of these changes), who served dukes, monarchs and emperors, had long been accustomed to relatively low ranking in the hierarchy of court servants (something which still chafed Mozart in the court of the Archbishop of Salzburg). But already in the 15th century things were changing.

Though court musicians might have to compete for place, the great were known by sound as well as sight. The trumpet was the instrument that signalled power – the power of the ultimate Judgment and the power of this world's judges. No court or great household would have been complete without its trumpeters, blaring praise and heralding arrivals. When Charles V was elected emperor the town clerk of Frankfurt recorded that twenty-two trumpeters blew their instruments, and ten years later, when the emperor met Clement VII, trumpets with drums and artillery complemented the hubbub of human voices in the city of Bologna. The sound of the trumpet was the sound of coming excitement, of welcome, of a great personage and the finery of high estate – enough to make any ordinary listener get ready to stop and stare. 'There is no heart so faint', wrote Montaigne, 'that the sound of our drums and trumpets will not warm it.'

The enhanced respect for the arts makes it possible to know more about artists, including what they looked like, thanks to the introspective drive of the period, which produced many self-portraits. To leave such a personal image in a religious sculpture or painting was not new – nor was there any intrinsic irreligiousness about claiming depicted proximity to saint or donor in a holy image. But some inscriptions in Renaissance works may bring home to the viewer with a jolt the artist's sense of personal triumph. Piero della Francesca placed his own name in *The Flagellation* in a Latin inscription on the step of Herod's throne, exactly on the level of Christ's feet. Mantegna, who did not know Greek, staked out humanist claims by setting his name in Greek letters alongside the figure of St Sebastian in his 1459 painting of that saint. And in the lantern of the Sigismund Chapel in Cracow, Bartolommeo Berrecci's name, set round the winged cherub, looks down on us from the centre of the vault.

Cultivation of the heroic was a Renaissance characteristic. It was rooted in a sense of scale, wonder at grandiosity, the larger than life, like that felt by 16th-century artists for the remains of colossal antique statues still housed on the Campidoglio in Rome. The making of monuments of enormous size was one way in which moderns advertised their ability.

Florentine heroes were biblical as well as classical, but they all had the quality of the superhuman, and their statues reflected this in scale.

Michelangelo's fourteen-foot marble *David* (p. 250), popularly known as 'the Giant', was the largest statue of its kind in existence when it was made early in the 16th century. Hercules, the Florentines' protector, appeared on the seal of the Signoria long before he took his place in the Piazza Signoria in a huge stucco statue (made to look like bronze) by Baccio Bandinelli (p. 50). This destroyed work, erected for the triumphal entry of the Medici pope Leo X in 1515, was even larger than Michelangelo's *David*. A generation later, when in 1545 Benvenuto Cellini took up Duke Cosimo de' Medici's commission to make his vast bronze of *Perseus* (p. 251), he was conscious of competing not so much with the ancients as with two of the greatest artists who had lived since Antiquity: Donatello and Michelangelo. The sheer technical accomplishment of casting a bronze statue of this size itself lent an element of the heroic to Cellini's work.

There is always the risk of vulgarity or the ridiculous in the outsize – or oversize – which perhaps charges our response to works that do not disappoint in this way, like the wonderful and long-admired equestrian statue of Marcus Aurelius on the Capitol in Rome (p. 86). The Renaissance experienced failures of both taste and execution in the pursuit of the heroic. The bronze equestrian monument commissioned from Leonardo to commemorate the condottiere, Francesco Sforza (p. 87), was to have been twice the size of Donatello's monument of Gattamelata (p. 87), but it was never realized. The stupendous grandiosity of Julius II's planned funerary monument (which may have contributed to the decision to replace the old St Peter's) also ran into the sands, and what eventuated is almost laughable, were it not also Michelangelo's 'tragedy of the tomb', which has left his great *Moses* (p. 262) in a position of such bathos.

If it is human to err, errant humanity shares the perennial longing to cheat death. Belief in the power of art to bestow immortality, or what Shakespeare called 'the living record' of the individual's memory, made many monuments, as well as poetry and eulogistic prose. Portraits in paint and stone, numberless effigies and tombs across the whole of Europe, the 'work of masonry ... marble ... and gilded monuments', testify to shared belief in the arts as conquerors of time, creators of fame as lasting as anything the destructive world can hope for.

> *'Gainst death, and all-oblivious enmity*
> *Shall you pace forth, your praise shall still find room,*
> *Even in the eyes of all posterity*
> *That wear this world out to the ending doom.*

Ironically, the power of art has proved such that in many cases it lives on, while the immortalized has disappeared and become nameless for ever. But perhaps that would not greatly have surprised either Michelangelo or Shakespeare.

'The work of Bartolommeo the Florentine': an inscription in the dome of the Sigismund Chapel, Cracow, 1517–33 (Poland's first experience of the Renaissance) proclaims the achievement of Bartolommeo Berrecci.

Julius II planned his own tomb, to be made by Michelangelo, as a huge free-standing monument with numerous life size and over-lifesize figures. In the event only Moses was ever finished, now forming the centre of the sadly reduced version that exists today, surrounded by sculpture by inferior artists (1545).

1. Dürer: self-portrait (1498).

2. Ghiberti: self-portrait on the bronze east doors of the Florence Baptistery (1425–52).

3. Parmigianino: self-portrait in a convex mirror (1523/4).

The artist's image

ARTISTS were long regarded merely as craftsmen exercising a skill. The change that placed them on an equality with poets, as inspired creators touched by the sacred spark, came with the Renaissance and was largely due to one writer and one artist. The writer was Giorgio Vasari, whose *Lives* put forward a view of art history that was to last for centuries – that the 'rebirth' of painting began with Giotto and culminated with 'the divine Michelangelo', the superhuman genius before whom all rules must bend. The ways in which artists chose to represent themselves in the Renaissance reflects this pattern. Ghiberti (2) and Krafft (4) show themselves as humble artisans, as in a sense do Holbein (6) and Titian (7), although the latter includes the golden chain of his imperial order. Dürer (1), Raphael (5) and Leonardo (8) give themselves a glamour above everyday life. Parmigianino's self-portrait in a mirror (3) is a typical piece of technical bravura. Michelangelo, most eccentric of all, depicts his own face in the flayed skin of St Bartholomew in *The Last Judgment* (9).

4. Adam Krafft: self-portrait at the base of the stone tabernacle of St Lorenz, Nuremberg (late 15th century).

Italian funerary monuments, 100–01

Funerary monuments of the north, 102–03

The Renaissance medal, 244–45

5. Raphael: self-portrait (*c.* 1506).

6. Holbein: self-portrait (1542).

7. Titian: self-portrait, detail (*c.* 1566).

8. Leonardo: self-portrait (*c.* 1512).

9. Michelangelo: detail from *The Last Judgment* showing his own face in the skin of St Bartholomew (1536–40).

The Renaissance medal

MEDALS are monuments in miniature, flattering the living and commemorating the dead. It was an art form in which the Renaissance directly challenged the achievement of the ancient world and surpassed it. Rome had immortalized her heroes on coins, the most collectable of antiques. Humanist Italy was ambitious to do the same. The genius of the medal was Pisanello, who virtually created it with his masterly profile portraits on the obverse and a variety of designs on the reverse, which can be personal emblems, like Alberti's (4), or allusions to historical events, like the Pazzi conspiracy that murdered Giuliano de' Medici (7). The fashion was soon imitated in the north, especially the Netherlands, where medals lost some of their simplicity but gained in technical sophistication. The portraits turned three-quarter (13) and then full-face (9), featuring the widest social range, from queens (9) to merchants' wives (15).

1. Niccolò Fiorentino: medal of Lorenzo the Magnificent (c. 1480).

2. Pisanello: drawing for a medal of Alfonso I of Naples (1448).

3, 4. Matteo de' Pasti: medal of Leon Battista Alberti, with his device, the winged eye, on the reverse (c. 1450).

5, 6. Sigismondo Malatesta and his mistress Isotta, whom he married in 1456 (mid-15th century).

7. Reverse of a medal of Giuliano de' Medici, with a view of the Pazzi murder (1478).

The northern humanists, 36–37

The northern monarchies, 70–71

The rulers of Italy, 72–73

Florence, 154–55

Sculpture in relief, 260–61

8. Portrait medal of Erasmus (1531).

9. Portrait medal of Queen Elizabeth, design by Nicholas Hilliard (late 16th century).

10. Steven van Herwijck: medal of Engelken Tols of Utrecht (1558).

11, 12. Jacques Jonghelinck: medal of Philip de Croy, Duke of Arschot, with his device, a hand holding a beehive, on the reverse (1567).

13. Friedrich Hagenauer: medal of Michael Mercator of Venloo (1539).

14, 15. Steven van Herwijck: medal of Richard Martin of London and his wife Dorcas Eglestone (1562).

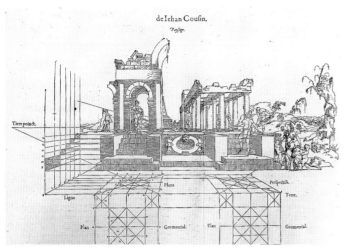

1. Jean Cousin the Younger: perspective diagram from *Livre de Perspective* (1560).

2. Jean Cousin the Younger: frontispiece from *Livre de Perspective* (1560).

3. Dürer: method of applying foreshortening by viewing the model through a grid (1538).

4. Masaccio: *The Trinity* (1425–28).

The mastery of space

FORESHORTENING is a technique for representing three-dimensional objects on a flat surface. Perspective is a technique for applying the same principles to the whole space of a composition as far as the horizon. It was the generation of Brunelleschi, Donatello and Masaccio, pioneers in so many aspects of the visual arts, that formulated these principles into a science. Once this had happened, painters took delight in exploiting their skill. Masaccio (**4**) places the Crucifixion in a correctly drawn barrel-vaulted space. In Austria Michael Pacher brought off a similar feat (**7**) but with Gothic vaulting. Mantegna (**8**) gave foreshortening an almost mystical dimension in his *Dead Christ*. Piero, who wrote a whole book on the subject, treated *The Flagellation* (**5**) – or, according to some, *The Dream of St Jerome* – almost as a demonstration of perspective theory. Uccello and Tintoretto were both, in different ways, fascinated by the mastery that perspective could confer, Uccello (**6**) naively displaying it for its own sake, Tintoretto (**9**) using it to dramatic purpose. Some artists, like the Frenchman Jean Cousin the Younger (**1, 2**), became such specialists that they set themselves almost impossible problems to solve.

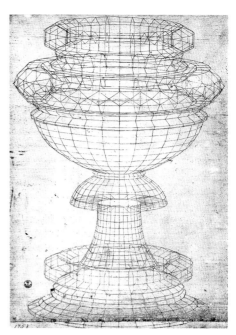

5. Piero della Francesca: *The Flagellation* (1456–57).

6. Uccello: design for a chalice (mid-15th century).

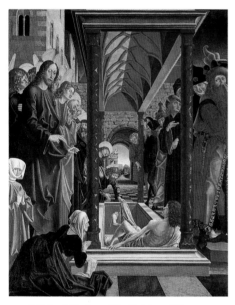

7. Michael Pacher: *The Raising of Lazarus*, detail (1481).

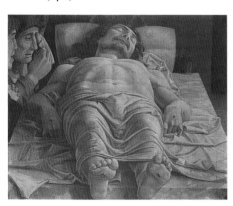

8. Mantegna: *Dead Christ* (c. 1500).

9. Tintoretto: *Discovery of the Body of St Mark* (c. 1562).

The Power of Art　247

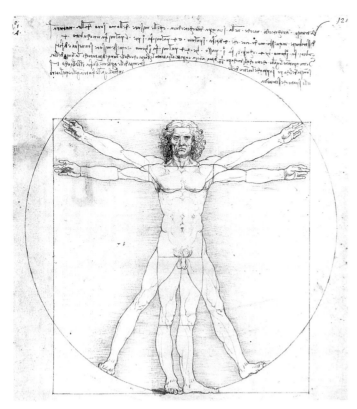

1. Leonardo da Vinci: *Vitruvian Man* (c. 1490).

The human form

THE naked human body had been virtually banished from art during the Middle Ages, when its associations were only with guilt and shame. The Renaissance rediscovered the body's beauty. Masaccio (3) and Dürer (2), still within the religious context of fallen Man, give the body dignity and strength. The pose of Masaccio's Eve, which looks so natural, is in fact copied from antique sculpture – the so-called 'Venus pudica', or 'modest Venus', with the hands placed over breasts and genitals. Mantegna's St Sebastian (4) is at the same time a Christian martyr and a pagan god, his body a generalized ideal of male beauty. It was typical of Leonardo that he should represent the male nude as a diagram (1): Vitruvius had stated as a rule of proportion that a man's body with arms outstretched could be inscribed in both a square and a circle. For the Venetian High Renaissance, anatomical accuracy counted for less than colour and atmosphere. Titian's mythological pictures (6), which he called *poesie* ('poems'), evoke a magical world of warm sensuality. With the Mannerist generation this tendency goes further and the body is seen wholly in terms of aesthetic and sexual allure. Parmigianino's Cupid (5) is a precocious adolescent, the face and figure ambiguous, the glance disturbingly direct; and Jean Cousin's knowing Eve (7) 'the first Pandora' is a far cry from Dürer's.

2. Dürer: *Adam and Eve* (1504).

3. Masaccio: *The Expulsion*, detail (1425–28).

Venus,
52–53

A new eroticism,
192–93

The heroic,
250–51

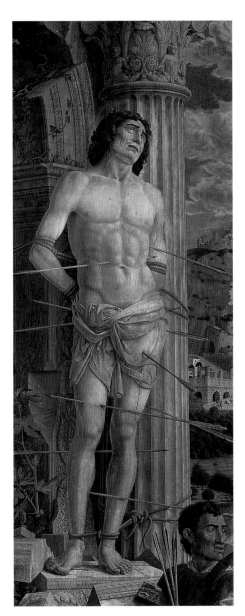

4. Mantegna: *St Sebastian* (1480).

6. Titian: *Danaë* (1553).

EVA PRIMA PANDORA

7. Jean Cousin the Elder: *Eva Prima Pandora* (c. 1550).

5. Parmigianino: *Cupid Carving his Bow* (1533).

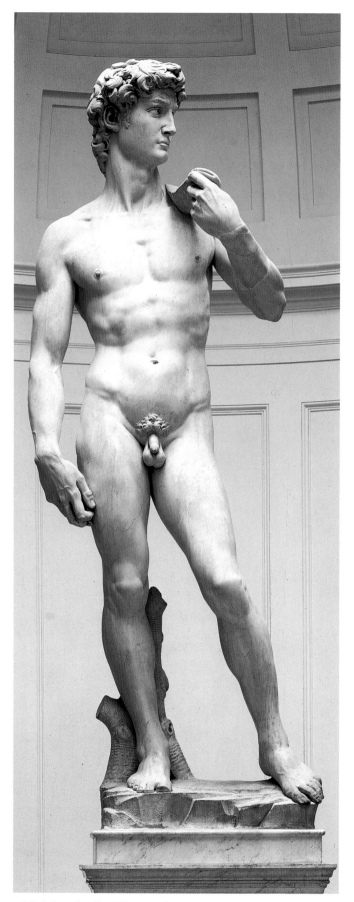

1. Donatello: *St George* (1416–20).   2. Donatello: *David* (1433).

The heroic

THE heroic ideal was one that crossed all cultural and religious boundaries and even blurred the fact that there were boundaries at all. Figures from the Old Testament and Christian history stand together with those from classical mythology. Moral strength is as dominant as physical. Donatello's St George (1) stands resolute, armed only with a shield. His David (2) broke with precedent in representing a biblical hero naked, a combination of the classical Apollo and Dionysus; the fight is over and Goliath's head lies at his feet. Michelangelo, like Donatello, shows David (3) naked, but chooses a moment before the fight, just as he is about to launch the stone from his sling. Commissioned by the Florentine state for the central square of Florence, it became a symbol of the republic (a fighter for freedom against a superior enemy) and is now almost a symbol of the Renaissance itself – larger than life (it is nearly 14 feet high), tensed for action but relaxed in pose, noble, confident, and invincible. Both Cellini's Perseus (4) and Castagno's David (5) have the same calm assurance that does not depend on weapons or muscle-power; they triumph, in Shakespeare's words, 'by sovereignty of nature'. A more academic exercise is Pollaiuolo's *Battle of the Nude Gods* (6). Other Italian artists of this extraordinary generation succeeded in the heroic vein, but it was one in which no one outside Italy seemed truly at home (7).

3. Michelangelo: *David* (1502–04).

The uses of myth, 48–49

The spell of the Antique, 54–55

The human form, 248–49

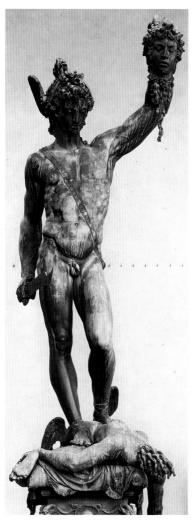

4. Benvenuto Cellini: *Perseus* (1545–54).

5. Castagno: *David* (c. 1450).

6. Antonio Pollaiuolo: *Battle of the Nude Gods* (late 15th century).

7. Hendrik Goltzius: *Manlius Torquatus* (c. 1586).

The Power of Art   251

1. Pirro Ligorio: ceiling in the Casino of Pius IV, the Vatican (1558–61).

2. Studio of Raphael: detail from the Vatican logge, Rome (1515–19).

3. Annibale Carracci: ceiling of the gallery of the Palazzo Farnese, Rome (1595–1604).

Italy: the language of decoration

JUST as Renaissance architecture demanded a whole new vocabulary of style (which came easily to Italians but had to be learned more painfully in the north), so the treatment of the interiors demanded a whole new concept of decorative design. Its inspiration was ultimately ancient Rome. The newly discovered rooms of Nero's 'Golden House' suggested the forms used by Raphael in his immensely influential Vatican logge (2); they had been found by excavation in so-called 'grottoes' – hence the name *grotteschi*. Almost all Renaissance decoration depended on painting, whether fresco or on canvas, usually contained in an architectural framework of stucco, which in Ligorio's Casino of Pius IV (1) becomes dominant. Raphael's Farnesina frescoes (5) use the story of Cupid and Psyche, those of the Carracci in the Palazzo Farnese (3) the more general theme of the loves of the gods. In the Palazzo Ducale of Venice (7) the subjects relate to the glory of the Venetian republic, while the more intimate studiolo of Francesco I of Tuscany (4) – the work of many artists – reflects his own recherché philosophical interests, including alchemy. Two Italians, Primaticcio and Rosso Fiorentino, took the style to France, where they created the gallery at Fontainebleau (6) for François I.

4. Studiolo of Francesco I, Palazzo Vecchio, Florence (1556–61).

Inside the palace, 80–81

Court entertainment, 98–99

The interior as work of art, 254–55

5. Raphael: loggia of Psyche in the Villa Farnesina, Rome (1515–17).

6. Primaticcio and Rosso Fiorentino: gallery of François I, Fontainebleau (1553–40).

7. Sala del Maggior Consiglio, Palazzo Ducale, Venice, with Tintoretto's *Paradiso* in the end wall (1577).

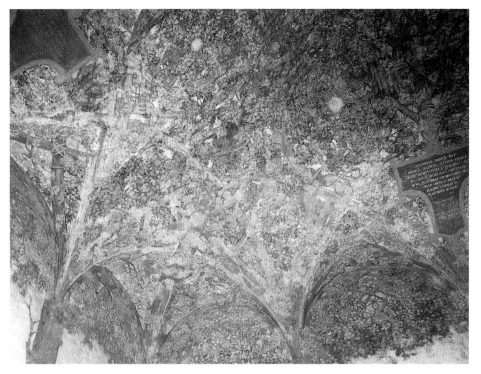

1. Leonardo: ceiling of the Sala delle Asse in the Castello Sforzesco, Milan (late 15th century).

2. Mantegna: Camera degli Sposi, Palazzo Ducale, Mantua (1470–74).

3. Baldassare Peruzzi: fresco in the Villa Farnesina, Rome (1516).

4. Mantegna: ceiling of the Camera degli Sposi, Palazzo Ducale, Mantua (1470–74).

Inside the palace, 80–81

The mastery of space, 246–47

Villa life, 284–85

5. Benozzo Gozzoli: detail from the *Journey of the Magi* in the chapel of the Palazzo Medici-Riccardi, Florence (*c.* 1459).

6. Correggio: dome of Parma Cathedral (1526–30).

7. Paolo Veronese: fresco in the Villa Barbaro, Maser (1561).

The interior as work of art

QUITE early in the Renaissance the idea arose of treating a whole room as a single artistic entity, with the decoration creating an illusory extension in which fictive men and women share the same space as the spectator. Perhaps the most successful example is Mantegna's Camera degli Sposi at Mantua (**2**), where members of the Gonzaga family appear with their friends, retainers, horses and dogs in an imaginary landscape, while above their heads an oculus opens to the sky (**4**) with peacocks and putti perching on the balustrade. Leonardo's illusionistic ceiling of trees in the castle of Milan (**1**) is a simpler conception, but Peruzzi, in the Villa Farnesina in Rome (**3**) opens out the wall to reveal a panorama of the city through columns. In the Palazzo Medici-Riccardi in Florence, Gozzoli treats the whole chapel as a setting for the *Journey of the Magi* (**5**), which ends at the altar where they adore the Virgin and Child. Mantegna's illusionist view from below (Italian *sotto in sù*) was eagerly developed by the painters of church domes, beginning with Correggio at Parma (**6**). Finally, in a domestic setting, is Veronese's charming detail of the girl peering round a non-existent door at the Villa Barbaro, Maser (**7**).

The Sistine ceiling

MICHELANGELO's scheme for the ceiling of the Sistine Chapel, painted at the command of Pope Julius II between 1508 and 1512, combines both methods of decorating an interior: a series of rectangular, self-contained pictures, and the illusion of opening up the whole vault to include the spectator in its fictive space. The panels showing scenes from Genesis begin at the altar end (left) and proceed in chronological order as follows: God separating the light from the darkness; God creating the Sun and the Moon

(God is seen twice here, approaching and disappearing, and as he disappears he creates the plants); the Congregation of the Waters; the Creation of Adam; the Creation of Eve; the Temptation and Expulsion; the Sacrifice of Noah; the Flood (with the Ark in the background); and the drunkenness of Noah. Michelangelo actually painted these scenes in the reverse order, and when he had reached half way realized that the scale was too small and increased it. The rest of the ceiling is divided by illusionistic transverse arches resting on plinths supported by pairs of 'sculpted' putti. On the plinths sit nude young men in various athletic poses. Lower down, between the plinths, sit those who foretold the coming of Christ – Hebrew prophets and pagan Sybils. (These are the largest figures on the ceiling.) In the triangular spandrels and semi-circular lunettes above the windows are the ancestors of Christ listed at the beginning of St Matthew's Gospel.

1. Leonardo da Vinci: caricature studies (*c.* 1495).

3. Giambologna: the Fountain of the Appenines in the garden of the Villa Demidoff, Pratolino, Italy (1569–81).

2. Quentin Massys: grotesque old woman, probably copied from a drawing by Leonardo (*c.* 1500). (This was the basis of Tenniel's Ugly Duchess in *Alice*.)

4. Shell figure from the grotto of Bastie d'Urfé, France (1535).

5. Woodcut from Sebastian Münster's *Cosmographia universalis* (1544) showing a man with one enormous foot, a woman with an eye in her forehead, a two-headed child, a man with his head in his chest and a dog-headed man.

The grotesque

THE word grotesque, as noted earlier (p. 252), originally referred to the kind of Roman ornament used by Raphael. It now has a different meaning: ugly, distorted, fantastic. In this sense it is more characteristic of the Gothic north than the Renaissance south and is indeed deeply alien to, even subversive of, ideals of classical harmony. Possibly for this reason it fascinated Leonardo, whose drawings of deformed faces (1) were copied with greater realism by Massys (2). Gardens were seen as a natural setting for the barbaric and the primitive (3, 4). But in other contexts the grotesque seems to emerge from the unconscious under cover of various excuses: travellers' tales from the unexplored regions of the world (5); Arcimboldi's strangely perceived affinity between vegetables and the human face (6); and in the extreme case of Hieronymus Bosch (7), allegories whose meaning has been lost – heaven, hell, the afterlife, or the orgiastic rites of a heretical sect?

6. Giuseppe Arcimboldi: *The Market-gardener* (late 16th century). To get the point of this extraordinary painting, turn the book upside down.

7. Hieronymus Bosch: detail from *The Garden of Earthly Delights* (c. 1500).

1. Donatello: *Miracle of the Eucharist*, an unbeliever's mule kneels before the consecrated host (1446–48).

2. Ghiberti: the young Jesus disputing with the doctors from the first Baptistery (north) doors (1403–24).

5. Agostino di Duccio: Angel from the Tempio Malatestiano, Rimini (1450–57).

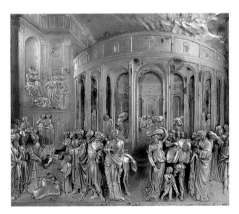

3. Ghiberti: the story of Joseph and his brothers in Egypt from the second Baptistery (east) doors (1425–52).

4. Jacopo della Quercia: the Creation of Eve and the Temptation from the portal of S. Petronio, Bologna (1425–38).

Italian funerary monuments, 100–01

The mastery of space, 246–47

Sculpture: a new dimension, 262–63

6. Peter Vischer the Younger workshop: bronze relief from the Fugger Chapel, St Anne's, Augsburg (1540).

7. Jean Goujon: two nymphs from the Fontaine des Innocents, Paris (1547–49).

8. Desiderio da Settignano: tabernacle in S. Lorenzo, Florence (1461).

Sculpture in relief

Late medieval relief sculpture was technically accomplished but lacking in drama. The Renaissance gave it a new vitality. The change can be seen in the work of one man, Lorenzo Ghiberti. In the first set of bronze doors that he made for the Florentine Baptistery (2) he keeps within Gothic conventions: a quatrefoil frame and figures arranged in a single plane. In the second (3) he enlarges the field, exploits recession in depth and depicts several episodes of the story in sequence. The supreme master of relief was Donatello, who in a depth of a few millimetres can give the impression of vast spaces – note the receding vaults behind the grille in the panel shown here (1). Jacopo della Quercia (4), within similar limitations, achieves a sensation of weight that anticipates Michelangelo; Agostino di Duccio (5) a lightness that is almost Hellenistic. Desiderio's tabernacle (8) combines perspective relief, forming a frame for the cupboard holding consecrated bread, with sculpture in the round. By the mid-16th century Germany (6) and France (7) had themselves fully absorbed the classical language of sculpture, though always remaining more decorative than dramatic.

1. Donatello:
St Mary Magdalene
(c. 1455).

2. Giambologna:
The Rape of the Sabines (1579–83).

3. Michelangelo: *Moses* (1513–16).

4. Bartolomeo Ammanati: Fountain of Neptune, Florence (1563–75).

5. Jacopo Sansovino: *Neptune* (1567).

Sculpture: a new dimension

No aspect of Renaissance art is more astonishing than the sudden flowering of sculpture. The impact of classical precedent, predictable in figures such as Neptune (4, 5), cannot alone account for it. Much of Donatello's work, seen on previous pages, is Roman in inspiration, but his long life was one of endless invention and unflagging brilliance, looking back to Gothic and forward (apparently) to expressionism. His late St Mary Magdalene (1) conveys an agonized intensity which leaves conventional beauty far behind. Michelangelo inherited Donatello's legacy, producing in works like his over-lifesize Moses (3) images of energy and power that reflect his own giant personality. After him Giambologna, among others, exploited the possibilities of dynamic movement involving the balance of bodies in motion (2). North of the Alps sculptors remained closer to the Gothic tradition, both in the nude (7) and especially in the virtuoso use of drapery (8, 9). The only parallel to Michelangelo, a century before him, is Claus Sluter, greatest of Burgundian sculptors, whose Moses (6) has comparable weight and authority.

8. Veit Stoss: *Virgin and Child* (late 15th century).

7. Tilman Riemenschneider: *Eve* (1491–93).

9. Tilman Riemenschneider: *St John the Evangelist* (1490–92).

6. Claus Sluter: *Moses* (1395–1403).

264

REBUILDING ANTIQUITY

❦

FROM the early years of the 15th century the search for the architecture of Antiquity accompanied the search for its literature. In both cases discovery and recovery went hand in hand with ideals of preservation and reconstruction. Just as Petrarch applied his scholarship to reconstituting the text and complete literary form of Livy, so Brunelleschi and others applied their investigations to recovering the architectural forms of ancient buildings. The destruction of ancient monuments and statues seemed as unforgivable as the neglect of precious manuscripts. Yet laments for losses continued. In the second decade of the 16th century, as in the second decade of the 15th, people were reported to be burning ancient marble to make lime, or quarrying buildings for dressed stone. The popes themselves were guilty of such pillage. The new bridge over the Tiber which Sixtus IV built to ease traffic congestion (after more than a hundred people had died in the crush on the Ponte S. Angelo during the 1450 Jubilee) used stone from the Colosseum.

Filippo Brunelleschi and Donatello went to Rome from Florence probably not long after 1401, in order to study ancient monuments. The two friends jointly carried on their investigations, making drawings and measurements of everything they could see, hiring labourers and arranging excavations to uncover design features (such as joints) which they could not otherwise reach. It was a pioneering venture. At the time it seemed that nobody was, or had for centuries been interested in ancient building methods, and Brunelleschi was deeply committed both to discovering the means by which the Romans had overcome complicated structural problems, and to the analysis of classical ornament and style.

Brunelleschi and Donatello were dubbed treasure-hunters by Romans who did not think of treasure in terms of detailed drawings. They were to learn better. Many others followed in the footsteps of the two Florentines. From Ciriaco d'Ancona in the 1430s to Maerten van Heemskerck (p. 279), Francisco de Holanda and Hendrik Goltzius in the 16th century, and long after, artists came to observe, learn and record, so that a great deal is known about the appearance of Rome through the Renaissance period.

What was seen and recorded above ground and recovered from below ground complemented the fresh knowledge of the page. Brunelleschi's observations about the characteristics of Doric, Tuscan, Ionic and Corinthian styles could be placed alongside Vitruvius (pp. 268–69). The text of Vitruvius' *De architectura*, which covered both the theory and practice of building, was the only technical treatise of its kind to survive from Antiquity, and Poggio's discovery of a manuscript at St Gallen in 1416 proved a great inspiration. Vitruvius became a positively biblical text book for Renaissance architects from Leon Battista Alberti to Christopher Wren. Alberti's own architectural treatise, *De re aedificatoria* (of the 1450s, though he worked on it until he died), was followed by a sequence of other architectural treatises, commenting on and emulating Vitruvius. The books of Sebastiano Serlio and Andrea Palladio proved enormously influential from the dates of their publication in the 16th century, and Vitruvius' own text, having been printed in its original

Ancient Rome *fascinated Antoine Caron, a 16th-century artist of the School of Fontainebleau. His* Massacre under the Triumvirate *(1566) is an unusual choice of subject – the Triumvirs were Octavius, Antony and Lepidus who staged a bloody revenge on the supporters of Brutus and Cassius after the murder of Julius Ceasar – and no doubt reflects the savagery that he had seen in the French Wars of Religion. (The fact that he was Catherine de Médicis' favourite painter gives it an uncannily prophetic look, though it was painted six years before the Massacre of St Bartholomew.) Caron invokes ancient Rome by crowding together all the well-known monuments. The Triumvirs sit in the middle of the Colosseum. Behind them stands the Pyramid of Cestius and behind that the Pantheon. To left and right are the Vatican obelisk and the Septizonium, a tower demolished under Sixtus V.*

Drawing of the Pantheon, Rome, by Domenico Ghirlandaio, with details of the sculptural decoration (15th century).

Title page of the first Italian translation of Alberti's De re aedificatoria, *1550, with the river-god of the Tiber in the foreground, and behind him an obelisk, the temple of Vesta and Trajan's Column.*

Latin in Rome about 1486, appeared in numerous vernacular editions (including four in Italian and others in French and German before 1590).

Countless Renaissance buildings, inspired in varying degrees and ways by the architectural models of Antiquity, had appeared across Europe by 1600 (pp. 108–11). In the first instance painters took the lead. They enjoyed the ability to present models of rebuilt Antiquity, portraying in paint or drawing ideal towns and churches of a kind yet to be realized in stone and mortar. The representation of architecture was central to the art of perspective. As Serlio put it in the 1540s, 'no perspective workman can make any work without architecture, nor the architecture without perspective' (pp. 246–47). The revolutionary new science which made it possible, as Vasari wrote in praise of Masaccio, to imitate in paint 'all the living things of nature ... just as nature produced them' so that 'they truly appear to be alive', found expression in new kinds of designed, perfected space. Painters showing their virtuosity in this new realism produced plenty of imaginary classicized buildings and townscapes.

The picture of an ideal city attributed to Piero della Francesca (p. 270), designed with mathematical precision like *The Flagellation* (p. 247), has the same effect on the viewer as that which Antonio Manetti reported of the panel of the Piazza del Duomo in Florence, painted by Brunelleschi as an optical demonstration; it seemed 'absolutely real'. The unpeopled clarity of this carefully calculated piazza conveys a sense of space so immediately present it seems to be awaiting the spectator's footfall. The converging lines, particularly those of the patterned pavement (in *The Flagellation* they are worked out with such precision that it has been possible to reconstruct its size and design), place us in a regally central position (like that of a Stuart king with the perfect seat for watching a court masque) from which to enter this city, designed for our unique presence. This civic space, modulated for our entry, makes our arrival its fulfilment. Something of this joyous sense of spatial completion can be experienced on entering the beautifully proportioned space and colour of Brunelleschi's Pazzi Chapel at S. Croce in Florence (p. 276).

The centrally planned domed church (pp. 274–75) was an ideal Renaissance form – bringing Vitruvius to correct Gothic imperfections – which to begin with was more widely mooted in paint than actualized on the ground. Many representations of episodes from the New Testament or lives of the saints envisaged these events taking place in the cleanly articulated colonnades of a *plein-air* chapel or a planned piazza. Such pure visions of arcaded town squares were rarely achieved in practice, even if Pius II's Pienza (p. 271) took a good step in that direction. But the cathedral in Pienza has nothing in common with the centrally planned, centrally placed domed buildings painted by Piero della Francesca, Pinturicchio and Perugino, the last of whom gives a striking example of a symmetrical temple flanked by triumphal arches in his Sistine Chapel fresco of *Christ Giving the Keys to St Peter* (p. 274). But not all such visions remained two-dimensional. The building of Giuliano da Sangallo's S. Maria delle Carceri in Prato (p. 108) started soon after Perugino's fresco, and though different in appearance it embodied essentially the same plan of central dome and projecting arms set within a square.

Painters like Mantegna and Perugino could construct at will in paint the triumphal arches and centralized buildings of an idealized Antiquity. In fact, of course, nobody in the Renaissance tried to build another Pantheon or arch of Septimius Severus – let alone a Colosseum. The recovered architectural knowledge of the ancient past inspired many new buildings and monuments across the continent – and eventually across the world – but they were not copies. The use of the ancient vocabulary and forms, in building as in writing, inspired fresh developments.

The Colosseum (pp. 278–79) came to epitomize Rome itself, as well as lending its features to numerous buildings in the shape of superimposed orders, storied loggias and arcaded courtyards. In a marble relief on the doorframe of Isabella d'Este's studiolo in Mantua, the figure of Poetry with her harp stands in front of the Colosseum, just as in Maerten van Heemskerck's self-portrait (p. 279) the painter's inspiration is yoked to that majestic ruin. The great dome of the Pantheon, the model for domed churches, also became the symbolic vault to lend the immortal lustre of classical fame (pp. 276–77).

Antiquity lived on metamorphosed into Renaissance terms. Pyramid and obelisk gained fresh currency (pp. 286–87). Sixtus V gave obelisks a new role by re-erecting them as conspicuous markers in his new street planning of Rome, as well as by moving the ancient obelisk at the Vatican. The city's Pyramid of Cestius, a well-known landmark, had dictated the position of Bramante's Tempietto at S. Pietro in Montorio. As architectural symbols of Antiquity, obelisk and pyramid travelled far in contributing the flavour of antique models. It was an eclectic Antiquity which went beyond Vitruvius, witness the Chigi chapel in S. Maria del Popolo, Rome, the tomb of William the Silent, Delft, and the proposal in London to replace the cross on the Cheapside monument by a pyramid.

Renaissance builders were at the mercy of both their sources and also their desires. Emulation of classical forms always had areas of uncertainty, in which the improving power of the imagination had to extrapolate from the basis of what could be known. That might lead to out-classicizing Antiquity, as in the case of the villa, for which there were no sure models in texts or on the ground until Herculaneum and Pompeii were recovered in a later period. Elsewhere, the greater the familiarity with ancient forms, the greater the possibilities of twisting and adapting them to inventive new uses – like the famous arches of the Forum, not only turned into Renaissance gateways, but ingeniously adapted to make frontages for churches, châteaux and houses, and designs for tombs (pp. 280–81).

The heirs of Brunelleschi and Bramante did their work so well that Antiquity came to be not so much rebuilt, as simultaneously excavated and extended. To go from the Roman Forum to the Campidoglio and St Peter's is to move between worlds that were indivisibly united and inescapably apart.

An ideal city (mid-15th century) features the Colosseum, the Arch of Constantine and an octagonal building not unlike the Florentine Baptistery.

The Colosseum forms the background to Giancristoforo Romano's relief of Poetry in the studiolo of Isabella d'Este at Mantua (1497–1505).

1. The Colosseum, Rome (1st century AD).

2. Alberti: façade of the Palazzo Rucellai, Florence (1446).

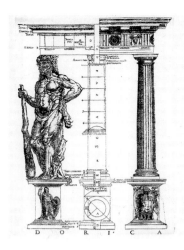

3, 4. Two woodcuts from John Shute's *First and Chief Groundes of Architecture* (1563).

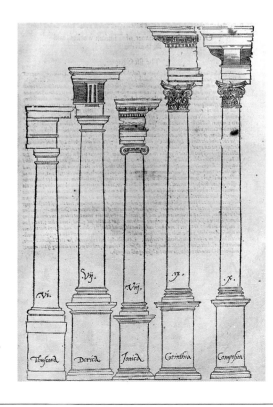

The classical orders

THE key to the classical style was the orders – the four types of column (5) whose use was governed by rules which dictated the proportion of height to width, the design of base, capital and entablature and how they could be placed in relation to each other. There were two sources of information for architects. One was the only surviving treatise on architecture by Vitruvius, who characterized Doric as 'masculine' and Ionic as 'feminine' (3, 4). The other was the actual remains of Roman buildings, the most influential of which was the Colosseum (1); where Doric, Ionic, Corinthian and Composite appeared one above the other. The first to use the three main orders on a palace was Alberti in the Palazzo Rucellai (2). The idea was taken up as an exciting novelty by architects in Spain (6), France (7) and England (8). Palladio (9) reduced the orders to a strict discipline, but by the later 16th century architects were already tiring of correctness and inventing new variants without classical precedent (10–12).

5. Sebastiano Serlio: the four orders of classical architecture with, at the beginning, the extra 'Tuscan' order. The columns are shown unfluted (1537).

6. The Palace of Charles V, Granada, Spain (1526).

7. Frontispiece of the Château of Anet, France; now in Paris (c. 1550).

8. Tower of the Orders, Bodleian Library, Oxford (c. 1620).

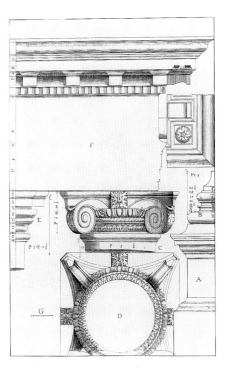

9. Palladio: the Ionic order from *Quattro libri dell'architettura* (1570).

10. Philibert de l'Orme: design for the 'French' order (1568).

11. Giulio Romano: Porta Citadella, Mantua (1540s).

12. Giulio Romano: detail from the Palazzo del Tè, Mantua (1527–34).

1. View of an ideal city attributed to Piero della Francesca (mid-15th century).

2, 3. Michelangelo: the Campidoglio, Rome (begun 1536).

Planned urban space

Renaissance town-planning was based less on antique models than on a love of geometry. Painters and architects were haunted by the idea of the perfect city. Piero della Francesca (1) was only one of those who explored it in their imagination. Filarete's fictitious Sforzinda (5) was actually worked out in some detail. Only rarely, however, could an entire town be planned as a single whole. One example is Palmanova (6), a fortified town designed from scratch by Giulio Savorgnano with an eye to symmetry as much as to defence. Another is in faraway Poland, where Zamosc (9) was laid out by an Italian engineer between 1581 and 1600. More normally urbanistic ideas had to be applied to a part only. Alberti's hierarchy of architectural types, distinguishing religious, civic and domestic uses, was partially realized at Pienza (7), replanned by Pius II in his own honour. Michelangelo restored to the Campidoglio (2, 3) its ancient function as the symbolic focus of secular Rome, while Vasari in Florence (4) experimented with long vistas of identical buildings ending with a screen onto the Arno. Pages 162–63 have shown how these ideas were taken up in France (8) and England.

4. Giorgio Vasari: the Uffizi, Florence (begun 1560).

The spell of the Antique, 54–55

Defensible spaces, 164–65

Triumphal arches, 280–81

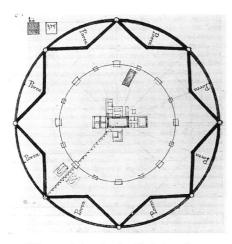

5. Filarete: design for the ideal city of Sforzinda (1460–64).

7. Main square of Pienza; cathedral on the left, bishop's palace on the right (mid-15th century).

6. Palmanova from the air.

8. Project for the Place de France, Paris, not executed (1641).

9. Main square of Zamosc, Poland, laid out by Bernardo Morando (1581–c. 1600).

Gothic survival

THE revival of classicism in the mid-15th century came naturally to Italy, where the classical tradition was so deeply rooted that it never really died. In the north, however, it had been forgotten or never known, and was introduced as an alien style, wholly Italian in its associations and at odds with the prevailing Gothic vocabulary. In both painting and architecture the result was often an uneasy mixture. Jan Gossaert (1) combines a classical foreground with a Gothic fountain and porch in the background. In Jean Fouquet's miniature (2) Gothic preserves its religious associations, as it long did (and still does), as a setting for the Virgin and Child, while the left part, more secular, is classical. Filarete (3) gives us Gothic windows under a classical arcade; Bremen Town Hall (5) clothes Gothic gables in classical dress; while at St Eustache in Paris (4) and Granada Cathedral (6), churches that are entirely Gothic in structure are re-styled in the classical idiom of columns and pilasters. At a humbler level, on an English tomb (7), up-to-date Renaissance putti happily share the task of supporting shields with medieval Gothic angels.

2. Page from the *Book of Hours of Etienne Chevalier* by Jean Fouquet (*c.* 1460).

1. Detail from Jan Gossaert, called Mabuse, *St Luke Drawing the Virgin* (1515).

3. Antonio Filarete: Ospedale Maggiore, Milan (*c.* 1460).

4. Interior of St Eustache, Paris (early 16th century).

6. Interior of Granada Cathedral (early 16th century).

5. Bremen Town Hall (16th century).

7. Detail from the De la Warr Tomb, Boxgrove, Sussex (1526).

1. The Pantheon, Rome (2nd century AD).

2. Antonio da Sangallo the Elder: S. Maria presso S. Biagio, Montepulciano (begun 1518).

The central-space church

CHURCHES with centralized plans – that is, symmetrical in all four directions – were unpopular with the clergy because they were liturgically impractical, but they had an irresistible appeal to architects, on both aesthetic and philosophical (Neoplatonic) grounds. Geometry, especially the circle, the perfect figure, was the visual expression of divine perfection, and hence ideally fitting for a place of worship. It also had the model of the best preserved of all antique buildings, the circular Pantheon (1), now transformed into a church. Finally, the Temple in Jerusalem, through a misidentification with the Dome of the Rock, was always represented as circular (4). Both Giuliano and Antonio da Sangallo had experimented with the symmetrical plan (2). Bramante had made it the basis for his new St Peter's (5, 6) and built his tiny Tempietto (7) in imitation of a Roman temple of Vesta. Leonardo, not an architect, probably knew Bramante in Milan. His sketches for centralized churches, exercises in pure form (3) must have been known in humanist circles: do they lie behind the mysterious church of S. Maria della Consolazione at Todi (8), for which no architect is known? With even less practicality, Palladio applied the centralized plan to domestic architecture. The four flights of stairs and four porticoes of the Villa Rotonda (9) are not in any way functional, but proved a tempting model for the future.

3. Leonardo da Vinci: sketch design for churches (c. 1490).

4. Perugino: detail from *Christ Giving the Keys to St Peter* with the Temple in the background (1481–82).

Christian classicism, 108–09

Planned urban space, 270–71

The rise of the dome, 276–77

5. Foundation medal for Bramante's St Peter's (1506).

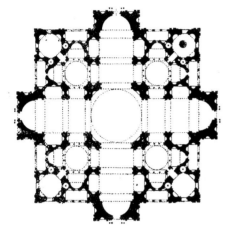

6. Bramante's plan for St Peter's (1506).

8. S. Maria della Consolazione, Todi (begun 1508).

7. Bramante: Tempietto in the cloister of S. Pietro in Montorio, Rome (1502).

9. Palladio: Villa Rotonda, near Vicenza (1550).

1. Brunelleschi: dome of Florence Cathedral (1419–46).

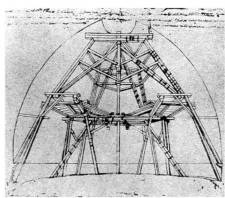

2. Scaffolding for the dome of Florence Cathedral (early 15th century).

3. Brunelleschi: the Pazzi Chapel, Florence (1429–46).

The rise of the dome

IN 1418 Filippo Brunelleschi was faced with a problem: how to cover the huge crossing space that had been somewhat optimistically left by the medieval architect of Florence Cathedral. His solution was a high octagonal dome on a drum (1), a structure that had no precedent, either classical or Byzantine, though the model of the Pantheon (p. 274) was important. Technically, it was an amazing feat, and exactly how it was done is still a mystery. The scaffolding had to rest on beams inserted into the masonry, as shown in a drawing probably from Brunelleschi's workshop (2). Others followed his lead. Bramante's S. Maria delle Grazie in Milan (4) was a simpler operation, but the dome he proposed for St Peter's (6) was even bigger than Florence. In the event it was built by Michelangelo (5), and immediately became a challenge and an inspiration to the whole of Europe. In Spain, the Escorial was finished by 1581. The first dome north of the Alps was in Belgium after 1600 (7), soon to be followed by France (8).

4. Bramante: dome of S. Maria delle Grazie, Milan (begun 1492).

5. Michelangelo: dome of St Peter's, Rome (designed *c.* 1560; completed after Michelangelo's death).

6. Bramante: design for the dome of St Peter's (1506).

7. Notre Dame, Scherpenheuvel, Belgium (1609).

8. Church of the Sorbonne, Paris (begun 1635).

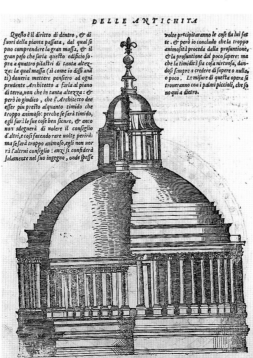

Rebuilding Antiquity   277

1. The Colosseum, Rome (1st century AD).

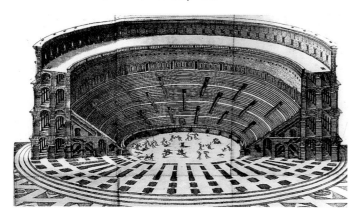

2. A Flemish drawing of the Colosseum (1584).

The Colosseum

THE Colosseum (1) was the biggest and among the best preserved of ancient Roman buildings. Famous throughout the Middle Ages, it was drawn or painted by every visiting artist (2, 3), and became almost an emblem of the city. Maerten van Heemskerck painted himself next to it (6), and Mantegna included it, along with the Pyramid of Cestius, in the background of the Camera degli Sposi (5). Architecturally it was highly influential, both for its superimposition of the orders and for the way it threaded a minor order supporting arches through the main order of semi-columns, a device adopted by Palladio, for example, in the Basilica at Vicenza (4). More remotely, it provided the model for Bruegel's *Tower of Babel* (7), where it rises into the clouds in an apparently infinite extension.

4. Palladio: Basilica, Vicenza (1546–50).

3. Antonio da Sangallo the Younger: section and view of the Colosseum (1504–05).

The ruins of Rome, 56–57

Rome, 156–57

The classical orders, 268–69

6. Maerten van Heemskerck: self-portrait with Colosseum in the background (1553).

5. Mantegna: detail from the Camera degli Sposi, Palazzo Ducale, Mantua (1470–74).

7. Pieter Bruegel the Elder: *The Tower of Babel*, detail (1563).

1. Botticelli: detail from *The Punishment of Cora* (1481–82).

3. Michelangelo: the Porta Pia, Rome (1561).

4. Entrance to the Castel Nuovo, Naples, with sculpture by Francesco Laurana (*c.* 1452–58).

2. The Arch of Constantine, Rome (4th century AD).

The ruins of Rome, 56–57

The classical orders, 268–69

Planned urban space, 270–71

5. Triumphal arch erected for the state entry of James I into London (1604).

7. Alberti: façade of the Tempio Malatestiano, Rimini (c. 1450).

8. Philibert de l'Orme: entrance to the Château of Anet (c. 1550).

6. Triumphal arch designed for the entry of Philip II into Brussels (1574).

Triumphal arches

A number of ancient triumphal arches survived more or less intact in Italian cities, potent symbols of Roman domination, the most famous being the Arch of Constantine (2). Botticelli incorporated it verbatim in one of his frescoes (1). In real life there was little call for triumphal arches, except temporary ones for the entry of great personages into cities (5, 6), which could, however, be of the greatest elaboration. Otherwise the form could be adapted for town-gates (3), the entrances to castles and châteaux (4, 8) and the façades of churches (7). The triumphal arch, thus revived by the Renaissance, was to have a long subsequent history, from the Brandenberg Gate in Berlin to British memorials of the First World War.

1. Palladio: Teatro Olimpico, Vicenza, with perspective scenery by Scamozzi (1586 and later).

The theatre

THE humanists were fascinated by Greek and Roman drama and longed to revive the plays in a classical setting. The ruins of several Roman theatres survived, and Vitruvius gave an account of the principles of their construction. But outdoor theatres on a Roman scale were not practical, nor was it at all clear how the plays were to be staged. Cesariano's reconstruction (2), based on his reading of Vitruvius, produced a building not unlike a small Colosseum. Palladio went to surviving theatres for this model; his reconstruction, published in an edition of Vitruvius (3), and his actual theatre at Vicenza (1) are as close as the Renaissance ever came to the real thing. Vitruvius also described three kinds of scenery – 'tragic', 'comic' (9) and 'rustic' – but they proved hard to reconcile with the actual buildings. Editions of Plautus and Terence (6, 8) sometimes tried to show how the plays would work in the theatre, and some stages in the Netherlands were built on the same lines (5). In England the Elizabethan theatre descended chiefly from inn-yards where plays were originally staged, but attempts were made to align them with the Vitruvian model – hence the circular shape and classical columns (4). A few later theatres, such as Inigo Jones' Cockpit-at-Court (7), adapted the classical form to a tiny scale, but the future lay with the proscenium theatre (10), where the only classical allusion would be the scenery.

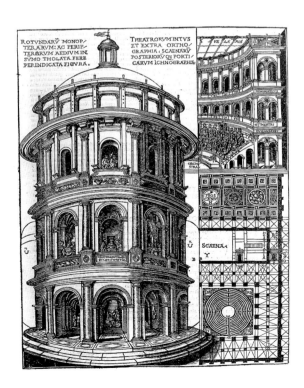

2. Cesariano: reconstruction of a Roman theatre from an edition of Vitruvius (1521).

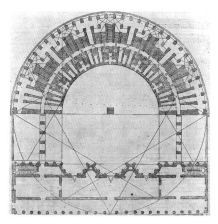

3. Palladio: reconstruction of a Roman theatre from Barbaro's edition of Vitruvius (1556).

4. The interior of the Swan Theatre, London (c. 1596).

5. A stage in Antwerp (1561).

COLISEVS SI VE THEATRVM

6. A Roman theatre from a Venetian edition of Terence (1497).

9. Sebastiano Serlio: 'comic scene' from Vitruvius (1569).

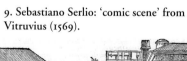

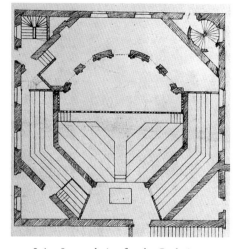

7. Inigo Jones: design for the Cockpit-at-Court Theatre, Whitehall, London (1629–30).

8. Illustration from a French edition of Terence (15th century).

10. Inigo Jones: proscenium stage with set for a tragic scene (early 17th century).

1. Villa Medici, Cafaggiolo (*c.* 1443–52).

2. Villa Medici, Careggi (remodelled by Michelozzo, 1430s).

4. Villa Medici, Fiesole, by Michelozzo (*c.* 1455).

3. Villa Medici, Poggio a Caiano, by Giuliano da Sangallo (1485).

5. Pratolino, villa built for Francesco I of Tuscany (*c.* 1570). Painting by Giusto Utens (1598).

The gentry at play, 96–97

The art of the garden, 170–71

Water for recreation and work, 234–35

6. Palladio: Villa Barbaro, Maser (1557–58).

7, 8. Palladio: front and rear elevation of the Villa Malcontenta on the Brenta (c. 1558–60).

Villa life

Aᴮᴼᵁᵀ the middle of the 15th century, a new style of living came into fashion among the gentry of central Italy. It began with the Medici. Members of that family took to spending part of the year in the country, sharing the pursuits of the rural inhabitants and congratulating themselves on getting away from the hot and crowded city – the beginning of an attitude that we take for granted today. At first they stayed at the old fortified farm-houses that had protected their estates in the later Middle Ages (1, 2). But reading Virgil's praise of country life and Pliny's account of his villas, they soon began to require something more refined, little country palaces where they could relax, entertain friends, read and hear music (3, 4, 5). Where Florence led, Venice followed. Palladio's villas on the Venetian mainland – part working farms, part country retreats – mark the apogee of the form (6, 7, 8). His publication of them in the *Quattro libri* meant that they could be imitated everywhere. England was among the first. The Queen's House at Greenwich (9) is essentially a grand villa, though it was not until the Palladian Revival in the 18th century that villas became as native to England as they were to Italy.

9. Inigo Jones: the Queen's House, Greenwich (1617).

1. Engraving by Domenico Fontana showing the Vatican obelisk standing in its original location next to the Sacristy of St Peter's with demonstrations of how it was to be moved (1590).

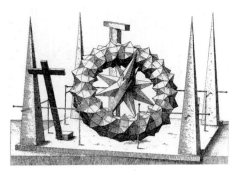

2. Jost Amman: regular solids, including the obelisk (1568).

3. The Vatican obelisk under scaffolding (1590).

4. The Vatican obelisk in its new location in front of St Peter's (1590).

The ruins of Rome, 56–57

Funerary monuments of the north, 102–03

Rome, 156–57

5. Tomb of William of Orange, Delft; detail from a painting by Bartolomeus van Bassen (1620).

7. Antoine Caron: detail from *Augustus and the Sybil* (late 16th century).

Obelisks: 'star-y-pointing pyramids'

R ENAISSANCE writers made no distinction between obelisks
and pyramids. Both came from Egypt, the source of
everything that was most ancient. The Romans had plundered
several Egyptian obelisks and set them up at key points in Rome,
where they remained all through the Middle Ages and where
Renaissance antiquarians tried in vain to read their hieroglyphs.
The most famous was that imported by Nero and erected in what
had been his Circus, to the south of St Peter's (1). In 1586 Pope
Sixtus V ordered Domenico Fontana to move it to its present
location in front of the basilica (4). It was an outstanding feat
of engineering (3), watched by thousands and recorded in a
sumptuous publication by the architect. Obelisks never lost their
association with Antiquity and the commemoration of the past.
One appears in the background of Antoine Caron's *Augustus
and the Sybil* (7), fancifully set in the Tuileries Gardens under
Catherine de Médicis. They rise over the tomb of William of
Orange at Delft (5) and are the main feature of William Cecil's
prodigy house at Burghley (6).

6. Courtyard of Burghley House, Stamford (1577–85).

1. Domenico Beccafumi: *The Fall of the Rebel Angels* (1524–25).

2. Bernardo Buontalenti: Porta delle Suppliche, Uffizi, Florence (1580).

3. Michelangelo and others: staircase of the Laurentian Library, Florence (*c.* 1520, completed 1550s).

Mannerism: an end or a beginning?

No artist is content to repeat what others have already done. The painters, architects and sculptors of the later 16th century in Italy had inevitably to move on. The style now called Mannerism represented a gain in complexity, wit, novelty and surprise. It lost in balance, repose and heroic dignity. The change is conventionally traced to Michelangelo, whose creative impulse was so strong that he seems often to be inventing difficulties in order to solve them. His staircase of the Laurentian Library in Florence (3) is unlike any staircase before it, in a room in which all the elements – walls, columns, consoles – conspicuously fail to

function as one would expect. It is therefore no great surprise when we find one of his followers, Bernardo Buontalenti, cutting a pediment in half and reversing the halves (2). However it may seem to later historians, this was not, for the architect, a denial or rejection of High Renaissance ideals, but a refinement of them. Painting followed the same path. Beccafumi's *Fall of the Rebel Angels* (1) does not aspire to clarity. It would be impossible to draw a plan of where all the figures are standing, nor is it obvious what everyone is doing or why. But these worries are in some ways more powerful, at least more disturbing, than certainty.

The Last Judgment, 146–47

The Sistine ceiling, 256–57

The grotesque, 258–59

Reference

Biographical Dictionary
Timelines · Map
Glossary · Gazetteer of Museums and Galleries
Bibliography · Sources of Illustrations
Index

BIOGRAPHICAL DICTIONARY

*This dictionary provides brief biographical information on the leading personalities in the book
and at the same time serves as an index to works by them or associated with them
(page number followed by illustration number) and notes on further reading.
Names in capital letters indicate cross-references to other entries.*

Abbate, Niccolò dell', *c.* 1509–71. Italian painter. He painted frescoes in Modena and Bologna and in 1552 travelled to France where he worked, under PRIMATICCIO's supervision, on the Mannerist decorations in FRANCOIS I's Palace of Fontainebleau. With Primaticcio and ROSSO FIORENTINO he is considered one of the leading figures of the First School of Fontainebleau.
Mythological Portrait of François I, 48–49 (4)
The Game of Tarot, 98–99 (6)
The Rape of Proserpine, 168–69 (3)

Agostino di Duccio, 1418–84. Italian sculptor. Born in Florence, he worked on ALBERTI's Tempio Malatestiano at Rimini, where with Matteo de' Pasti he carved the relief panels of the interior. He later moved to Perugia, where he worked on the façade of the Oratory of S. Bernardino, and to Bologna and Florence. His style is characterized by delicacy and charm.
Madonna and Child, 132–33 (5)
Tempio Malatestiano, Rimini: angel, 260–61 (5); Diana, relief of, 25; Sign of Cancer, the Crab, 216–17 (8)
John Pope-Hennessy, *The Virgin and Child by Agostino di Duccio*, 1952

Alberti, Leon Battista, 1404–72. Italian architect and writer. Alberti represents the ideal Renaissance 'universal man': a learned humanist, a practised writer, skilled in all the arts, a man of the world and a courtier. His influence was twofold – as a theorist and as a designer. His writings cover an amazing diversity of topics: architecture (*De re aedificatoria*, the Renaissance equivalent of Vitruvius, dealing with all aspects of building, in theory and practice); painting (*Della pittura*); sculpture (*De statua*); perspective (*Prospettiva*); archaeology (*Descriptio urbis Romae*); mathematics (*Ludi*); and ethics (*Momus*, *Della famiglia* and *Della tranquillità dell'anima*). Alberti also wrote comedies, played musical instruments, painted and sculpted. His fame as an architect rests on four buildings, none of which was finished in the way he intended: the Tempio Malatestiano, Rimini; S. Sebastiano and S. Andrea, Mantua; and the Palazzo Rucellai, Florence. Following BRUNELLESCHI's lead, Alberti combined geometry (involving calculated mathematical proportions) with the use of the classical orders. He was the first to apply the orders to a palace front and to use the triumphal arch as a motif in a church façade. His completion of the façade of S. Maria Novella, Florence,

introduced the idea of scrolls connecting the lower and upper storeys.
Medal by Matteo de' Pasti, 244–45 (3, 4)
De re aedificatoria, title page of, 266
Palazzo Rucellai, Florence, 268–69 (2)
S. Andrea, Mantua, 110–11 (3)
S. Maria Novella, Florence, 108–09 (1)
Tempio Malatestiano, Rimini, 280–81 (7)
F. Borsi, *Leon Battista Alberti: The Complete Works*, 1989

Alexander VI, Pope, 1431–1503. Pope from 1492. Born Rodrigo BORGIA in Spain, he was the nephew of Pope Callixtus III. His papacy has become a byword for corruption and venality. Most of his energies went into expanding his temporal power in Italy and enriching his sons Giovanni and Cesare and his daughter Lucrezia. He was, however, a lavish patron of the arts. BRAMANTE, RAPHAEL and MICHELANGELO all worked for him, and PINTURICCHIO immortalized him in the frescoes of the so-called Borgia Apartments in the Vatican.
Portrait by Pinturicchio, 66–67 (2)
Arnold Harris Mathew, *The Life and Times of Rodrigo Borgia, Pope Alexander VI*, 1912
M. Mallett, *The Borgias*, 1981

Alfonso V, medal by Cristoforo di Geremia, 15th century.

Alfonso V, 1432–81. King of Portugal from 1438. His reign saw the beginning of the great age of Portuguese exploration.
Portrait by Nuño Gonçalves, 70–71 (7)
A. Ryder, *The Kingdom of Naples under Alfonso the Magnanimous*, 1976
———, *Alfonso the Magnanimous, King of Aragon, Naples and Sicily, 1396–1458*, 1990

Alsloot, Denis van, died 1628. Flemish painter.
The Ommeganck Procession, 90–91 (2)
James Laver, *Isabella's Triumph*, 1947

Altdorfer, Albrecht, *c.* 1480–1538. German painter. Born and died at Regensburg, he belonged to the 'Danube School', working in a northern tradition but influenced by Italian art through engravings and above all through DURER; he seems never to have gone to Italy. His subjects included Old and New Testament scenes, landscapes, mythology and classical history.
Battle of the Issus, 84–85 (4), 168–69 (5)
Couple Embracing, 192–93 (4)
Landscape of the Danube near Regensburg, 166–67 (9)
St George and the Dragon, 168–69 (4)
Emil Waldmann, *Albrecht Altdorfer*, 1923
Christopher S. Wood, *Albrecht Altdorfer and the Origins of Landscape*, 1993

Amman, Jost, 1539–91. Swiss artist. He settled in Nuremberg and became a prolific illustrator of the Bible and other subjects.
Allegory of Commerce, 232–33 (6)
Regular solids, sketch of, 286–87 (2)
Sculptor's workshop, 186–87 (3)

Ammanati, Bartolomeo, 1511–92. Italian sculptor and architect. Greatly influenced by MICHELANGELO, his most famous sculptural commission was the Fountain of Neptune in the Piazza della Signoria, Florence. His architectural work in Florence included the Ponte S. Trinita, and the enlargement of the Palazzo Pitti.
Fountain of Neptune, Florence, 262–63 (4)

Andrea del Sarto, 1486–1530. Italian painter. Born and trained in Florence under PIERO DI COSIMO, Sarto epitomizes the transition from the High Renaissance style of RAPHAEL to that of Mannerism. He was the master of ROSSO FIORENTINO and PONTORMO. FRANCOIS I invited him to come to Paris but he returned to Florence after a year. Technically perfect, Sarto combined Venetian colour with Florentine *disegno*, producing mostly religious works that were both charming and powerful. He worked chiefly in oil, but carried out fresco cycles in the cloisters of the Scalzi and SS. Annunziata, Florence.
Madonna of the Harpies, 132–33 (2)
Sydney J. Freedberg, *Andrea del Sarto*, 1963
John Shearman, *Andrea del Sarto*, 1965

Angelico, Fra, active 1417–died 1455. Italian painter. Born and trained in Florence, he entered the Dominican convent of S. Marco about 1420 and spent the rest of his life in the service of his order. His paintings, although taking account of the innovation of MASACCIO, look back to the Middle Ages in the simple directness of their Christian message. They range from large-scale compositions involving hosts of saints and angels to the austere suffering Christs that he painted in the cells of his Dominican brethren.

Bosco ai Frari Altarpiece, 136–37 (5)
St Lawrence Distributing Alms, 126–27 (1)
Saints Cosmas and Damian, 198–99 (5)
The Transfiguration, 144–45 (3)
Giulio C. Argan, *Fra Angelico: Biographical and Critical Study*, 1955
John Pope-Hennessy, *Fra Angelico*, 2nd ed., 1974

Sofonisba Anguissola, self-portrait, 1561.

Anguissola, Sofonisba, *c.* 1532–1625. Italian painter. She was a member of a noble family from Cremona, allowed by her father to study painting with a local artist – something quite exceptional for a gentlewoman. In 1554 she travelled to Rome, where she sketched the antiquities, and also met MICHELANGELO. Mainly occupied with portraiture of herself and her family, she also undertook important commissions, such as portraying the Duke of Alba. Invited to the court of PHILIP II in 1559, she spent several years in Spain where she taught painting to the Queen and produced many fine royal portraits. One of the first women painters to achieve fame, she was included by VASARI in his *Lives*.

Bernardino Campi painting her portrait, 194–95 (2)

Antonello da Messina, 1430–79. Italian painter. Though he was born and died in Messina, Antonello travelled widely – to Florence, Rome and Venice – and is credited by VASARI with learning the technique of oil painting from Flemish artists and introducing it to Italy. He certainly knew the work of Petrus CHRISTUS, and his *S. Cassiano*

Altarpiece in Venice (only a fragment survives) profoundly influenced Giovanni BELLINI and the whole Venetian School.

Stefano Bottari, *Antonello da Messina*, 1957
Giorgio Vigni, *All the Paintings of Antonello da Messina*, 1963

Arcimboldi, Giuseppe, 1527–93. Italian painter. Chiefly remembered for his inventive and witty paintings of fantastic heads composed from vegetables, flowers and other natural objects. Originally from Milan, he spent many years as a painter at the HABSBURG courts of Vienna and Prague.

The Market-gardener, 258–59 (6)

Aretino, Pietro, 1492–1556. Italian author. Aretino's talent for amusing satire made him welcome at the courts of Pope LEO X in Rome and Giovanni de' MEDICI in Florence until he made these cities too hot for himself and retreated to Venice. Here he prospered by blackmail, pornography and comedy, and attracted a wide circle of friends, including TITIAN.

Portrait by Titian, 38–39 (7)
James Cleugh, *The Divine Aretino*, 1965
Christopher Cairns, *Pietro Aretino and the Republic of Venice*, 1985

Ariosto, Ludovico, 1474–1533. Italian poet. Although he wished to devote his life to literary studies, his father made him study law and in 1500, at his father's death, he was required to assume responsibility as head of a large family. He entered the service of the ESTE family in Ferrara in 1501, undertaking military, administrative and diplomatic roles over many years. He is famous for his romantic epic, *Orlando furioso*, a poem first published in 1516, but continually revised by Ariosto throughout his life. Written in the eight-line Italian stanza, *ottava rima*, it continues the theme of Boiardo's *Orlando innamorato* into which Ariosto also wove a celebration of the Este family. Based on the medieval stories of Charlemagne and his knights, it transforms the heroic atmosphere into one of love and magic, treated with a mixture of irony and humour. Episodes from it were favourite subjects for decorative paintings. In 1525 Ariosto was finally able to settle quietly in Ferrara and concentrate on studying and writing. He also made a contribution to the development of drama, writing vernacular comedies in imitation of Latin models.

Portrait by Palma Vecchio, 38–39 (1)
Orlando furioso, title page of, 38–39 (14)
Robert Griffin, *Ludovico Ariosto*, 1974
Robert J. Rodini, *Ludovico Ariosto, an Annotated Bibliography of Criticism*, 1984

Ascham, Roger, 1515–68. English humanist and writer. Educated at Cambridge, he was a distinguished scholar and was appointed reader in Greek at St John's College in 1538. He was a tutor to the young Princess Elizabeth, and later travelled widely in Europe

while serving as secretary to the English ambassador to CHARLES V. He is known for *The Schoolmaster*; a book written in clear English prose and published posthumously in 1570, which concentrates chiefly on the learning of Latin. He also wrote *Toxophilus* (1545), the first book on archery in English, which is written in a dialogue form.

Lawrence Vincent Ryan, *Roger Ascham*, 1963
Jerome Steele Dees, *Sir Thomas Elyot and Roger Ascham*, 1981

Francis Bacon by William Marshall, early 17th century.

Bacon, Francis, 1561–1626. English philosopher and writer. Educated at Cambridge, he subsequently studied law and entered parliament in 1584. He held a number of important official appointments in the reigns of ELIZABETH I and JAMES I, finally becoming Lord Chancellor in 1618. His career as a statesman ended in 1621 when he faced charges of corruption, and he devoted the rest of his life to philosophy and literature. His *Novum organum* (1620), based on a belief that investigation and experiment could lead to universal knowledge, gives him a claim to be considered one of the fathers of the modern scientific method. He wrote other works on philosophy and law, and is also remembered for his wide-ranging *Essays* (final edition 1625).

Anthony Quinton, *Francis Bacon*, 1980
Ian Box, *The Social Thought of Francis Bacon*, 1989

Baldassare Estense, active 15th century. Italian painter and medallist who worked mostly in Milan.

Family of Umberto de' Sacrati, 190–91 (7)

Baldovinetti, Alesso, 1425–99. Italian painter. A member of a wealthy Florentine family, he was apprenticed for a short period to DOMENICO VENEZIANO, and his carefully detailed religious panels are characterized by elegant and refined figures. For his wall paintings he used a technically unstable combination consisting of true fresco overlaid with tempera details. A few of his frescoes survive in deteriorated condition and most, like the *Nativity* in SS. Annunziata, Florence, have entirely lost their tempera overpainting.

Ruth W. Kennedy, *Alesso Baldovinetti, A Critical and Historical Study*, 1938

Baldung Grien, Hans, 1485–1545. German painter and engraver. Probably trained by DÜRER in Nuremberg, he settled in Strasbourg where he eventually became a city councillor. In common with his German contemporaries, he produced not only paintings but also a large number of drawings, woodcuts and prints. Although he painted religious subjects, most notably the large-scale polyptych for the high altar in Freiburg Cathedral, many secular works and portraits also feature in his output. Always highly inventive, his later work is dominated by grim allegories of life and death, and representations of the supernatural.

Das Buch Granatapfel, title page of, 116–17 (3)
The Knight, the Maiden and Death, 200–01 (7)
The Nativity, 130–31 (2)
Vanity, 46–47 (10)

James H. Marrow and Alan Shestack (eds), *Hans Baldung Grien, Prints and Drawings*, 1981

Bandinelli, Baccio, 1493–1560. Italian goldsmith, sculptor and painter. The leading sculptor in Florence after MICHELANGELO's departure for Rome in 1534, he enjoyed the patronage of Cosimo I de' MEDICI. His emulation of Michelangelo can be seen in *Hercules and Cacus*, a free-standing composition placed in the Piazza della Signoria, Florence, to counterbalance Michelangelo's *David*. The exaggerated musculature and deeply drilled features of the piece aroused satirical comment. Bandinelli's skill was better suited to low-relief carving, as seen in a memorable series of *Prophets* for the choir of Florence Cathedral. An accomplished draughtsman, he also produced engravings and paintings.

Hercules and Cacus, 50–51 (3)

Barbaro, Daniele, 1513–70. Italian scholar and patron. Member of a noble Venetian family, Barbaro served as ambassador to England, commissioned a villa from PALLADIO and published an edition of Vitruvius with Palladio's drawings.

Portrait by Veronese, 34–35 (3)

Bartolommeo, Fra, *c.* 1472–1517. Italian painter. Trained in Florence by Cosimo ROSSELLI, he became a Dominican friar under the influence and teaching of SAVONAROLA. Having taken Holy Orders, he resumed his career and worked, as Fra ANGELICO had before him, in the painting workshop of S. Marco, Florence. Following visits to Venice in 1508 and Rome in 1515, his colours became richer and his compositions more

monumental. Reducing worldly detail to a minimum, and concentrating on the depiction of the holy characters, his religious paintings are imbued with great reverence and awe. His influence, particularly felt in clarity of composition and a deeply folded drapery style, was spread through the circulation of his numerous drawings.

Leader Scott, *Fra Bartolommeo*, 1922

Bassano, Jacopo (Jacopo da Ponte), *c.* 1510–92. Italian painter. The most talented member of a dynasty of artists from Bassano in the Veneto. At first influenced by Venetian masters, he made a speciality of crowded scenes with shepherds and animals, and in his middle years he produced some highly individual Mannerist compositions. In his later work he developed considerable skill in the depiction of night scenes.

Earthly Paradise, 182–83 (4)

Battiferri, Laura, 1523–89. Italian poet. She spent most of her life in Florence and was in contact with the foremost humanists and intellectuals of the age. Her collection of madrigals, sonnets and other verse, *Primo libro delle opere toscane* (1560), received critical acclaim from leading literary figures, including TASSO. She was married to the architect and sculptor, AMMANATI.

Portrait by Bronzino, 194–95 (3)

Beccafumi, Domenico, *c.* 1486–1551. Italian painter. A major Sienese Mannerist, although his early style reflects his knowledge of Quattrocento Sienese masters. Visits to Rome and Florence in his late twenties proved extremely important for Beccafumi, most significantly through contact with the works of RAPHAEL and MICHELANGELO. Returning to Siena, he evolved his own style characterized by deep, dusky shadows contrasted dramatically against bright colour and light effects. Apart from religious subjects, he frescoed scenes from Greek and Roman history in Siena Town Hall, and produced designs for the marble pavement of Siena Cathedral.

The Fall of the Rebel Angels, 288 (1)

Bella, Stefano della, 1610–64. Italian engraver.

Entry of the Polish Ambassadors into Rome, 90–91 (5)

Bellini, Gentile, active *c.* 1460–died 1507. Italian painter. Elder brother of Giovanni BELLINI, he trained in the Venetian workshop of his father, Jacopo BELLINI, and painted a series of history paintings (since destroyed) for the Doge's Palace, Venice. From 1478 to 1481 he was at the court of Sultan Mehmet II in Constantinople and some notable portraits of the sultan feature among the paintings he produced there. He is chiefly remembered for his carefully observed anecdotal paintings of the ceremony and pageantry of Venice, such

as the *Procession of the Reliquary of the True Cross*, which gives a detailed rendering of St Mark's Square and incorporates portraits of members of the lay brotherhood taking part.

Portrait of Sultan Mehmet II, 58–59 (7)
Cardinal Bessarion Presenting a Reliquary of the True Cross, 58–59 (2)
Procession of the Reliquary of the True Cross, 88–89 (2)
St Mark Preaching in Alexandria, 58–59 (6)

Bellini, Giovanni, 1428–1516. Italian painter, younger son of Jacopo BELLINI. He was the outstanding Venetian master of his day who was largely responsible for turning Venice into a leading centre of artistic production, capable of rivalling Florence. His influence was immense, not only on his own pupils, GIORGIONE and TITIAN, but also on artists who visited Venice, such as DÜRER and Fra BARTOLOMMEO. His early style was close to that of his brother-in-law, MANTEGNA, and he was also influenced by ANTONELLO DA MESSINA; his style continued to evolve throughout a long active career into one uniquely personal. He is renowned for several specific types of religious composition: the half-length serene Madonna and Christ Child, where the Holy figures are set behind a parapet and are framed by an exquisite landscape; the half-length *pietà* with Christ supported by the Virgin and St John (a composition derived from Jacopo Bellini's sketchbook and DONATELLO's reliefs of the theme); and a series of large altarpieces of the Madonna and Child with Saints. This last group represents a remarkable development of the *sacra conversazione* and includes altarpieces for the Venetian churches of S. Giobbe and S. Zaccaria. He perfected a refined and smooth oil-painting technique, enabling him to create natural lighting effects and to achieve brilliant, saturated colours. A number of remarkable images attest to his consummate skill as a portraitist. His late work *Feast of the Gods* (1514) shows him integrating mythological figures into his favoured element of landscape, and reveals that he was aware of the pastoral themes being explored by his former pupils.

Allegory of Inconstancy, 46–47 (3)
Baptism of Christ, 134–35 (4)
Madonna of the Meadow, 166–67 (5)
Madonna of the Pomegranate, 132–33 (4)
Sacred Allegory, 46–47 (1)
S. Giobbe Altarpiece, 136–37 (4)
The Transfiguration, 144–45 (6)

Philip Hendy and Ludwig Goldscheider, *Giovanni Bellini*, 1945
Giles Robertson, *Giovanni Bellini*, 1968

Bellini, Jacopo, active 1424–died 1470/1. Italian painter. A Venetian artist who probably trained with GENTILE DA FABRIANO, and worked with him in Florence in 1424. Few of his paintings survive but two important sketchbooks (now in the Louvre and the British Museum) show his extraordinary range of subject-matter. They also attest to his outstanding skill as a draughtsman and display his complete mastery of perspective. These exquisite silverpoint sketchbooks provided rich compositional sources not only for his sons, Gentile and Giovanni BELLINI, but also for his son-in-law MANTEGNA, and other artists working in Venice.

Christiane L. Joost-Gaugier, *Jacopo Bellini, Selected Drawings*, 1980
Colin Eisler, *The Genius of Jacopo Bellini*, 1988

Pietro Bembo, woodcut, 16th century.

Bembo, Pietro, 1470–1547. Italian humanist, scholar and poet. He was born into a noble Venetian family. A great Latin scholar, and a student of Greek, he nonetheless proposed that the sweet and fluid Tuscan dialect should be adopted instead of Latin by contemporary writers. His most notable work is *Gli Asolani* (1505), a story with lyrics and dialogue on the nature of love. Highly significant for the development of Italian literature, Bembo was also a noted collector of antiquities and paintings. In 1539 he was made cardinal by Pope PAUL III and later became Bishop of Bergamo. He features as a character in CASTIGLIONE's *Courtier*.

Portrait by Raphael, 34–35 (2)
Prose della volgar lingua, title page of, 26

The Prettiest Love Letters in the World, Letters between Lucrezia Borgia and Pietro Bembo, trans. by Hugh Shankland, 1987

Benedetto da Maiano, 1442–97. Florentine sculptor. He is best known for his narrative reliefs on pulpits and tombs and for his charming groups of the Virgin and Child. He ventured into architecture to work on the design of the Palazzo Strozzi. Giovanni da Maiano of the same family worked in England for Cardinal Wolsey.

Bergognone, Ambrogio see **Borgognone**

Bernardino of Siena, 1380–1444. Franciscan preacher, who adopted the monogram of Jesus (IHS) on his badge. He was canonized in 1450.

Preaching in the Piazza del Campo, Siena, 116–17 (1)

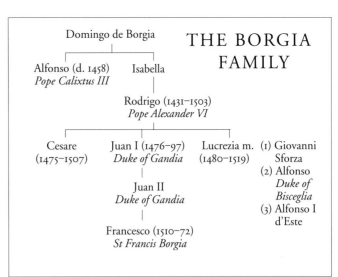

THE BORGIA FAMILY

Domingo de Borgia
|
Alfonso (d. 1458) — Isabella
Pope Calixtus III
|
Rodrigo (1431–1503)
Pope Alexander VI
|
Cesare (1475–1507) — Juan I (1476–97) *Duke of Gandia* — Lucrezia m. (1480–1519) — (1) Giovanni Sforza (2) Alfonso *Duke of Bisceglia* (3) Alfonso I d'Este
|
Juan II *Duke of Gandia*
|
Francesco (1510–72) *St Francis Borgia*

Cesare Borgia, woodcut from Paolo Giovio's Elogia virorum bellica virtute illustrium, *Basle, 1577.*

I. Origo, *The World of San Bernardino*, 1963
Raymond de Roover, *San Bernardino of Siena and Sant' Antonio of Florence*, 1967

Berrecci, Bartolommeo, died 1537. Italian architect, who came to Cracow about 1530 at the invitation of Sigismund I to build the St Sigismund Chapel in Cracow Cathedral, the first Renaissance building in Poland.

St Sigismund Chapel, Cracow, 108–09 (5), 110–11 (10), inscription on dome, 241

Berruguete, Alonso, *c.* 1485–1561. Spanish sculptor and painter, son of the artist Pedro Berruguete. During more than a decade spent in Italy after 1504, he met MICHELANGELO and saw the early Mannerist paintings of PONTORMO and ROSSO FIORENTINO. On his return to Spain he was appointed royal painter to CHARLES V, although he actually concentrated more on sculpture, producing several carved altarpieces which display his agitated and contorted figural style. His work provided an important and influential injection of Mannerism into Spain.

Bessarion, Cardinal, 1403–72. Byzantine theologian and humanist. An archbishop of the Eastern Church, he travelled to Italy with the Byzantine Emperor on a mission to promote unity with the Western Church. He remained in Italy and was made a cardinal of the Roman Church in 1439. An outstanding scholar, he promoted the study of Greek and helped found the Platonic Academy in Florence.

Portrait, presenting a reliquary of the true cross, by Gentile Bellini, 58–59 (2)

John Monfarani, *Byzantine Scholars in Renaissance Italy, Cardinal Bessarion and other Emigrés*, 1995

Boccaccio, Giovanni, 1313–75. Italian author and humanist. Son of a Florentine merchant, he was sent to Naples where his literary interests were aroused and inspired by the sophisticated environment of the court of King Robert. Called back to Florence, where

he survived the Great Plague, he wrote a number of works in verse and prose including the immensely popular and influential *Decameron*. This consists of 100 tales, remarkable for their breadth of subject-matter and tone, exchanged by ten young Florentine aristocrats. Often bawdy and irreverent, at times poignant, the range of stories includes deceit, adultery, compassion and ideal love. Its defiance of convention, both literary and moral, its fresh observation of human behaviour and its humour made it widely influential – for instance on Chaucer. In the 16th century BEMBO cited its language as a model of Italian vernacular prose. Boccaccio is also noted as one of the earliest humanists. Following the lead of his friend PETRARCH, he made a close study of the Latin classics, wrote a book on the genealogy of the gods, and tried to learn Greek. He also wrote a biography of Dante and a commentary on part of the *Divine Comedy*.

Decameron: 15th-century illustration, 192–93 (5); illustration by Botticelli, 38–39 (12)

V. Branca, *Boccaccio: the Man and his Works*, 1976
Judith Powers Serafini-Sanli, *Giovanni Boccaccio*, 1982

Borgia family. Spanish family which produced two popes, a ruthless tyrant, a romantic heroine and a saint. When Cardinal Alfonso Borgia (d. 1458), from Catalonia, was elected pope in 1455 as Calixtus III several of his relatives accompanied him to Rome, among them his nephew Rodrigo who became Pope ALEXANDER VI. Alexander's son Cesare (1475–1507) was one of the cruellest and most efficient of Italian Renaissance power politicians, serving as the model for MACHIAVELLI's 'Prince'. His sister Lucrezia (1480–1519), much maligned by later chroniclers, spent much of her life presiding over the cultured ESTE court of Ferrara. Alexander's great-grandson Francesco (1510–72) somewhat redeemed the family's reputation by becoming General of the Jesuits and being canonized in 1671.

Portrait of Alexander VI by Pinturicchio,
66–67 (2)
Borgia Apartments, the Vatican, fresco in,
44–45 (3, 7)
Rachel Erlanger, *Lucrezia Borgia*, 1979
M. Mallett, *The Borgias*, 1981

Borgognone, Ambrogio, active 1481–died 1523. Italian painter. He worked almost entirely in Milan and nearby Pavia. His religious works are in the northern Italian tradition and display knowledge of the painting of FOPPA, also active in Milan. He painted many frescoes and altarpieces for the Certosa at Pavia.

Bosch, Hieronymus, *c.* 1450–1516. Netherlandish painter who spent most of his life in 'sHertogenbosch, the town from which his name derives. The chronology of his work is unclear, but some religious paintings, notably a *Crucifixion* in Brussels, suggest the early influence of Rogier van der WEYDEN. He is chiefly remembered for paintings which include fantastic demonic creatures and disturbing details of human depravity; the most famous of which is the large triptych of *The Garden of Earthly Delights* in the Prado, Madrid. While many of his bizarre symbolic images are undoubtedly moralizing and allegoric, today many defy interpretation. An artist of unique creative imagination, his work was popular in his lifetime and attracted the attention of several discriminating 16th-century collectors, including PHILIP II of Spain.
The Garden of Earthly Delights, 258–59 (7)
James Snyder, *Hieronymus Bosch*, 1980
Linda Harris, *The Secret Heresy of Hieronymus Bosch*, 1995

Botticelli, Sandro, 1445–1510. Italian painter whose allegorical works, particularly *The Birth of Venus* and the *Primavera*, are today among the most famous images of Italian Renaissance art. His elegantly draped figures are reminiscent of the graceful forms of his master, Fra Filippo LIPPI, but Botticelli's paintings, characterized by a marked ethereal quality, are delineated with a distinctive fluid outline. One of the artists called to Rome by SIXTUS IV in 1481 to fresco the Sistine Chapel, he contributed scenes from *The Life of Moses* and *The Temptation of Christ*. The rest of his active career was spent in Florence, closely bound up with MEDICI patronage, and some of his mythological canvases are visual representations of the humanist ideas of FICINO and the Medici academic circle. Botticelli's tender images of the Madonna and Child were extremely popular and inspired many inferior copies. Towards the end of the century Botticelli was attracted to the preaching of SAVONAROLA, and a more expressive and powerful force discernible in his later works may represent his spiritual response to the religious unrest in Florence.
Adoration of the Magi, 72–73 (1)
The Birth of Venus, 52–53 (6)

The Calumny of Apelles, 46–47 (5)
Decameron by Boccaccio, illustration to the, 38–39 (12)
Lamentation over the Dead Christ, 142–43 (3)
The Mystic Nativity, 130–31 (5)
Pallas Athene and the Centaur, 46–47 (9)
Primavera, 54–55 (6), 228–29 (4)
The Punishment of Cora, 280–81 (1)
Lionello Venturi, *Botticelli*, 1961
Ronald Lightbown, *Sandro Botticelli*, 1978

Botticini, Francesco, *c.* 1446–97. Italian painter. Little is known of this Florentine artist and craftsman, who imitated the style of other painters, including BOTTICELLI. Several paintings are attributed to him, most notably an unusually large panel of the *Assumption*, in which the artist displays considerable skill in a perspectival representation of the dome of Heaven.

Bourdichon, Jean, *c.* 1457–1521. French painter and illuminator chiefly remembered for his famous illuminated manuscript *Les Grandes heures de la Reine Anne de Bretagne*, which was completed in 1508.
David MacGibbon, *Jean Bourdichon, a Court Painter of the Fifteenth Century*, 1933

Bouts, Dieric, *c.* 1415–75. Netherlandish painter. Born in Haarlem, his painting reflects the strong influence of Rogier van der WEYDEN. He is first recorded in Louvain, near Brussels, the main centre of his artistic activity and where he painted his most famous work, a large-scale triptych of the *Sacraments*, for Louvain Cathedral. His *Entombment* in the National Gallery, London, is a rare survival of a painting on linen canvas using a glue medium; a very common technique in the 15th century but one extremely prone to atmospheric damage. His attention to detail, elaborate costumes and attractive landscape backgrounds give his paintings charm, but he does not pretend to dramatic power.
The Last Supper, 138–39 (1)

Bracciolini, Poggio, 1380–1459. Italian humanist and scholar. He developed his considerable capacity for Latin scholarship in the humanist circles of late 14th-century Florence and, as papal secretary, attended the Council of Constance (1414–18). While travelling in northern Europe he searched monastic libraries for previously lost classical manuscripts and his significant discoveries of works by Cicero and Quintilian caused great excitement among classical scholars. He became well known as the author of works in Latin, mostly moral and religious but also including a book of jokes, the *Facetiae*. He wrote a history of Florence during his years as Chancellor of the city.
Portrait in manuscript, 34–35 (6)
William Shepherd, *The Life of Poggio Bracciolini*, 1837

Tycho Brahe, 1586.

Brahe, Tycho, 1546–1601. Danish astronomer. He made an outstanding contribution to the science of astronomy through decades of rigorous observation and calculation, which enabled him to plot the position of the planets accurately – this proved an essential basis for later discoveries. He enjoyed the sponsorship of King Frederick II in Denmark but towards the end of his life moved to RUDOLF II's Prague court, where he left the legacy of his life's work to his assistant, Johannes KEPLER.
Quadrant and observatory, 214–15 (6)
James Gerald Crowther, *Six Great Astronomers*, 1961
John Louis Emil Dreyer, *Tycho Brahe: a Picture of Scientific Life and Work in the Sixteenth Century*, reprint, 1963

Bramante, Donato, 1444–1514. Italian architect. One of the foremost figures of the Roman High Renaissance whose dignified and monumental style proved profoundly influential on numerous followers. Born near Urbino, he worked initially as an illusionistic painter, and his first architectural commissions date from after 1479, when he entered the service of Duke Lodovico SFORZA. His rebuilding of S. Maria presso S. Satiro in Milan reflects his knowledge of ALBERTI and includes a convincing *trompe-l'oeil* barrel-vaulted chancel. From about 1500 he was in Rome where his complete understanding of classical forms is revealed in the small, circular Tempietto at S. Pietro in Montorio, which features a central cella surrounded by a Doric peristyle, built on the supposed site of St Peter's martyrdom. A seminal building of the Italian Renaissance, the Tempietto was included by both SERLIO and PALLADIO in their architectural treatises. Under the demanding patronage of JULIUS II, Bramante drew up plans for the rebuilding of St Peter's Basilica. His centrally planned design was begun and formed the basis for MICHELANGELO's final building, though drastically altered. Considerable work took place on the Belvedere Courtyard, a vast scheme of two- and three-storey logge which Bramante designed to link the Vatican Palace to the Villa Belvedere. His Palazzo Caprini (also known as the House of Raphael), a two-storey town house featuring a rusticated ground floor surmounted by an elegant *piano nobile*, provided the model for secular buildings in Rome and throughout Italy.

Belvedere Courtyard, the Vatican, 156–57 (5)
House of Raphael, Rome, 156–57 (2)
S. Maria delle Grazie, Milan, 110–11 (4), 276–77 (4)
S. Maria presso S. Satiro, Milan, chancel of, 110–11 (2)
St Peter's: design for the dome of, 17, 276–77 (6); foundation medal for, 274–75 (5); plan for, 274–75 (6)
Tempietto, Rome, 274–75 (7)

Peter Murray, *Bramante's Tempietto*, 1972
Arnaldo Bruschi, *Bramante*, 1977

Sebastian Brant by Hans Burgkmair, c. 1508.

Brant, Sebastian, 1457–1521. German satirical poet. His long poem in rhyming couplets, *Narren schuff* (*Ship of Fools*), published in 1494, castigated sin and folly in their various guises, from adultery and selling forged relics to book-collecting and failing to follow doctor's orders. It became immensely popular, partly because of its woodcut illustrations.

Broederlam, Melchior, active 1381–died 1409. French painter. He worked at the court of the Duke of Burgundy from 1387 and was in Paris in the 1390s. He painted two wings of an altar, combining elements from both Flemish realism and French courtly painting.

Bronzino, Agnolo, 1503–72. Italian painter. A Florentine Mannerist, influenced by MICHELANGELO, he was a pupil and assistant to PONTORMO, although he developed a less tortured style than that of his master. Principally noted for his sophisticated

Pieter Bruegel the Elder, engraving, 1572.

portraits, many commissioned by the MEDICI family, he also painted religious and allegorical works, as well as a large-scale fresco cycle in the Palazzo Vecchio, Florence. His easel paintings are characterized by cool tones, a smooth enamel-like surface, an air of studied artificiality, and what one critic has called 'icy obscenity'.

Portrait of Laura Battiferri, 194–95 (3)
Portrait of Lucrezia Panciatichi, 94–95 (2)
Andrea Doria as Neptune, 48–49 (2)
Venus, Cupid, Folly and Time, 192–93 (2)

Arthur K. McComb, *Agnolo Bronzino, his Life and Works*, 1928
Charles McCorquodale, *Bronzino*, 1981

Bruegel family. Flemish painters. Pieter Bruegel the Elder (active 1551–died 1569) is first recorded in the Antwerp Painters' Guild in 1551, he then travelled for two years in Italy. The beauty of the Alps and the Italian countryside, which he recorded in exquisite drawings, inspired him far more than exposure to Italian painting. He was employed by an engraver on returning to Antwerp, where he saw copies of BOSCH's prints, and where his own compositions, including the *Seven Deadly Sins*, were later published. From the mid-1560s he lived in Brussels, where his works were eagerly sought by collectors. He was a celebrated landscapist and a witty observer of traditional Flemish life which he captured in his characteristic peasant scenes. A painter of moral and satirical subjects, some of his works, such as *The Massacre of the Innocents*, may allude to the plight of the Netherlands under Spanish rule. His two sons, Pieter Bruegel the Younger (c. 1564–1638) and Jan Bruegel the Elder (1568–1625) were also successful painters; the first made copies of his father's works, the second specialized in landscapes.

Jan Bruegel the Elder: *Battle of the Issus*, 84–85 (2)
Earthly Paradise, 182–83 (3)
Forge in the Mountain, 236–37 (3)

Landscape with Flooded Road and Windmill, 178–79 (7)
The Sense of Hearing, 220–21 (3)
Pieter Bruegel the Elder:
The Census at Bethlehem, 184–85 (9)
The Cripples, 200–01 (8)
Peasant Woman, 194–95 (7)
The Tower of Babel, 278–79 (7)
Pieter Bruegel the Younger:
Village Wedding, 180–81 (3)

Walter S. Gibson, *Bruegel*, 1977
Wolfgang Stechow, *Bruegel*, 1990

Brunelleschi, Filippo, 1377–1446. The most celebrated Italian architect of the early Renaissance, he was originally trained as a sculptor and goldsmith, and was runner-up to GHIBERTI in the 1401 sculptural competition for the Florentine Baptistery doors. His keen interest in mathematical enquiry resulted in his demonstration of single-point perspective, a key tool in Renaissance art which was later codified by ALBERTI in *Della pittura*. He was revered in his own time as the architect whose outstanding engineering skills solved the seemingly impossible construction problems of the Florentine Cathedral dome – a symbol of immense civic pride. His own architecture draws on classical and Tuscan Romanesque motifs to produce a rational style characterized by decorative restraint, in sharp contrast to the elaborate variety of the Gothic style. His elegant loggia of the Foundling Hospital is often cited as the first Renaissance building and was followed by a series of outstanding works, including the two Florentine basilican churches of S. Lorenzo and S. Spirito. The small centrally planned Old Sacristy at S. Lorenzo is a seminal work which epitomizes his style – based on careful proportion and visual harmony, it features his favoured internal articulation of grey sandstone detailing against simple white stucco. Considered as one of the creators of the Renaissance style, Brunelleschi's influence on succeeding generations cannot be overstated.

Florence Cathedral: dome of, 276–77 (1); scaffolding for the dome of, 276–77 (2)
Foundling Hospital, Florence, 174
Pazzi Chapel, Florence, 276–77 (3)
S. Lorenzo, Florence, 110–11 (1)
S. Spirito, Florence, 110–11 (5)

A. Manetti, *The Life of Brunelleschi*, 1970
Eugenio Battisti, *Brunelleschi*, 1981

Bruni, Leonardo, c. 1370–1444. Italian humanist and statesman. A noted scholar of Latin and Greek, he was Chancellor of Florence from 1427 and wrote a history of the Florentine people. His Latin translations of classical Greek texts encouraged the study of Greek literature, and he wrote biographies of the Italian poets Dante, PETRARCH and BOCCACCIO. His tomb monument by Bernardo ROSSELLINO in S. Croce, Florence, is remarkable for its classical iconography.

Tomb, 32

H. Baron, *From Petrarch to Leonardo Bruni*, 1968
G. Griffiths, J. Hawkins and D. Thompson, *The Humanism of Leonardo Bruni*, 1987

Bruno, Giordano, 1548–1600. Italian philosopher. Bruno's mind was wide-ranging and adventurously speculative. Seeking a theological framework, he joined first the Dominicans, then the Calvinists, then the Lutherans, but none could tolerate his fiercely individual opinions. He became a successful freelance writer and lecturer, wandering through France, England and Germany before unwisely returning to Italy. Without promoting any coherent body of doctrine, Bruno was willing to entertain highly unorthodox ideas, such as the Copernican solar-system, the infinite number of worlds, the magical efficacy of the art of memory, and a World Soul that included the human race and God. This was inevitably seen as a rejection of the authority of the Church. In Rome he was tried for heresy, excommunicated and burnt at the stake, a martyr if not to science, at least to freedom of thought.

Frances A. Yates, *Giordano Bruno and the Hermetic Tradition*, 1964
John Bossy, *Giordano Bruno and the Embassy Affair*, 1991

Buchanan, George, 1506–82. Scottish humanist. After 35 years in France and Portugal, teaching (MONTAIGNE, among others), promoting the Reformation and writing Latin verse, he returned to Scotland in 1561 and was appointed tutor to Mary, Queen of Scots. He was, however, among those who helped to convict her of Darnley's murder. Important as a Reformer and teacher, he was above all outstanding as a Latin stylist.

Budé, Guillaume, 1467–1540. French scholar and humanist. Educated in several disciplines, including theology, philosophy and medicine, he was also a noted Greek scholar. He served as French ambassador in Rome and later, while royal librarian to FRANCOIS I, was responsible for assembling an important royal collection of manuscripts. He instigated the foundation of the Collège de France, in Paris (1530), a centre for advanced Greek, Latin and Hebrew studies, which proved fundamental to the revival of classical learning in France. Budé's own scholarship, in such works as *De Asse* (1514) and *Commentarii linguae Graecae* (1529), was also instrumental in promoting the study of classical language and literature.

Portrait by François Clouet, 36–37 (4)
D. O. McNeil, *Guillaume Budé and Humanism in the Reign of Francis I*, 1975

Bull, John, *c.* 1562–1628. English composer and musician, celebrated as an outstanding keyboard player and an important composer of keyboard music, especially for the virginals. In 1582 he was appointed organist at Hereford Cathedral, later becoming the first Professor of Music at Gresham College in London, and travelling in France and Germany. He left England in 1613, and spent his remaining years in Brussels and subsequently in Antwerp.

Walker Cunningham, *The Keyboard Music of John Bull*, 1984

Bullant, Jean, *c.* 1520–78. French architect. He studied the ancient buildings of Rome while travelling in Italy in the early 1540s, and later used some of his drawings of classical motifs in an architectural textbook *Reigle générale d'architecture des cinq manières de colonnes* (1564). His own architecture, a highly personal form of Mannerism, is marked by accurate classical detailing, but often used in unusual or unclassical ways – such as his pavilion at Ecouen which features the first use in France of the giant order. In 1570 he was appointed architect to Catherine de MEDICIS, and was engaged on several projects including the enlargement of the Château of Chenonceau and the building of the Hôtel de Soissons.

Buontalenti, Bernardo, *c.* 1536–1608. Italian architect, engineer and designer. A multi-talented Mannerist architect, he was active almost entirely in the service of the Grand Ducal court in Florence. His engineering skills were put to work not only on construction and hydraulic schemes, but also to provide fireworks, moving scenery, and waterworks for elaborate court entertainments. His architecture includes the façade of S. Trinita, Florence, and a doorway in the Uffizi, Florence, the Porta delle Suppliche, with its fantastic and highly original pediment. At Pratolino he built a villa for Francesco I (since destroyed) and equipped its huge garden with spectacular water-effects and fountains.

Porta delle Suppliche, Florence, 288 (2)

Burgkmair, Hans the Elder, 1473–1531. German painter and woodcut designer, probably trained by SCHONGAUER. He settled in his native Augsburg, although he made several visits to northern Italy, particularly Venice, which were formative on his style. He painted several large altarpieces characterized by warm colours and monumental figures, and was also a skilled portraitist, producing penetrating images of his sitters contrasted against dark monochrome backgrounds. He worked for several publishers, providing bold woodcut designs to illustrate printed texts.

Portrait of Sebastian Brant, 295
Boyar ambassadors at the court of Maximilian I, 82–83 (3)

Byrd, William, 1543–1623. English composer and musician. He became organist of Lincoln Cathedral in 1563 and later served as joint-organist of the Chapel Royal. One of the foremost composers of polyphonic choral church music, as well as music for keyboard instruments, he was a founder of the English Madrigal School. For over 20 years during ELIZABETH I's reign Byrd, and his master Thomas TALLIS, enjoyed the monopoly of issuing printed music.

Joseph Kerman, *The Masses and Motets of William Byrd*, 1981
Oliver Neighbour, *The Consort and Keyboard Music of William Byrd*, 1984

Calvin, Jean, 1509–64. French theologian and Reformer. A scholar of great intellect, he studied theology, law and Greek at universities in France. By 1533 he had broken from the Catholic Church to become a proponent of the doctrines of reform and in 1536 he published *The Institutes of the Christian Religion*, his learned and logical justification of Protestantism based on Scriptural evidence. Written in Latin, but soon translated into French, his book was a major factor in the spread of Protestantism in France. From 1541 he lived in Geneva, where he worked tirelessly for the rest of his life, establishing and administering the Reformed Church of Geneva, a highly disciplined and strictly supervised organization which became a model for other reformed groups. Calvin believed there was no measure of human choice in redemption, and that an omnipotent God predestined the chosen people (the elect) for salvation while the rest, condemned to damnation, were powerless to change their fate.

Portrait, 114–15 (6)
Der Heilige Brotkorb, title page of, 120–21 (2)
W. Monter, *Calvin's Geneva*, 1967
T. H. L. Parker, *John Calvin*, 1975

Cano, Alonso, 1601–67. Spanish painter, sculptor and architect. A leading artist in 17th-century Spain, he produced large and complex painted altarpieces set in elaborate architectural and sculptural frameworks. His reputation as an architect rests on his striking design for the façade of Granada Cathedral which, although built after his death, was completed as he intended.

Granada Cathedral, 108–09 (6)
H. E. Wethey, *Alonso Cano, Painter, Sculptor and Architect*, 1955

Caravaggio (Michelangelo Merisi da Caravaggio), 1571–1610. Italian painter. He received his early training in Milan but by 1592 was recorded in Rome, where his first works were mainly still-life and flower paintings. Through influential patronage he was commissioned to decorate the Contarelli Chapel in S. Luigi dei Francesi in Rome. Here he painted two huge pendant canvases of *The Calling of St Matthew* and *The Martyrdom of St Matthew*, involving the spectator in the drama and using his characteristic *chiaroscuro* to exciting narrative effect. He seems to have invented the device of setting his scenes in darkness illuminated by a single shaft of light, destined to be very influential on Baroque art. Although he was enthusiastically supported by a number of intellectual collectors, his rigorous realism did not find universal approval and several of his religious commissions, such as *The Death of the Virgin*, were adjudged indecorous. His erotic and sensuous images of young men, which, like the *Victorious Amor*, were commissioned for private collections, are considered to mirror his own sexuality. Caravaggio's dramatic and uncompromising style was matched by his turbulent life. Frequently in trouble with the authorities, in 1606 he fled from Rome after killing a man in a fight. He continued to paint in Naples and Malta, but died of fever on his return journey to Rome in 1610.

Howard Hibbard, *Caravaggio*, 1989
Alfred Moir, *Caravaggio*, 1989

Caron, Antoine, *c.* 1520–*c.* 1599. French painter. Caron was the leading French exponent of the School of Fontainebleau, inheriting the style of PRIMATICCIO and ROSSO FIORENTINO and making it even more mannered and theatrical, often with backgrounds of fantastic architecture.

Augustus and the Sybil, 286–87 (7)
Massacre under the Triumvirate, 264

Carpaccio, Vittore, *c.* 1460/5–1525. Italian painter. Born in Venice, possibly a pupil of Gentile BELLINI, Carpaccio is best known for several cycles of large-scale narrative paintings commissioned by Venetian charitable brotherhoods. The scenes, which are from the lives of saints and martyrs, are often set against identifiable Venetian backgrounds. Packed with carefully observed details of everyday life and customs in his native city, they have a simple anecdotal interest, a delight in beautiful objects and a direct charm that have made them perennially popular.

The Arrival of St Ursula and her Virgins at Cologne, 178–79 (1)
The Lion of St Mark, 158–59 (4)
Miracle of the Reliquary of the Cross, 198–99 (2)

Terisio Pignatti, *Carpaccio: Biographical and Critical Study*, trans. by J. Emmons, 1958
Francesco Valconover, *Carpaccio*, 1989

Carracci family. An Italian family of painters from Bologna of whom the most noted members were two brothers Annibale and Agostino, and their cousin Lodovico. Lodovico (1555–1619) was influenced by the work of CORREGGIO in Parma and painted several large altarpieces as well as collaborating with his cousins on frescoes in Bolognese palaces. He was the leading figure in the Carracci Academy set up in Bologna by the three cousins in 1582, which trained many of the leading 17th-century painters and laid great stress on draughtsmanship. Annibale (1560–1609) was one of the most famous painters of his day who sought a return to the classicism of the High Renaissance masters, particularly RAPHAEL. Called to Rome by Cardinal Odoardo FARNESE in 1595, his masterpiece is the vast frescoed ceiling of the Palazzo Farnese Gallery which depicts the *Loves of the Gods*. The high level of illusionism which includes painted false architecture, statues and medallions also features *quadri riportati*, and proved a major source of inspiration for Baroque ceiling painters. Agostino (1557–1602) worked mainly in Bologna and Parma. He was trained as an engraver, although he also painted altarpieces, and from 1597 to 1599 worked with Annibale in Rome on the Farnese Gallery ceiling.

Annibale Carracci:
Venus and Anchises, 52–53 (3)
Ceiling of Farnese Gallery, Rome, 252–53 (3)

D. Posner, *Annibale Carracci*, 1971
Drawings and Prints by Carracci, 1973

Casa, Giovanni della, 1503–56. Italian archbishop and writer. He pursued a successful career as an ecclesiastical administrator but is chiefly remembered for his witty and popular manual of etiquette, *Il galateo*, which is concerned with the manners and behaviour of polite society as opposed to the higher courtly circles of CASTIGLIONE's *Courtier*. Published posthumously in 1558, the manual enjoyed popular acclaim and was soon translated into several languages.

Castagno, Andrea del, active *c.* 1421–died 1457. Italian painter. Tuscan by birth, Castagno is recorded as painting frescoes in Venice early in his career, but after 1444 he returned to Florence, where he remained for the rest of his life. His painting style is linked with Quattrocento Florentine developments in both painting and sculpture, and in turn his work became influential on later artists. In his masterpiece, the *Last Supper* fresco which dominates the refectory of S. Apollonia, Florence, he exploits a limited colour range to its full potential, and portrays monumental figures deriving ultimately from MASACCIO's example. His fresco series of *Famous Men and Women*, and the equestrian portrait of *Niccolò da Tolentino*, are bold and linear, representing a convincing pictorial equivalent to DONATELLO's sculpture.

David, 250–51 (5)
The Trinity with St Jerome, 128–29 (1)

Marita Horster, *Andrea del Castagno: Complete Edition with a Critical Catalogue*, 1980
John R. Spencer, *Andrea del Castagno and his Patrons*, 1991

Castiglione, Baldassare, 1478–1529. Italian humanist, author and diplomat. Born near Mantua, he received a classical education and later served at the courts of the GONZAGA in Mantua and the MONTEFELTRO in Urbino. Sent as papal nuncio to Spain in 1524, Castiglione died in Toledo five years later. His famous book, *The Courtier*, started in 1508 but not published until 1528, is set in Urbino and written in the form of fictional dialogues between prominent and cultivated members of the court. In the course of several genial discussions they seek to establish the requisite qualities of the ideal court gentleman and gentlewoman. The book was significant in popularizing humanist ideas and was regarded as a manual of etiquette.

Portrait by Raphael, 38–39 (3)

J. Cartwright, *Baldassare Castiglione*, 1908
Peter Burke, *The Fortunes of the Courtier*, 1995

Catena, Vincenzo, *c.* 1475–1531. Italian painter. Catena is first recorded, rather surprisingly, in partnership with GIORGIONE, although his earliest works are firmly based on compositions by Giovanni BELLINI. A painter of religious subjects and portraits, it was only after the death of Giorgione that his paintings reflected Giorgione's influence, particularly in the treatment of landscape settings. Catena was a man of means, having an independent income and moving within Venetian humanist circles.

Giles Henry Robertson, *Vincenzo Catena*, 1954

Caxton, William, *c.* 1422–91. English printer, translator and businessman. Trained in London as a cloth merchant, he left for Bruges in 1445 and spent over 30 years trading successfully in the Netherlands. It was only in middle age, while pursuing his own translation and writing interests in Cologne, that Caxton learned about printing techniques. On his return to London in 1476, he introduced into England the method of printing with movable type which enabled the production of cheaper, multiple copies of books. Caxton's texts were important for the dissemination of literary works and also for the promotion of a standard form of printed English.

Chaucer's *Canterbury Tales*, 208–09 (2)
Colophon, 206–07 (3)

Richard Deacon, *A Biography of William Caxton*, 1976
N. F. Blake, *William Caxton and English Literary Culture*, 1991

Cellini, Benvenuto, 1500–71. Italian goldsmith and sculptor. He wrote an immensely readable autobiography which encompasses his artistic activities and includes frequent references to his sexual proclivities and a colourful first-hand account of the Sack of Rome. The first two decades of his career were spent mainly in Rome and from 1540 he was employed in France by FRANCOIS I, for whom he made a celebrated gold salt-cellar. In 1545, back in his native Florence, he entered into acrimonious rivalry with BANDINELLI and received the MEDICI commission for *Perseus*, a highly acclaimed success and a remarkable feat of bronze casting. He wrote treatises on goldsmithery and sculpture, and although mainly noted for his gold and bronze work, also produced some sculpture in marble.

Perseus, 250–51 (4)
Salt-cellar, 236–37 (9)

Charles Hope and Alessandro Nova (eds), *The Autobiography of Benvenuto Cellini*, 1983
John Pope-Hennessy, *Cellini*, 1985

Celtis, Conrad, 1459–1508. German humanist and poet, who promoted classical scholarship in Germany and founded a centre of humanist study in Vienna. He wrote Latin odes and love poems, musical masques, and published scholarly works with a strong patriotic tone.

Portrait, 36–37 (9)

Lewis W. Spitz, *Conrad Celtis, the German Arch-Humanist*, 1957

Cervantes Saavedra, Miguel de, 1547–1616. Spanish novelist and poet, who is a major figure in world literature. Celebrated chiefly for his novel *Don Quixote*, he wrote poetry throughout his life and contributed to the development of Spanish drama as the author of many plays. He was seriously wounded at the Battle of Lepanto (1571) and later, captured by pirates, endured five years imprisonment in Algiers before eventually returning to Spain in 1580. The first part of *Don Quixote*, a complex novel satirizing chivalric ideals and woven with much humour and pathos, was published in 1605 to immediate popular acclaim. In the knight himself Cervantes created a pattern of unworldly goodness, and in his squire Sancho Panza one of earthy realism and proverbial wisdom. The second part of *Don Quixote* which was equally successful appeared in 1615. Cervantes also explored shorter forms of literary fiction, most notably in his *Novelas ejemplares* (*Exemplary Novels*, 1613) in which he addressed a wide variety of themes.

Portrait by Juan de Jauregui, 38–39 (6)

R. L. Predmore, *Cervantes*, 1973

Charles V, 1500–58. King of Spain from 1516 until 1556 and Holy Roman Emperor from 1519 until 1556. At the death of his grandfather MAXIMILIAN I, he became ruler of the vast Holy Roman Empire which included Spain, the Netherlands, the HABSBURG domains of Germany and Austria, the Kingdom of Naples and areas of Spanish America. A staunch Catholic and passionately determined to defend his territorial inheritance, his rule was marked by a constant struggle to hold together his empire, particularly in the face of the Protestant Reformation and FRANÇOIS I's claims to Burgundy. His armies sacked the city of Rome in 1527 but he finally made peace with Pope CLEMENT VII, and was crowned Holy Roman Emperor in 1530 by the pontiff in Bologna. When he abdicated in 1556, the kingdoms of Spain and the Netherlands passed to his son, PHILIP II of Spain and the title of emperor passed to his brother FERDINAND I. Charles V retired to a monastery in Spain, where he spent the last years of his life. During his reign humanist scholarship flourished in Spain in spite of the restraints imposed by religious orthodoxy. Of his patronage of the arts, TITIAN's portraits and his innovative, but unfinished, palace at Granada may be mentioned.

Portrait by Titian, 62, 68–69 (5)
Portrait in intaglio, 68–69 (1)
Portrait with Pope Clement VII by Vasari, 66–67 (6)
Bruges, entry into, 90–91 (1)
Confession of Augsburg, 114–15 (7)
Coronation by Pope Clement VII by Vasari, 68–69 (6)
Enthronment by Giulio Clovio, 68–69 (7)
Netherlands, entertainment in, 98–99 (3)
Parade helmet, 222–23 (5)
Palace at Granada, 268–69 (6)
Tomb by Pompeo Leoni, 102–03 (2)

R. Tyler, *The Emperor Charles V*, 1956
M. F. Alvarez, *Charles V, Elected Emperor and Hereditary Ruler*, 1975

Charles VIII, 1470–98. King of France from 1483. He was aged only 13 when he succeeded to the throne and was dominated for many years by his politically astute sister, Anne, who arranged his advantageous marriage to Anne of Brittany. His reign was characterized by peace in France but his ill-advised invasion of Italy (1494), to assert his remote claim to the Kingdom of Naples, began the HABSBURG–VALOIS Wars.

Florence, entry into, 82–83 (4)

Roger Doucet, *France under Charles VIII and Louis XII*, 1957

Charles VIII, medal by Niccolò Fiorentino, 15th century.

Chigi, Agostino, 1465–1520. Sienese banker who acted as financier for several popes. He built the Villa Farnesina in Rome, patronized PERUZZI and RAPHAEL and set up a Greek printing press.

F. Gilbert, *The Pope, his Banker and Venice*, 1991

Christian II, 1481–1559. King of Denmark, Norway and Sweden from 1514. Although a violent and unscrupulous man, Christian took an interest in art and learning, meeting DÜRER, MASSYS and ERASMUS, some of whose ideas he put into practice.

Portrait by Cranach, 70–71 (2)

Christian IV, 1577–1648. King of Denmark and Norway from 1588. His rule was overshadowed by the problems of the Thirty Years War, from which he tried, without success, to reap some advantage for Denmark. He was, however, one of Europe's most active patrons of architecture, building or rebuilding the castles of Frederiksborg, Rosensborg and Kronborg, as well as a large number of public buildings, and founding several planned towns, including Christiania (named after himself), now Oslo.

Frederiksborg Castle, ballroom of, 80–81 (5)

Christine de Pisan, 1365–c. 1434. French poet and writer. Born in Venice, she was raised at the French court where her scholarly father was astrologer to Charles the Wise. She was widowed in her mid-twenties and, with three small children, turned to writing to support her family. Chiefly known for *La Cité des dames* (1405), a history of virtuous and courageous women, she also wrote many poignant verses of personal grief at the loss of her husband, and poems of courtly love. Her illustrious patrons included the duc de Berry and Philip the Bold, and she wrote a biography of Charles the Wise. She is the earliest woman writer to celebrate female strengths and qualities.

Reinterpreting Christine de Pizan, 1992

Christus, Petrus, active 1442–died 1472/3. Flemish painter. He was the major painter in Bruges after the death of Jan van EYCK, and although he was probably not in the city during Van Eyck's lifetime, his painting is strongly based on the older master's work. An artist of religious subjects and portraits, his work is often minutely detailed and highly finished. His interest in the definition of space can be noted in his portraits where, by placing the sitter in front of a window or within a room, he creates the believable depth of an interior setting, at the same time as providing a formal context for his subject.

Madonna and Child, 132–33 (3)

Maryan W. Ainsworth, *Petrus Christus, Renaissance Master of Bruges*, 1994

Chrysoloras, Manuel, c. 1353–1415. Greek scholar, who was sent to Italy by the Byzantine Emperor to obtain support against the Ottomans. He subsequently spent much of his life in the west, where he championed the study of Greek literature and sought union between the Eastern and Western Churches. As well as teaching Greek in Florence, he also translated works of Plato and Homer.

Portrait, 58–59 (5)

Ciriaco d'Ancona, c. 1390–1455. Italian antiquarian. A merchant with a passionate interest in antiquities, he was one of the first collectors to bring gems and manuscripts from Greece and Egypt into Italy. Some of his notes and drawings of Greek antiquities have survived, and are often our earliest record.

Hagia Sophia, Constantinople, 58–59 (1)

Clement VII, Pope, 1478–1534. Pope from 1523. Born Giulio de' MEDICI, he was raised by his grandfather, Lorenzo de' Medici the Magnificent and was promoted in his ecclesiastical career by his cousin, Pope LEO X. A handsome and learned humanist, his papacy is marked by the problems surrounding the rising tide of Protestantism; the issue of HENRY VIII's marriage annulment; and the political struggles between the Emperor CHARLES V and FRANÇOIS I. At the Sack of Rome in 1527, he took refuge in the

Pope Clement VII by Sebastiano del Piombo, 1523–34.

Castel Sant'Angelo but was later reconciled to Charles V and crowned him Holy Roman Emperor in 1530. His intellectual and aesthetic taste promoted his discriminating patronage of RAPHAEL, MICHELANGELO and SEBASTIANO DEL PIOMBO.

Portrait by Vasari, 66–67 (6)
As cardinal by Raphael, 66–67 (5)
Charles V: crowning, 68–69 (6); entombment of, 68–69 (7)

Pierre Crabitès, *Clement VII and Henry VIII*, 1936

Clouet family. French painters. Jean (died 1540) was employed by the Duke of Burgundy, and was later Court Painter to the King of France. He was succeeded in this post by his son François (c. 1510–72) in 1541. It is probable that he visited Italy early in his career, as his mannered portraits, for example of the French royal family, suggest the influence of BRONZINO. He also painted a number of sensual images, such as the depiction of a royal mistress in *Lady in her Bath*.

François Clouet:
    Portrait of Guillaume Budé, 36–37 (4)
    Portrait of Charles IX, 92–93 (6)
    Portrait of Elizabeth of Austria, 94–95 (5)
    The Pharmacist Pierre Quthe, 228–29 (3)
Jean Clouet:
    Portrait of François I, 70–71 (1); on horseback, 86–87 (2)

Three hundred French Portraits Representing Personages of the Courts of Francis I, Henry II and Francis II by Clouet, 1875
P. Mellen, *Jean Clouet*, 1971

Clovio, Giulio, 1498–1578. Italian painter and miniaturist. He was born in Croatia, migrating to Italy at the age of 18 and working for Cardinal Grimani.

The Aztecs, 198–99 (4)
Charles V, manuscript illumination of, 68–69 (7)
Corpus Christi Procession, 88–89 (3)

John William Bradley, *The Life and Works of Giulio Clovio*, 1891

Colet, John, 1467–1519. One of the leading English theologians and humanists of the first generation. Son of a prosperous mercer, he was educated at Oxford and then spent three years travelling and studying in France and Italy, where he came in contact with the new critical techniques of biblical scholarship, learned Greek and met BUDE, ERASMUS and others. Ordained a priest in 1498, he became Dean of St Paul's Cathedral in 1504 and five years later, with his inherited wealth, founded St Paul's School – where he insisted on Greek, Latin and philosophy being taught. He was renowned as a preacher, particularly on the New Testament, and was the author of several unpublished religious commentaries. A friend of MORE, Colet was by temperament a Reformer, but he died before the Reformation made it necessary to take sides.

Portrait by Holbein, 36–37 (3)

R. P. Adams, *The Better Part of Valor. More, Erasmus, Colet and Vives on Humanism, War and Peace, 1496–1535*, 1962
John B. Gleason, *John Colet*, 1989

Colleoni, Bartolomeo, 1400–76. Italian condottiere. A generous patron of the arts, he is commemorated by the Colleoni Chapel in Bergamo by Amadeo and by an equestrian monument in Venice by VERROCCHIO.

Equestrian monument by Verrocchio, 86–87 (7)

The Life of Bartolomeo Colleoni of Anjou and Burgundy, 1891

Colonna, Francesco, 1433–1527. An Italian Dominican friar, of somewhat dubious character, who wrote the dream romance, *Hypnerotomachia Poliphili*. The elegant 1499 edition of the book, produced by the Aldine Press, is a masterpiece of printing in which exquisite woodcuts (by an unidentified artist) are specifically linked to narrative details of the text.

Hypnerotomachia Poliphili: **pages from, 208–09 (5, 6); woodcut from, 170–71 (3)**

Linda Fierz-David, *The Dream of Poliphilo*, 1950

Columbus, Christopher (Cristobal Colón), c. 1446–1506. Italian navigator. As early as the 1470s, by studying all the available geographical information, Columbus reached the belief that the earth was a sphere and therefore the Indies could be reached by sailing west. But he was not able to find patrons willing to invest in an expedition until 1492: Ferdinand and Isabella of Spain. He eventually made four voyages across the Atlantic, discovering and exploring most of the West Indian islands and part of the coast of South America, but never realized that he had found a whole new continent.

Portrait by Ghirlandaio, 210–11 (9)

Felipe Fernandez-Armerto, *Columbus*, 1991
The Christopher Columbus Encyclopedia, 1992

Nicolaus Copernicus, woodcut by Tobias Stimmer, 1543.

Copernicus, Nicolaus, 1473–1543. Polish astronomer. Educated at universities in Poland and Italy, he settled in Frauenburg (Frombork) in the early 1500s, where he was canon of the cathedral. By 1514 his astronomical studies had led him to draw the almost unbelievable conclusion that the earth and other planets revolved on their own axes in orbit around the sun, contradicting the Ptolemaic model, accepted by the Church, in which the earth (and by extension mankind) was at the centre of the universe. Unwilling to provoke controversy, Copernicus put this forward as a formal assumption designed to simplify the mathematics, rather than as a physical hypothesis. Nevertheless, it had the profoundest effects, not only on astronomical science but on the whole of western thought. Initially he circulated his theories in manuscript form but his complete works *De revolutionibus orbium coelestium, libri VI* (*On the Revolution of the Celestial Spheres*) were published in 1543.

Portrait, 214–15 (5)

Fred Hoyle, *Nicolaus Copernicus*, 1973

Corneille de Lyon, active 1533/4–died 1574. Naturalized French painter. A native of The Hague, he moved to Lyon, where he converted to Catholicism and took French citizenship. He was painter to the French court under HENRI II and specialized in small-scale, finely detailed, portraits, against monochrome backgrounds. Although many such works are attributed to him, only one autograph painting is known.

Correggio (Antonio Allegri), 1494–1534. Italian painter. Born near Parma, he emerged as a major artist of the High Renaissance. The influence of LEONARDO is apparent in his altarpieces and mythological pictures where he uses a technique of soft, atmospheric shading (*morbidezza*) which was his main appeal to later generations. By contrast, his fresco style indicates his awareness of MICHELANGELO and

RAPHAEL, possibly from a visit to Rome. He worked mainly in Parma, beginning with the enigmatically symbolic frescoes in the Camera di S. Paolo. His dome frescoes for S. Giovanni Evangelista and the Cathedral in Parma are his most original and influential works. In both these churches he negates the solidity of the dome architecture and presents the viewer with an illusionistic image of the vault of Heaven, full of clouds, angels and floating saints, achieved through his imaginative use of foreshortening and perspective, prefiguring the achievements of 17th-century Baroque ceiling painters.

Jupiter and Io, 192–93 (6)
Parma Cathedral, dome of, 254–55 (6)

Cecil Gould, *The Paintings of Correggio*, 1977
David Alan Brown, *The Young Correggio and his Leonardesque Sources*, 1981

Corvinus, Matthias see **Matthias Corvinus**

Cossa, Francesco del, *c.* 1436–78. Italian painter. A leading artist of the 15th-century school of Ferrara which was centred around the ESTE court. His altarpieces show the strong influence of MANTEGNA, with stony landscapes and sculptural figures. By contrast, his fresco cycle in the Palazzo Schifanoia, Ferrara, has an elegance reminiscent of International Gothic. The frescoed allegories in the Room of the Months include deities, zodiacal signs and seasonal labours which relate closely to examples found in northern illuminated manuscripts.

The Month of April, 52–53 (1)
The Triumph of Venus, 54–55 (2)

Benedict Nicolson, *The Painters of Ferrara, Cosmè Tura, Francesco del Cossa, Ercole de' Roberti and others*, 1950

Costa, Lorenzo, *c.* 1460–1535. Italian painter. Trained in Ferrara, he was strongly influenced by ROBERTI, of whom he was possibly a pupil, and by TURA. He spent over 20 years in Bologna, working for the powerful Bentivoglio family, and, in 1506, moved to the GONZAGA court in Mantua, where he was appointed court painter in succession to MANTEGNA. Although many of his altarpieces date from his Bolognese years, he continued to paint religious subjects, allegorical themes and portraits at the Mantuan court.

Cousin family. French artists. Jean Cousin the Elder (*c.* 1490–1560) worked mainly as a designer and painter of stained glass, and he also designed tapestries. He had a successful career, working initially in his native Sens and, from 1538, in Paris. His son Jean Cousin the Younger (1522–94) was mainly active as a book illustrator and glass painter. His most famous surviving painting is *The Last Judgment* in the Louvre, which shows the influence of Florentine Mannerism.

Jean Cousin the Elder:
 Eva Prima Pandora, 248–49 (7)
Jean Cousin the Younger:
 Livre de Perspective, 246–47 (1, 2)

Coverdale, Miles, 1488–1569. English bishop and translator. Educated at Cambridge and ordained as a priest in 1514, he was committed to reform of the English Church and was strongly attracted to Lutheran views. In 1529 he visited Hamburg, where he is said to have helped TYNDALE translate part of the Old Testament into English, and then moved to Antwerp where he began his own translation of the entire Bible, based largely on previous versions. Back in England he supervised the printing of the 'Great Bible' – the English version CRANMER introduced into churches which was an important instrument in reforming religious practices (his translation of the Psalms is still used). Having been removed from his position as Bishop of Exeter at the accession of the Catholic Queen MARY I, he left England to return only at the beginning of ELIZABETH I's reign.

Coverdale's Bible, 118–19 (8)

Henry Guppy, *Miles Coverdale and the English Bible, 1488–1568*, 1935
Henry John Cowell, *The Coming of the English Bible. Biographical Notes Concerning John Wycliffe, William Tindale, Miles Coverdale*, 1944

Cranach family. German painters and printmakers. Lucas Cranach the Elder (1472–1553) was called to Wittenberg in 1505 by Frederick the Wise of Saxony, and remained in the city for over 45 years, serving as court painter to three Electors. Often described as a Reformation artist because of his position at the court and his friendship with LUTHER, he in fact received patronage from both Protestants and Catholics. His bold portraits, in which the individual dominates and fills the picture plane, represent an important visual record of the major personalities of court and city during his long career. The full-length portrait seems to have been his invention. Cranach also specialized in a unique type of mythological scene with slender and erotic female nudes in the guise of goddesses or classical heroines. His depiction of beautiful female saints, heavily jewelled and clothed in rich fabrics, was also highly unusual. His sons, Lucas Cranach the Younger (1515–86) and Hans (died 1537), took over the family workshop after his death, and continued to produce work in the style of their father.

Lucas Cranach the Elder:
 Portrait of Christian II of Denmark, 70–71 (2)
 Portrait of Henry the Pious, Duke of Saxony, 92–93 (1)
 Portrait of Luther, 114–15 (4)
 Portrait of Philip Melanchthon, 36–37 (6)
 Deer Hunt of the Elector Frederick the Wise, 96–97 (2)
 Venus and Cupid, 52–53 (7)
 Luther preaching at Wittenberg, 116–17 (6)
 Protestants and Catholics, woodcut of, 120–21 (4)
Lucas Cranach the Younger:
 Portrait of Joachim II of Brandenburg, 70–71 (4)
 Judith with the Head of Holofernes, 196–97 (2)
 The Last Supper, 120–21 (1)

Pierre Descargues, *Lucas Cranach the Elder*, 1968
N. Nikulin, *Lucas Cranach*, trans. by V. Fatayev, 1976

Thomas Cranmer by Gerhard Flicke, 1546.

Cranmer, Thomas, 1489–1556. English scholar and archbishop. A theologian of considerable learning and a fellow of Jesus College, Cambridge, he was strongly committed to reformation of the English Church. Drawn into the circle of HENRY VIII during the negotiations for the king's divorce from Catherine of Aragon, he visited Rome in a delegation to the pope and as Archbishop of Canterbury from 1533 (becoming the first Protestant English primate) supported the king as supreme head of the Church of England. At the accession of the Catholic Queen MARY I, Cranmer was removed from his archbishopric, charged with heresy and burned at the stake. His contribution to reform continued to be felt through his introduction of the English Bible into churches and the compilation of the Book of Common Prayer.

Jasper Ridley, *Thomas Cranmer*, 1962
Paul Ayris and David Selwyn (eds), *Thomas Cranmer, Churchman and Scholar*, 1993

Crivelli, Carlo, active *c.* 1457–died 1494. Italian painter. Born in Venice, he spent most of his life in central Italy where he pursued a successful career painting altarpieces. He combines Paduan influences, apparent in classical architectural settings and a gaunt style of figure, with a Gothic feel for highly patterned and minutely detailed fabrics, fruits and flowers. His work is also noted for a lavish use of gold, a smooth enamel-like finish, and raised plaster effects on such details as haloes.

G. Rushforth, *Crivelli*, 1910

Cronaca, Il (Simone del Pollaiuolo), 1457–1508. Florentine architect who spent some years in Rome. His major works are in Florence: the courtyard of the Palazzo Strozzi and parts of the Palazzo Vecchio.

David, Gerard, born before 1470–died 1523. Flemish painter probably trained in Haarlem. He spent most of his active career in Bruges, where he was the leading artist after the death of MEMLINC, but he also travelled to Antwerp after 1515 and may have been in contact with MASSYS. In the northern tradition his paintings are full of carefully observed and minutely detailed objects and textures, but his figure types became more rounded and monumental in his later works. Several of his paintings are noted for their exquisite wooded landscapes, an element which he also depicted on the wings of triptychs.
Baptism of Christ, 134–35 (2)
William Henry James Weale, *Gerard David, Painter and Illuminator*, 1905

De Brosse, Solomon, 1571–1626. French architect. He built three grand châteaux, including the Luxembourg in Paris (1615) for Marie de Médicis which was deliberately based on AMMANATI's courtyard of the Palazzo Pitti, Florence. His façade of the church of St Gervais in Paris (1616) is an inventive adaptation of classical superimposed orders.
St Gervais, Paris, 108–09 (7)
Rosalys Coope, *Solomon de Brosse*, 1972

De l'Orme (Delorme), Philibert, *c.* 1510–70. French architect. He spent three years in Rome from 1533, moving in diplomatic and humanist circles and studying classical buildings. On his return to France he designed the Château of Anet for DIANE DE POITIERS and was appointed superintendent of buildings to HENRI II, undertaking among various projects the design of FRANÇOIS I's tomb at St Denis. The monumental style of his work stands in contrast to the decorated architecture of his contemporary, LESCOT. He wrote an architectural treatise in nine books, *L'Architecture* (1567) modelled in part on Vitruvius and ALBERTI, but modified by his own practical appreciation of building practice.
L'Architecture, allegory from, 22
Château of Anet: chapel, 110–11 (8); entrance, 280–81 (8)
The 'French' order, design for, 268–69 (10)
Hôtel Bulliond, Lyon, France, 188–89 (5)
Tomb of François I, St Denis, 102–03 (10)
Anthony Frederick Blunt, *Philibert de l'Orme*, 1958

Del Duca, Giacomo, *c.* 1520–1604. Italian architect and sculptor. He was one of MICHELANGELO's most talented and innovative assistants in Rome, and completed the dome of St Peter's after Michelangelo's death. His independent Roman work includes the Porta San Giovanni and the cupola of S. Maria di Loreto. In the early 1590s he returned to his native Sicily where he became architect to the city of Messina.
The Gesù, Rome, 108–09 (2)

Della Robbia family. The founder of the dynasty was Luca (1400–82), a sculptor who worked on a singing gallery in Florence Cathedral and bronze doors to the sacristy, in *c.* 1430 he perfected a technique of glazing terracotta which became extremely popular. His nephew Andrea (1435–1525) made the famous children on BRUNELLESCHI's Foundling Hospital. Luca's sons carried on the firm until the late 16th century.
Luca della Robbia: Medal of Savonarola, 327 Teachers and students, 42–43 (4)
Della Robbia workshop: Ospedale del Ceppo, Pistoia, friezes from, 126–27 (2, 3, 7)
John Pope-Hennessy, *Luca della Robbia*, 1980
Fiamma Domestici, *Della Robbia, a Family of Artists*, 1992

Desiderio da Settignano, 1430–64. Italian sculptor. Born near Florence into a family of stone masons and sculptors, he was probably trained in the workshop of Bernardo ROSSELLINO. His sculpture, although undoubtedly displaying affinity with some of DONATELLO's more lyrical early pieces, displays exceptional grace and is often described as 'sweet'. His skill can be seen in the exquisite decorative detailing on his first major independent commission, the tomb monument of Carlo MARSUPPINI in S. Croce, Florence. He became famous in his own short lifetime, particularly for his portrait busts of women and children, and for tender low-relief images of the Madonna and Child – all of which were very influential and were soon copied by far less skilled sculptors.
S. Lorenzo, Florence, tabernacle in, 260–61 (8)

Deutsch, Niklaus Manuel see **Manuel (Deutsch), Niklaus**

Diane de Poitiers, 1499–1566. The beautiful mistress of HENRI II of France, her power was such that she presided at the royal court despite the presence of the queen, Catherine de MEDICIS. Politically she was strongly anti-Protestant. She cultivated her great interest in letters and arts, being the patron of many poets, including RONSARD. Her Château of Anet, to which she was forced to retire after the king's death, was built by Philibert DE L'ORME.
Jehanne d'Orliac, *The Moon Mistress, Diane de Poitiers*, trans. by F. M. Atkinson, 1931

Domenico Veneziano, active *c.* 1438–61. Italian painter. GENTILE DA FABRIANO and PISANELLO were probably influential on his early work. In 1439 he painted a fresco cycle in S. Egidio in Florence, a project on which PIERO DELLA FRANCESCA worked as an assistant. His masterpiece is the *St Lucy Altarpiece*, an early *sacra conversazione* remarkable for the spatial complexities of its architectural framework and the notable colour composition, including pinks, greens and whites, which are subtly modified by shadows cast from a consistent and rational light source.

Hellmut Wohl, *The Paintings of Domenico Veneziano: A Study in Florentine Art of the Early Renaissance*, 1980

Donatello (Donato di Niccolò Bardi), 1386–1466. Italian sculptor. The outstanding figure in the development of sculpture in 15th-century Florence who, with BRUNELLESCHI and MASACCIO, is recognized as one of the creators of the Renaissance style. Responsible for major innovations in both figure and relief sculpture, he worked in marble, stone, bronze and wood. The gravity and realism of his early monumental marble figures – like the seated St John the Evangelist for the façade of Florence Cathedral and St Mark for the Orsanmichele – are in stark contrast to the elegant and decorative forms of the International Gothic style. A pioneer in the use of linear perspective, he displayed his interest and mastery of spatial effects in several contrasting relief forms. The Feast of Herod, a bronze panel for the Siena Baptistery font, features a complex arrangement of architectural settings uniting several narrative episodes, whereas in his *St George and the Dragon* relief he creates depth with devices such as a receding colonnade and a row of trees whose apparent depth defies the remarkably shallow (*schiacciato*) carving of the marble surface. In a successful partnership with MICHELOZZO he designed many important tomb monuments. His fame brought him prestigious commissions in Padua where he produced a celebrated equestrian monument of the GATTAMELATA, and the Santo Altar. Donatello's influence was immense and multi-faceted – his lyrical pieces found favour with the Florentine 'sweet style' sculptors, MICHELANGELO praised his monumental figures, and many northern Italian painters, including MANTEGNA, responded to his remarkable narrative reliefs in Padua.
David, 250–51 (2)
Miracle of the Eucharist, 260–61 (1)
St George, 250–51 (1)
St George and the Dragon, 240
St Mary Magdalene, 262–63 (1)
Anti-Pope John XXIII, tomb of, 100–01 (3)
Bust of a young man, 44–45 (6)
Gattamelata, equestrian monument to, 86–87 (8)
Frederick Hartt, photographs by David Finn, *Donatello, Prophet of Modern Vision*, 1974
Bonnie A. Bennett and David G. Wilkins, *Donatello*, 1984

Donne, John, 1572–1631. English author and preacher, a leading poet of what was later called the Metaphysical School. Educated at Oxford and Cambridge, he travelled widely in Europe before embarking on a career in law. He was born into a Roman Catholic family, but a difficult personal religious struggle eventually led him to embrace the Anglican faith, and he was ordained a priest in 1615. He became a royal chaplain and was Dean of St Paul's Cathedral from 1621, noted as one of the most effective and learned preachers of his age. His work divides into the passionate love

ANNO DNI. 1591.
ÆTATIS SVÆ

John Donne, engraving by William Marshall, 1591.

poetry of his youth and the equally passionate religious poetry of his later years. Both have the same tense, immensely personal quality, expressed in highly wrought, intellectual imagery, often drawing on the latest philosophical and scientific concepts.

George Parfitt, *John Donne, a Literary Life*, 1989
John Carey, *John Donne, Life, Mind and Art*, new ed., 1990

Andrea Doria, medal by Leone Leoni, 16th century.

Doria, Andrea, 1466–1560. Italian statesman and admiral. A member of a noble Genoese family, he was the most skilled naval commander of his age. With Spanish support, he forced the French from Genoa in 1527 and established order and stability in the city-state. Genoa regained its economic and political power under his leadership, and became a centre of considerable cultural activity.

Andrea Doria as Neptune by **Bronzino**, 48–49 (2)

Dossi, Dosso, active 1512–died 1542. Italian painter. Little is known about his early training, but the warm tones and pastoral nature of many of his paintings denote his knowledge of RAPHAEL and GIORGIONE, whose romanticism and feeling for magical landscape he developed. He worked mainly at the Court of Ferrara, where he also made designs for tapestries and festival decorations.

Felton Gibbons, *Dosso and Battista Dossi, Court Painters at Ferrara*, 1968

Dowland, John, 1562–1626. English musician and composer. A leading figure in the development of accompanied vocal compositions, he wrote many celebrated songs for lute accompaniment which were performed throughout Europe. He travelled widely and was the most famous lutenist of his day, holding at various times official appointments as court lutenist to the King of Denmark and to Charles I in Great Britain.

Diana Poulton, *John Dowland*, new ed., 1982

Drake, Francis, *c.* 1545–96. English admiral and navigator. In 1577 he led an expedition to pass the Straits of Magellan and prey upon the Spanish land on the west coast of America. He sailed north as far as California before crossing the Pacific back to England in 1580. This was the first English circumnavigation of the globe. Drake later acquired further fame by his part in the defeat of the Spanish Armada in 1588.

Portrait, 210–11 (8)

George Malcolm Thomson, *Sir Francis Drake*, 1988
John Cummins, *Francis Drake*, 1995

Du Bellay, Joachim, 1522–60. French poet. With RONSARD he was a leading figure in a literary group, La Pléiade, which sought to promote modern French poetry based on classical models and his *Défense et illustration de la langue française* (1549) asserted that French literature could produce work to rival that of the Italians. He wrote the first love sonnets in the French language, *L'Olive* (1549–50), which were influenced by PETRARCH. A learned Latinist, he spent several years in Rome in the company and service of his cousin, Cardinal Jean du Bellay, and in 1558 produced two collections of poems, *Antiquités de Rome* and *Regrets*.

G. Dickinson, *Du Bellay in Rome*, 1960
David Hartley, *Patriotism in the Work of Joachim Du Bellay*, 1993

Du Cerceau, Jacques Androuet the Elder, *c.* 1520–*c.* 1585. French architect and engraver. Little of his architecture was built, although he designed the châteaux of Verneuil and Charleval. He was well known in his lifetime for engravings of fantastic Mannerist architectural ornament, and towards the end of his life published two volumes of *Les Plus excellents bastiments de France* (1576 and 1579). They are important sources of information on many 16th-century buildings, although Du Cerceau's imaginative creativity often led him to add his own style of ornament to his engravings of other architects' buildings, or even to complete their plans as he saw fit.

Dürer, Albrecht, 1471–1528. German painter and engraver. Dürer's outstanding influence had two main strands: firstly, he was a major force in the transmission of Italian Renaissance ideas to northern Europe (and subsequently influenced both northern and southern artists through dissemination of his own graphic output) and secondly, he was one of the first northerners to promote the status of the creative artist. Trained in Nuremberg as a painter and printmaker, he travelled to other German cities before visiting Venice in 1494 and again from 1505 to 1507, where he was influenced by MANTEGNA's engravings and the paintings of Giovanni BELLINI, at the same time absorbing the intellectual preoccupations of humanism. He became court painter to the Emperor MAXIMILIAN I in 1512 and to CHARLES V in 1520, painting portraits of both, as well as portraits of many notable personalities of the age. He also excelled in large-scale religious painting and portraits of his family, his friends and himself. More than anything else he probably owed his fame to his woodcuts and copper engravings. His prints, either original subjects or inventive variations on traditional themes, are marked by expressive sculptural figures, delineated in clear, fine detail. Many, like the *Apocalypse*, the two *Passions*, or single plates like *Melancholia*, are forceful and dramatic, and involve several levels of meaning. Some of his drawings and very naturalistic watercolours record people and scenes encountered on his travels in Europe and a detailed diary survives of his journey in the Netherlands in 1520.

Self-portrait, 27, 242–43 (1)
Portrait of Maximilian I, 68–69 (2); woodcut of, 317
Adam and Eve, 248–49 (2)
Adoration of the Magi, 198–99 (7)
Adoration of the Trinity, 104
The Great Piece of Turf, 228–29 (6)
Hercules, 50–51 (5)
Melancholia, 46–47 (7)
The Nativity, 130–31 (4)
Rhinoceros, 182–83 (7)
St Jerome, 30
Study of a Hare, 182–83 (5)
View of Arco, 166–67 (8)
Method of applying foreshortening, 246–47 (3)
A syphilitic, woodcut of, 224–25 (7)
Triumphal arch for Maximilian I, 20

Erwin Panofsky, *Albrecht Dürer*, 1955
Jane Campbell Hutchison, *Albrecht Dürer, a Biography*, 1990

Edward VI, 1537–53. King of England from 1547. The only son of HENRY VIII, he was given a thorough humanist education by, among others, Roger ASCHAM, imbibing extreme Protestant views and inheriting his father's role as supreme head of the Church. But his death at the age of 16 meant that he had little personal influence.

Coronation procession, 90–91 (3)

J. Loach and R. Tittler (eds), *The Mid-Tudor Polity, c. 1540–1560*, 1980
Nigel Heard, *Edward VI and Mary, a mid-Tudor Crisis*, 1990

Elizabeth I, the 'Rainbow Portrait', by Marcus Gheeraerts the Younger, 1600–03.

Elizabeth I, 1533–1603. TUDOR Queen of England from 1558. Elizabeth was one of the most learned and accomplished women of her age, thoroughly grounded in Greek and Latin (by William Grindal and Roger ASCHAM) and speaking several other languages fluently. Her notorious parsimony, however, prevented her from initiating any costly enterprises. She built no palaces and commissioned few works of art, though she encouraged her subjects to do so. The fact that her reign is considered the Golden Age of the English Renaissance is largely a happy accident. In music (TALLIS, BYRD) and above all in literature (SHAKESPEARE, JONSON, MARLOWE, SPENSER, SIDNEY) she provided inspiration but little more.

Portrait by the workshop of Hilliard, 94–95 (6)
Portrait medal, 244–45 (9)
Dutch ambassadors, receiving, 82–83 (7)
Elizabeth ruling the waves, 212–13 (3)
Entertainment for, 64
Model of a coach presented by her to Tsar Boris Godunov, 178–79 (9)
Christopher Haigh, *Reign of Elizabeth I*, 1988
Neville Williams, *The Life and Times of Elizabeth I*, 1992

Elsheimer, Adam, 1578–1610. German painter and printmaker. Trained in Frankfurt, he worked mainly in Italy and he spent the most important period of his career, from 1600 until his death, in Rome. Predominantly a painter of exquisite atmospheric landscapes, often depicting classical themes and peopled by tiny figures, he was interested in portraying mysterious effects of light. His practice of working in oil on small copper panels resulted in a jewel-like finish combined with a high level of detail. His work was popular and very influential, not only in Rome, where Rubens and Claude were acquainted with him, but also elsewhere in Europe where his compositions were widely disseminated as prints.
Keith Andrews, *Adam Elsheimer*, 1977

Erasmus, Desiderius, 1466–1536. Dutch scholar and humanist. Ordained as an Augustinian monk, he received permission to study in Europe and became one of the greatest scholars of the northern Renaissance. He made several visits to England, being in close contact with MORE and COLET, and was Professor of Greek in Cambridge. He also worked in Venice with Aldus MANUTIUS. In 1521 he settled in Basle. As an educationalist, Erasmus made available a whole range of classical and patristic texts in first or improved editions, and popularized them in works intended for ordinary readers, particularly, the *Adagia* of 1523 (sayings from classical authors). In 1516 he published the first edition of the Greek New Testament, applying the same textual rigour, which led him into controversy since it questioned the authority of the Vulgate. He never left the Catholic Church, however critical he was of its corruption and some of its practices, and however sympathetic in certain respects to LUTHER's reforms. His *Manual of the Soldier of Christ* (1504) tries to go back to primitive Christian morality. His gift for amusing satire – often at the expense of monks and religious superstition – which enlivens his *Colloquies* (1522) and *The Praise of Folly* (*Encomium Moriae*, 1509) made him widely read and very influential. Erasmus' moody, undogmatic and humorous personality comes through in his numerous letters.

Portrait by Holbein, 36–37 (5)
Portrait medal, 244–45 (8)
***Adagia*, title page of**, 36–37 (1)
M. M. Phillips, *Erasmus and the Northern Renaissance*, rev. ed., 1981
Richard J. Schoeck, *Erasmus of Europe, the Prince of Humanists*, 1993

Este family. Rulers of Ferrara. Leonello (1407–50), Borso (1413–71) and Ercole I (1433–1505) were brothers. Ercole, Duke of Ferrara from 1471 to 1505, married Eleanora of Aragon and consolidated Ferrarese power. His daughters, Isabella (1474–1539) and Beatrice (1475–97), both outstandingly gifted and cultured women, married into the GONZAGA and SFORZA families. His son, Alfonso I (1486–1534), who succeeded to the dukedom, married Lucrezia BORGIA.

Portrait of Leonello d'Este by Pisanello, 72–73 (4)
J. Cartwright, *Isabella d'Este, Marchioness of Mantua*, 1903

Eworth, Hans, active 1540–died 1573. Flemish painter. Probably from Antwerp, he was a leading court artist in England during the mid-16th century. Showing little interest in three-dimensional effects, his portraits are very decorative and patterned, with finely detailed fabrics contrasted against pale skin tones. In one of his most unusual works, *Sir John Luttrell Saved from Drowning*, he portrays his subject as part of an elaborate allegorical scene, which suggests that Eworth was aware of the contemporary artistic developments of the Italian painters of the School of Fontainebleau.

Queen Elizabeth and the Three Goddesses, 48–49 (7)
Sir John Luttrell, 46–47 (8)

Eyck, Jan van, active 1422–died 1441. The most famous and influential early Flemish painter who although not responsible for 'inventing' oil painting, as often claimed, nonetheless perfected the technique to achieve a level of minute detailing and clarity of colour previously unimagined. He worked in The Hague for John of Bavaria and then as court painter to Philip the Good of Burgundy, for whom he also undertook several diplomatic missions, and from 1430 he lived in Bruges. Mystery still surrounds the works of Jan's older brother, Hubert (died 1426). No paintings are attributed entirely to Hubert but the Eyckian masterpiece *Adoration of the Lamb* in Ghent Cathedral bears an inscription stating that it is the work of both brothers. With 12 painted panels and closing shutters it is remarkable for its rich colour, abundant goldwork, detailed landscape and complex iconographic programme. Jan van Eyck's technical capacity to model with light and colour, and his detailed depiction of surfaces and textures are apparent not only in his altarpieces but also in several striking, unidealized portraits. His extraordinary technical mastery of detail had a crucial effect on the whole Netherlandish School, distinguishing it radically from that of Italy.

Betrothal portrait of Giovanni Arnolfini and his Wife, 190–91 (3)
God the Father, 128–29 (3)
Madonna with Chancellor Rolin, 166–67 (10)
Carol J. Purtle, *The Marian Paintings of Jan van Eyck*, 1982
Craig Harbison, *Jan van Eyck*, 1991

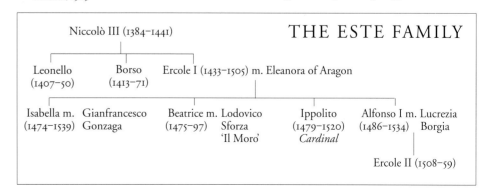

THE ESTE FAMILY

Niccolò III (1384–1441)

Leonello (1407–50) Borso (1413–71) Ercole I (1433–1505) m. Eleanora of Aragon

Isabella m. Gianfrancesco Gonzaga (1474–1539) Beatrice m. Lodovico Sforza 'Il Moro' (1475–97) Ippolito (1479–1520) *Cardinal* Alfonso I m. Lucrezia Borgia (1486–1534)

Ercole II (1508–59)

Farnese family. Although already noble, the family fortunes were founded by Giulia Farnese, the mistress of Pope ALEXANDER VI. Her brother Alessandro was made a cardinal, later becoming Pope PAUL III. Paul's son Pierluigi (1503–47) was given the duchy of Parma, and his son Ottavio married into the family of CHARLES V. Ottavio's son Alessandro (1545–92) was the Duke of Parma who commanded PHILIP II's army in the Netherlands.

Corpus Christi Procession from *The Hours of Cardinal Alessandro Farnese* by Giulio Clovio, 88–89 (3)

FERDINAND· D·G· ROMAN· IMP· SEMPER· AVG·
GERMAN· VNGAR· BOHEMIÆ· DALM·CROAT·REX
ARCHID·AVSTRIÆ· DVX·BVRGVND·COM·TIROLIS·ZC

Ferdinand I by Martin Rota, 1575.

Ferdinand I, 1503–64. Holy Roman Emperor from 1558. He was the brother of CHARLES V, who granted him the HABSBURG lands in Germany and Austria and whom he succeeded as emperor. His reign was spent struggling with the religious division in the wake of the Reformation, in which he upheld the Catholic cause.

Portrait in intaglio, 68–69 (1)
Listening to nuncio in Vienna, 116–17 (4)
Paula Sutter Fichter, *Ferdinand I of Austria*, 1982

Ferdinand II, 1578–1637. Holy Roman Emperor from 1619. Grandson of FERDINAND I and a HABSBURG, he succeeded his cousin RUDOLF II and MATTHIAS. From 1619 onwards he was involved in the Thirty Years War as leader of the Catholics.

Ficino, Marsilio, 1433–99. Italian philosopher and author. A distinguished classical scholar, he was a key figure in the development of Italian humanism. Under the munificent patronage of Cosimo de' MEDICI, he translated from Greek to Latin all the known works of Plato, which gave many Renaissance scholars access to Plato's philosophy for the first time. Ficino developed his own belief that there were elements of harmony between Plato's philosophy and the Christian faith, a notion of great importance in Renaissance humanist thought. In addition to his major philosophical work, *Theologia platonica*, completed in 1474, he translated and wrote commentaries on many Greek texts, as well as many of the Hermetic writings, key works in Renaissance magic. For many years he was at the centre of an informal Platonic Academy based in a Medici villa outside Florence.

Medal by Niccolò Fiorentino, 44–45 (4)
Portrait by Ghirlandaio, 44–45 (2)
Portrait by Rosselli, 44–45 (1)
Life and Works of Plotinus, 34–35 (9)
P. O. Kristeller, *The Philosophy of Marsilio Ficino*, 1943

Filarete (Antonio Averlino), *c.* 1400–69. Italian architect, sculptor and theorist. Possibly trained in sculpture under GHIBERTI in Florence, he was commissioned by Pope Eugenius IV to execute a set of bronze doors for St Peter's Basilica in Rome. In 1451 he entered the service of the Duke of Milan, Francesco SFORZA, building part of the Ospedale Maggiore in the city, to his own complicated, half-Gothic design. He built little and is chiefly remembered for his *Trattato d'architettura*, which includes plans for an ideal and fantastic centrally planned Renaissance city called Sforzinda. Partly based on his knowledge of ALBERTI's theories and including much of his own invention, the treatise circulated widely in manuscript form – and was described as 'ridiculous' by VASARI.

Ospedale Maggiore, Milan, 272–73 (3)
Sforzinda, design for, 270–71 (5)
J. R. Spencer, *Filarete's Treatise on Architecture*, 1965

Filelfo, Francesco, 1398–1481. Italian scholar. In the 1420s he visited Constantinople and learned Greek, which he taught in Florence until a quarrel obliged him to flee to Milan. Here he was employed by both the VISCONTI and the SFORZA.

Leslie Alfred Sheppard, *A Fifteenth-century Humanist, Francesco Filelfo*, 1935

Floris (de Vriendt) family. Flemish family of artists. The two most notable members of the family, the brothers Cornelis (1514–75) and Frans (1516–70), both spent several years in Italy and on their return to Antwerp were conspicuous exponents of Mannerism. Cornelis is chiefly remembered as architect of the Town Hall in Antwerp, an impressive classicizing building which reveals his mastery of Italian forms. Frans, a painter, was deeply influenced by MICHELANGELO, having witnessed in Rome the unveiling of *The Last Judgment* in the Sistine Chapel. In Antwerp he ran a successful studio specializing in large-scale religious and mythological scenes which typically include complex compositions of muscular and powerful figures. He also painted some intense and forceful portraits.

Cornelis Floris: Antwerp Town Hall, 160–61 (4)

Foppa, Vincenzo, *c.* 1428–1515/16. Italian painter. Born in Brescia, he worked mainly in Milan and Pavia, and was the leading artist in Lombardy before the arrival of LEONARDO. Although revealing an appreciation of the artistic developments of Giovanni BELLINI and MANTEGNA, his paintings are characterized by a more expressive and muscular type of figure, and also by a unique and subtle tonal range. Throughout a long and productive career he painted frescoes and altarpieces, many commissioned by the Dukes of Milan.

Fouquet, Jean, *c.* 1420–81. French painter and illuminator. Little is known of his early life but in 1447 he is recorded as having painted a portrait of Pope Eugenius IV in Rome. The following year he returned to his native Tours, working for CHARLES VIII and eventually being appointed as royal painter. His authenticated works include 60 exquisitely detailed miniatures for a large Book of Hours, and other illuminated manuscripts. His visit to Italy encouraged an interest in perspective and classical details, which he combined with the northern tradition of minute and carefully observed details.

Book of Hours of Etienne Chevalier, 272–73 (2)
Klaus Günther Perls, *Jean Fouquet*, 1940
C. Winkworth, *Jean Fouquet and his Time*, 1947

Foxe, John, 1516–87. English Protestant priest and author. He lived abroad during the reign of MARY I, returning in 1559 and publishing a record of her persecutions of Protestants, *Acts and Monuments of these Latter and Perilous Days* (known as the *Book of Martyrs*) in 1563.

Book of Martyrs, 120–21 (3)
W. Haller (ed.), *Foxe's Book of Martyrs and the Elect Nation*, 1963
Neville Williams, *John Foxe the Martyrologist, his Life and Times*, 1975

Francesco di Giorgio Martini, 1439–1502. Italian architect, painter, sculptor and theorist. A native of Siena, his activity in painting and sculpture was mainly confined to his early career, and by 1477 he entered the service of Federigo da MONTEFELTRO in Urbino, as a military engineer and architect. Employed on many fortification schemes, and possibly on some projects in the Palazzo Ducale, his chief work of architecture was S. Maria del Calcinaio, Cortona, a Latin cross church of great refinement, subsequently much altered. His influential architectural treatise, *Trattato di architettura civile e militare*, although based in part on Vitruvius and ALBERTI, was of a more practical nature, dealing with aspects of military architecture, city planning and religious symbolism in church building.

Catapult, 164–65 (1)
A. S. Weller, *Francesco di Giorgio*, 1943
Gustina Scaglia, *Francesco di Giorgio*, 1992

Franciabigio (Francesco di Cristofano), *c.* 1482–1525. Italian painter. A Florentine artist, he was influenced by ANDREA DEL SARTO for whom he worked as an assistant. He was most successful as a painter of portraits, but also undertook fresco work in Florence.

Susan Regan Mackillop, *Franciabigio*, 1974

Francken, Franz, 1578–1647. Flemish painter, who spent most of his life in Antwerp, specializing in battles, scenes of the chase and landscapes.

Cabinet of Curiosities, 60–61 (7)

François I, 1494–1547. VALOIS King of France from 1515. François was one of the trio of kings (with HENRY VIII and CHARLES V) who sought to dominate Europe in the first half of the 16th century. A major part of that dominance was cultural, manifested in the ostentatious display of the Field of Cloth of Gold; in the Italianate palaces that he commissioned (Chambord, Château de Madrid); in his invitation to France of Italian artists such as SERLIO, CELLINI, ROSSO FIORENTINO, PONTORMO and LEONARDO; and in his encouragement of literature and learning – founding the Collège de France and assisting BUDE, MAROT and others.

Portrait by François Clouet, 70–71 (1)
Portrait by Jean Clouet, 86–87 (2)
Portrait by Niccolò dell' Abbate, 48–49 (4)
Field of Cloth of Gold, 82–83 (6)
With Charles V, 68–69 (7)
Gallery of François I, Fontainebleau, by Primaticcio and Rosso Fiorentino, 252–53 (6)
Tomb, 102–03 (10)

R. J. Knecht, *Francis I*, 1982
———, *French Renaissance Monarchy, Francis I and Henry II*, 1984

François I in old age, c. 1550.

Frederick III, 1415–93. Holy Roman Emperor from 1440 until 1490. Son of Ernst of HABSBURG. With the advice of Aeneas Sylvius Piccolomini, later Pope PIUS II, he signed the Concordat of Vienna, 1448, pledging German loyalty to the papacy. He was the last emperor to be crowned in Rome, but was virtually deposed by his son MAXIMILIAN I in 1490.

Betrothal to Eleanor of Portugal by Pinturicchio, 82–83 (2)
Coin cabinet, 60–61 (2)

Martin Frobisher by Cornelius Ketil, 1577.

Frobisher, Martin, *c.* 1535–94. English navigator. Between 1576 and 1578 he led three expeditions across the Atlantic in search of a northwest passage to China. They failed, but he was able to explore northern Canada.

Peter Dawlish, *Martin Frobisher*, 1956
W. A. Kenyon, *Tokens of Possession, the Northern Voyages of Martin Frobisher*, 1975

Fugger family. German bankers and merchants who wielded enormous financial and political power during the 15th and 16th centuries in Europe. The dynastic foundations, laid in the mid-14th century in Augsburg, were based initially on the textile industry. By the end of the 15th century various members of the family had established trading and banking strongholds in Rome, Venice and Innsbruck, as well as controlling mining monopolies in Austria and Czechoslovakia. Jakob Fugger the Rich (1459–1525), head of the family at the end of the 15th century, supported MAXIMILIAN I and financed the election of CHARLES V. He was severely criticized by LUTHER for his financial activities. Jakob's successor was Anton (1493–1560), an acute businessman who secured loans for Charles V and PHILIP II of Spain. After Anton's death the business slowly declined, although the personal wealth of the Fugger family was ensured by vast land and property holdings.

Portrait of Christoph Fugger, 232–33 (5)
Jakob Fugger in his office, 232–33 (4)
Fugger Chapel, Augsburg: design for, 19; relief by Vischer, 260–61 (6)

Gabrieli, Giovanni, 1557–1612. Italian composer and musician. He was the nephew of the composer, singer and organist, Andrea Gabrieli. He studied with him and, after a period spent in Munich, succeeded Andrea as organist at St Mark's Basilica. His music became very well known in Europe and he had several German and Austrian patrons. A composer of sacred music, including choral and instrumental settings for the liturgy, his most famous works are the *Sacrae symphoniae*. Later he became a highly respected teacher.

D. Arnold, *Giovanni Gabrieli*, 1974
———, *Giovanni Gabrieli and the Music of the Venetian High Renaissance*, 1979

Gaffurio, Franchino, 1451–1522. Italian musician. He was *maestro di capella* at Milan Cathedral for nearly 40 years, but is better known for his publications, which relate music to Neoplatonic number theory, than for his compositions.

Lecturing, 220–21 (5)
De harmonica musicorum, 220–21 (9)
Claudet Palisca (ed.), *The Theory of Music, Franchino Gaffurio*, 1993

Galileo Galilei, early 17th century.

Galilei, Galileo, 1564–1642. Italian scientist and astronomer. A noted mathematician, he was fascinated with optical science and developed scientific instruments, particularly telescopes. His astronomical observations led him to endorse the notion of a heliocentric planetary system, put forward by COPERNICUS. The publication of his *Dialogue Concerning the Two Chief World Systems – Ptolemaic and Copernican* (1632) brought him into conflict with the Church, and he was tried and held under house arrest for having supported and taught Copernican theory. Famous in his own lifetime, he made major contributions to experimental enquiry, especially in physical and astronomical science. His other major published work was *Dialogue Concerning the Two New Sciences* (1638).

Moons of Jupiter, observations on, 214–15 (8)
Telescopes, 214–15 (7)

Pietro Redondi, *Galileo: Heretic*, trans. by R. Rosenthal, 1988
Michael White, *Galileo Galilei*, 1991

Garcilaso de la Vega, *c.* 1501–36. Spanish poet. A nobleman from Toledo whose life was spent in the military and diplomatic service of CHARLES V, he epitomizes the Renaissance ideal of the cultivated soldier-courtier. He travelled widely in his career, moving in cultured courtly circles, and of great significance to his poetic achievements were the friendships he formed with Italian literary figures, including TASSO and BEMBO. His Spanish verse, particularly love sonnets based on Petrarchan models and three pastoral poems, was important in introducing Italianate forms into Spanish literature. He was fatally wounded fighting with the imperial troops in a battle in southern France, aged only 35.

Elias L. Rivers, *Garcilaso de la Vega, Poems, a Critical Guide*, 1980

Gattamelata (Erasmo da Narni), 1370–1433. Italian condottiere in the service of Venice. Subject of an equestrian monument in Padua by DONATELLO.

Equestrian monument by Donatello, 86–87 (8)

Geertgen tot Sint Jans, *c.* 1455/65–1485/95. Dutch painter. Active in Haarlem during the late 15th century; no contemporary documents exist to provide details of his life. His name literally means 'Little Gerard of St John' which points to his connection with a lay brotherhood at the monastery of St John in Haarlem, where he painted two panels for the high altar. A body of work is attributed to him on stylistic grounds, particularly through his distinctive figures, with smooth, oval-shaped faces, who engage in simple and sincere devotion.

Gemistus Plethon, George, 1355–1452. Byzantine philosopher and humanist. He was an adviser to the Byzantine Emperor and between 1438 and 1445 attended the church councils in Italy where union of the Greek and Latin Churches was sought. His important contribution to Florentine humanism through his treatise *On the Differences between Aristotelian and Platonic Philosophies* (1439) aroused interest in the study of Plato, and may have prompted Cosimo de' MEDICI's foundation of the Platonic Academy in Florence.

Gentile da Fabriano, active 1408–died 1427. Italian painter. First recorded in Venice in 1408 working on frescoes in the Doge's Palace, he was a major exponent of the courtly International Gothic style of painting, and was already famous in 1422 when called to Florence by Palla Strozzi to paint his most celebrated work, *The Adoration of the Magi*. This large altarpiece, sumptuous and lavish in its use of applied gold and expensive pigments, stands in absolute contrast to the exactly contemporary work of MASACCIO. It presents a crowded procession of men and animals massed behind the three richly clad kings – a composition which was very

influential on later representations of the Epiphany. Gentile also worked in Siena and Orvieto, and died in Rome while working for Pope Martin V on frescoes in the Lateran Basilica which have since been destroyed.

Keith Christiansen, *Gentile da Fabriano*, 1982

Gerhaert van Leyden, Nicolaus, active 1462–died 1473. Netherlandish sculptor. Although his name implies Dutch origins, little is known of his early life or training, and most examples of his sculpture are found in Germany. He worked mainly in stone, carving several important tomb monuments and some notable portrait busts. Called to Vienna, his final commission was the red marble tomb of Emperor FREDERICK III, featuring a deeply undercut and realistic effigy, which is characteristic of his figural style.

Gerolamo dai Libri, 1474–1555. Italian painter and miniaturist of the School of Verona. He was a follower of Domenico Morone and like many Veronese painters was strongly influenced by MANTEGNA. His religious subjects are often set against ethereal landscape backgrounds.

Gesualdo, Don Carlo, *c.* 1560–1613. Italian composer and musician. A Neapolitan prince, he is chiefly remembered for his dramatic and expressive madrigals, which were published in six books between 1594 and 1611, and reprinted several times in his own lifetime. Highly original and possibly too forward looking for his era, his works did not inspire any contemporary followers. He was also famous for ordering the murder of his unfaithful first wife and her lover.

Denis Arnold, *Gesualdo*, 1984
G. Watkins, *Gesualdo, the Man and his Music*, 2nd ed., 1991

Gheeraerts family. Flemish painters who settled in London. Marcus Gheeraerts the Elder (*c.* 1525–before 1591) fled from Bruges in 1568. He may have painted a portrait of Queen ELIZABETH I. His son, Marcus Gheeraerts the Younger (1561–1636), worked from his father's London workshop which was also shared by Isaac OLIVER. He enjoyed considerable success as a portraitist in the court circles of both Elizabeth I and JAMES I. Although his portraits are far more naturalistic than his father's rather stiff and formal images, they are still characterized by fine detailing of features and patterning of fabrics.

Marcus Gheeraerts the Elder: *Procession of Knights of the Garter*, 90–91 (4)
Marcus Gheeraerts the Younger: **Portrait of Elizabeth I**, 303

Ghiberti, Lorenzo, 1378–1455. Italian sculptor of outstanding creative and technical skill whose bronze masterworks are two celebrated sets of doors for the Florentine Baptistery. The north doors (1403–24) portray scenes from the Life of Christ and the east doors (1425–52), called

the 'Gates of Paradise' by MICHELANGELO, depict subject matter from the Old Testament. The commission for the north doors was decided by a sculptural competition in 1401 in which Ghiberti triumphed over BRUNELLESCHI and other sculptors. His development from elegant and fluid International Gothic forms to an equally refined but more classical sculptural style can be traced through the individual panels of these doors, which represent 50 years of his career. His large workshop, which required a dedicated foundry, was a major force in the artistic training of many young assistants including DONATELLO, FILARETE, MICHELOZZO and UCCELLO. His other work includes three bronze figures for the Orsanmichele in Florence and relief panels for the Siena Baptistery font. In his later years he wrote three *Commentarii*, one of which includes his autobiography.

Self-portrait from baptistery doors, 242–43 (2)
Jesus disputing with the doctors, 260–61 (2)
Story of Joseph, 260–61 (3)

Ludwig Goldscheider, *Ghiberti*, 1949
Richard Krautheimer and Trude Krautheimer-Hess, *Lorenzo Ghiberti*, 1970

Domenico Ghirlandaio, woodcut from Vasari's Lives, *1568.*

Ghirlandaio, Domenico, *c.* 1448–94. Italian painter who was an outstanding practitioner of fresco technique and decorated the family chapels of many rich Florentine merchants. The most notable of his fresco cycles, in the Sassetti Chapel of S. Trinita and the vast chancel space of S. Maria Novella in Florence, and the Sistine Chapel in Rome, include many portraits of the patrons' families, depicted typically as groups of spectators at the religious events. A master of clear narrative composition, Ghirlandaio's engaging frescoes are also visual documents of great interest, showing contemporary dress, customs and several specific views of the city. He was primarily a painter of fresco but his tempera altarpiece, *The Adoration of the Magi*, is justly recognized as a masterpiece. He ran a large, busy studio, in which MICHELANGELO was an apprentice.

Ficino, Cristoforo Landino, Poliziano and Giovanni de' Becchi, fresco of, 44–45 (2)
The Last Supper, 138–39 (2)
Miracle of St Francis, 154–55 (2)
The Nativity, 130–31 (6)
Old Man and Boy, 176–77 (8)
Visiting the Sick, 200–01 (5)
Pantheon, Rome, drawing of, 266

Emma Micheletti, *Domenico Ghirlandaio*, 1990

Giambologna (Giovanni Bologna), 1529–1608. Flemish sculptor, real name Jean Boulogne. Trained in Belgium, he arrived in Italy in the 1550s, becoming not only the leading sculptor in Florence, his main centre of activity, but also an artist renowned throughout Europe. Inspired both by classical models and the work of MICHELANGELO, he extended the boundaries of free-standing marble sculpture to encompass multiple viewpoints and vigorous movement, achieved through expressive Mannerist figure compositions. This development is exemplified in *The Rape of the Sabines*, where three spiralling, entwined figures are carved with extraordinary technical skill from a single marble block. Equally talented in bronze, he produced single figures (including *Mercury*), narrative reliefs and large-scale equestrian monuments. Bronze statuettes, cast from his models, were eagerly sought by collectors.

Mercury, 236–37 (8)
The Rape of the Sabines, 262–63 (2)
Fountain of the Appenines, Pratolino, 258–59 (3)

C. Avery, *Giambologna, the Complete Sculpture*, 1987
Mary Weitzel Gibbons, *Giambologna, Narrator of the Catholic Reformation*, 1995

Gibbons, Orlando, 1583–1625. English composer and musician. Acknowledged as the outstanding keyboard player of his day, he was organist at the Chapel Royal of JAMES I, and subsequently organist at Westminster Abbey. He made an important contribution to musical composition for virginals and viols, and is remembered also for his church music and fine madrigals.

Edmund Horace Fellowes, *Orlando Gibbons. A Short Account of his Life and Work*, 1925
———, *Orlando Gibbons and his Family*, 2nd ed., 1951

Giocondo, Fra Giovanni, *c.* 1433–1515. Italian humanist, architect and engineer. A scholarly friar who had considerable influence on the buildings of other architects through his drawings of classical ruins and his technical expertise in engineering and construction. After several years working in Naples, he went to Paris where he designed the Notre-Dame bridge. He worked on fortification and hydraulic projects for the Republic of Venice, and after the death of BRAMANTE was called to Rome as a technical

consultant on the construction of the new St Peter's. His reputation as a classical scholar was enhanced by the publication in 1511 of his edition of Vitruvius, which was the first illustrated and annotated version of *De architectura*.

Giorgione, *c.* 1478–1510. Italian painter. He was an innovative artist, of great significance to Venetian painting, yet enigma surrounds his short life and his few accepted paintings. A pupil of Giovanni BELLINI, in 1506 he was recorded in partnership with CATENA and in 1508 he worked on frescoes on the exterior of the Fondaco dei Tedeschi, Venice – a project in which TITIAN was also employed. None of his works is fully documented although the *Castelfranco Madonna*, Castelfranco Cathedral, is an accepted attribution in which he develops the *sacra conversazione* by a remarkable organization of spatial relationships which places the Madonna and Child on a high, inaccessible throne. Giorgione's major contribution to Venetian art was the pastoral landscape theme, as in *La Tempesta*, where he explored the power and moods of nature. He is also noted for his use of rich, saturated colours. Following his early death from plague in 1510, some of his paintings were completed by Titian and SEBASTIANO DEL PIOMBO, and this has further complicated the assessment of Giorgione's œuvre.

Armed Warrior with his Squire, 222–23 (2)
La Tempesta, 166–67 (2)
The Three Ages of Man, 176–77 (4)
La Vecchia, 176–77 (3)

Terisio Pignatti, *Giorgio da Castelfranco, Called Giorgione*, trans. by Clovis Whitfield, 1971
Hugh Hood, *Five New Facts about Giorgione*, 1987

Giovanni di Paolo, active 1420–died 1482. Italian painter. He was a prolific artist who, with SASSETTA, was one of the leading painters in 15th-century Siena. He was mainly influenced by earlier Sienese masters, and his work has a Gothic feel both in representation of space and a slender, elongated type of figure. He continued to use a considerable amount of gold leaf and decorative detailing in his paintings.

Dante's *Paradiso*, illustration to, 38–39 (11)

John Pope-Hennessy, *Giovanni di Paolo, 1403–1483*, 1937
———, *Paradiso, the Illuminations to Dante's Divine Comedy*, 1993

Giulio Romano (Giulio Pippi), *c.* 1499–1546. Italian Mannerist architect and painter. Born and trained in Rome, he became a key member of RAPHAEL's workshop, and completed the master's unfinished works in the Vatican. His major architectural work was undertaken in Mantua but before he left Rome he built the Villa Lante (1518–20) and the Palazzo Maccarani (*c.* 1520); the latter incorporates his first unorthodox use of classical elements. In

Mantua he was commissioned by Federico GONZAGA to build the Palazzo del Tè (1527–34), a single-storey villa surrounding a courtyard. In the Palazzo his revolutionary juxtaposition of smooth and rusticated surfaces, large over-emphasized keystones and witty slipped triglyphs are intended to amuse and shock. Equally bizarre is his completely frescoed room in the Palazzo, the Sala dei Giganti, where illusionistic collapsing columns and falling rocks seem to envelop the spectator as the Giants' domain is destroyed by Jupiter's thunderbolts.

The Bath of Mars and Venus, 52–53 (8)
The Holy Family with St Anne, 190–91 (1)
The Marriage of Cupid and Psyche, 236–37 (4)
Palazzo del Tè, Mantua, 268–69 (12)
Porta Citadella, Mantua, 268–69 (11)

Frederick Hartt, *Giulio Romano*, 2 vols, 1958

Goes, Hugo van der, active 1467–died 1482. Flemish painter, probably born in Ghent where he entered the Painters' Guild in 1467. The large scale of most of his work is rather unusual and he combines the northern tradition of carefully observed detail and rich colour with the impressive monumentality of his figures and background settings. His paintings have an intense devotional feeling ranging through all his characters from elegant floating angels and serene Madonnas, to adoring Magi and swarthy shepherds. His remarkable *Portinari Altarpiece*, painted for the merchant Tommaso Portinari, was despatched to Florence in 1483 and proved influential on many Italian artists, most notably GHIRLANDAIO. In 1475 he entered an Augustinian monastery near Brussels as a lay-brother, where he continued to paint until finally seized by a melancholic mental illness.

Lamentation over the Dead Christ, 142–43 (4)
The Nativity (*Portinari Altarpiece*), 130–31 (3)

Goltzius, Hendrik, 1558–1617. Dutch painter and engraver. He went to Italy *c.* 1590 and evolved an individual Mannerist style, sometimes using colour wood-blocks.

Manlius Torquatus, 250–51 (7)

Gonçalves, Nuño, active 1450–died 1471. The leading Portuguese artist of the 15th century, who was court painter to ALFONSO V, King of Portugal, from 1450. His only surviving works are six large panels from an altarpiece painted for the Convent of São Vicente, Lisbon. The four narrower panels each represent St Vincent surrounded by different ranks of Portuguese society, such as members of the royal court and the clergy. He was an artist of superb technical skill and the fine detail of these scenes, combined with the realism of his figures, points to a strong affinity with Flemish art.

Alfonso V, King of Portugal, Kneeling before St Vincent, 70–71 (7)

THE GONZAGA FAMILY

Francesco (1388–1407)
|
Gianfrancesco I (1394–1444)
|
Lodovico (1412–78) m. Barbara of
Brandenburg
|
Federico I (1439–84)   Francesco
| *Cardinal*
Gianfrancesco (1466–1519) m. Isabella d'Este
|
Federico (1500–40)

Federico Gonzaga by Titian, c. 1525.

Gonzaga family. Rulers of Mantua from
the early 14th century until 1627. Francesco
(1388–1407) built the castle of Mantua
and initiated the family's collection of
manuscripts. His grandson, Lodovico
(1412–78) received a scholarly education
from VITTORINO DA FELTRE, as well as
being trained as a military leader, and
attracted many humanists to his court.
A keen patron of architecture, he planned
several major rebuilding schemes in Mantua
and commissioned from ALBERTI the churches
of S. Sebastiano and S. Andrea. He was
also patron of MICHELOZZO's vast Rotunda
of SS. Annunziata in Florence. MANTEGNA
was painter to the Mantuan court from 1460,
and depicted Lodovico and his family in
courtly scenes in the Camera degli Sposi
in the Palazzo Ducale. His grandson
Gianfrancesco (1466–1519) was also primarily
a military leader, but his wife Isabella d'ESTE
made Mantua one of the most brilliant courts
of Italy. These interests were inherited by
their son Federico (1500–40) who employed

GIULIO ROMANO at the Palazzo del Tè.
Several members of the family became
cardinals.
Lodovico Gonzaga and his family by Mantegna,
72–73 (6)
Hunters and Dogs of the Gonzaga Court,
96–97 (1)
S. Brinton, *The Gonzaga – Lords of Mantua,* 1927
Kate Simon, *A Renaissance Tapestry, the Gonzaga of
Mantua,* 1988

Gossaert, Jan see **Mabuse**

Goujon, Jean, *c.* 1510–68. French sculptor.
He had a scholarly interest in the Antique,
and his sculptural style, which shows the
influence both of classical models and the
Mannerism of the School of Fontainebleau,
is characterized by elegant figures swathed in
distinctive, decorative drapery. His mature
work was mainly in collaboration with
the architect LESCOT, and his sculptural
decoration formed a key element of the
architecture. He provided figures and
decorative friezes for the Cour Carrée at the
Louvre, and his technical skill and invention
can be appreciated in a series of graceful
shallow-relief nymphs for the Fontaine
des Innocents, Paris. He illustrated and
wrote an introduction to the first French
edition of Vitruvius.
Fontaine des Innocents, 260–61 (7)
Reginald Lister, *Jean Goujon: his Life and Work,*
1903

Gozzoli, Benozzo, 1420–97. Italian painter.
A Florentine by birth, he was in Rome
between 1448 and 1450 working as Fra
ANGELICO's chief assistant on a fresco cycle
in the Nicholas V Chapel in the Vatican.
His own masterpiece is a frescoed chapel
in the Palazzo Medici-Riccardi, Florence,
which depicts the Journey of the Magi, and
extends GENTILE DA FABRIANO's handling
of the same theme into a majestic and
continuous procession encircling the chapel
walls. The stately pageant, which according
to tradition includes a number of portraits
of the MEDICI family and their circle,
takes place within a carefully observed
and detailed Tuscan landscape, with villages,
trees, animals and birds realistically depicted.
As well as frescoes, Gozzoli also painted
altarpieces.
Journey of the Magi, 254–55 (5)
St Augustine Teaching in Rome, 42–43 (7)
Robert M. A. Rowe, *Benozzo Gozzoli,* rev. ed., 1967

Graf, Urs, *c.* 1485–1527. Swiss goldsmith,
draughtsman and engraver. He produced
a large number of drawings, woodcuts
and engravings in the style of DÜRER and
BALDUNG, but often depicting low-life
subjects. A rogue and brawler, repeatedly
in trouble with the authorities, he often left
Basle to fight as a mercenary soldier in both
Italy and France. In his clear and flowing
style he recorded images which include
the stark reality of death in battle, witty

observations of courtesans and soldiers, and
satirical images and allegories. He provided
many woodcuts for book illustrations, and
signed most of his work with his distinctive
monogram.

Greco, El (Domenikos Theotokopoulos),
1541–1614. Although born and trained in
Crete, at that time a Venetian territory, he is
generally considered a Spanish painter. He
spent some time as a pupil of TITIAN in
Venice and by late 1570 was in Rome. He
left Italy for Spain in 1577 and spent the
rest of his life in Toledo, frustrated in his
attempts to become a court painter to
PHILIP II. Deeply affected by a number of
influences – Byzantine art, the Venetian
works of Titian and TINTORETTO, and the
Roman Mannerism of MICHELANGELO –
El Greco developed a dramatic style
which was entirely suited to the fervent
Counter-Reformation spirit of Toledo. The
elongation of his figures, rendered in fluid
brushstrokes and a strikingly unique palette,
deprives his bodies of physical solidity but
gives them an intense spirituality, so that he
is unequalled as a painter of mystical and
visionary subjects. He was also an excellent
and sensitive portraitist.
Baptism of Christ, 134–35 (5)
Crucifixion, 140–41 (6)
The Dream of Philip II, 124–25 (5)
David Davis, *El Greco,* 1976
El Greco, the Complete Paintings, trans. by Jane
Carroll, 1980

Grien, Hans Baldung see **Baldung**

Grolier de Servières, Jean, 1479–1565.
French patron and bibliophile. He became
one of the treasurers of France and was a
generous patron to many artists. His interest
in books, and particularly in fine book-
binding, led him to support MANUTIUS'
Aldine Press in Venice, and he was later
instrumental in promoting the craft of
book-binding in France. His own library
contained more than 3,000 volumes, each
distinctively bound and personalized with
Latin inscriptions in gold-tooled lettering.

Grünewald, Matthias (Mathis Gothardt),
active 1500–died 1528. A German painter
of powerful religious images whose portrayal
of the emotional and physical anguish
of Holy figures is heightened by his use
of intense colour. He undertook many
commissions in Alsace and Germany, one
of the most noted being the *Isenheim Altarpiece,* made for the chapel of a hospital. A
structurally complex altarpiece, with twelve
panels, which include an *Annunciation* and
a *Nativity,* and the striking image of the
pain-wracked Christ of the *Crucifixion.*
Crucifixion, 140–41 (4)
The Resurrection, 144–45 (2)
G. Schoenberger, *The Drawings of Mathis
Gothardt Nithart called Grünewald,* 1948
N. Pevsner and M. Meir, *Grünewald,* 1958

Guarino da Verona, medal by Matteo de' Pasti, c. 1440–46.

Guarino da Verona, 1374–1460. Italian teacher. He learned Greek in Constantinople and established himself at Ferrara in 1429, making it a centre of humanist education, and attracting many students from other countries, including Great Britain. His syllabus of Greek and Latin composition in prose and verse, the study of grammar and the close reading of classical texts was to be influential for the next 400 years.

Gutenberg, Johannes, *c.* 1400–68. German printer. He invented the method of printing with movable type, which was a landmark in the development of printing. In 1455, after long years of experiment and realization of his invention in both Mainz and Strasbourg, he was involved in legal proceedings brought by his financial partner, Johannes Fust, which resulted in Fust gaining control of all of Gutenberg's printing equipment and type. Although no texts exist which bear Gutenberg's name it is accepted that he produced the earliest book printed with movable type, the masterly 42-line Bible (or the Mazarin Bible) of 1455.
The 42-line Bible, 206–07 (1)

Habsburg family. The longest lasting and most widespread of European dynasties. Their possessions in Austria led to their election as Holy Roman Emperors in the 13th century, and this became virtually hereditary in the family from 1438 to 1806. During the Renaissance they also increased their power outside the Empire. MAXIMILIAN I married the heiress of Burgundy and Flanders. His son Philip I (1478–1506) married the daughter of Ferdinand and Isabella of Spain, and their son CHARLES V accordingly inherited both Spain and the Netherlands, as well as being elected emperor. Charles, however, assigned Germany and Austria to his brother FERDINAND I (later emperor, to be followed by his own descendants), and Spain to his son PHILIP II. From this time the destinies of the Spanish and Austrian Habsburgs were separate, the first lasting until 1700, the second until 1918.
A. Wandruszka, *The House of Habsburg*, 1964
Andrew Wheatcroft, *The Habsburgs*, 1995

Hawkwood, John, *c.* 1320–94. English mercenary soldier employed by Pisa, Milan and finally Florence. Subject of a memorial fresco by UCCELLO in Florence Cathedral.
Equestrian portrait by Uccello, 86–87 (3)
J. Temple-Leader and G. Marcotti, *Sir John Hawkwood*, 1889

Heemskerck, Maerten van, 1498–1574. Dutch painter, one of the leading Mannerists in 16th-century Holland. When he visited Italy between 1532 and 1536 he was overwhelmed by the Roman Mannerism of MICHELANGELO. He drew extensively, making studies of both ancient and modern Rome with details of buildings, sculptures, paintings, and city views, which supplied motifs throughout the rest of his career in Haarlem. Two of his surviving sketchbooks, now in Berlin, provide extremely valuable documentary evidence of the fabric of 16th-century Rome.
Self-portrait with Colosseum, 278–79 (6)
New St Peter's under construction, 156–57 (3)
Roman sarcophagus and sphinxes, 56–57 (6)
I. Veldman, *Maerten van Heemskerck and Dutch Humanism in the Sixteenth Century*, 1977

Heere, Lucas de, 1531–81. Flemish painter who spent much of his life in England.
Allegory of the Tudor Succession, 70–71 (6)

Henri II, 1519–59. VALOIS King of France from 1547. He succeeded his father FRANCOIS I, and his policy was largely

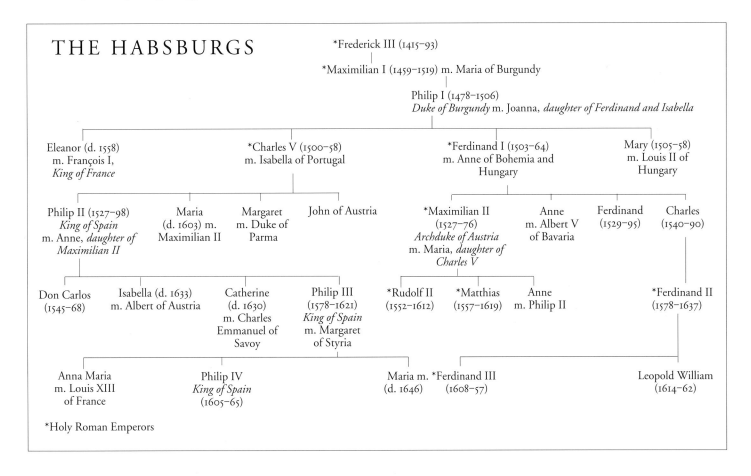

THE HABSBURGS

*Frederick III (1415–93)

*Maximilian I (1459–1519) m. Maria of Burgundy

Philip I (1478–1506)
Duke of Burgundy m. Joanna, *daughter of Ferdinand and Isabella*

Eleanor (d. 1558)
m. François I,
King of France

*Charles V (1500–58)
m. Isabella of Portugal

*Ferdinand I (1503–64)
m. Anne of Bohemia and
Hungary

Mary (1505–58)
m. Louis II of
Hungary

Philip II (1527–98)
King of Spain
m. Anne, *daughter of
Maximilian II*

Maria
(d. 1603) m.
Maximilian II

Margaret
m. Duke of
Parma

John of Austria

*Maximilian II
(1527–76)
Archduke of Austria
m. Maria, *daughter of
Charles V*

Anne
m. Albert V
of Bavaria

Ferdinand
(1529–95)

Charles
(1540–90)

Don Carlos
(1545–68)

Isabella (d. 1633)
m. Albert of Austria

Catherine
(d. 1630)
m. Charles
Emmanuel of
Savoy

Philip III
(1578–1621)
King of Spain
m. Margaret
of Styria

*Rudolf II
(1552–1612)

*Matthias
(1557–1619)

Anne
m. Philip II

*Ferdinand II
(1578–1637)

Anna Maria
m. Louis XIII
of France

Philip IV
King of Spain
(1605–65)

Maria m. *Ferdinand III
(d. 1646)   (1608–57)

Leopold William
(1614–62)

*Holy Roman Emperors

Henri II, medallion by Germain Pilon, mid-16th century.

determined by his powerful mistress, DIANE DE POITIERS. In 1531 he married Catherine de MEDICIS. During his reign, affairs in France were dominated by financial and religious issues, including the spread of Calvinism.

Death of, 200–01 (1)

R. J. Knecht, *French Renaissance Monarchy, Francis I and Henry II,* 1984

Henri IV by Jean Rabel, c. 1580.

Henri IV (Henry of Navarre), 1553–1610. King of France from 1589. As a leading Protestant nobleman he played a central role in the final phases of the French Wars of Religion, and although he became a Catholic on accession to the French throne, he ensured the protection of the Protestants by the Edict of Nantes (1598). He restored a measure of stability and order to France and consolidated royal authority. In 1610 he was murdered by a Roman Catholic fanatic.

Desmond Seward, *The First Bourbon, Henry IV, King of France and Navarre,* 1971
Mark Greengrass, *France in the Age of Henri IV,* 2nd ed., 1995

Henry VIII, 1491–1547. TUDOR King of England from 1509. Henry's divorce, leading to his break with the pope, the foundation of the Anglican Church and the dissolution of the monasteries, was catastrophic for English culture. It ended religious painting and sculpture and severely curtailed religious architecture. In his Catholic youth, however, Henry had encouraged intellectuals such as Fox, Linacre, COLET, ERASMUS and MORE, the last of whom was to die for opposing him. And later he promoted the first Bible in English, the 'Great Bible' (1539), and was instrumental in introducing Italian Renaissance sculpture and architecture (TORRIGIANO, Nonsuch Palace).

Portrait by Holbein, 92–93 (2)
Field of Cloth of Gold, 82–83 (6)
'Great Bible', title page of, 118–19 (9)
'Musick', 220–21 (2)
Parliament, 74–75 (3)
Warship, 212–13 (6)

J. J. Scarisbrick, *Henry VIII,* 1968
D. R. Starkey, *The Reign of Henry VIII: Personalities and Politics,* 1985

Henry the Navigator, 1394–1460. Portuguese prince, son of John I. Not strictly a navigator at all, he organized voyages of exploration down the west coast of Africa, the beginning of Portugal's overseas empire.

Portrait of Alfonso V with Henry the Navigator behind him, 70–71 (7)

John Ure, *Prince Henry the Navigator,* 1977
P. E. Russell, *Prince Henry the Navigator and the Fall of a Culture Hero,* 1984

Herrera, Juan de, *c.* 1530–97. Spanish architect. Details of his architectural training are not known but he pursued an academic interest in mathematics and science throughout his life. In 1563 he was appointed assistant to Juan Bautista de Toledo, designer of PHILIP II's Escorial Palace near Madrid. After Toledo's death Herrera oversaw the massive construction project of the Escorial and designed its church and infirmary. The Palace of Aranjuez (1569) and the Exchange in Seville (1582) epitomize his severe Italianate style, which was very influential and became known as *estilo desornamentado.*

The Escorial, 78–79 (11)

Catherine Wilkinson-Zerna, *Juan de Herrera, Architect to Philip II of Spain,* 1993

Hilliard, Nicholas, 1547–1619. English miniaturist and goldsmith. Born in Exeter, he spent much of his childhood in Geneva. Having served his goldsmith's apprenticeship he further developed his career by specializing in miniature painted portraits, which often formed part of elaborate jewelled lockets. Small enough to fit in the hand and painted from life, they show every rich and minute detail of faces, fabrics and jewels of the period. Hilliard portrayed Queen ELIZABETH I and many

of her courtiers in this form. He wrote a *Treatise on the Art of Limning* (miniature painting) in which he also acknowledged his admiration of HOLBEIN.

Portrait of George Clifford, Earl of Cumberland, 222–23 (7)
Portrait medal of Queen Elizabeth, design for, 244–45 (9)
Portrait of Queen Elizabeth by the workshop of Hilliard, 94–95 (6)
Young Man amid Roses, 92–93 (3)

Erna Auerbach, *Nicholas Hilliard,* 1961
Roy Strong, *Nicholas Hilliard,* 1975

Hoby, Sir Thomas, 1530–66. English diplomat whose translation of CASTIGLIONE's *Cortegiano* (*The Courtier*) was first published in 1561.

Tomb, 102–03 (5)

Edgar Powell (ed.), *The Travels and Life of Sir Thomas Hoby,* 1902

Holbein, Hans (the Younger), 1497–1543. German painter. Born in Augsburg, where he was trained by his father, Hans Holbein the Elder, he moved to Basle in 1515 and was engaged in painting portraits and religious subjects, as well as producing woodcuts. Although he visited England for about two years from 1526, he did not settle permanently in London until 1532, probably entering the service of the TUDOR court soon afterwards, to draw and paint many members of its circle. His famous iconic images of HENRY VIII (surviving in part through drawings) portray the awesome bulk of the king dominating the picture plane. Holbein's realistic depiction of physical features and his technically superb rendering of fabrics and textures found full expression in his masterpiece, *The Ambassadors* (1533) – a work combining a double portrait with complex iconography and symbolism.

Self-portrait, 242–43 (6)
Portrait of Amerbach, 36–37 (7)
Portrait of Robert Cheeseman, 96–97 (3)
Portrait of Christina of Denmark, 94–95 (3)
Portrait of John Colet, 36–37 (3)
Portrait of Erasmus, 36–37 (5)
Portrait of Henry VIII, 92–93 (2)
Portrait of Sir Thomas More, 36–37 (2)
The Ambassadors, 202
Dead Christ, 142–43 (2)
Nicolas Kratzer, Astronomer to Henry VIII, 214–15 (3)
The Painter's Wife and Children, 190–91 (5)
Parnassus, 48–49 (6)
Clock, design for, 230–31 (2)
Henry VIII's 'musick', 220–21 (2)
Ship, drawing of, 212–13 (4)

John Rowlands, *Holbein,* 1985
Helen Langdon, *Hans Holbein,* rev. ed., 1993

Holl, Elias, 1573–1646. German architect. Born into an Augsburg family of masons, he became the leading Renaissance architect in Germany, building in a style characterized by clearly defined classical forms and decorative restraint. He became a master mason in 1596 and in 1600 experienced Italian architecture on a visit to Venice. In 1602 he was appointed official mason of Augsburg, and for the next three decades built numerous civic buildings including schools, city gates, warehouses and a hospital. His masterpiece is the imposing Town Hall (1614–20), a unique design in which he placed great emphasis on the centre of the façade and contrasted it against simple flanking bays.

Augsburg Town Hall, 160–61 (1)

Ignatius see **Loyola**

James I, attributed to John de Critz, c. 1605.

James I, 1566–1625. King of Great Britain from 1603. He was politically and religiously moderate, though his grand scheme for restoring peace to Europe by marrying his daughter to the Elector Palatine, the Protestant leader, and his son to the Infanta of Spain did not succeed. James considered himself an intellectual and wrote several books. But as a patron he is remembered more for taking the theatrical company to which SHAKESPEARE belonged under his protection and for commissions to Inigo JONES.

Christopher Durston, *James I*, 1993
Michael Brown, *James I*, 1994

John XXIII, Anti-Pope, *c.* 1370–1419. Anti-Pope from 1410 until 1415. He was elected during the Great Western Schism (1378–1417) when factions within the Catholic Church elected rival claimants to the Throne of St Peter. The Council of Constance finally healed the Schism by seeking the abdication of the three rival popes and duly electing Pope Martin V, but John XXIII's flight from the city resulted in his four-year imprisonment on unsubstantiated charges. His wall tomb, by DONATELLO and MICHELOZZO, is in the Florentine Baptistery.

Tomb by Donatello and Michelozzo, 100–01 (3)

Inigo Jones, after Van Dyck, 17th century.

Jones, Inigo, 1573–1652. English architect who was responsible for introducing the architectural style of Renaissance Italy into England. Probably apprenticed in London to the artist Marcus GHEERAERTS the Younger, he visited Italy between 1598 and 1603, at that time being described as a 'picture-maker'. For several years he was a prominent figure at court where he designed elaborate and fantastic scenery, costumes and mechanical stage devices for royal masques, quite unlike anything seen before in England. In 1613 he again went to Italy, this time in the company of the notable collector and courtier Lord Arundel, undertaking an intense cultural tour which increased his knowledge not only of ancient monuments, but also Renaissance architecture, particularly the buildings of PALLADIO. In 1615 he was appointed Surveyor of the King's Works, and during more than 25 years service to the Crown built his famous classically inspired buildings which were in striking contrast to the existing fabric of TUDOR London. His masterpiece is the Banqueting House, Whitehall (1619–22), a solid and harmonious Palladian building with a two-tier classical façade fronting a single volume double-cube interior. He also built the Queen's House, Greenwich (begun 1616 but not finished until 1635), and the Prince's Lodging, Newmarket (1619–22). He designed the first regular and symmetrical London square at Covent Garden, flanked by uniform façades and featuring the small church of St Paul's, one of the first new Protestant churches in England.

Tempe Restored, **costume design for, 98–99 (5)**
Banqueting House, Whitehall, 162–63 (1)
Cockpit-at-Court Theatre, design for, 282–83 (7)
Earl of Arundel's sculpture gallery, 60–61 (4)
Old St Paul's, added portico, 162–63 (3)
Old Somerset House, portico, 162–63 (2)
Proscenium stage, 282–83 (10)
Queen's House, Greenwich, 284–85 (9)
St Paul's, Covent Garden, 108–09 (10)
John Harris and Gordon Higgott, *Inigo Jones, Complete Architectural Drawings*, 1989
John Peacock, *The Stage Designs of Inigo Jones*, 1995

Jonson, Ben, 1572–1637. English dramatist. A contemporary of SHAKESPEARE, Jonson's major contribution to the development of English drama is a series of moralizing comedies which include *Volpone* (1606), *The Alchemist* (1610), and *Bartholomew Fair* (1614). Although his technique depended on generalized types ('humours') rather than individuals, he achieved a marked sense of realism in many works – *Bartholomew Fair*, for example, being set in the London of his day, adhering to unity of time and place, and featuring the comic knavery of low-life rogues and pretentious fools. Proud of his humanist learning, he produced two Roman tragedies (*Sejanus* and *Cataline*) but their dependence on classical texts compromise their vitality. He was also a lyric poet and was renowned for his elaborately produced court masques, some featuring scenery and costumes by Inigo JONES.

Rosalind Miles, *Ben Jonson, his Life and Work*, 1986
David Riggs, *Ben Jonson, a Life*, 1989

Pope Julius II, drawing by Raphael, 1511–12.

Julius II, Pope, 1443–1513. Pope from 1503. The papacy of the forceful and influential Giuliano della Rovere, nephew of SIXTUS IV, was stamped by his outstanding personality. A diplomat and administrator of great skill, he consolidated papal authority by reducing the power of the Roman commune, and did much to restore the papal territories, often taking an active and leading military role in battles. A discerning patron while still a cardinal, once elevated to the papacy he sought to remodel Rome, and commemorate himself, through the work of the greatest artists of the High Renaissance. Among his most famous commissions were the Sistine Chapel ceiling frescoes and his own tomb from MICHELANGELO, the plan for a new St Peter's Basilica and vast architectural works in the Vatican Palace from BRAMANTE, and the magnificent series of frescoes by RAPHAEL in the Vatican Stanze.

Portrait by Melozzo da Forlì, 14
Portrait by Raphael, 66–67 (4)
Tomb, 241
F. Gilbert, *The Pope, his Banker and Venice*, 1980
Christine Shaw, *Julius II, the Warrior Pope*, 1993

Kepler, Johannes, 1571–1630. German astronomer. After the death of Tycho BRAHE he was appointed RUDOLF II's astrologer and mathematician, inheriting Brahe's priceless records of the planets. Accepting COPERNICUS' heliocentric model of the solar system, Kepler was able to calculate the orbits of the planets, showing that they were ellipses rather than circles, thus laying the foundation for Newton's definitive account of the laws of planetary motion.
Carola Baumgardt, *Johannes Kepler: Life and Letters*, 1952
Arthur Koestler, *The Watershed, a Biography of Johannes Kepler*, 1960

Keyser, Hendrick de, 1565–1621. Dutch architect and sculptor. He worked mainly in Amsterdam where he built the Amsterdam Exchange and two important Protestant churches, the Zuiderkerk (begun 1606) and the Westerkerk (begun 1620). His sculptural masterpiece is the tomb of William the Silent in the Nieuwe Kerk, Delft, with a celebrated and serene marble effigy which features a virtuoso display of skilled carving in the costume's neck ruff and buttoned tunic. His son, Thomas (1596–1667), became an excellent portraitist, and three of his other sons were sculptors. His most celebrated pupil was Nicholas STONE, who later became his son-in-law.

Krafft (Kraft), Adam, 1455/60–1508/9. German sculptor. His known works are all in Nuremberg, where his masterpiece is the 60-feet (18-metre) high stone tabernacle of the Sacrament in the church of St Lorenz. Its architectural framework, a Gothic profusion of slender pinnacles and elaborate tracery, contrasts with the uncluttered and naturalist compositions of the narrative panels and relief figures of saints. Three astonishingly realistic and vigorous life-size male figures support the base of the tabernacle and one of these crouching men is a self-portrait of Krafft.

Self-portrait from the tabernacle of St Lorenz, Nuremberg, 242–43 (4)

Kulmbach, Hans von, *c.* 1480–1522. German painter. A close follower of DÜRER, he was also influenced by Jacopo de' Barbari, a Venetian who worked for some years in Germany and was influential on Dürer. A refined and delicate colourist, he painted altarpieces in Nuremberg and Cracow, and also designed and painted stained glass.

Kyd, Thomas, *c.* 1558–94. English dramatist and poet. His most famous work *The Spanish Tragedy*, an early example of a revenge tragedy, was first published in 1592 and was one of the most popular plays of its day.
Arthur Freeman, *Thomas Kyd, Facts and Problems*, 1967
Peter Murray, *Thomas Kyd*, 1969

Lamberti, Niccolò, 1393–1434. Italian sculptor born in Florence but working most of his life in Venice.
Tomb of Onofrio Strozzi, 100–01 (2)

Landino, Cristoforo, 1424–92. Italian philosopher and writer. A scholar of Latin and Greek, and a noted teacher, he held the chair of poetry and rhetoric at the Studio Fiorentino, where his pupils included FICINO and POLIZIANO. His major work, the *Disputationes camaldulenses* (1474), takes the form of four discussions, each lasting one day, held between leading Florentine humanists. The dialogues include a debate on the nature of the active and contemplative life between ALBERTI and Lorenzo de' MEDICI the Magnificent. Landino also wrote important commentaries on PETRARCH, Dante and Virgil.
Portrait by Ghirlandaio, 44–45 (2)
With Federigo da Montefeltro, 32

Lassus, Orlando, *c.* 1532–94. Flemish composer and choirmaster, who holds a central position in the development of Renaissance music. In his early twenties he was choirmaster at the Lateran Basilica, Rome, and subsequently travelled extensively in Europe. From 1557 he was in the service of the ducal court in Munich. Celebrated for his development of choral technique and the emotional expression of his work, his *œuvre* of both church and secular compositions was vast. His musical setting of the *Seven Penitential Psalms* (published in 1565) is one of his most noted works.
Book of madrigals, 220–21 (8)

Le Breton, Gilles, active 1527–died 1553. French master mason. A craftsman of great technical skill and practical knowledge, his active career was spent chiefly in the service of FRANÇOIS I at Fontainebleau, and he was the first to introduce the classical style into France. He interpreted the king's plans for the enlargement of the Château and probably designed several elements himself, including the entrance court and the Porte Dorée.

Lemercier, Jacques, *c.* 1582–1654. French architect. His classical style was inspired by a seven-year period of study in Rome (1607–1614). In 1624 he was commissioned by Louis XIII to extend the Cour Carrée of the Louvre, Paris. He extended the building in harmony with LESCOT's wing, and added the central Pavillon de l'Horloge, where twin

caryatids support the pediment. For Cardinal Richelieu he built the Palais Cardinal (later the Palais Royal), the Church of the Sorbonne, and the Château and town of Richelieu. Only one block of the once enormous Château still exists, but the small town of Richelieu, built on a rectangular grid plan, survives little changed and provides an interesting example of 17th-century town planning. Lemercier also designed town houses and his Hôtel de Liancourt (1623) provided a model for many later Parisian hôtels.

Pope Leo X, attributed to Giulio Romano or Sebastiano del Piombo, 1513–21.

Leo X, Pope, 1475–1521. Pope from 1513. The second son of Lorenzo de' MEDICI the Magnificent, Giovanni de' Medici was groomed for high ecclesiastic office from a tender age and was admitted to minor orders aged only eight. His elevation to the papal throne just 30 years later seemed to augur an era of stability for Rome. In keeping with his Medici background, he was a keen humanist and attracted distinguished scholars and writers to the papal court. His renewal of JULIUS II's indulgence to provide funds for the rebuilding of St Peter's Basilica prompted LUTHER's protest in Wittenberg which led eventually, after Leo's death, to the full consequences of the Protestant Reformation.
Portrait by Raphael, 66–67 (5)
Janet Cox-Rearick, *Dynasty and Destiny in Medici Art, Pontormo, Leo X and the Two Cosimos*, 1984

Leonardo da Vinci, 1452–1519. Italian artist, writer, engineer and scientist of outstanding invention and versatility. He trained in the Florentine workshop of VERROCCHIO and his early work includes the serene *Annunciation*, set before an atmospheric landscape. His extraordinary level of preparation, and innovative method of modelling in monochrome before adding colour, can be seen in his large unfinished *Adoration of the Magi* (1481). Through such preparation he developed his highly influential *sfumato* effect of softly formed contours which became a hallmark of the Milanese School. By 1483 he was in Milan working for the SFORZA family, where his first commission was for *The Virgin of the Rocks*, in which he depicts the holy figures in a fantastic landscape bathed by a mysterious light. The innovative *Last Supper* in S. Maria delle Grazie, Milan, was one of his most influential compositions, but his experimental technique of working in oil on dry plaster meant that the painting had already begun to deteriorate within his own lifetime. He undertook preparatory work and made a huge model for an equestrian monument to Francesco Sforza, but this project was abandoned when the French invaded Milan in 1499. He returned to Florence in 1500 and in the following years produced, among other works, the *Mona Lisa*, and versions of *The Virgin and Child and St Anne*. His last years were restless – he spent time in Rome and Florence, and eventually moved to France in 1517 under the patronage of FRANCOIS I. He painted little towards the end of his life but was active in many fields, devoting himself to scientific experiment and minute observation of nature. Large numbers of his notebooks and drawings, many in the Royal Library, Windsor, are testimony to his unparalleled enquiring mind and his extraordinary intellect. Their main subjects are anatomy (Leonardo dissected bodies and made meticulous records of the internal organs); botany; the movement of water, often with the idea of controlling rivers; war machines and flying machines, which show ingenuity but are mostly quite impracticable; and architecture, projecting centrally planned churches (which may have influenced BRAMANTE). Leonardo was not a scholar and seems to have taken little interest in classical literature and culture. He was therefore not a typical humanist, but the reputation he earned in his own lifetime was immense

Leonardo da Vinci, woodcut from Vasari's Lives, *1568.*

and he was instrumental in promoting the notion of the artist as an intellectual thinker, as opposed to a manual craftsman.

Self-portrait, 242–43 (8)
Allegory, 46–47 (2)
Lady with the Ermine, 182–83 (2)
The Last Supper, 138–39 (3)
Mona Lisa, 194–95 (5)
The Virgin of the Rocks, 168–69 (1)
Vitruvian Man, 248–49 (1)
Anatomical drawing, 226–27 (2)
Caricature studies, 258–59 (1)
Church designs, sketch for, 274–75 (3)
Foetus, drawing of, 226–27 (4)
Fortress, plan for, 164–65 (3)
Hanged man, sketch of, 65
Monument to Gian Giacomo Trivulzio, sketch of, 86–87 (6)
Mortars discharging shells, 222–23 (3)
Oak leaves and acorns, and lily, 228–29 (1, 2)
Sala delle Asse in the Castello Sforzesco, Milan, ceiling, 254–55 (1)
Warrior dressed in fantastic armour, 222–23 (4)

M. Kemp, *Leonardo da Vinci*, 1981
The Complete Paintings of Leonardo da Vinci, intro. by L. D. Ettlinger, notes and catalogue by Angela Ottino della Chiesa, 1985

Leoni, Pompeo, 1533–1608. Italian sculptor, who went to Spain and became court artist to PHILIP II. His most famous works are the royal tombs in the Escorial.

Tomb of Charles V, 102–03 (2)

Pompeo Leoni in the Collection of the Hispanic Society of America, etc., 1928
Beatrice Gilman Proske, *Pompeo Leoni*, 1956

Lescot, Pierre, c. 1515–78. French architect who was fundamental to the development of French classicism, which blends the clarity and symmetry of classical structure with decorative elements. His collaboration on several projects with the sculptor GOUJON confirms that decoration was integral to the architectural style and not perceived as applied ornament. His most famous surviving work is one wing, the model for all the rest, of the Cour Carrée of the Louvre, Paris (begun 1546). Here Lescot's deep understanding of classical models is complemented by Goujon's refined sculptural decoration.

Lescot wing of the Louvre, 78–79 (10)

Leyden, Lucas van, 1489/94–1533. Netherlandish engraver and painter. He showed prodigious technical skill as an engraver from an early age and is now chiefly remembered for his graphic work which includes religious subjects, caricatures and some highly original allegories. He met both DURER and MABUSE during his travels in the Netherlands. A number of large painted triptychs date from the last years of his life.

Ellen S. Jacobowitz and Stephanie Loeb Stepanek, *The Prints of Lucas van Leyden and his Contemporaries*, 1983
Elise Lawton Smith, *The Paintings of Lucas van Leyden*, 1992

Ligorio, Pirro, c. 1510–83. Italian architect. In the shadow of MICHELANGELO Ligorio developed a highly sophisticated Mannerist style of his own, best seen in the Casino of Pius IV in the Vatican. He probably designed the gardens of the Villa d'Este at Tivoli.

Casino of Pius IV, the Vatican, 252–53 (1)
Villa d'Este, gardens, 234–35 (2)

G. Smith, *The Casino of Pius IV*, 1977

Limbourg (Limburg) family. Flemish illuminators. The three brothers Paul, Herman and Jean, all born after 1385 and dead by 1416, are the most celebrated late Gothic illuminators. Initially apprenticed to a Parisian goldsmith, they entered the service of the Duke of Burgundy and by 1411 were working for the Duke's brother on the famous *Très Riches heures du Duc de Berry*. This sumptuous Book of Hours represents the epitome of the courtly and sophisticated International Gothic style, and although it includes naturalistic details of landscape and animals, its overall effect is rich and decorative. Characterized by attention to finely delineated detail and clear, bright colours, the work was very influential on early Netherlandish painting.

Lippi, Filippino, 1457–1504. Italian painter, the son of Fra Filippo LIPPI. His early style was strongly influenced by BOTTICELLI, whose Florentine workshop he entered in 1469 after the death of his father. His first major commission was to complete the Brancacci Chapel fresco cycle in S. Maria del Carmine, Florence, where the work of MASACCIO and MASOLINO had been left incomplete for nearly 50 years. He received other prestigious fresco commissions in Rome and Florence, proving his ability in large-scale composition and often setting his scenes in classical architectural settings. Renowned also for his altarpieces, he enjoyed a very successful career.

Katherine B. Neilson, *Filippino Lippi*, 1938

Lippi, Fra Filippo, c. 1406–69. Italian painter. His eventful life contrasts strongly with the gracious and serene religious images for which he is famous. As a young orphan, he was sent to a Florentine friary and despite being unsuited to the religious life, took Holy Orders. His abduction of a nun, and the subsequent birth of their son, Filippino LIPPI, caused great scandal and it was only through the support of the MEDICI that he was able to marry and legitimize his family. While his earlier painting style derived from MASACCIO, Lippi's later works became far more lyrical, characterized by beautiful Madonnas and elegant figures in flowing and diaphanous drapery. Although chiefly known for his altarpieces and panels, he also painted a celebrated series of frescoes in Prato Cathedral, which show a feeling for narrative and drama.

Jeffrey Ruda, *Filippo Lippi Studies*, 1982
———, *Fra Filippo Lippi, Life and Work with a Complete Catalogue*, 1993

Lombardo family. A family of architects and sculptors who were active mainly in Venice. Pietro (*c.* 1435–1515) is credited with introducing the Tuscan Renaissance style of architecture into Venice, a fine example of which is the small marble-clad church of S. Maria dei Miracoli which he built with the assistance of his sons, Tullio (*c.* 1455–1532) and Antonio (*c.* 1458–*c.* 1516). All three family members worked on large architectural tomb monuments, often based on a triumphal arch form and including classicizing motifs and many sculpted figures. Among the most notable of these works in Venice are the Monument to Pietro Mocenigo by Pietro Lombardo, and Tullio Lombardo's tomb of Andrea Vendramin.

Tullio Lombardo:
  Tomb of Guidarello Guidarelli, 100–01 (9)
  Tomb of Andrea Vendramin, 100–01 (7)

Lorenzo Monaco (Piero di Giovanni), *c.* 1370–1425. Italian painter and illuminator. Probably of Sienese origin, he entered the Camaldolensian monastery of S. Maria degli Angeli in Florence, where he eventually became deacon. Working mainly for his own religious order, he painted illuminated manuscripts, frescoes and altarpieces. His crowded compositions and emphasis on luxury accessories, like clothes and jewelry painted in realistic detail, bring him close to International Gothic. In late 14th-century tradition, gilding still featured prominently in his altarpieces, but he was also a colourist of considerable talent, achieving brilliant contrasting and complementary colour effects using rich, jewel-like pigments.

Marvin Eisenberg, *Lorenzo Monaco*, 1989

Lotto, Lorenzo, 1480–1556. Italian painter. Born in Venice, Lotto was an original and independent painter, who spent his unsettled life working throughout northern and central Italy. Often employing his brilliant saturated colours in tender and melancholy religious works, he was also a portraitist of considerable skill and humanity. His own account book and diary, which document details of his life from 1538, reveal a troubled disposition and a deep religious conviction. He sought refuge towards the end of his life in the sanctuary at Loreto.

Portrait of Andrea Odoni, 60–61 (3)
Messer Marsilio and his Wife, 190–91 (4)

Bernard Berenson, *Lorenzo Lotto*, 1956
Piero Bianconi, *All the Paintings of Lorenzo Lotto*, trans. by P. Colacicchi, 1963

Loyola, St Ignatius, 1491–1556. Spanish founder of the Jesuit Order. A worldly and noble knight who, during convalescence from a serious battle wound, underwent a spiritual conversion which changed his life. He made a pilgrimage to the Holy Land, but returned to Europe in 1523 to prepare for his life's work by several years of intensive study at universities in Spain and France. With a few followers, under strict vows of poverty, chastity and obedience, he travelled to Rome and in 1540 his Society of Jesus received papal recognition from PAUL III. The order grew rapidly, and with its dedication of ministry to the sick and suffering, and its zealous mission of Catholic conversion, it proved a major force in the Counter-Reformation and in the Catholic reform movement. Loyola's *Spiritual Exercises*, formulated early in his conversion, were widely practised as a guide to prayer and meditation.

Portrait by Juan de Roelas, 124–25 (2)

Philip Caraman, *Ignatius Loyola*, 1990
John C. Olin, *The Catholic Reformation, Savonarola to Ignatius Loyola, Reform in the Church*, 1992

Luini, Bernardino, active 1512–32. Italian painter. He was a prolific and successful artist, who worked mainly in Milan and other cities in Lombardy. His style was derived from LEONARDO, and many of his paintings are rather sentimental versions of that master's religious compositions.

Salome, 196–97 (4)

Luther, Martin, 1483–1546. German Protestant Reformer. He left the University of Erfurt to enter an Augustinian friary in 1505, and two years later was ordained a priest. On a visit to Rome in 1510 he was shocked by the lavish and princely lifestyle of the pope, and the corruption and abuse he perceived in the ecclesiastical hierarchy. During years of teaching theology at Wittenberg, and through a thorough study of the scriptures, he became convinced that salvation was a gift granted by God alone and was purely a matter of faith unaffected by the sacraments or acts of penance. In October 1517, spurred by his total opposition to the sale of indulgences in Germany, which he saw as a means for the Catholic Church to finance the excesses of the papacy, he prepared 95 theses on this question, which were promptly published and printed. In 1521 the pope, exasperated by Luther's continued defiance of papal authority, finally excommunicated him and the Emperor CHARLES V summoned Luther to the Diet of Worms hoping that he would recant. He refused, however, and took refuge in the Wartburg under the protection of the Elector of Saxony. Here he translated the New Testament into German. During the next decade, with the support of the north German princes, his breach with Rome hardened and the Confession of Augsburg, presented to the emperor in 1530, was the first statement of Lutheran doctrine. In later life Luther finished the translation of the whole Bible, which is one of the classics of the German language.

Portrait by Cranach, 114–15 (4)
Luther's Bible, 118–19 (3)
The 95 theses, allegorical painting of, 114–15 (1)
Preaching at Wittenberg, 116–17 (6)

A. G. Dickens, *Martin Luther and the German Nation*, 1974
Gerhard Brendler, *Martin Luther*, 1991

Lyly, John, 1554–1606. English dramatist and writer. He was the author of the moralistic novels *Euphues: The Anatomy of Wit* (1578) and *Euphues and His England* (1580) written in a self-consciously learned, artificial and elegant prose from which the term 'Euphuism' derives. After 1580 he concentrated on playwriting, making an important contribution to the development of prose dialogue in some of the first high comedy to be written in the English language.

George Kirkpatrick Hunter, *John Lyly, The Humanist as Courtier*, 1962
Joseph W. Houppert, *John Lyly*, 1975

Mabuse (Jan Gossaert), *c.* 1478–1532. Flemish painter. Recorded as a member of the Painters' Guild in Antwerp in 1503, he accompanied Philip of Burgundy to Rome in 1508 on a visit which proved influential on his art. Although his painting remained substantially northern in character, he adopted Italianate architectural settings and introduced Renaissance motifs into his compositions. He also painted many fine portraits, and in his later work explored the representation of the male and female nude, both in religious and classical themes.

St Luke Drawing the Virgin, 272–73 (1)
Virgin of Louvain, 132–33 (7)

Arthur Annesley Ronald Firbank, *An Early Flemish Painter*, 1969

Machiavelli, Niccolò, 1469–1527. Italian political theorist who was employed by the Florentine republic from 1498. He was particularly engaged with supervision of the city's militia but also undertook several diplomatic assignments, including missions to MAXIMILIAN I and JULIUS II. He was embittered by his summary dismissal from public service in 1512 when the MEDICI returned from exile but, despite being cleared of conspiracy against the Medici, his earnest hope of a return to political office was never fulfilled. During his retirement on his farm near Florence he produced the political writings for which he is remembered. In *Il Principe* (*The Prince*, 1513) he argued that if a ruler wished to retain power, his decision-making should be based on the expediency of actual circumstance, not on moral or ethical ideals. He recognized the psychological forces inherent in political strategy, and based his theories not only on his own experience of government, but also on the study of examples from ancient history. His other works include *A History of Florence*, *The Art of War*, and the comedy *Mandragola*.

Portrait by Santi di Tito, 38–39 (2)

J. R. Hale, *Machiavelli and Renaissance Italy*, 1972
Quentin Skinner, *Machiavelli*, 1981

Magellan, Ferdinand, *c.* 1480–1521. Portuguese navigator. His early years were spent in the service of Portugal in the East Indies, but in 1514 he entered the service of CHARLES V of Spain, with the intention of achieving what COLUMBUS had failed to do and reach the Indies by sailing west. He set out in 1519, passed the straits which bear his name and crossed the Pacific. But in the Philippines he was killed in a fight with the natives. The remnants of the expedition, under Sebastiano del Cano, returned to Spain in 1522, the first circumnavigators of the globe.

Portrait, 210–11 (7)

Alan Blackwood, *Ferdinand Magellan*, 1985

Malatesta family. They dominated the city-state of Rimini during the 14th and 15th centuries, owing their ascendancy mainly to military prowess. Sigismondo (1417–68), Lord of Rimini from 1432, is often considered a model Renaissance soldier-prince due to his reputation both as a famous condottiere and an ambitious patron of the arts. Many accusations of depravity and corruption were made against him, particularly by his avowed enemy, Pope PIUS II, who excommunicated him in 1461. Sigismondo commissioned ALBERTI to transform the Gothic church of S. Francesco in Rimini into the splendid Tempio Malatestiano, which is adorned internally with a fine sculptural programme by AGOSTINO DI DUCCIO. He was succeeded by his son Roberto.

Marble relief of Roberto Malatesta, 86–87 (6)
Medal of Sigismondo Malatesta and his mistress, Isotta da Rimini, 244–45 (5, 6)
Portrait of Sigismondo Malatesta by Piero della Francesca, 72–73 (7), 182–83 (8)

P. Jones, *The Malatesta of Rimini*, 1974

Mantegna, Andrea, *c.* 1431–1506. One of the leading Italian artists of the 15th century whose classicizing and sculptural style influenced numerous north Italian painters. His exposure to the Paduan sculpture reliefs of DONATELLO in the church of S. Antonio at Padua and contact with the work of his father-in-law, Jacopo BELLINI, affected his development much more than the teaching of his master, Squarcione. A learned classicist, his archaeological interest is revealed in the antique architectural settings of many paintings, and in the details of his re-creation of the Roman world in the *Triumphs of Caesar*, while his mastery of perspective is shown in the startling foreshortening of the *Dead Christ*. His earliest masterpiece, the frescoes in the Eremitani Church, Padua, were destroyed in 1944. From 1460 he was court painter to the GONZAGA family and his frescoes in the Camera degli Sposi in the Mantuan Palazzo Ducale include narrative scenes with Gonzaga portraits and the celebrated illusionistic ceiling oculus featuring court ladies and playful putti peering down at the spectator. His 'stony' or 'metallic' style and outstanding draughtsmanship were entirely suited to engraving, of which he was an early and highly talented exponent.

Lodovico Gonzaga and his family, 72–73 (6)
Agony in the Garden, 168–69 (2)
Dead Christ, 246–47 (8)
Death of the Virgin, 166–67 (6)
Hunters and Dogs of the Gonzaga Court, 96–97 (1)
Martyrdom of St Christopher, 56–57 (5)
Parnassus, 48–49 (5)
St Sebastian, 248–49 (4)
S. Zeno Altarpiece, 136–37 (3)
Triumphs of Caesar, 56–57 (7)
Camera degli Sposi, Palazzo Ducale, Mantua, 254–55 (2, 4), 278–79 (5)

Renata Cipriani, *All the Paintings of Mantegna*, trans. by P. Colacicchi, 1963
Jane Martineau (ed.), *Andrea Mantegna*, 1992

Manuel (Deutsch), Niklaus, *c.* 1484–1530. Swiss painter and writer. He lived in his native Berne, although often called Deutsch, and his artistic career was mainly conducted between 1515 and 1520. He produced portraits, mythological and religious paintings, and expressive drawings influenced by DÜRER, often showing a preoccupation with the theme of death. A strong supporter of the Reformation, he wrote several plays in the 1520s which were highly critical of the Church of Rome. The last years of his life were predominately devoted to political activities and his duties as an elected member of the city council at Berne.

Aldus Manutius, early 16th century.

Manutius, Aldus (the Elder), 1449–1515. Italian printer and typographer who in 1495 founded the famous Venetian Aldine Press which produced the first printed copies of many Latin and Greek classics. He collaborated with scholars on the preparation of classical texts, ensuring that the high quality of his printing was enhanced by textual accuracy. His clear and inexpensive, small-sized editions proved extremely popular and apart from classical authors he published works by BEMBO, PETRARCH and ERASMUS, and the *Hypnerotomachia Poliphili* of COLONNA. The Aldine Press flourished for over a century, being continued after the death of Aldus Manutius the Elder by his brothers-in-law, the Asolani, then by his son Paulus (1512–74) and finally by his grandson Aldus Manutius the Younger (1547–97).

Emblem, 206–07 (2)
Epitome, page from, 208–09 (4)
Hypnerotomachia polifili, 208–09 (5, 6)

M. Lowry, *The World of Aldus Manutius*, 1979

Marguerite of Navarre, 1492–1549. French humanist patron and writer, who was the sister of FRANCOIS I. After the death of her first husband she married Henri II of Navarre, and established a celebrated court at Nérac to which she attracted leading humanists and literary figures, and where she afforded protection to French religious reformers. Her most famous work is the *Heptameron*, a series of tales recounted by travellers, which takes its form from BOCCACCIO's *Decameron*.

Paul Rival, *The Madcap Queen. The Story of Marguerite of Navarre*, trans. by Marvin McCord Lowes, 1930
S. W. Putnam, *Marguerite of Navarre*, 1936

Marlowe, Christopher, 1564–93. English dramatist and poet. His career is mysterious and he was very probably employed as a secret agent by the government. In London from 1587 he began a highly successful career as a playwright but his turbulent personal life, mirrored in his plays, ended violently when he was fatally wounded (or, more probably, assassinated) in a London tavern brawl in 1593. Although his period of literary activity lasted only six years he made a vital contribution to English literature. In *Tamburlaine*, *Edward II* and *Dr Faustus* he largely created poetic drama, excelling also as a narrative poet and as a translator (Ovid's *Amores*).

Della Hilton, *Christopher Marlowe and the New London Theatre*, 1993
Charles Nicolls, *The Reckoning*, 1994

Marmion, Simon, *c.* 1420–89. French painter and illuminator. Strongly influenced by Flemish painters, especially Rogier van der WEYDEN, he was recorded at Amiens, Lille and Valenciennes. Although no documented paintings exist, the shutters for the *St Bertin Altarpiece* are attributed to him on stylistic grounds, and reveal his considerable skill as a colourist. He was also an illuminator of manuscripts.

Marot, Clement, 1496–1544. French poet. Marot was a successful court poet under FRANCOIS I but lacked courtly discretion and compromised himself by sympathizing with the Protestants. As a writer, he moved French poetry away from strict rules and disciplines towards freer, more natural forms, using Italian humanist models to treat modern and religious themes.

H. P. Clive, *Clement Marot, an Annotated Bibliography*, 1983
Annwyl William, *Clement Marot*, 1990

Marsuppini, Carlo, 1399–1453. Italian humanist and statesman. A noted scholar of Greek, he moved in Florentine humanist circles and became Chancellor of Florence after the death of BRUNI. His tomb monument, a masterpiece of carving and design by DESIDERIO DA SETTIGNANO, faces that of Bruni in S. Croce, Florence.

Mary I by Antonio Mor, 1554.

Mary I, 1516–58. Queen of England from 1553. Daughter of HENRY VIII and Catherine of Aragon, Mary TUDOR was fanatically Catholic. She restored the old religion, married PHILIP II of Spain and had nearly 300 Protestants executed for heresy.
D. M. Loades, *The Reign of Mary Tudor: Politics, Government, and Religion in England, 1533–1558*, 1979
R. Tittler, *The Reign of Mary Tudor*, 2nd ed., 1991

Masaccio (Tommaso di Ser Giovanni), 1401–*c.* 1428. Italian painter who was responsible for introducing a new style of painting into early 15th-century Florence, and who is acknowledged as one of the undisputed founders of Renaissance art. His representation of the human figure as a three-dimensional and realistic form broke new ground in painting, and paralleled DONATELLO's achievements in monumental figure sculpture. His famous and highly influential frescoes in the Brancacci Chapel, Florence, reveal not only his compositional and narrative skills, but also his effective and innovative use of modelling with light and shadow. His fresco of *The Trinity* in the Florentine church of S. Maria Novella presents an illusionistic barrel-vaulted chapel space which conforms strictly to single-point perspective, and draws the spectator to participate in the scene.
The architectural setting and sophisticated

perspective of *The Trinity* point to a design collaboration with his friend BRUNELLESCHI. Masaccio was commissioned in 1425 to paint a large altarpiece for S. Maria del Carmine, Pisa, of which the central scene of the *Madonna and Child* is in the National Gallery, London. Although the gold background and gilded punch-work of this panel reflect established practices, the work nonetheless heralds new directions in painting. The sculptural Madonna, the perspectival effects of the throne and the Child's halo, and the consistent treatment of light falling from one source are all innovations which presage future artistic developments. Despite his early death in Rome, probably from the plague, Masaccio left a rich legacy for many later artists.
Crucifixion, 140–41 (2)
The Expulsion, 248–49 (3)
Madonna and Child, 132–33 (1)
Tribute money, 23
The Trinity, 246–47 (4)
Ugo Procacci, *All the Paintings of Masaccio*, 1962
Bruce Cole, *Masaccio and the Art of Early Renaissance Florence*, 1980

Masolino (Masolino da Panicale), *c.* 1383–*c.* 1447. Italian painter. Born near Florence, he is chiefly remembered for his collaboration with MASACCIO on the fresco cycle in the Brancacci Chapel in Florence. His independent work did not follow the robust and monumental style of Masaccio, and in his fresco commissions in Rome and northern Italy he depicts elegant figures and decorative effects of landscape, painted in clear and cool tones. His work is an interesting blend of early 15th-century artistic trends because, while revealing a preference for the refined style of LORENZO MONACO and GHIBERTI, he also took great interest in experimenting with perspectival effects.
Paul Joannides, *Masaccio and Masolino, a Complete Catalogue*, 1993

Massys, Quentin, 1465/6–1530. Flemish painter. Born at Louvain, he was admitted to the Antwerp Painters' Guild in 1491 and by the beginning of the 16th century was the leading painter in the city. His religious works, usually depicting dignified and elegant saints, are precisely delineated in rich colours, but he also experimented with caricature and grotesque, and was noted as a portraitist. Landscape elements appear in many of his works and are derived from PATENIER, who was his close friend in Antwerp. Their association seems to have been mutually effective with Massys providing the figures in some of Patenier's paintings.
Portrait of Pierre Gilles, 36–37 (8)
Grotesque old woman, 258–59 (2)
Larry Silver, *The Paintings of Quintin Massys, with a Catalogue Raisonné*, 1984

Matthias, 1557–1619. HABSBURG Holy Roman Emperor from 1612. Son of MAXIMILIAN II, he succeeded his brother RUDOLF II in 1612. He moved the capital from Prague to Vienna, but was an ineffective ruler, largely responsible for the revolt of Bohemia that led to the Thirty Years War.
Portrait in intaglio, 68–69 (1)

Matthias Corvinus, marble relief by Giancristoforo Romano, 1489.

Matthias Corvinus (Matthias Hunyadi), 1440–90. King of Hungary. An energetic and capable ruler, he secured Hungary against the Turks and conquered large parts of Austria. Passionately interested in the arts and scholarship, Matthias was responsible for introducing the Renaissance into Hungary, inviting several Italians to his court to work on his palaces of Buda and Visegrád, commissioning painting and sculpture from Italian artists including DONATELLO and Filippino LIPPI, and founding a famous library full of Italian manuscripts of classical texts.
Rózsa Feuer-Tóth, *Art and Humanism in Hungary in the Age of Matthias Corvinus*, trans. by Györgi Jakobi, 1990

Maximilian I, 1459–1519. Holy Roman Emperor from 1493. At the death of his father, Emperor FREDERICK III in 1493, he became ruler of the HABSBURG domains in Germany and Austria. He had also secured claims to Burgundy and the Netherlands by his marriage in 1477 to Maria, the daughter of Charles the Bold of Burgundy. During much of his rule he was engaged in wars in Italy, mainly against the French, while attempting to consolidate the vast Habsburg Empire. He was a personal friend of many artists and scholars and had his portrait painted by DÜRER.

Maximilian I, woodcut by Dürer, c. 1518–19.

Maximilian II, engraving, 1566.

Maximilian II, 1527–76. Holy Roman Emperor from 1564. Eldest son of the HABSBURG Emperor FERDINAND I. After an active diplomatic career under his father and uncle CHARLES V, he succeeded to the empire in 1564. Maximilian was no religious bigot and tried hard to hold the balance between his Catholic and Protestant subjects.

Medici family. Family of Florentine bankers and businessmen who came to dominate Florence in the mid-15th century, though they did not have any formal authority or title until 1537. More important, however, is their cultural ascendancy. It was under Medici leadership that Florence became the cradle of humanism, and the city that more than any other promoted advances in scholarship and the arts, a legacy whose significance it is impossible to exaggerate. The family fortunes were founded by the elder Cosimo 'Pater Patriae' (1389–1464) to be extended and strengthened by his son Piero (1414–69) and grandson LORENZO the Magnificent. Lorenzo's brother Giuliano was murdered by political rivals, but his son Giovanni became Pope LEO X and his nephew Giulio CLEMENT VII. After the upheavals of the 1520s and 1530s Florence was constituted a duchy. Cosimo I (1519–74), descended from a collateral branch, became Duke of Florence and then in 1569 Grand Duke of Tuscany. Two of the more obscure members of the family have tombs by MICHELANGELO in the New Sacristy (Medici Chapel) of S. Lorenzo. And Lorenzo the Magnificent's great-granddaughter CATHERINE married HENRI II of France.

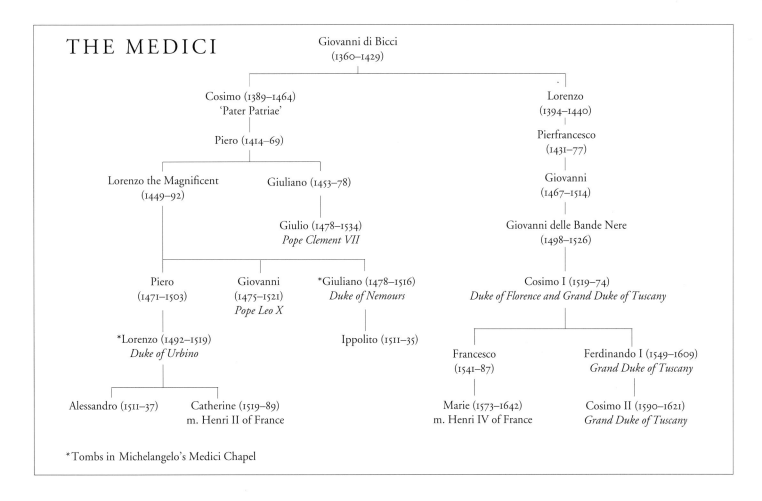

THE MEDICI

Giovanni di Bicci
(1360–1429)

Cosimo (1389–1464)
'Pater Patriae'

Lorenzo
(1394–1440)

Piero (1414–69)

Pierfrancesco
(1431–77)

Lorenzo the Magnificent
(1449–92)

Giuliano (1453–78)

Giovanni
(1467–1514)

Giulio (1478–1534)
Pope Clement VII

Giovanni delle Bande Nere
(1498–1526)

Piero
(1471–1503)

Giovanni
(1475–1521)
Pope Leo X

*Giuliano (1478–1516)
Duke of Nemours

Cosimo I (1519–74)
Duke of Florence and Grand Duke of Tuscany

*Lorenzo (1492–1519)
Duke of Urbino

Ippolito (1511–35)

Francesco
(1541–87)

Ferdinando I (1549–1609)
Grand Duke of Tuscany

Alessandro (1511–37)

Catherine (1519–89)
m. Henri II of France

Marie (1573–1642)
m. Henri IV of France

Cosimo II (1590–1621)
Grand Duke of Tuscany

*Tombs in Michelangelo's Medici Chapel

Cosimo de' Medici, marble relief by Andrea del Verrocchio, c. 1464.

Duke Cosimo I by Vasari, 72–73 (2)
Giuliano de' Medici: with Poliziano by
    Ghirlandaio, 176–77 (1); reverse of a medal of,
    244–45 (7)
Lorenzo de' Medici with philosophers and
    scholars by Vasari, 34–35 (8)
Adoration of the Magi, members of the family in,
    72–73 (1)
Tombs by Michelangelo, 100–01 (5, 6)
Nicolai Rubinstein, *The Government of Florence
    under the Medici*, 1966
J. R. Hale, *Florence and the Medici: the Pattern of
    Control*, 1977

*Lorenzo the Magnificent, terracotta bust by
Andrea del Verrocchio, c. 1485.*

Medici, Lorenzo the Magnificent, de'
1449–92. Perhaps the key figure in the whole
Renaissance. He promoted the study of the
classics, employing Pico della MIRANDOLA,
Marsilio FICINO and Angelo POLIZIANO to
edit and translate Greek and Latin texts. He
encouraged the search for Roman antiquities,
assembling a collection where generations of
sculptors learned their art. He patronized
painters, including BOTTICELLI, GOZZOLI
and GHIRLANDAIO, and initiated some of the
most fruitful architectural commissions.
Lorenzo the Magnificent, medal of, 244–45 (1)

*Catherine de Médicis, medallion by Germain
Pilon, mid-16th century.*

Médicis, Catherine de, 1519–89. Queen of
France from 1547. Daughter of Lorenzo de'
MEDICI, Duke of Urbino, she married the
future HENRI II in 1533, ruling as regent after
the death of her husband and older son. She
was mainly responsible for the massacre of
Protestants on St Bartholomew's Day (1572).
Tapestry: showing jousting, 96–97 (5);
    showing meeting of French and Spanish
    royal families, 64

Melanchthon, Philip, 1497–1560. German
Reformer, theologian and educationalist. A
man of deep religious conviction, he was an
outstanding classical scholar who, at the age
of 21, was appointed Professor of Greek at
Wittenberg University. He became a close
friend and supporter of LUTHER; wrote
the first systematic work on Lutheran
evangelical theology (*Loci communes rerum
theologicarum*, first edition 1521); and led the
Reformation cause in Wittenberg while
Luther took refuge in the Wartburg. His
Confession of Augsburg, a statement of
Lutheran beliefs which was presented to
the Diet of Augsburg in 1530, was rejected
by the Catholic authorities but also drew
criticism from some Protestants for being
too conciliatory. Apart from his leading role
in the Reformation, Melanchthon was also
an active educationalist who promoted a
humanist programme of study and was
responsible for a thorough reorganization
of the German educational system.
Portrait by Cranach, 36–37 (6)

Melozzo da Forlì, 1438–94. Italian painter.
Little is known of the early life of this
painter born near Ravenna, although his
work shows the influence of PIERO DELLA
FRANCESCA, whom he met at the court of
Urbino. His few surviving frescoes confirm
his complete understanding of perspective
effects, and combine monumental and
clear compositions with strong colour. He
received important commissions from Pope
SIXTUS IV and his circle, including the
decoration of the sacristy of S. Marco in
Loreto where his innovative foreshortening
transforms the interior of the dome into the
vault of heaven, with prophets seated on
the cornice and angels, as seen from below,
apparently hovering in space. *Sotto in sù*,
this type of illusionist treatment of dome
decoration, was an important model for
later artists, particularly CORREGGIO.
*Pope Sixtus IV Della Rovere appointing Platina as
    Papal Librarian*, 66–67 (3), 328
Sixtus IV Inspecting his Library, 14

Memlinc, Hans, active 1465–died 1494.
Flemish painter. Although born in Germany
he is first recorded in 1465 as a citizen of
Bruges, the city in which he spent the rest
of his life. He is traditionally thought to
have trained under Rogier van der WEYDEN,
although his work lacks the emotional
content of that master. He was technically a
highly skilled artist and produced smoothly
finished paintings characterized by a feeling
of serenity and elegance. His *Donne Triptych*
in the National Gallery, London, epitomizes
his richly coloured and minutely observed
style. Apart from painting many altarpieces,
with the collaboration of a large workshop,
he was also noted as a talented portraitist.
Georges Henri Dumont, *Hans Memlinc*, trans. by
    Haydn Barnes, 1967

Michelangelo Buonarroti, 1475–1564.
Italian painter, sculptor and architect.
Michelangelo's forceful personality
dominated the whole of the Italian (and
European) Renaissance. The quality termed
terribilatà by his contemporaries – emotional
intensity, physical power, dramatic
excitement – is unmistakable in all his work,
work which embraced all the visual arts
throughout a career that spanned nearly 70
years at the very centre of artistic patronage.
His influence on succeeding generations was
immense and (partly because of VASARI's
hero-worship) he stands at the beginning of
the Romantic – and still current – view of
the artist as an exceptional being, above
ordinary conventions, whose mission is to
express his unique genius to the uttermost.
Michelangelo learned painting in the
workshop of GHIRLANDAIO and sculpture
in the MEDICI Garden. In 1496 he went to
Rome and won immediate acclaim for his
pietà in St Peter's. Back in Florence he
received further major commissions
including *David* (1502–04). JULIUS II
summoned him back to Rome to make his

Michelangelo, fresco by Vasari, mid-16th century.

tomb (of which only *Moses* and two *Slaves* were completed) and to paint the ceiling of the Sistine Chapel (1508–12). This enormous fresco combines scenes from *Genesis*, portraits of the prophets who foretold Christ, Christ's ancestors and nude athletes representing perfect beauty, thus epitomizing the whole cultural programme of humanism. In 1516 he returned to Florence at the command of LEO X to build the Laurentian Library and the Medici Chapel of S. Lorenzo, which contains the tombs of two minor Medici dukes consisting of two statues and the figures of *Night, Day, Dawn* and *Evening*. In 1534 he settled permanently in Rome, where his works included *The Last Judgment* on the altar wall of the Sistine Chapel, two frescoes in the Cappella Paolina, and the supervision of the basilica of St Peter's, where he drastically modified the building begun by BRAMANTE, thickening the piers of the central crossing and designing the present dome. His other architectural works in Rome are the Palazzo Farnese (begun by Antonio da SANGALLO the Younger) and the Porta Pia (finished by Giacomo DEL DUCA). Even this catalogue does not exhaust Michelangelo's talents. He left a large corpus of fine drawings and a collection of sonnets in Italian which bear witness to his deep interest in philosophy and religion.

Bacchus in Galli's garden, 60–61 (5)
Battle of Cascina, 84–85 (3)
The Creation of Adam, 128–29 (4)
Crucifixion, 140–41 (3)
David, 250–51 (3)
Ganymede, 196–97 (5)
The Last Judgment, 146–47 (3)
Leda and the Swan, 192–93 (3)
Moses, 262–63 (3)
Pietà, 142–43 (6)
The Campidoglio, 270–71 (2, 3)
Florence, sketches for the fortification of, 164–65 (4)
Laurentian Library, Florence: 42–43 (8); staircase, 288 (3)

Medici tombs, 100–01 (5, 6)
Palazzo Medici-Riccardi, Florence, 78–79 (1)
Porta Pia, Rome, 280–81 (3)
St Bartholomew's skin from *The Last Judgment*, 242–43 (9)
St Peter's, Rome, dome, 276–77 (5)
Sistine Chapel, the Vatican, ceiling, 256–57
Tomb of Julius II, 241

Giulio Carlo Argan and Bruno Contardi, *Michelangelo Architect*, 1993
George Bull, *Michelangelo*, 1995

Michelozzo Michelozzi (di Bartolommeo), 1396–1472. Italian sculptor and architect. He was born in Florence, but little is known of his early training; by 1417 he was a bronze-working assistant in GHIBERTI's studio. In 1425 he entered a 'sculptural' partnership with DONATELLO – a very successful association which lasted for eight years and resulted in important commissions, particularly for tomb monuments. Although Michelozzo was more involved with the structural aspects of these large-scale monuments, he was also an accomplished marble carver, as can be seen on the relief panels of the Aragazzi Monument in Monte-pulciano. His most famous buildings, built in Florence under the patronage of Cosimo I de' MEDICI, were the Palazzo Medici, a landmark in palace design; the priory of S. Marco where the simplicity and elegance of his architecture were complemented by Fra ANGELICO's devotional frescoes; and the rotunda added to the SS. Annunziata, a work of surprising originality and daring. Michelozzo also designed several of the Medici's country villas.

Palazzo Medici-Riccardi, Florence, 78–79 (1)
S. Marco, Florence, library of, 33
Tomb of Anti-Pope John XXIII, 100–01 (3)
Villa Medici, Careggi, 284–85 (2)
Villa Medici, Fiesole, 284–85 (4)

Harriet McNeal Caplow, *Michelozzo*, 1977
R. W. Lightbown, *Donatello and Michelozzo, an Artistic Partnership and its Patrons in the Early Renaissance*, 1980

Mino da Fiesole, 1429–84. Italian sculptor. Possibly trained by MICHELOZZO, he was influenced by his contemporary, DESIDERIO DA SETTIGNANO, although technically far less skilled. Much of his tomb and monumental sculpture is charming though derivative but he produced several very successful portrait busts, including one of Piero de' MEDICI. He undertook sculptural commissions in Florence, Rome and Naples.

Montaigne, Michel Eyquem de, 1533–92. French essayist. He received a carefully supervised humanist education which was then followed by studying law. Soon after the death of his father in 1568, he retired from his legal career and moved to the family Château of Montaigne to devote his life to study and leisure – although he undertook some diplomacy for HENRI IV and served as Mayor of Bordeaux from 1581 to 1585. He is celebrated for his *Essais* (two

books published in 1580, with a third volume in 1588) in which he treats a wide range of themes. Their subjects are often suggested by passages in his favourite classical authors, whom he quotes liberally. But his ultimate criterion is his own experience, revealing so much about his personal life that he is often cited as the first modern man.

Portrait, 38–39 (4)

Keith Cameron (ed.), *Montaigne and his Age*, 1981
Max Gauna, *The Dissident Montaigne*, 1989

Federigo da Montefeltro, coin by Sperandio da Mantova, 1474.

Montefeltro, Federigo da, 1422–82. Ruler of Urbino from 1444, and Duke from 1474, he was a member of the Montefeltro family which had dominated the city-state of Urbino since the 13th century. An outstanding condottiere, he was also a learned scholar, avid collector of manuscripts and inspired patron of the arts, whose humanist court was second to none. He supervised the transformation of the medieval palace at Urbino into a ducal palace of vast proportions. Externally the palace presents a fortified aspect but internally contains elegant apartments decorated by leading artists, including PIERO DELLA FRANCESCA. The palace also features Luciano Laurano's harmonious courtyard and Federigo's studiolo which contains exquisite *trompe-l'oeil* decoration of inlaid wood. CASTIGLIONE's *Courtier* is set at the court of Urbino during the reign of Federigo's son, Guidobaldo.

Portrait by Piero della Francesca, 72–73 (5)
With Cristoforo Landino, 32
Marquetry panel from his studiolo, 222–23 (6)

P. Rotondi, *The Ducal Palace of Urbino*, 1969
Judith Hook, *A Renaissance Prince, Federico di Montefeltro*, 1979

More, Sir Thomas, 1477–1535. English humanist and statesman. Born in London, he received a classical education and embarked on a successful career in law. Although he decided against taking Holy Orders, his whole life was marked by his deeply held religious convictions, and his family home became an informal centre of learning and virtue. His *Utopia* (1516) is an idealistic essay on the perfect social and political state, which conceals a satirical attack on contemporary conditions. Fully employed in the service of HENRY VIII, he made important contributions to diplomatic and court life, and was eventually appointed Lord Chancellor in 1529. When he refused to take an oath denying the pope's supreme position as head of the church, in the aftermath of Henry VIII's break with Rome, More was accused of high treason and beheaded. In 1935 he was canonized by the Roman Catholic Church.

Portrait by Holbein, 36–37 (2)
Utopia, woodcut from, 38–39 (8)
A. G. Fox, *Thomas More: History and Providence*, 1982
Richard Marius, *Thomas More*, 1984

Moroni, Giovanni Battista, active 1546/7– died 1578. Italian painter. Born near Bergamo, he was a pupil and assistant to Moretto da Brescia. Although his religious works owe a great debt to Moretto, he surpassed his master in portraiture, becoming an acknowledged specialist in that field. His portraits focus on the realistic depiction of the individual sitter often offset against a simple tonal background.
Portrait of a Gentleman, 92–93 (5)

Mostaert, Jan, *c.* 1472/3–1555/6. Dutch painter. An artist of religious subjects and portraits, he may have worked for Margaret of Austria, the Regent of the Netherlands, but is also recorded in his home town of Haarlem. His attributed paintings are carefully detailed and smoothly finished, and are closely linked stylistically to the work of GEERTGEN TOT SINT JANS.
The Egg Dance, 180–81 (2)
West Indian Landscape, 210–11 (10)

Mytens, Daniel, *c.* 1590–*c.* 1648. Dutch painter, who spent much of his life in England before returning to Holland in *c.* 1635. He was court painter to Charles I, but was eclipsed by the arrival of Van Dyck.
The Earl of Arundel in his sculpture gallery in London, 60–61 (4)

Niccolò Fiorentino (Nicolo Spinelli), 1430–1514. Italian medallist. He worked in Florence most of his life, but also visited the court of Philip the Bold in Burgundy.
Medal of Charles VIII, 298
Medal of Marsilio Ficino, reverse of, 44–45 (4)
Medal of Lorenzo the Magnificent, 244–45 (1)
Medal of Pico della Mirandola, 322
Medal of Angelo Poliziano, reverse of, 44–45 (5)
Medal of Giovanna Tornabuoni, reverse of, 54–55 (5)

Nostradamus (Michel de Nostre-Dame), 1503–66. French astrologer and physician. In 1555 he published his *Centuries*, a series of prophetic verses couched in such allusively obscure language that they were held *post facto* to have predicted a large number of historical events. They still provide amusement for some.
Herman Irwell Woolf, *Nostradamus, His Life and Prophecies*, 1944
Kazimierz Chodkiewicz, *Oracles of Nostradamus*, 1965

Oliver, Isaac, *c.* 1560/5–1617. French painter who settled in England. Born in Rouen, he was brought to England by his parents in 1568, and was trained in London under HILLIARD and in the late 1580s and 1590s spent time in Italy. In England he achieved great success, becoming a serious rival to Hilliard towards the end of the century, and enjoying royal patronage under JAMES I. His small portraits are often imbued with a sense of melancholy, and his figures are more naturalistic than his master's. While mainly a portrait miniaturist, he also painted small religious subjects and classical scenes.

Pacher, Michael, 1435–1498. Austrian painter and sculptor, whose workshop produced many painted and carved altarpieces for churches throughout the Tyrol. He probably travelled to Italy early in his career, as some of his altarpieces show a knowledge of perspective and the influence of MANTEGNA, but his work also displays northern characteristics reminiscent of Rogier van der WEYDEN. His masterpiece is the *St Wolfgang Altarpiece* in Upper Austria.
The Coronation of the Virgin, 128–29 (2)
The Raising of Lazarus, 246–47 (7)
Nicolò Rasmo, *Michael Pacher*, trans. by Philip Waley, 1971

Palestrina, Giovanni Pierluigi da, *c.* 1525– 94. Italian composer. He was organist and choirmaster at Palestrina Cathedral by the age of 20, and in 1550 was appointed choirmaster to the Vatican. He occupied a series of important positions in Rome under Pope Julius III. In 1562 the Council of Trent decreed that musical settings of the mass should not be so complicated that the words became inaudible. Palestrina managed to obey this instruction while at the same time preserving his rich polyphonic style. He was the model for later Counter-Reformation sacred music, achieving sonority through unaccompanied voices without the lavish instrumentation popular in Venice.
Autograph music, 220–21 (6)
Herbert Kennedy Andrews, *An Introduction to the Technique of Palestrina*, 1958
Malcolm Boyd, *Palestrina's Style*, 1973

Palissy, Bernard, *c.* 1510–90. French potter, who invented an extraordinary style of ornamenting plates and dishes in relief with reptiles, fishes, snails, etc., that were highly coloured and very lifelike. Palissy's works illustrate a vein of the grotesque that is alien to most other Renaissance ideals.
Cecilia Lucy Brightwell, *Palissy, the Huguenot Potter*, 1921

Andrea Palladio in his late sixties by Giambattista Maganza, 1576.

Palladio, Andrea, 1508–80. One of the most famous of all Italian architects whose classically inspired designs and theoretical publications exerted unprecedented influence on subsequent architecture throughout Europe. Born in Padua, and trained as a mason, he spent two years from 1545 in Rome studying, with archaeological precision, the buildings of Antiquity. His renowned series of harmonious and strictly symmetrical villas in the Veneto, which include La Rotonda (1550) and La Malcontenta (*c.* 1558–60), broadly conform to a design of a central block fronted by a columnar pedimented portico (which he was the first to apply to a secular building) and flanked by low wings of farm buildings. A number of fine palaces in Vicenza also feature among his domestic architectural achievements. Palladio's Venetian churches, S. Giorgio Maggiore and Il Redentore, are noted for their luminous interiors and majestic façades composed of interlocking temple fronts. The Teatro Olimpico at Vicenza was an attempt to re-create a Roman theatre, though its perspective street-set was built after his death. His *Quattro libri dell'architettura* (1570), which include illustrations of his own buildings, were fundamental in disseminating knowledge of his style.

Basilica, Vicenza, 278–79 (4)
Ionic order, from *Quattro libri*, 268–69 (9)
Palazzo Chiericati, Vicenza, 78–79 (5)
Roman theatre, reconstruction of, 282–83 (3)
S. Giorgio Maggiore, Venice, 108–09 (8), 110–11 (6)
Teatro Olimpico, Vicenza, 282–83 (1)
Villa Barbaro, Maser, 284–85 (6)
Villa Malcontenta, near Vicenza, 284–85 (7, 8)
Villa Rotonda, near Vicenza, 274–75 (9)
J. S. Ackerman, *Palladio*, 2nd ed., 1977
Bruce Boucher, *Andrea Palladio, the Architect in his Time*, 1994

Palma Giovane, 1544–1628. Italian painter. Venetian-born great-nephew of PALMA VECCHIO, he was an assistant of TITIAN from 1570, working with the master on his last works. His own paintings, usually large-scale religious and narrative subjects, are closer to the style of TINTORETTO. A prolific painter and draughtsman, he received commissions for decorative schemes in Venetian palaces and churches, and also from patrons elsewhere in Europe. After Tintoretto's death he was the leading artist in Venice.

Palma Vecchio, *c.* 1480–1528. Italian painter. Born north of Bergamo, he spent most of his life in Venice and was influenced by GIORGIONE and the early works of TITIAN. He painted religious and allegorical scenes set in extensive landscape, but is most noted for his half-length portraits of women, in which he idealized a type of blonde Venetian beauty. He used clear and brilliant tones for these sensuous images, highlighting the opulence and texture of rich fabrics and jewels in contrast to delicate tones of flesh and hair.

Portrait of Ariosto, 38–39 (1)

Philip Rylands, *Palma Vecchio*, 1992

Pannartz, Arnold, died *c.* 1476. German printer, who with Conrad SWEYNHEYM set up the first printing press in Italy at Subiaco.

Cicero's *De oratore*, 208–09 (1)

Parmigianino (Francesco Mazzola), 1503–40. Italian painter. Principally influenced by the works of CORREGGIO in his native Parma, in 1524 he travelled to Rome where contact with the achievements of RAPHAEL and MICHELANGELO were also important to his artistic development. A major force in the early evolution of Mannerism, his intensely personal style is characterized by the studied elegance and sophistication of his elongated figures, and by loose, flowing brushstrokes delineating drapery and landscapes. He painted altarpieces and portraits as well as frescoes, of which the most notable are in S. Maria della Steccata, Parma. His compositions became widely known through the dissemination of his own etchings.

Self-portrait in a convex mirror, 242–43 (3)
Cupid Carving his Bow, 248–49 (5)
Madonna with the Long Neck, 132–33 (5)

Sydney J. Freedberg, *Parmigianino: his Works in Painting*, 1950
Arthur Ewart Popham, *Catalogue of the Drawings of Parmigianino*, 1971

Patenier, Joachim, active 1515–died before 1524. Netherlandish painter. He spent his active career in Antwerp and was predominantly a painter of landscapes, a genre of which he was one of the first practitioners. Although figures appear in his compositions, they are usually eclipsed by his fantastic, rocky scenery, painted in cool tones and often featuring atmospheric lighting effects.

Crossing the Styx, 168–69 (6)
The Rest on the Flight to Egypt, 166–67 (3)

Paul III, Pope, 1468–1549. Pope from 1534. A learned humanist with refined artistic taste, Paul III (Alessandro FARNESE) laid important foundations for religious reform, most significantly by instigating the Council of Trent (1545–63). He consolidated papal authority and encouraged the new religious orders, granting papal recognition to the Jesuits in 1540. His Palazzo Farnese, Rome, begun by Antonio da SANGALLO the Younger and completed by MICHELANGELO, was regarded as the epitome of a princely Renaissance palace. Under the pope's patronage Michelangelo also frescoed *The Last Judgment* in the Sistine Chapel and remodelled the important civic site of the Campidoglio. His long papacy marked a period of stability and urban growth in Rome, but his advancement of his illegitimate children was cause for criticism.

Portrait by Titian, 66–67 (7)

Pope Paul III, detail from a portrait by Titian, 1543.

Perugino, Pietro (Pietro Vanucci), *c.* 1446–1523. Italian painter. Born near Perugia, he is the best representative of the Umbrian School. By 1472 he was in Florence in VERROCCHIO's workshop, where LEONARDO was also apprenticed. He was among a number of artists called to Rome by Pope SIXTUS IV to fresco the Sistine Chapel walls, and his *Christ Giving the Keys to St Peter* epitomizes his clearly organized and uncluttered style, with figures set well into the foreground against an architectural or landscape setting. He became very successful, running more than one workshop to fulfil commissions for altarpieces and frescoes. RAPHAEL was one of his pupils in Perugia from about 1500 to 1504. Stylistically he made few changes throughout his career, painting serene, often sentimental, Saints and Madonnas in a limited and recognizable range of poses which became repetitive towards the end of his life.

Christ Giving the Keys to St Peter, 274–75 (4)
Crucifixion, 140–41 (1)

Pietro Vannucci, *The Masterpieces of Perugino*, 2nd ed., 1930
Richard T. James, *Perugino*, 1952

Peruzzi, Baldassare, 1481–1536. Italian architect and painter. Born and trained in Siena, Peruzzi became a senior assistant to BRAMANTE in Rome in 1503. His early masterpiece is the Villa Farnesina (1506–11), an elegant suburban villa in Rome which was decorated with exquisite frescoes by the leading artists of the day, including RAPHAEL and SEBASTIANO DEL PIOMBO. On the first floor Peruzzi frescoed the Salone delle Prospettive (1517–18) with illusionistic perspectives featuring *trompe-l'oeil* marble columns and painted vistas of Roman landscapes. Imprisoned at the Sack of Rome in 1527, he returned to his native Siena where he became official architect to the Sienese Republic. In his last years he produced the masterly design for the Palazzo Massimo alle Colonne, Rome (begun 1533), which incorporates two family palaces on a shared site, one being distinguished externally by its famous curved, porticoed façade. Peruzzi's drawings and theories became known through the publications of his pupil SERLIO.

Villa Farnesina, Rome, fresco in, 254–55 (3)

W. W. Kent, *The Life and the Works of Baldassare Peruzzi of Siena*, 1925

Pesellino (Francesco di Stefano), *c.* 1422–57. Italian painter. A Florentine artist, influenced by Fra Filippo LIPPI, his only documented painting, *The Trinity with Saints*, was completed by Fra Filippo Lippi following Pesellino's early death. A body of work is attributed to him on stylistic grounds.

Petrarch (Francesco Petrarca), 1304–74. Italian humanist and poet. Son of an exiled Florentine notary who had settled in Avignon, home of the papal court. He travelled widely in France and Italy, but Provence remained his base for over 40 years. While he was educated in law and eventually took minor Holy Orders, his major interest was the study of the Latin classics and he did much to establish authentic texts by collecting manuscripts, and was one of the first humanists to try to learn Greek. Petrarch also wrote a celebrated series of sonnets inspired by his ideal love for a woman called Laura, about whom little is known. His poetic works, collectively known as the *Canzoniere*, earned him considerable fame and he became the first poet of modern times to be crowned Poet Laureate in Rome.

Portrait in his study, 34–35 (4)
Livy, manuscript of, copied by Petrarch, 34–35 (1)
Simone Martini's illustration in his copy of Virgil, 34–35 (7)
Trionfi, illustration to, 200–01 (3)

John Larner, *Italy in the Age of Dante and Petrarch, 1216–1380*, 1983
Nicholas Mann, *Petrarch*, 1984

Philip II, 1527–98. King of Spain from 1556. Most of Philip's energies went into governing his immense empire. His intellectual interests embraced humanism, but always within strict Catholic orthodoxy. Architecturally his tastes were austere (witness his great palace, the Escorial, overseen by HERRERA); in painting, rather surprisingly, much less so – he particularly liked TITIAN's nudes.

Portrait by Sanchez Coello, 92–93 (7)
Portrait by Titian, 70–71 (8)
The Dream of Philip II by El Greco, 124–25 (5)
Netherlands, entertainment in, 98–99 (3)
Triumphal arch, 280–81 (6)

Geoffrey Parker, *Philip II*, 1988
Geoffrey Woodward, *Philip II*, 1992

Pico della Mirandola, medal by Niccolò Fiorentino, c. 1495.

Pico della Mirandola, Giovanni, 1463–94. Italian philosopher and author. Born into a noble Lombard family, he possessed outstanding intellect, mastering many disciplines and languages before concentrating on philosophy. While other Renaissance humanists saw underlying common ground in Platonic and Christian thought, Pico sought wider unity by also exploring Hebrew and Arabic writings, including the Cabbala and works of Averroes. Aged only 24, he went to Rome and published 900 *Conclusiones* (theses) which he invited scholars to debate publicly with him. The papacy's condemnation of some of his theses as heretical forced him to flee the city before any debate took place. With FICINO Pico was a leading intellectual in the Platonic Academy in Florence but was increasingly attracted towards the study of theology, becoming a friend and follower of SAVONAROLA. His major work, *Oratio de dignitate hominis*, proposes that the human individual has no fixed place in creation and possesses a measure of liberty and free choice.

Portrait by Rosselli, 44–45 (1)

Piero della Francesca, active 1439–died 1492. Italian painter whose style is noted for its sense of monumentality and stillness, and for particular sensitivity to effects of light.

Although little is known of his early life, Piero is recorded in Florence in 1439 working on the lost fresco cycle in S. Egidio with DOMENICO VENEZIANO, who seems to have been a formative influence on his subtle skill as a colourist. In 1442 he returned to his native Borgo S. Sepolcro, where he painted *The Resurrection* in a room in the town hall, and during a long career worked for many of the most discriminating patrons in central Italy. Among his most famous works are panels of *The Flagellation* and *The Baptism of Christ*, and the frescoed chancel of S. Francesco, Arezzo, depicting the *Legend of the True Cross*. He expounded his mathematical and perspectival theories in *De prospectiva pingendi* and *De quinque corporibus regularibus*.

Portrait of Sigismondo Malatesta: 72–73 (7); before St Sigismund, 182–83 (8)
Portrait of Federigo da Montefeltro, 72–73 (5)
The Baptism of Christ, 134–35 (1)
Defeat of Chosroes by Heraclius, 84–85 (1)
The Flagellation, 246–47 (8)
Hercules, 50–51 (1)
Legend of the True Cross, 16
Madonna della Misericordia, 106
The Nativity, 130–31 (1), 166–67 (4)
The Resurrection, 144–45 (4)
Ideal city, 270–71 (1)

The Complete Paintings of Piero della Francesca, intro. by Peter Murray, 1985
Ronald Lightbown, *Piero della Francesca*, 1992

Piero di Cosimo, 1462–1521. Italian painter. A pupil of Cosimo ROSSELLI, he went to Rome in 1481 to assist his master with fresco decoration of the Sistine Chapel. He spent most of his life in his native Florence becoming, according to VASARI, progressively eccentric and reclusive. Something of the idiosyncrasy of his character is reflected in his highly original and fantastic interpretation of mythological subjects, which made up the majority of his output. While stylistically influenced by Florentine masters, his works attest to his great affinity with nature and animals. Piero was also noted for designing impressive festive decorations for processions and ceremonies.

R. Langton Douglas, *Piero di Cosimo*, 1946

Pilon, Germain, 1537–90. French sculptor. His early style, characterized by elegant and elongated Mannerist figures, is dependent on PRIMATICCIO's stucco decoration at Fontainebleau but he developed towards a more naturalistic and emotional style, seen particularly on the marble gisants of HENRI II and Catherine de MEDICIS on their tomb at St Denis. The tomb, on which he worked from 1563 until 1570, also features kneeling figures of the monarchs in bronze. He was appointed royal sculptor in 1568, and produced many portrait busts of the French royal family.

Henri II: medallion of, 310; monument for the heart of, 54–55 (7)
Catherine de Médicis, medallion of, 318

Pinturicchio, self-portrait, 1501.

Pinturicchio, Bernardo, c. 1454–1513. Italian painter. Born and trained in Perugia, he worked in Rome with PERUGINO on frescoes in the Sistine Chapel and subsequently decorated the Borgia Apartments in the Vatican palace for Pope ALEXANDER VI. His last major commission, on which he worked for many years, was the impressive fresco cycle in the Piccolomini Library in Siena Cathedral, which chronicles the life of PIUS II in several large narrative scenes which Pinturicchio organized within a fictive architecture framework.

Portrait of Pope Alexander VI, 66–67 (2)
Aeneas Sylvius Piccolomini Sets Out for the Council of Basle, 166–67 (1)
Arithmetica, 218–19 (7)
Arrival of Pope Pius II Piccolomini at Ancona, 66–67 (1)
Betrothal of Frederick III and Eleanor of Portugal, 82–83 (2)
Borgia Apartments, the Vatican, fresco in, 44–45 (3, 7)

Evelyn M. Phillips, *Pintoricchio*, 1901
Corrado Ricci, *Pintoricchio*, trans. by F. Simmonds, 1902

Pisanello (Antonio Pisano), c. 1395–1455. Italian medallist and painter. Assistant and heir to GENTILE DA FABRIANO, he was employed at many of the major Italian courts, where his sophisticated and decorative International Gothic style of painting reflected the taste of patrons such as the GONZAGA and ESTE families. Only a few of his frescoes and panel paintings survive but his sketchbooks, full of exquisite detailed drawings, of animals, birds, costumes and fabrics, confirm his exceptional skill as a draughtsman. He is particularly noted as the first, and most original, Renaissance medallist. Commissioned for commemorative and diplomatic use by aristocratic and humanist patrons, his bronze medals characteristically show a bold profile portrait, with an heraldic or symbolic device on the reverse. They usually bear an inscription, and often Pisanello's own name.

Alfonso I, drawing for a medal of, 244–45 (2)
Portrait of Leonello d'Este, 72–73 (4)
Medal of Vittorine da Feltre, 334
Portrait of Filippo Maria Visconti, 72–73 (3)
St George and the Princess, 76–77 (2)
Court dress, design for, 65

Enio Sindona, *Pisanello*, trans. by J. Ross, 1961
Giovanni Paccagnini, *Pisanello*, trans. by Jane Carroll, 1973

Pius II, Pope, 1405–64. Pope from 1458. An able papal secretary, scholar and writer, Aeneas Sylvius Piccolomini did not take Holy Orders until 1446, by which time he had visited most of Europe. By the time of his election as pontiff his love of worldly pleasures was subdued, but his humanist and artistic interests were unabated. Pius commissioned a fresco cycle celebrating his life from PINTURICCHIO to decorate the Piccolomini Library in Siena Cathedral and employed Bernardo ROSSELLINO on the ambitious project to remodel his native village into the papal town of Pienza. During his papacy he campaigned for a new crusade against the Turks, but his death prevented fruition of the plan. Pius II's memoirs, the *Commentarii*, give a unique and candid insight not only into his own thoughts and actions, but also into corrupt practices within the Church hierarchy.

Arrival of Pope Pius II Piccolomini at Ancona by Pinturicchio, 66–67 (1)
Pius II Sets Out for the Council of Basle by Pinturicchio, 166–67 (1)

Memoirs of a Renaissance Pope: the Commentaries of Pius II, trans by F. A. Gragg, 1959

Plantin, Christophe, c. 1520–89. French printer and bookseller who settled in Antwerp from 1549. His successful business soon became renowned for its excellent typography and the quality of its engraved illustrations. Plantin received the support of PHILIP II of Spain for his master project, the publication of the *Biblia polyglotta* (Polyglot Bible) in five languages which appeared in eight volumes between 1568 and 1572. He also printed scientific and other learned texts, and under his own initiative produced the first dictionary of the Dutch language.

Colin Clair, *Christopher Plantin*, 1960

Pleydenwurff, Hans, active 1450–died 1477. German painter who worked in Nuremberg.

The Resurrection, 144–45 (1)

Poliziano, Angelo, 1454–94. Poet and philologist. He received a wide humanist education in Florence, including the study of Plato under FICINO. Less intensely intellectual than Ficino or PICO DELLA MIRANDOLA, he possessed outstanding ability in both Latin and Greek, talents which brought him into the MEDICI household as tutor to Cosimo de' Medici's son, Piero. A leading Renaissance poet in

both Latin and vernacular Italian, his *Stanze per la giostra*, written for Giuliano de' Medici, probably provided the learned framework upon which BOTTICELLI based his mythological paintings for the Medici family. From 1480 he was professor of Greek and Latin at the University in Florence where he continued his researches into classical texts and language.

Medal by Niccolò Fiorentino, 44–45 (5)
Portrait by Ghirlandaio, 44–45 (2), 176–77 (1)
Portrait by Rosselli, 44–45 (1)

Pollaiuolo family. Antonio (c. 1432–98) and his younger brother Piero (c. 1441–96) ran a large Florentine workshop which produced paintings, sculpture, stained glass and goldsmiths' work. Antonio's interest in anatomy and the representation of the active human figure is revealed in his engraving *Battle of the Nude Gods*, and is also a theme which appears in the brothers' huge collaborative panel painting, *The Martyrdom of St Sebastian*. From 1484 the brothers were in Rome where they produced two highly acclaimed papal monuments, the bronze tomb of SIXTUS IV and a wall tomb and monument to Pope Innocent VIII.

Antonio Pollaiuolo:
Battle of the Nude Gods, 250–51 (6)
Hercules, 50–51 (4)
Hercules and Antaeus, 50–51 (6)
Equestrian monument to Francesco Sforza, design for, 86–87 (4)
Tomb of Pope Sixtus IV, 100–01 (1)

Maud Cruttwell, *Antonio Pollaiuolo*, 1907
Leopold D. Ettlinger, *Antonio and Piero Pollaiuolo: A Complete Edition with a Critical Catalogue*, 1978

Pontormo, Jacopo (Carucci), 1494–1556. Italian painter. Of Tuscan origin, he trained in various Florentine workshops, including that of ANDREA DEL SARTO who proved a formative influence on his early work. He and his contemporary, ROSSO FIORENTINO, were the main creators of Mannerism. A profoundly religious man, his works are highly expressive and his use of brilliant colour follows MICHELANGELO's example. His *Deposition Altarpiece* in S. Felicita, Florence, is considered a key Mannerist work and he produced a celebrated and intense fresco cycle of Christ's Passion in the Certosa at Galluzzo. His diary reveals a solitary, neurotic nature and one of his few friendships was with his pupil BRONZINO.

Frederick M. Clapp, *Jacopo Carucci da Pontormo, His Life and Work*, 1916
J. C. Rearick, *The Drawings of Pontormo*, 1964

Pordenone (Giovanni Antonio de Sacchis), 1483–1539. Italian painter. Chiefly remembered for his dramatic and expressive frescoes, he was born in northern Italy and later moved to Venice where, for a brief period, his work rivalled that of TITIAN. He probably made a visit to Rome, as the monumentality of his figures suggests the influence of MICHELANGELO, while the

illusionism of his ceiling frescoes reflects a knowledge of the northern Italian example of MANTEGNA. He worked extremely rapidly in a fluid, sometimes coarse, fresco technique which mirrored the energy and immediacy of his powerful images. His most famous frescoes are scenes from Christ's Passion in Cremona Cathedral.

Primaticcio, Francesco, 1504–70. Italian painter, designer and architect. Trained under GIULIO ROMANO in Mantua, the major part of his career was spent in France where he was employed by FRANCOIS I as an artist and interior designer at the Palace of Fontainebleau. Collaborating with ROSSO FIORENTINO, he developed a sumptuous and sophisticated style of decor combining panelling, painting and high-relief stucco work. Principally remembered for this rich and impressive Mannerist decoration at the palace, which originated the French School of Fontainebleau, he also undertook some architectural work in France towards the end of his career.

Gallery of François I, Fontainebleau, 252–53 (6)

Quercia, Jacopo della, 1374/5–1438. Italian sculptor. Probably trained by his father, he was the leading Sienese sculptor of the early 15th century. Although unsuccessful in the 1401 competition to design the bronze doors for the baptistery in Florence, he went on to receive major commissions in Siena, Lucca and Bologna. His early tomb monument of Ilaria del Carretto at Lucca is a landmark in Renaissance sculpture, combining the elegance of a Gothic effigy with distinct classical motifs of garland-carrying putti. In his relief work, such as the Fonte Gaia, Siena, he concentrated on the depiction of expressive human figures, and unlike GHIBERTI and DONATELLO, showed little interest in the exploration of perspective effects. His late work on the portal of S. Petronio in Bologna shows his relief style distilled to great dramatic effect. Stripped of all extraneous detail and dominated by sturdy, muscular figures, nude or swathed in heavy drapery, he produced an individual and powerful interpretation of scenes from *Genesis*, which subsequently very proved influential on the young MICHELANGELO.

Portal of S. Petronio, Bologna, 260–61 (4)
Tomb of Ilaria del Carretto, Lucca, 100–01 (8)

Charles Seymour, *Jacopo della Quercia*, 1973

Rabelais, François, c. 1494–1553. French humanist, physician and satirist. In 1520 he is recorded as a Franciscan friar in Poitou but his study of Greek was viewed with great disapproval and he obtained permission to transfer to a nearby Benedictine monastery. Rabelais travelled to several universities, renounced his monastic habit and studied medicine in Paris, a discipline of which he became an eminent practitioner and teacher. The targets of his satire in his long mock-epics *Pantagruel* (1532) and *Gargantua* (1534) are scholastic pride, monastic ignorance and legal absurdity. Their exuberant invention and gross humour made them popular, but they also involve a vast parade of learning and beneath it all a serious purpose in revealing true religion and morality.

Pantagruel, **woodcut from**, 38–39 (9)
Donald M. Frame, *François Rabelais, a Study*, 1977
M. A. Screech, *Looking at Rabelais*, 1988

Raimondi, Marcantonio, *c*. 1480–1534. Italian engraver. Of Bolognese origin, he visited Venice in 1506, where he saw the work of DURER, and in 1507 moved to Rome. He was the first to make engraved copies of works by famous artists including RAPHAEL, MICHELANGELO and GIULIO ROMANO, a major factor in disseminating knowledge of the Italian masters throughout Europe.

Sir Walter Raleigh, 1602.

Raleigh, Sir Walter, *c*. 1554–1618. A favourite of ELIZABETH I, by whom he was knighted in 1585, Raleigh fought against the rebels in the Irish Rebellion of 1580 and undertook several expeditions of discovery and colonization in north America. He fell from favour when knowledge of his secret marriage reached the queen. At JAMES I's accession he was accused of plotting against the king and in 1603 he and his wife were imprisoned in the Tower of London. Raleigh was released from prison in 1616 to lead a further voyage to the Orinoco in search of gold, but on his return from the failed expedition he was executed. He wrote poetry and accounts of his voyages of discovery, and during his imprisonment started his *History of the World* (1614) of which only the first volume was completed.

Andrew Sinclair, *Sir Walter Raleigh and the Age of Discovery*, 1984
Norman Lloyd Williams, *Sir Walter Raleigh*, 1988

Raphael, woodcut from Vasari's Lives, *1568.*

Raphael (Raffaello Sanzio), 1483–1520. Italian painter and architect, in whose art the ideals of the High Renaissance found complete expression. Born in Urbino, he trained in Perugia with PERUGINO – the influence of his master is clear in such early works as *The Marriage of the Virgin*. In 1504 he arrived in Florence, where he began a series of serene Madonnas – for example the *Madonna of the Meadow* – which, although related to LEONARDO's pyramidal compositions of the same theme, are set in calm, harmonious landscapes quite unlike Leonardo's dark, fantastic settings. Within four years Raphael had achieved considerable success in Florence and his fame had spread, so that by 1508 he was in Rome, having been given the prestigious commission to decorate the Vatican Stanze for Pope JULIUS II. The first room he frescoed includes the famous scenes of *The School of Athens* and the *Disputà*. Other papal commissions were for the tapestries lining the walls of the Sistine Chapel, for which he produced his large-scale *Cartoons* (1516), and the decoration of the Vatican logge, which were very influential on later decorative art. Raphael responded to the art of MICHELANGELO by developing a more monumental type of human form, but this did not entail sacrificing the grace and dignity of his figures, as epitomized in the brilliantly coloured fresco of *Galatea*, painted for Agostino CHIGI in the Villa Farnesina. Not only his outstanding artistic talent, but also his affable nature endeared Raphael to patrons, and he had to employ a large number of assistants to fulfil his numerous commissions. Under Pope LEO X he began a comprehensive survey of the antiquities of Rome and after the death of BRAMANTE in 1514, he was appointed architect of St Peter's Basilica. In his architectural designs, as in his paintings, he displayed a strong affinity with classical and antique models. Raphael also proved himself to be a sensitive portraitist,

portraying, among others, Pope Leo X and Baldassare CASTIGLIONE. His last work, *The Transfiguration*, points forward to Mannerism, a tendency to be developed by his star pupil GIULIO ROMANO. Raphael's sudden death aged 37 was the cause of great public mourning and the highly esteemed artist was buried in the Pantheon, Rome.

Self-portrait, 242–43 (5)
Portrait of Pietro Bembo, 34–35 (2)
Portrait of Baldassare Castiglione, 38–39 (3)
Portrait of Pope Julius II, 66–67 (4), 311
Portrait of Pope Leo X, 66–67 (5)
La Gravida, 176–77 (1)
Madonna of the Baldacchino, 136–37 (6)
The School of Athens, 40–41, 218–19 (2)
Sistine Madonna, 132–33 (6)
The Transfiguration, 144–45 (5)
Venus, Ceres and Juno, 48–49 (1)
Vatican logge, 252–53 (2)
Villa Farnesina, Rome, loggia of Psyche, 252–53 (5)
Villa Madama, Rome, 156–57 (7)

Roger Jones and Nicholas Penny, *Raphael*, 1983
James Beck, *Raphael*, 1987

René of Anjou, medal by Pietro da Milano, 1461.

René of Anjou, 1409–80. French Duke of Anjou and Bar, Count of Provence and Piedmont, who made several unsuccessful attempts to assert his claim to the Kingdom of Naples. He was a keen patron of the visual arts and literature, and wrote French prose on courtly and romantic themes.

Reuchlin, Johannes, 1455–1522. German humanist and writer. A noted classical scholar, he corresponded with other leading humanists including ERASMUS, FICINO and PICO DELLA MIRANDOLA. He is chiefly celebrated for *De rudimentis Hebraicus* (*On the Fundamentals of Hebrew*, 1506) a landmark in Hebrew scholarship which was a crucial tool for subsequent Old Testament studies. Reuchlin also championed the preservation of Hebrew literature when it was threatened with suppression by the Dominicans of Cologne. An author and translator of many texts, he favoured religious reform but, unlike his nephew MELANCHTHON, died before he had to commit himself to the Reformers or the Catholic Church.

Riccio (Andrea Briosco), 1470–1532. Italian sculptor. Originally trained as a goldsmith, he is noted for his exquisitely detailed bronze statuettes which were extremely popular among the humanist collectors of his native Padua. His bronze masterpiece is the *Paschal Candlestick* (1507–16) in the Santo in Padua which stands over 12 feet (3.5 metres) high, and includes classically inspired reliefs and figures.

Bronze candelabrum, 236–37 (6)

Ried, Benedikt, *c.* 1454–1534. Bohemian architect. The last of the great central European Gothic architects, Ried is best known for the church of Kutna Hora and the Vladislav Hall of Prague Castle, both masterpieces of complex vaulting. In the latter, however, he also used an accomplished Renaissance classical style, probably acquired in Hungary, for many of the doorways and windows, and in one place twisted the fluted pilasters into a spiral that can only be called Mannerist.

Church of St George, Prague, porch, 160–61 (8)
Vladislav Hall, Prague Castle, 24, 160–61 (9)

Riemenschneider, Tilman, *c.* 1460–1531. German sculptor. Riemenschneider stands at the end of the German Gothic tradition, but his highly individualized figures, simplified drapery and humanist sympathies bring him close to the Italian Renaissance. He worked mostly in wood.

Eve, 262–63 (7)
St John the Evangelist, 262–63 (9)
Nora Purtscher-Wydenbruck, *Gothic Twilight. The Life of Tilman Riemenschneider*, 1939
Justus Bier, *Tilman Riemenschneider, his Life and Work*, 1982

Roberti, Ercole de', active 1479–died 1496. Italian painter. Youngest of the three major Ferrarese painters of the 15th century influenced by MANTEGNA, his work is stylistically close to the other two masters, TURA and COSSA. His few surviving paintings are particularly marked by a rigorous portrayal of gaunt and suffering saints and hard, almost metallic drapery. From 1486 he was court painter at the ESTE court in Ferrara.

Pietà, 142–43 (5)
Benedict Nicolson, *The Painters of Ferrara, Cosmè Tura, Francesco del Cossa, Ercole de' Roberti and others*, 1950
Joseph Manca, *Art of Ercole de Roberti*, 1992

Rojas, Fernando de, *c.* 1465–1541. Spanish author, celebrated for his only known work

the *Tragicomedia de Calisto y Melibea* (1499) which is popularly called *La Celestina*. A 16-act romantic drama, later expanded to 21 acts, its main theme of a tragic love story is interwoven with numerous bawdy and knavish incidents featuring a large cast of colourful characters. Written in prose dialogue and never intended for performance, its freedom of language and action had a great influence on the subsequent development of both drama and the novel.

Calisto and Melibea, **title page of**, 26
Stephen Gilman, *The Spain of Fernando de Rojas*, 1972
Peter Norman Dunn, *Fernando de Rojas*, 1975

Pierre de Ronsard, 16th century.

Ronsard, Pierre de, 1524–85. French poet. Born into a noble family, he served as a royal page, but when an illness in 1540 prevented him pursuing a diplomatic career he turned his considerable intellect to the study of Latin and Greek literature. He was a leading figure of the literary group La Pléiade, which included DU BELLAY and other writers, whose aim was to reform French literature and produce poetry in the French language which could compare with classical precedents. His contribution to reform was felt through his poetic language, particularly lyrical when extolling the beauty of nature and his native landscape. His wide-ranging output included odes, love-sonnets and essays – often sophisticated and classically inspired but nonetheless presented with great human insight and a compassionate personal voice.

Margaret M. McGowan, *Ideal Forms in the Age of Ronsard*, 1985
Kathleen Anne Perry, *Another Reality, Metamorphosis and the Imagination in the Poetry of Ovid, Petrarch and Ronsard*, 1990

Rosselli, Cosimo, 1439–1507. Italian painter who, with PERUGINO, BOTTICELLI and other artists, was called to Rome in 1481 by Pope SIXTUS IV to fresco the side walls of the Sistine Chapel. He ran a workshop in Florence; two of his best-known pupils were PIERO DI COSIMO and Fra BARTOLOMMEO.

Neoplatonic scholars, fresco of, 44–45 (1)

Rossellino family. Bernardo (1409–64) was a talented sculptor who ran a Florentine workshop where he trained his younger brother Antonio (1427–79) and probably DESIDERIO DA SETTIGNANO. Bernardo's sculptural masterpiece is the wall-tomb of the humanist chancellor of Florence, Leonardo BRUNI, in S. Croce. From the mid-1440s he was mainly employed as an architect and his contact with ALBERTI, particularly as architect on site at the Palazzo Rucellai, was clearly formative on his own style when he came to remodel the small town of Pienza for PIUS II. Pienza remains a rare and outstanding example of Quattrocento town planning where the hierarchy of buildings and harmony of design closely mirror Albertian architectural theory. Antonio displayed great skill in marble-bust portraiture and sculpted the acclaimed marble tomb of the Cardinal of Portugal in S. Miniato al Monte, Florence.

Tomb of the Cardinal of Portugal, 100–01 (4)
Anne Markham Schulz, *The Sculpture of Bernardo Rossellino and his Workshop*, 1977

Rosso Fiorentino, woodcut from Vasari's Lives; 1568.

Rosso Fiorentino (Giovanni Battista di Jacopo), 1494–1540. Italian painter. A key figure in the development of Florentine Mannerism, he was an assistant in the workshop of ANDREA DEL SARTO, and was a contemporary of PONTORMO. His easel paintings are noted for contorted compositions and flat applications of bright colour. He worked for various periods in

Florence, Rome and northern Italy and in 1530 travelled to France to join PRIMATICCIO working on large-scale decorative projects in the gallery of the royal palace at Fontainebleau for FRANÇOIS I. The Mannerist style which the Italian painters developed in the palace exerted considerable influence on French painting, and became known as the School of Fontainebleau.

Gallery of François I, Fontainebleau, 252–53 (6)

David Franklin, *Rosso in Italy, the Italian Career of Rosso Fiorentino*, 1994

Rudolf II by Hans von Aachen, 1600–03.

Rudolf II, 1552–1612. Holy Roman Emperor from 1576. The grandson of CHARLES V, he was educated in Spain at the court of PHILIP II, but his unstable character made him an ineffective ruler of the HABSBURG Empire, and eventually he was forced to abdicate in favour of his brother, MATTHIAS. His court in Prague reflected his bizarre personality, and attracted numerous eccentrics as well as distinguished scholars and scientists. His interests ranged from magic and the occult, to scientific enquiry and art. The noted astronomers BRAHE and KEPLER were under his patronage, and he employed many painters, including ARCIMBOLDI and SPRANGER, as court artists. He amassed several thousand paintings, including works by LEONARDO, BRUEGEL and CORREGGIO, made vast collections of fossils, skeletons, coins and scientific instruments, and maintained a large menagerie.

Portrait by Adrian de Vries, 68–69 (3)
Portrait in intaglio, 68–69 (1)

R. J. W. Evans, *Rudolf II and his World*, 1973

Rustici, Vicenzo, 1556–1632. Italian painter.

Bullfighting and other Games in the Piazza del Campo, Siena, 96–97 (8)

Salutati, Coluccio, 1331–1406. Italian humanist and statesman. He became Chancellor of Florence in 1375, and for over 30 years was a key figure at the centre of the political and administrative affairs of the city. A keen humanist, he wrote on literary and philosophical subjects, influenced a number of pupils including BRUNI, and formed a library of manuscripts.

B. L. Ullmann, *The Humanism of Coluccio Salutati*, 1963
R. G. Witt, *Coluccio Salutati and his Public Letters*, 1976

Sangallo family. A Florentine family of architects, sculptors and painters, of whom the most notable members were two brothers, Giuliano (*c.* 1443–1516) and Antonio da Sangallo the Elder (*c.* 1453–1534), and their nephew, Antonio da Sangallo the Younger (1485–1546). Giuliano found favour as leading architect to Lorenzo de' MEDICI the Magnificent. Two of the most important works to result from this patronage were the Villa Medici at Poggio a Caiano, an important Renaissance villa which consciously evokes the villa architecture of Antiquity, and S. Maria delle Carceri, Prato, a Greek-cross church which reflects Giuliano's complete understanding of BRUNELLESCHI's centrally planned structures. Antonio the Elder collaborated with his brother on many fortification projects but his independent masterpiece was the monumental pilgrimage church of S. Maria presso S. Biagio at Montepulciano, which is based on a Greek-cross plan and fully exploits its dominant hill-top site. Antonio the Younger received his early training in Florence from his uncles and joined BRAMANTE's workshop in Rome in 1503, where initially he worked as a carpenter and draughtsman. Under the patronage of Cardinal Alessandro Farnese (later Pope PAUL III) he built the massive and imposing Palazzo Farnese, Rome, a three-storey rectangular

Antonio da Sangallo the Younger, woodcut from Vasari's Lives, *1568.*

building surrounding a central square courtyard. (After his death the palazzo was modified and completed by MICHELANGELO.) Although Antonio da Sangallo the Younger became architect of St Peter's after the death of RAPHAEL, his plans for the basilica were not executed. As papal architect, however, he undertook many projects for both CLEMENT VII and Paul III, and also proved himself a highly skilled military architect in such buildings as the Fortezza da Basso in Florence.

Antonio da Sangallo the Elder: S. Maria presso S. Biagio, Montepulciano, 274–75 (2)
Antonio da Sangallo the Younger: The Colosseum, section and view of, 278–79 (3)
Palazzo Farnese, Rome, 21
Aristotile da Sangallo: Section of a Florentine house, 188–89 (1)
Giuliano da Sangallo: Palazzo Strozzi, 154–55 (4)
S. Maria delle Carceri, Prato, 108–09 (4)
Villa Medici, Poggio a Caiano, 284–85 (3)
Giuliano da Sangallo (after): Drawings of Roman architecture and sculpture, 56–57 (8)
Hagia Sophia, copy of Ciriaco d'Ancona's drawing, 58–59 (1)

Nicholas Adams (ed.), *The Architectural Drawings of Antonio da Sangallo the Younger and his Circle*, 1994

Sanmicheli, Michele, *c.* 1484–1559. Italian architect whose expertise encompassed military, ecclesiastic and domestic commissions. Born in Verona, by 1500 he was in Rome, where he was influenced by the achievements of BRAMANTE and RAPHAEL. Back in the Veneto after the Sack of Rome, he became an outstanding military architect, employed by the Venetian Republic. He fused Bramante's grave classicism with his own Mannerist tendencies, producing a series of striking and monumental fortresses and city gates, such as the Porta Palio, Verona (1548–50). His palace architecture, while reflecting Roman High Renaissance models, was stamped with a strong individuality, particularly evident on the rich sculptural façade of the Palazzo Bevilacqua, Verona. The Cappella Pellegrini at S. Bernardino, Verona, has a highly original circular plan based on the Pantheon, while his Palazzo Grimani in Venice is one of the dominant accents of the Grand Canal.

Sano di Pietro, 1405–81. Italian painter, one of the leading representatives of the early Sienese school.

Allegory of Good Government, 74–75 (1)
S. Bernardino preaching in the Piazza del Campo, Siena, 116–17 (1)

Sansovino, Jacopo, 1486–1570. Italian architect and sculptor. Born in Florence and trained by Andrea Sansovino, whose name he adopted, he also formed close contacts with the SANGALLO family. In Rome from 1505 until 1527, principally practising as a sculptor, he returned to Florence to work on the temporary architectural structures for LEO X's ceremonial entry into the city. He settled permanently in Venice after 1527, where he achieved fame as a sculptor of monumental tombs, but where his greatest achievement was the remodelling and monumentalization of Piazza S. Marco by a series of noble civic buildings. These buildings, including the Zecca and the Library of St Mark's (c. 1540–54) and the loggia of the Campanile (1538–40) are inventive and impressive developments of High Renaissance architecture. His other architectural work includes Venetian palaces and churches, and his most famous sculptures are two huge figures of *Mars* and *Neptune* which flank the Sala dei Giganti in the Doges' Palace.

Jacopo Sansovino by Tintoretto, mid-16th century.

Baptism of Christ, 134–35 (3)
Neptune, 262–63 (5)
The Campanile of St Mark's, Venice, loggia, 158–59 (6)
Palazzo Corner, Venice, 158–59 (3)
St Mark's Library and the Mint, Venice, 158–59 (2)
Deborah Howard, *Jacopo Sansovino, Architecture and Patronage in Renaissance Venice*, 1975
Bruce Boucher, *The Sculpture of Jacopo Sansovino*, 1991

Sassetta (Stefano di Giovanni), active *c.* 1423–50. Italian painter who was one of the leading artists in 15th-century Siena. While his work attests to the heritage of Trecento Sienese masters, it also combines International Gothic elegance with an interest in creating spatial effects through the use of complex architectural settings or bold rocky landscapes.
John Pope-Hennessy, *Sassetta*, 1939

Savonarola, Fra Girolamo, 1452–98. Italian friar and theologian. A sudden conversion led Savonarola to leave his native Ferrara and enter a Dominican monastery in Bologna in 1475. Noted as a fervent and eloquent preacher, he became prior of the Florentine convent of S. Marco at Lorenzo de' MEDICI's invitation. Soon, however, he became an

Savonarola, medal by Luca della Robbia, 1495.

outspoken critic of the Medici and the Florentine republic, accusing them of corruption and abuse of power. In protest against luxury he encouraged the public burning of books, pictures and 'vanities' deemed immoral, as well as paintings and musical instruments. His virulent attacks were also directed at corruption in the church and despite being excommunicated, following his call for Pope ALEXANDER VI's deposition, he continued to preach. He eventually antagonized all factions to the extent that both the Florentine government and the papal authorities sought his permanent removal. Charges of heresy were brought against him in 1498 and he was hanged and burned in Florence.
R. Ridolfi, *The Life of Girolamo Savonarola*, trans. by Cecil Grayson, 1959
D. Weinstein, *Savonarola and Florence*, 1970

Schongauer, Martin, *c.* 1435–91. German engraver and painter. Famous throughout Germany in his lifetime, his style was strongly influenced by Rogier van der WEYDEN, and his engravings were admired by DÜRER. Remembered now chiefly for his prints and drawings, he also executed altarpieces and wall paintings.
Prints of Martin Schongauer, 1971

Sebastiano del Piombo, 1485–1547. Italian painter. Born in Venice, his early paintings show the influence of GIORGIONE, in whose workshop he may have trained. In 1511 he was called to Rome by Agostino CHIGI to work on the fresco decoration of the Villa Farnesina, where RAPHAEL and PERUZZI were also employed. MICHELANGELO, with whom he developed a close friendship, had a strong influence on his artistic development, and Sebastiano's painting of the *Flagellation* in S. Pietro in Montorio, Rome, is based on a drawing provided by Michelangelo. One of the first artists to return to the city after the Sack of Rome, he was made Keeper of the Papal Seal ('Piombo') in 1531, and with the

exception of some fine portraits, he painted far less after this date.
Portrait of Pope Clement VII, 299
Pietà, 142–43 (8)
Michael Hirst, *Sebastiano del Piombo*, 1981

Seisenegger, Jacob, 1505–67. Austrian painter.
Portrait of Elizabeth of Austria aged four, 94–95 (7)
Ferdinand I listening to the papal nuncio, 116–17 (4)

Serlio, Sebastiano, 1475–1555. Italian architect, painter and theorist. He is renowned for his architectural treatise, *L' Architettura* (six books published between 1537 and 1551; book seven published posthumously in 1575), which includes volumes on the classical orders, perspective, domestic buildings and churches. Serlio's architectural background in Rome, in the environment of BRAMANTE, RAPHAEL and his acknowledged teacher PERUZZI, was crucial to the formation of his ideas, and he included drawings by all three masters in his volume devoted to antiquities. *L' Architettura* was the first modern treatise to include illustrations, it had a strong practical basis and proved highly significant in disseminating knowledge of Italian High Renaissance architecture. Serlio was in France from 1540, under the patronage of FRANÇOIS I, where he designed the Grande Ferrare and the Château at Ancy-le-Franc.
'Comic scene' from Vitruvius, 282–83 (9)
Orders of architecture, 268–69 (5)

Francesco Sforza by G. Briago, 1454.

Sforza family. Rulers of Milan. Francesco (1401–66) was a condottiere who served the last of the VISCONTI dukes of Milan, married his daughter and eventually took over the dukedom for himself. His achievements were celebrated by FILELFO in an epic about his military deeds (*Sforziade*), by FILARETE in a Utopian city (*Sforzinda*) and by LEONARDO,

THE SFORZA FAMILY

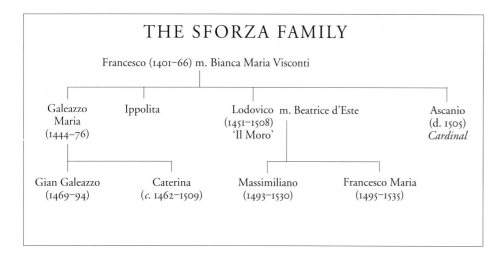

Francesco (1401–66) m. Bianca Maria Visconti

- Galeazzo Maria (1444–76)
- Ippolita
- Lodovico (1451–1508) 'Il Moro' m. Beatrice d'Este
- Ascanio (d. 1505) *Cardinal*

- Gian Galeazzo (1469–94)
- Caterina (c. 1462–1509)
- Massimiliano (1493–1530)
- Francesco Maria (1495–1535)

---

who made an equestrian monument in clay, never cast. His son Lodovico (1451–1508), known as 'Il Moro', made the fatal decision to encourage CHARLES VIII's invasion of Italy. Lodovico extricated himself from this situation, but was defeated by Charles' successor Louis XII and died in a French prison. He too had scholarly and artistic interests and is remembered above all as the patron of Leonardo and BRAMANTE. The Sforzas never recovered power in Milan, but Lodovico's niece Caterina (c. 1462–1509) led a violent and colourful life in Rome, politically ambitious, personally abrasive and sexually uninhibited.

Design for Equestrian Monument to Francesco Sforza by Antonio Pollaiuolo, 86–87 (4)

E. Breisach, *Caterina Sforza, a Renaissance Virago*, 1967
Gregory Lubkin, *A Renaissance Court, Milan under Galeazzo Maria Sforza*, 1994

Shakespeare, William, 1564–1616. English dramatist, who spent all his working life as an actor and playwright in London. Shakespeare's links with humanist culture and the Italian Renaissance are many and deep. If by Ben JONSON's standards he had 'small Latin and less Greek', by those of the 20th century he had quite a lot of Latin and perhaps even a little Greek, as well as being able to read Italian and French. *The Rape of Lucrece* and *Venus and Adonis* are based on Ovid, *The Comedy of Errors* on Plautus and the Roman plays (*Julius Caesar, Antony and Cleopatra* and *Corialanus*) on Plutarch. Other plays, including *Othello* and many of the comedies, are drawn from 15th- and 16th-century Italian stories and have Italian settings. His imagery is rich in mythological allusions and he even mentions one contemporary Italian painter, GIULIO ROMANO. At a more general level, his emphasis on the uniqueness of the individual, his apparent indifference to religious dogma, his endless curiosity about human motivation and character and his ability to empathize with a whole range of contradictory moral attitudes, all bring him close to the ideal of the 'universal man'. On the other hand, he shows

no particular respect for the ancient world, is dismissive of pedantry and impatient with formal literary categories. Hardly any aspect of Shakespeare conforms to established Renaissance criteria (hence the hostility that he aroused in orthodox critics), yet his achievement is impossible to imagine without it.

Portrait from the First Folio, 38–39 (5)
Titus Andronicus, contemporary drawing, 198–99 (3)

E. K. Chambers, *Shakespeare, a Study of Facts and Problems*, 1930
S. Schoenbaum, *Shakespeare's Lives*, new ed., 1993

Sidney, Sir Philip, 1554–86. English poet and courtier. He was educated at Christ Church, Oxford, and between 1572 and 1575 travelled widely in Europe studying languages and the arts. An accomplished and well-loved figure, he was the embodiment of the ideal Renaissance courtier; an image further romanticized following his fatal wounding in battle. His untimely death prompted great mourning and many literary tributes, including an elegy by his friend SPENSER. Sidney's chief contribution to English

Sir Philip Sidney, late 16th century.

literature was *Arcadia*, a romantic prose-fiction, considered an early precursor of the novel. He wrote a series of love sonnets, *Astrophel and Stella*, and an important work of literary criticism, *Apology for Poetry*.

Dorothy Connell, *Sir Philip Sidney, the Maker's Mind*, 1977
Katherine Duncan-Jones, *Sir Philip Sidney*, 1991

Signorelli, Luca, 1441–1523. Italian painter. Trained, according to VASARI, by PIERO DELLA FRANCESCA, he then moved to Florence where the work of Antonio POLLAIUOLO greatly influenced his style. His interest in anatomy, musculature and representation of the human figure in action can be seen in his masterpiece, a frescoed chapel of the *Last Judgment* (1499–1504) in Orvieto Cathedral. In one scene, the dramatic and crowded nude composition of *The Damned Consigned to Hell*, foreshortened figures of the condemned tumble onto a writhing mass of tortured sinners and demons. His great skill as a draughtsman is confirmed in his drawings and preparatory figure studies.

The Damned Consigned to Hell, 146–47 (2)

Gloria Kury, *The Early Work of Luca Signorelli, 1465–1490*, 1978
Antonio Paolucci, *Luca Signorelli*, 1990

Pope Sixtus IV by Melozzo da Forlì, mid-15th century.

Sixtus IV, Pope, 1414–84. Pope from 1471. Born Francesco della Rovere, he was a learned Franciscan whose papacy was marked by an unprecedented level of nepotism. He greatly enlarged the Vatican Library, added to the papal collection of antiquities and had the Sistine Chapel built and partly frescoed. A great self-publicist, he lavished the papal arms and numerous inscriptions to his munificence throughout Rome, and commissioned a large series of frescoes in celebration of his own life. The iconography on his free-standing bronze tomb by the POLLAIUOLO brothers refers to his humanist learning.

In Raphael's *Sistine Madonna*, 132–33 (7)
Sixtus IV della Rovere Appointing Platina as Papal Librarian by Melozzo da Forlì, 66–67 (3)
Sixtus IV Inspecting his Library by Melozzo da Forlì, 14
Tomb by Antonio Pollaiuolo, 100–01 (1)

Pope Sixtus V, bronze medal, 1589–90.

Sixtus V, Pope, 1525–90. Pope from 1585. The Franciscan Felice Peretti was a vigorous and reforming pope, who in his short papacy sought to change the face of Rome through the building of new roads, restoration of the water supply, erection of obelisks and fountains, and major work on the Lateran and Vatican Palaces. His considerable political and social achievements included ridding Rome of bandits and organizing efficient food distribution, but his attempt to restore the papal finances by stringent cuts in expenditure effectively crippled the Roman economy. He commissioned his favoured papal architect, Domenico Fontana, to built the sumptuous and vast Sistine Chapel in S. Maria Maggiore in Rome.

Portrait, 156–57 (1)
Street plan for Rome, 156–57 (4)

Ugo Balzani, *Rome under Sixtus V*, vol. 3, *Cambridge Modern History*, 1902

Sluter, Claus, active *c.* 1380–died 1406. Sculptor of Dutch origin who worked mainly for Duke Philip the Bold on the sculptural programme for the Charterhouse of Champmol, near Dijon. Little survives of his work on the portal and calvary, but the base of the latter, the so-called *Well of Moses*, featuring six monumental prophets, shows Sluter's bold and realistic style which is in absolute contrast to International Gothic trends and prefigures DONATELLO's realism by a generation. He also designed the tomb of Duke Philip the Bold, although it was mostly executed by his nephew, Claus de Werve. In 1404 Sluter retired to the monastery of St Etienne in Dijon.

Moses, 262–63 (6)
Tomb of Philip the Bold, Dijon, 102–03 (9)

Kathleen Morand, photographs by David Finn, *Claus Sluter, Artist at the Court of Burgundy*, 1991

Smythson, Robert, *c.* 1536–1614. English architect. First recorded as chief-mason at Longleat, Wiltshire, in the late 1560s, his architectural masterpiece is Wollaton Hall, Nottinghamshire, which is one of the finest examples of Elizabethan Renaissance style. He was probably the architect of Hardwick Hall, Derbyshire, and other houses have been attributed to him on stylistic grounds.

Design for a garden, 170–71 (5)

M. Girouard, *Robert Smythson, the Elizabethan Country House*, 1983

Edmund Spenser, 1598.

Spenser, Edmund, *c.* 1552–99. English poet. He studied at Pembroke Hall, Cambridge, from 1569 until 1576, and towards the end of this period translated many sonnets by PETRARCH and DU BELLAY. In London he formed a literary group 'Aeropagus' with SIDNEY and other poets, which addressed such topics as the adaptation of classical poetic models to English vernacular forms. From 1580 he held a number of official posts in Ireland, returning to England only a year before his death. His smaller works, including *The Shepheardes Calendar* and *Epithalamion*, amply demonstrate his lyrical fluency. In his major work, *The Faerie Queen*, a medievalizing and chivalric celebration of ELIZABETH I and her court, he consciously emulated the Italian epic poems of ARIOSTO and TASSO. The overall structure of the poem, which involves the adventures of a series of knights personifying Christian virtues, might have been easier to grasp if he had completed more than six of the projected 12 books. Its great merits are the melody of its language, the richness of its imagery and the magical atmosphere that it evokes. His adaptation of the Italian *ottava rima* to a nine-line English stanza found favour with many later poets.

Anthea Hume, *Edmund Spenser, Protestant Poet*, 1984
Gary Waller, *Edmund Spenser, a Literary Life*, 1994

Spranger, Bartholomeus, 1546–1611. Flemish painter. Trained in Antwerp, he spent several years in Rome and Parma where he was influenced by the work of CORREGGIO and PARMIGIANINO. He evolved a Mannerist style which typically presented slender and elegant nudes in compositions of studied intricacy, painted with a gleaming enamelled finish. In 1581 he was appointed court painter to RUDOLF II in Prague, and remained in the city for the rest of his life. His works became widely known through engravings by GOLTZIUS.

Hercules, Dejinira and the Dead Nessus, 50–51 (7)
Venus, Mercury and Cupid, 52–53 (9)

Stephen Batóry, 1533–86. King of Poland from 1579. He kept the Turks at bay, waged a successful war against Russia and introduced the Jesuits into Poland.

Stimmer, Tobias, 1539–84. German printer and engraver.

Portrait of Copernicus, 214–15 (5), 299
The Ages of Man, 176–77 (6, 7)

Stone, Nicholas, 1583–1647. English sculptor and mason. His work was initially influenced by several years spent as an assistant to Hendrick de KEYSER in Amsterdam and his style later developed through contact with Charles I's collection of antique sculpture when he was Master Mason to the Crown. His tomb monuments are numerous and varied, ranging from simple slabs to impressive architectural structures featuring busts, kneeling or reclining figures, marked by naturalism in his early work but later becoming more classical. His monument to John DONNE in St Paul's Cathedral includes an unusual upright shrouded effigy, while his monument to Francis Holles in Westminster Abbey is the first English work to be influenced by MICHELANGELO.

Tomb of Francis Holles, 102–03 (4)

Albert Edward Bullock, *Some Sculptural Works of Nicholas Stone*, 1908
John Havill, *Nicholas Stone, Statuary Mason and Architect*, 1982

Stoss, Veit, 1440/50–1533. German sculptor. Like RIEMENSCHNEIDER, Stoss stands midway between Gothic and Renaissance, and even looks forward to Baroque. His masterpiece is the high altar of St Mary, Cracow.

Virgin and Child, 262–63 (8)

Arthur Burkhard, *The Cracow Altar of Veit Stoss*, 1972

Strada, Jacopo da, died 1588. Italian scholar and collector. He worked for many years on an (unfinished) dictionary in 11 languages. He designed the Antiquarium in Munich for Albrecht V of Bavaria.

Portrait by Titian, 60–61 (1)
Munich Antiquarium, 60–61 (6)

Striegel, Bernhard, *c.* 1446–1528. German painter employed by MAXIMILIAN I.
Portrait of Sibylla von Freyberg, 94–95 (4)
The Family of Maximilian I, 190–91 (2)

Strozzi family. Important Florentine family, frequently in conflict with the MEDICI. Among them were bankers, military commanders and leading patrons of the arts.
Tomb of Onofrio Strozzi, 100–01 (2)
Carolyn Renfrew, *The Last of the Strozzi*, 1923
M. M. Bullard, *Filippo Strozzi and the Medici*, 1980

Sweynheym, Conrad, d. 1476. German printer, who with Arnold PANNARTZ set up the first printing press in Italy at Subiaco.
Cicero's De oratore, 208–09 (1)

Thomas Tallis, 1530.

Tallis, Thomas, *c.* 1515–85. English composer. Although he spent most of his life composing music for the Anglican liturgy, Tallis seems to have had strong Catholic sympathies. A complete master of harmonic and contrapuntial technique and of the fashionable Continental styles, he shows a spontaneity and brilliance that were to mould English music for the next century. His most famous work, *Spem in alium*, is a motet in 40 parts.

Tasso, Torquato, 1544–95. Italian poet and writer. Educated at the court of Urbino, he undertook literary studies at university in both Padua and Bologna, and in 1565 travelled to Ferrara to serve at the ESTE court. His most famous work, one of the great Italian epic poems, is *Gerusalemme liberata*, an attempt to apply Virgilian epic grandeur to a Christian theme. Written in *ottava rima* (an eight-line stanza), its subject matter is the capture of Jerusalem during the First Crusade. Although written by 1575 it was not published until 1581 and Tasso, constantly plagued by doubts about its literary merit and critical standing against classical models, continued to revise the text. His self-doubting and melancholy nature

Torquato Tasso, 16th century.

and a violent outburst at the Ferrarese court, resulted in his seven-year enforced detention in a hospital under Duke Alfonso d'Este's orders. Eventually seeking refuge in Mantua under the protection of Duke Vincenzo GONZAGA, his last years are marked by a restless wandering between cities and courts. Tasso's other writing includes a pastoral play with classical and Neoplatonic overtones, *Aminta* (1573); a tragedy, *Il re Torrismondo* (1587) and discourses on literature and literary theory.
Gerusalemme liberata, 38–39 (13)
C. P. Brand, *Torquato Tasso: a Study of the Poet and his Contribution to English Literature*, 1965
Robert L. Montgomery, *The Reader's Eye, Studies in Didactic Literary Theory from Dante to Tasso*, 1979

Tetzel, Johann, 1465–1519. German Dominican preacher, who aroused the enmity of LUTHER for his sale of indulgences.
Caricature, 114–15 (3)

Tintoretto (Jacopo Robusti), 1518–94. Italian painter. With VERONESE, he was the leading artist in Venice after the death of TITIAN. He worked in a notably fluid technique which, combined with bold lighting effects and dramatic movement, gives his paintings an exciting sense of immediacy. He employed surprising compositional devices in many works, like the swooping, foreshortened St Mark in *St Mark Freeing the Slave* or the startled princess rushing towards the spectator in *St George and the Dragon*. His most famous commissions were the painting cycle for the Scuola di S. Rocco, Venice (1564–87), which includes many large canvases of scenes from the Old and New Testaments, and the decoration of the Palazzo Ducale after the fire of 1577, which includes his *Paradiso*.

Tintoretto, self-portrait, 1588.

Portrait of Jacopo Sansovino, 327
The Creation of the Animals, 128–29 (5)
Crucifixion, 140–41 (5)
Discovery of the Body of St Mark, 246–47 (9)
The Labyrinth of Love, 170–71 (6)
The Last Supper, 138–39 (4)
Paradiso, 252–53 (7)
Susanna and the Elders, 196–97 (6)
The Taking of Parma, 84–85 (6)
Anna Pallucchini, *Tintoretto. The Life and Work of the Artist*, 1971
David Rosand, *Painting in Cinquecento Venice: Titian, Veronese, Tintoretto*, 1982

Titian (Tiziano Vecellio), 1480–1576. Italian painter. The greatest Venetian artist of the 16th century who influenced not only his contemporaries, but also succeeding generations of painters. He was widely celebrated in his own lifetime and his work was eagerly sought by leading Italian and European patrons, including Alfonso d'Este, CHARLES V and PHILIP II. He was a pupil of Giovanni BELLINI and his early work attests to his deep admiration of GIORGIONE, whose pastoral themes he developed in paintings such as *Sacred and Profane Love*. Titian's reputation was established by his huge altarpiece of *The Assumption of the Virgin* in the Frari, Venice – a key work of the Venetian High Renaissance. This was followed by the *Pesaro Altarpiece*, displaying a bold diagonal composition and monumental architectural setting which redefined the artistic boundaries of the *sacra conversazione*. In 1533 Titian became court painter to Charles V, and in later years made two visits to the Imperial Court in Augsburg. His artistic creativity covered religious, allegorical and mythological subject matter. Canvases such as *Pope Paul III Farnese with his Nephews* confirm his perception and sensitivity in portraiture. Titian revolutionized painting technique by his use of oil glazes to create

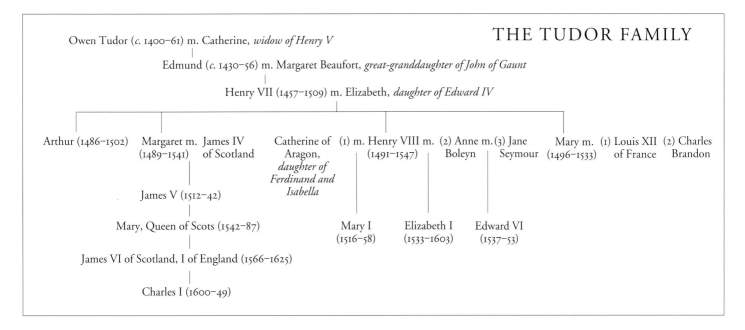

THE TUDOR FAMILY

Owen Tudor (*c.* 1400–61) m. Catherine, *widow of Henry V*

Edmund (*c.* 1430–56) m. Margaret Beaufort, *great-granddaughter of John of Gaunt*

Henry VII (1457–1509) m. Elizabeth, *daughter of Edward IV*

Arthur (1486–1502)   Margaret m. James IV (1489–1541) of Scotland   Catherine of Aragon, *daughter of Ferdinand and Isabella*   (1) m. Henry VIII m. (2) Anne m. (3) Jane (1491–1547) Boleyn Seymour   Mary m. (1) Louis XII (2) Charles (1496–1533) of France Brandon

James V (1512–42)

Mary, Queen of Scots (1542–87)   Mary I (1516–58)   Elizabeth I (1533–1603)   Edward VI (1537–53)

James VI of Scotland, I of England (1566–1625)

Charles I (1600–49)

---

rich and subtle effects, and his reputation as a colourist embraces his use of colour as a powerful means of artistic expression. Towards the end of his career, particularly in his series of mythological scenes (*poesie*) for Philip II, his handling of paint became increasingly free and he exploited the textural potential of canvas in an entirely original way.

Self-portrait, 242–43 (7)
Portrait of Pietro Aretino, 38–39 (7)
Portrait of Charles V, 68–69 (5); on horseback, 62
Portrait of Federico Gonzaga, 308
Portrait of Isabella of Portugal, 94–95 (1)
Portrait of Jacopo da Strada, 60–61 (1)
Portrait of Pope Paul III, 321
Portrait of Philip II, 70–71 (8)
The Assumption of the Virgin, 124–25 (6)
Bacchanal, 54–55 (4)
The Council of Trent, 114–15 (8)
Danäe, 248–49 (6)
Diana and Actaeon, 174
Pietà, 142–43 (7)
Pope Paul III Farnese with his Nephews, 66–67 (7)
Religion Succoured by Spain, 124–25 (4)
Sacred and Profane Love, 46–47 (6)
Saints Sebastian and Roch, 107
Tarquin and Lucretia, 196–97 (1)
The Vendramin Family, 190–91 (6)
Venus and Adonis, 52–53 (5)
Venus of Urbino, 52–53 (2)

Ugo Fasolo, *Titian*, trans. by Patrick Geagh, 1981
David Rosand, *Titian*, 1987

Torrigiano, Pietro, 1472–1528. Italian sculptor. Born in Florence, he was a pupil of the MEDICI court sculptor, Bertoldo. According to VASARI, Torrigiano broke MICHELANGELO's nose in a jealous assault and was thus exiled from Florence. In England, between 1511 and 1518, he undertook several significant commissions, including the tomb of King Henry VII and Elizabeth of York in Westminster Abbey, London, which is considered

his masterpiece. His last years were spent in Spain, where he modelled some impressive portrait busts in terracotta, a medium in which he was particularly skilled.

Henry VII, effigy, 70–71 (5)
Tomb of Henry VII and Queen Elizabeth, 102–03 (8)

Tory, Geoffroy, *c.* 1480–*c.* 1533. French grammarian and printer. He contributed to the development of typography, promoting the use of the Roman letter against Gothic, and printed many significant Books of Hours. In *Champfleury* (1529), his famous work of philology, he not only proposed improvements to the French language, including the use of accents and other marks of punctuation, but also expounded mystical theories about the origin and meaning of the letters of the alphabet. He championed the use of the French language for learned texts and in 1530 was made *imprimeur du roi* by FRANCOIS I.

Initial letters, 208–09 (9)

Trivulzio, Gian Giacomo, 1441–1518. Italian condottiere. He served with the invading French army against his own city of Milan and commissioned a monument to himself, unrealized, from LEONARDO.

Sketch of the monument by Leonardo, 86–87 (5)

Tudor family. English royal family, tracing its descent to Owen Tudor, who (probably) married Catherine, widow of Henry V, and whose son Edmund married Lady Margaret Beaufort, a Plantagenet. Their son Henry seized the throne from Richard III and reigned as Henry VII. The crown then descended lineally to his son HENRY VIII, and his children EDWARD VI, MARY I and ELIZABETH I, after which it passed via his sister Margaret to JAMES I.

Edward VI's coronation procession, 90–91 (3)
Elizabeth I: portrait, 212–13 (3); portrait medal, 244–45 (9); coach presented to Tsar, 178–79 (9); receiving Dutch ambassadors, 82–83 (7)
Henry VII: effigy, 70–71 (5); tomb, 102–03 (8)
Henry VIII: Field of Cloth of Gold, 82–83 (6); 'Great Bible', 118–19 (9); parliament under, 74–75 (3); warship, 212–13 (6)
Allegory of the Tudor Succession, 70–71 (6)

P. Williams, *The Tudor Regime*, 1979
John Guy, *Tudor England*, 1988

Tura, Cosimo, *c.* 1430–95. Italian painter. Strongly influenced by MANTEGNA, he was the founder of the School of Ferrara and court artist to the ESTE family for whom he produced religious and allegorical paintings, tapestry designs and festival decorations. Paduan influences have been deduced from his wiry figures and hard sculptural settings, but this is softened by an interest in fantastic architectural elements and rich decorative effects. As one of the first Italian painters to make effective use of oil paint, he achieved colours of great intensity and brilliance.

Allegorical figure, 46–47 (4)

Benedict Nicolson, *The Painters of Ferrara, Cosmè Tura, Francesco del Cossa, Ercole de' Roberti and others*, 1950
Eberhard Ruhmer, *Tura*, 1958

Tyndale, William, *c.* 1490/4–1536. English humanist and translator. A scholar of note, he may have spent about twelve years at Oxford (and then gone to Cambridge). He was convinced that ordinary Christians should be given the opportunity to read the Bible, but his resolution to translate them into English brought him into conflict with the authorities, who in England associated vernacular scripture with heresy. Tyndale pursued this objective in Germany, where he met LUTHER and where his New Testament was first printed in Cologne in 1525. He was denounced by the Catholic authorities but

William Tyndale, from his First Revision of the New Testament, 1534.

avoided capture, continuing to campaign for Protestant reforms and beginning his translation of the Old Testament. In 1536 he was arrested in Antwerp, charged with heresy, and burned at the stake. Subsequent English versions of the Bible, in particular the Authorised Version, were based on his learned, accurate and often poetic translations.

Portrait, 118–19 (6)
St John's Gospel, opening page of his translation, 118–19 (7)
C. Morris, *Political Thought in England: Tyndale to Hooker*, 1965
David Daniell, *William Tyndale, A Biography*, 1994

Uccello, Paolo, 1397–1475. Italian painter. He was recorded as a young apprentice in GHIBERTI's sculptural workshop and by 1414 was a member of the painters' guild. His main centre of artistic activity was Florence, although from 1425 to 1431 he worked as a mosaicist in Venice. The three panels of the *Rout of San Romano* painted for the MEDICI family (now in London, Paris and Florence) exemplify his unique style, which combines his fascination with geometry and foreshortening with the patterning and elegance of the International Gothic. His complete mastery of linear perspective is revealed in his remarkable drawings and he applied his skill to dramatic effect in the monochromatic fresco of *The Deluge* in the Green Cloister of S. Maria Novella, Florence.

Rout of San Romano, 84–85 (5)
Chalice, drawing of, 246–47 (5)
Equestrian portrait of Sir John Hawkwood, 86–87 (3)
John Pope-Hennessy, *The Complete Work of Paolo Uccello*, 1969
Franco and Stefano Borsi, *Paolo Uccello*, 1994

Sir Henry Unton, 1586.

Unton, Sir Henry, *c.* 1557–96. English gentleman and diplomat. He served as a soldier in the Netherlands and was English ambassador in Paris.

Memorial painting: banquet, 98–99 (7); burial, 200–01 (2)
Angela Cox, *Sir Henry Unton, Elizabethan Gentleman*, 1982

Utens, Giusto, died 1609. A Flemish painter who was first recorded in Italy in 1588, he is known as the artist of 14 lunettes, commissioned by Grand Duke Ferdinando I de' MEDICI, to decorate the *salone* of the Villa Medici at Artimino, near Florence. Each canvas in the series presents a topographical view of a different Medici property, shown within ordered gardens and surrounding countryside. Apart from their considerable aesthetic appeal, these canvases are valuable sources of information on the architecture of Medici villas.

The Boboli Gardens, 170–71 (1)
Villa of Pratolino, 234–35 (7), 284–85 (5)

Valdés family. Twin brothers, Alfonso (*c.* 1490–1532) and Juan (*c.* 1490–1541), who both became noted humanists. They were born into an influential and intellectual Spanish family; and corresponded with ERASMUS, whose humanist ideals they supported. Alfonso worked as secretary to CHARLES V and served at the Diet of Worms, which sought reconciliation between LUTHER and the Catholic Church. Juan left Spain soon after writing his *Diálogo de la doctrina cristiana* (1529) and spent his remaining years in Italy. He also wrote a humanist treatise on the Spanish language *Diálogo de la lengua* (*c.* 1535).

John Edward Longhurst, *Erasmus and the Spanish Inquisition: the Case of Juan de Valdes*, 1950

Valkenborch, Lucas van, 1535–97. Flemish painter.
Spring, 96–97 (4)

Valla, Lorenzo, 1407–57. Italian humanist and philosopher. Disappointed in his aim of securing employment in the papal court, he

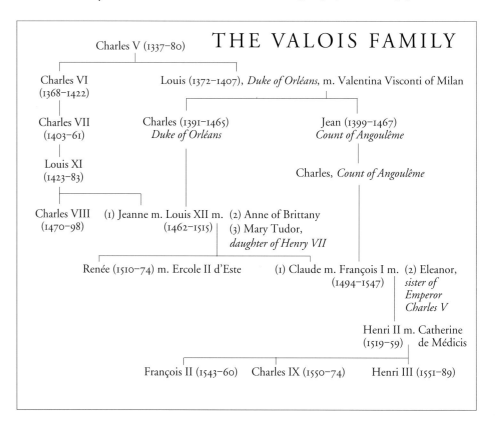

THE VALOIS FAMILY

Charles V (1337–80)

Charles VI (1368–1422) — Louis (1372–1407), *Duke of Orléans*, m. Valentina Visconti of Milan

Charles VII (1403–61) — Charles (1391–1465) *Duke of Orléans* — Jean (1399–1467) *Count of Angoulême*

Louis XI (1423–83) — Charles, *Count of Angoulême*

Charles VIII (1470–98) — (1) Jeanne m. Louis XII m. (2) Anne of Brittany (1462–1515) (3) Mary Tudor, *daughter of Henry VII*

Renée (1510–74) m. Ercole II d'Este — (1) Claude m. François I m. (2) Eleanor, (1494–1547) *sister of Emperor Charles V*

Henri II m. Catherine (1519–59) de Médicis

François II (1543–60) Charles IX (1550–74) Henri III (1551–89)

left his native Rome and eventually became a royal secretary at the court of Alfonso, King of Naples. His most famous treatise *De falso credita et ementita Constantini donatione* (1440) denied the authenticity of the Donation of Constantine by learned philological argument which showed that the crude Latin of the text could not date from the age of Constantine. His treatise thus attacked the very foundation of papal temporal power in Rome. He applied his learned analysis and close textual scrutiny to other revered sources, including the Vulgate, published works of philosophy and wrote a very successful Latin grammar, *Elegantiae linguae Latinae*, which was published in 1471.

Tomb, 34–35 (5)

Valois family. Kings of France. The direct line from Charles VI (1368–1422) died out with CHARLES VIII, and the crown passed through various branches, all descended from Charles V (1337–80), though there was always a connection by marriage: Louis XII (1462–1515) married a daughter of Louis XI (1423–83), FRANÇOIS I a daughter of Louis XII. The Valois were also connected by marriage to other European royal families – Louis XII with the TUDORS, François with the HABSBURGS – as well as to Italian ducal families – Louis, Duke of Orléans (1372–1407) with the VISCONTI, HENRI II with the MEDICI, and Renée (1510–74) with the ESTE. At the death of Henri III (1574–89) there was no direct heir, and the crown passed to a distant connection, HENRI IV, the first of the Bourbons, who ruled France until the Revolution.

R. Vaughan, *Valois Burgundy*, 1975
Keith Cameron (ed.), *From Valois to Bourbon, Dynasty, State and Society in Early Modern France*, 1989

Valturius, Roberto, 1405–75. Italian diplomat and secretary, who spent most of his life in the service of the MALATESTA family in his native Rimini. He is chiefly remembered for his *De re militari* (12 books on the art of war), a significant treatise on contemporary warfare and weaponry, lavishly illustrated with fine woodcuts and dedicated to Sigismondo Malatesta.

Vasari, Giorgio, 1511–74. Italian painter, architect and writer, who is predominantly remembered as the author of the *Lives of the Most Eminent Painters, Sculptors and Architects* (first published in 1550; followed by a much enlarged edition in 1568). Of immeasurable art-historical importance, the *Lives* combine biographical information with anecdote and critical judgment. Vasari charts Italian art as a progressive development from Cimabue and Giotto to a culmination of excellence in MICHELANGELO, whom Vasari revered both as artist and man. Vasari was an immensely productive artist in his own right, aided by assistants and much favoured by the patronage of Grand Duke Cosimo I de'

Vasari, self-portrait, mid-16th century.

MEDICI. His most noted paintings are fresco cycles in the Palazzo Vecchio, Florence, and the Palazzo della Cancelleria, Rome, while his finest architectural achievement is the Uffizi, Florence.

Ceremony of the Candles, 154–55 (6)
Duke Cosimo I of Florence Studying Plans, 72–73 (2)
Giostra del Saracino in Via Largo, 188–89 (2)
Joust in the Piazza S. Croce, 96–97 (7)
Lorenzo de' Medici with Philosophers and Scholars, 34–35 (8)
The Painter's Studio, 238
Pope Clement VII and the Emperor Charles V, 66–67 (6)
Procession in the Piazza S. Giovanni, 88–89 (1)
Lives, frontispiece, 9
Mercato Vecchio, Florence, 186–87 (8)
The Uffizi, Florence, 270–71 (4)

T. S. R. Boase, *Giorgio Vasari, the Man and the Book*, 1979
Leon Satkowski, *Giorgio Vasari, Architect and Courtier*, 1993

Vasco da Gama, c. 1460–1524. Portuguese navigator. In 1497 he was chosen by Emanuel I of Portugal to lead an expedition that was to round the Cape of Good Hope and explore what lay beyond. In May 1498 he reached Calicut – he was the first European to establish a sea-route to India. A later expedition met with a hostile reception, and Da Gama was sent out again in 1502. Having suppressed all opposition with the utmost brutality, he returned with a rich treasure to Lisbon. Da Gama went back to India in April 1524, dying there at the end of that year.

Portrait, 210–11 (6)

Henry Hersch Hart, *Sea Road to the Indies. An Account of the Voyages and Exploits of the Portuguese Navigators, Together with the Life and Times of Dom Vasco da Gama*, 1952
Kingsley Garland Jayne, *Vasco da Gama and his Successors, 1460–1580*, 1970

Veronese (Paolo Caliari), 1528–88. Italian painter. Trained in his native Verona, he arrived in Venice in 1553 and became a leading figure in Venetian art, painting huge canvases and frescoes, packed with figures and incident. He excelled in large-scale ceiling paintings, usually of mythological or allegoric subjects, where he displayed his daring and witty *sotto in sù* illusionistic effects. He decked most of his figures in the rich costumes of Venetian high-fashion, and even his religious scenes are set in the material splendour of 16th-century Venice. Questioned by the Inquisition over the propriety of his representation of a *Last Supper* (which included 'buffoons, drunkards, dwarfs, Germans and other riff-raff'), he strongly defended the notion of artistic licence, although he eventually changed the title of the work to *Feast in the House of Levi*.

Portrait of Barbaro, 34–35 (3)
Feast in the House of Levi, 198–99 (6)
The Marriage at Cana, 220–21 (4)
Venus and Adonis, 52–53 (4)
The Wife of Zebedee Interceding with Christ, 124–25 (1)
Villa Barbaro, fresco in, 254–55 (7)

R. Cocke, *Veronese's Drawings*, 1984
W. R. Rearick, *The Art of Paolo Veronese*, 1988

Verrocchio, Andrea del, 1435–88. A major Italian sculptor, he was also a gifted painter and a draughtsman of exceptional skill. He ran a large, productive workshop in Florence where LEONARDO was his most famous pupil. Particularly renowned for his bronze-casting skills, his most noted works are the sculptural group of the *Incredulity of St Thomas* on the Orsanmichele, Florence, and the monument to Bartolomeo COLLEONI in Venice, which although it emulates DONATELLO's GATTAMELATA, extends the possibilities of the equestrian monument in pose and balance. His paintings and smaller bronze works (such as the *Putto with a Dolphin*) are characterized by considerable refinement and charm.

Cosimo de' Medici, marble relief of, 318
Lorenzo the Magnificent, bust of, 318
Equestrian monument to Bartolomeo Colleoni, 86–87 (7)

Gunter Passavant, *Verrocchio*, trans. by Katherine Watson, 1969
Charles Seymour, *The Sculpture of Verrocchio*, 1971

Vesalius, Andreas (Andries van Wesel), 1514–64. Flemish anatomist and physician. Educated at Louvain and Paris, he furthered his medical studies at Padua University, where he became a teacher. He studied human anatomy through the minute scientific dissection of human cadavers. In 1543 he published *De humani corporis fabrica libri septem* (*The Seven Books on the Structure of the Human Body*), an extremely important anatomical textbook which contained fine engravings accurately reproduced from his own scientific drawings. From 1544 he served as a physician to the household of CHARLES V and in 1559 he moved to Madrid as physician to PHILIP II.

Portrait, 226–27 (5)

De humani corporis fabrica libri septem, flayed figure from, 226–27 (6)

Harvey Williams Cushing, *A Biography-Bibliography of Andreas Vesalius*, 2nd ed., 1962

Charles Donald O'Malley, *Andreas Vesalius of Brussels*, 1964

Vespasiano da Bisticci, 1421–98. Italian bookseller and businessman. Owner of a manuscript-copying business in Florence, renowned for the elegance and accuracy of its calligraphy, he provided manuscripts to a prestigious clientele, including such discriminating collectors as Duke Federigo da MONTEFELTRO of Urbino. Retiring in 1482, when the demand for hand-copied texts had declined, he wrote a series of lively biographical sketches which provide a fascinating and direct source of information about many prominent 15th-century figures whom he knew as customers and friends.

Vite, trans. by W. G. and E. Waters as *The Vespasiano Memoirs*, 1926

Amerigo Vespucci, 16th century.

Vespucci, Amerigo, 1454–1512. Italian navigator. His voyages on behalf of the royal families, first of Spain and then of Portugal, took him to Brazil, whose coast he explored in 1501 almost as far as the Strait of Magellan. His account of this expedition was used by Martin Waldseemüller for his world map of 1507, which christened the new continent America, thus giving Vespucci an immortality that is perhaps greater than he deserved.

In Waldseemüller's map, 150

Faith Yingling Knoop, *Amerigo Vespucci*, 1969

Vignola, Giacomo Barozzi da, 1507–73. Italian architect. Trained in painting and architecture at Bologna, by 1530 he was in Rome where he made significant

contributions to architectural design and theory. In two small churches he introduced the oval dome; in S. Andrea in Via Flaminia (1554) the ground plan is rectangular but in S. Anna dei Palafrenieri (1572–73) he expressed the oval in the ground plan as well. His church of the Gesù, the Jesuits' mother church in Rome, responded to the requirements of the Council of Trent, and became a model for many new churches both in Italy and elsewhere in Europe. Vignola's secular architecture includes his collaboration with VASARI and AMMANATI on the Villa Giulia in Rome and the circular courtyard of the Palazzo Farnese at Caprarola. His treatise on the Orders, *Regola delli cinque ordini d'architettura* (1562) became one of the most popular and widely used architectural textbooks.

The Gesù, Rome, 110–11 (7)

James S. Ackerman and Wolfgang Lotz, *Vignoliana*, 1965

Vischer family. German family of sculptors and bronze-founders. Their outstanding work is the bronze shrine of St Sebald at Nuremberg, a huge and elaborately decorated architectural canopy surrounding the reliquary of the saint. Although designed in 1488 by Peter Vischer the Elder (*c.* 1460–1529), much of the work was completed after 1512 by two of his sons, Hermann (1486–1517) and Peter Vischer the Younger (1487–1528), who had both travelled in Italy. The St Sebald Shrine is, therefore, an interesting combination of German Gothic style with Italianate architectural features and sculptural motifs such as putti and garlands. They also provided two statues for the tomb of Emperor MAXIMILIAN I at Innsbruck.

Hermann Vischer:
  Shrine of St Sebald, Nuremberg, drawing, 20
Peter Vischer the Elder:
  Shrine of St Sebald, Nuremberg, 20, 50–51 (2)
  Tomb of Maximilian I, Innsbruck, 102–03 (6)

Peter Vischer the Younger workshop:
  Bronze relief from the Fugger Chapel, Augsburg, 260–61 (6)

Visconti family. Rulers of Milan from the 13th century until 1447. Their position was established by the cruel and ruthless Bernabo (1323–85) and strengthened by his nephew Giangaleazzo (1351–1402), a man equally unscrupulous, but a generous patron of scholarship and the arts. Under him the Visconti extended their rule over the whole of Lombardy, parts of Piedmont and for a time parts of Tuscany and Umbria. His second son Filippo Maria (1392–1447) recovered much of the territory lost by his elder brother. When he died the dukedom passed to the husband of his daughter Bianca Maria, Francesco SFORZA.

Daniel Meredith, *Bueno de Mesquita, Giangaleazzo Visconti, Duke of Milan, 1351–1402*, 1941

Vittorino da Feltre, medal by Pisanello, c. 1446.

Vittorino da Feltre, 1378–1446. Italian educationalist. He founded a school in Mantua in 1427 which became a model of humanist teaching until the 19th century.

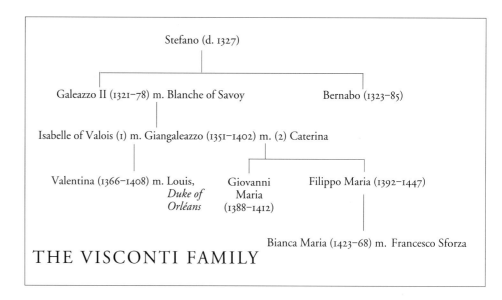

Stefano (d. 1327)

Galeazzo II (1321–78) m. Blanche of Savoy

Bernabo (1323–85)

Isabelle of Valois (1) m. Giangaleazzo (1351–1402) m. (2) Caterina

Valentina (1366–1408) m. Louis, *Duke of Orléans*

Giovanni Maria (1388–1412)

Filippo Maria (1392–1447)

Bianca Maria (1423–68) m. Francesco Sforza

THE VISCONTI FAMILY

Vittorino combined practice in Greek and Latin composition, grammar, rhetoric and dialectic with training in mathematics and philosophy, moral instruction, social accomplishment and physical well-being, qualities underlying CASTIGLIONE's recipe for the complete Renaissance gentleman.

Vivarini family. Venetian family of painters. Antonio (*c.* 1415–76/84) usually produced paintings in collaboration with other artists, most notably his brother-in-law Giovanni d'Alemagna (active 1441–died 1449/50) and later his own brother Bartolomeo (*c.* 1432–*c.* 1499). These works were typically large-scale altarpieces, depicting traditional Gothic-style saints, framed by elaborate gilded carpentry. When Bartolomeo worked independently (from the 1460s) he moved towards a style based on MANTEGNA's more sculptural forms. Alvise (*c.* 1445–1503/5) was the son of Antonio, although he probably trained with his uncle Bartolomeo, and his paintings developed in line with the influence of Giovanni BELLINI.
John Steer, *Alvise Vivarini, his Art and Influence*, 1982

Vivès, Juan Luis, 1492–1540. Spanish humanist and scholar, who spent his life outside Spain. He reacted against scholasticism and advocated a humanistic and scientific system of education based on empirical knowledge and experience. During the period from 1519 to 1523, when he was Professor of Humanities at Louvain, he became friends with ERASMUS and BUDÉ. Vivès wrote a book to guide the education of MARY I, and spent several years in England, where he lectured at Oxford, but left for the Netherlands in 1527 having lost favour due to his opposition to HENRY VIII's divorce. The last years of his life were devoted to writing on education and philosophy – *On the Right Method of Instruction for Children* (1523), *Twenty Books on Disciplines* (1531) and *Three Books on the Soul and on Life* (1538).
Portrait, 36–37 (10)
R. P. Adams, *The Better Part of Valor. More, Erasmus, Colet and Vives on Humanism, War and Peace, 1496–1535*, 1962

Philip C. Dust, *Three Renaissance Pacifists, Essays in the Theories of Erasmus, More and Vives*, 1988

Vries, Adrian de, *c.* 1550–1626. Dutch sculptor who worked in Prague for RUDOLF II.
Portrait of Rudolf II, 68–69 (4)

Weyden, Rogier van der, *c.* 1400–64. Flemish painter. The leading Flemish artist of the mid-15th century, he was probably trained in the workshop of Robert Campin in Tournai and also influenced by the paintings of Jan van EYCK, though his work differs from the earlier master by being highly emotional and spiritually charged. In 1425 he was appointed city-painter in Brussels and apart from a visit to Italy in 1450, he spent the rest of his life in the city. His two major paintings are on a huge scale – the *Deposition* in Madrid and *The Last Judgment* at Beaune. His religious paintings convey a profound emotional quality, achieved through the facial expressions and poses of tender Madonnas and grieving saints. Several sensitive portraits also exist which attest to a sympathetic and penetrating portrayal of his sitters.
The Catholic Sacraments, 112–13 (1, 2, 3)
The Descent from the Cross, 142–43 (1)
The Last Judgment, 146–47 (1)
The Virgin and Child with Saints, 136–37 (2)
M. Davies, *Rogier van der Weyden*, 1972
Lorne Campbell, *Van der Weyden*, 1979

Witz, Konrad, *c.* 1400–44/6. German painter who worked mainly in Switzerland, producing a number of altarpieces which confirm his knowledge of Jan van EYCK. In his last work *The Miraculous Draught of Fishes*, he includes a realist, detailed landscape which is not just a typical Swiss view, but the depiction of a specific and recognizable site on Lake Geneva.
The Miraculous Draught of Fishes, 166–67 (7)

Wynkyn de Worde (Jan van Wynkyn), active *c.* 1476–died 1535. Alsatian printer and businessman. Born in the Duchy of Lorraine, he was probably brought to

London by CAXTON as his skilled craftsman and assistant. Worde, who was neither a translator nor a writer, took over control at Caxton's death and proved a shrewd businessman. His importance in printing was his recognition that there was demand for cheaper books, and he served this market by producing popular and smaller-sized editions covering many subjects including histories, romances and books for children.
H. R. Plomer, *Wynkyn de Worde and his Contemporaries*, 1925

Zarlino, Gioseffo, 1517–90. Italian composer and theoretician. A Franciscan friar, he studied music in Venice and became choirmaster of St Mark's Basilica. His published theoretical writings, the most famous being *Le istitutioni harmoniche*, were important in the development of Renaissance music.

Zwingli, Huldreich, 1484–1531. Swiss Protestant Reformer. Educated at university in Vienna and Basle, he served as a parish priest and an army chaplain before moving to Zurich in 1518, where he was the leading figure in the Swiss Reformation. A follower of ERASMUS, he developed his theological beliefs and zealous conviction for reform through humanist enquiry, the writings of LUTHER, and a profound study of the Scriptures. An energetic Reformer and a powerful preacher, he established Zurich as a centre of Protestantism, dramatically simplifying religious practice. His prescribed observance of moral behaviour prefigured that imposed by CALVIN in Geneva. Luther and Zwingli disagreed over the 'presence' of Christ in the Eucharist; Luther maintained Christ's real presence in the bread and wine, while Zwingli held that the bread and wine were symbolic reminders of Christ's body and blood. Zwingli was killed in a battle at Kappel, fighting in a religious war against Catholic forces.
Portrait, 114–15 (5)
G. R. Potter, *Zwingli*, 1976
W. P. Stephens, *The Theology of Huldrych Zwingli*, 1986

TIMELINES OF RENAISSANCE

	HISTORY	IDEAS	LITERATURE
1400	**Innocent VII** elected pope (1404) **Gregory XII** elected pope (1406) **Alexander V** elected pope (1408)	Birth of **Nicholas of Cusa** (1401) Death of **Salutati** (1406) Birth of **Lorenzo Valla** (1407)	Death of **Chaucer** (1400)
1410	**Sigismund** elected emperor (1411) **Henry V** becomes King of England (1413) Battle of Agincourt (1415) **Martin V** elected pope; end of the Great Schism (1417)	Council of Constance begins (1414) **Poggio** discovers lost texts of Cicero, Lucretius, Quintilian and Vitruvius (1414) Death of **Manuel Chrysoloras** (1415) **John Huss** burnt at the stake (1415)	Death of **Froissart** (1410) **Thomas à Kempis'** *Imitation of Christ* (1414)
1420	**Charles VII** becomes King of France (1422) **Henry VI** becomes King of England (1422) **Leonardo Bruni** appointed Chancellor of Florence (1427)	**Poggio** discovers unique copy of Petronius (1423) *Aeneid* first translated into a modern language, Spanish (1427) **Guarino da Verona** teaches Greek at Ferrara (1429) **Plautus'** plays rediscovered (1429)	
1430	**Eugenius IV** elected pope (1431) **Joan of Arc** burnt at the stake (1431) **Cosimo de' Medici 'Pater Patriae'** assumes power in Florence (1434) **Albert II** elected emperor (1437) Council of Ferrara-Florence (1438)	Birth of **Marsilio Ficino** (1433) **Ciriaco d'Ancona** visits Athens (1436) **Biondo's** *Decades* (1437) **Valla's** *Disputatione dialectiae* (1439)	Birth of **François Villon** (1431)
1440	**Frederick III** elected emperor (1440) **Federigo da Montefeltro** becomes Ruler of Urbino (1444) **Nicholas V** elected pope (1447) Battle of Kossovo (1448) Birth of **Lorenzo de' Medici the Magnificent** (1449)	Birth of **Nebrija** (1440) **Valla** exposes Donation of Constantine as forgery (1440) Death of **Leonardo Bruni** (1444) Death of **Vittorino da Feltre** (1446)	**Gutenberg** invents movable type (1440)

HISTORY AND CULTURE

ART

ARCHITECTURE

Births of **Rogier van der Weyden** and **Luca della Robbia** (1400) **Ghiberti** begins first Florentine Baptistery doors (1401) Birth of **Masaccio** (1401) **Sluter's** *Well of Moses,* Champmol (*c.* 1402) Birth of **Fra Filippo Lippi** (1406)	Birth of **Filarete** (1400)	**1400**
Très Riches Heures (1411) Birth of **Dieric Bouts** (1415)	**Brunelleschi's** Foundling Hospital, Florence (1418) **Brunelleschi's** S. Lorenzo, Florence (1418) **Brunelleschi's** Dome of Florence Cathedral begun (1419)	**1410**
Birth of **Fouquet** (1420) **Ghiberti** begins second set of Florentine Baptistery doors (1425) Death of **Gentile da Fabriano** (1427) Birth of **Giovanni Bellini** (1428) Death of **Masaccio** (1428)	**Brunelleschi's** Pazzi Chapel, Florence, begun (1429)	**1420**
Births of **Antonello da Messina** and **Desiderio da Settignano** (1430) Birth of **Mantegna** (1431) **Van Eyck's** *Ghent Altarpiece* (1432) **Donatello's** *David* (1433) Births of **Verrocchio** and **Michael Pacher** (1435) **Fra Angelico** works on frescoes at S. Marco, Florence (1436) Death of **Jacopo della Quercia** (1438) Birth of **Francesco di Giorgio** (1439)	**Brunelleschi's** S. Spirito, Florence, begun (1436)	**1430**
Death of **Jan van Eyck** (1441) Birth of **Signorelli** (1441) **Donatello's** *Gattamelata* (1444) Birth of **Botticelli** (1445) Birth of **Perugino** (1446) Birth of **Ghirlandaio** (1448)	Birth of **Mauro Coducci** (1440) Birth of **Bramante** (1444) Palazzo Ducale, Urbino, begun (1444) **Alberti's** Palazzo Rucellai, Florence (1446) Death of **Brunelleschi** (1446) **Michelozzo's** Palazzo Medici-Riccardi, Florence, begun (1446)	**1440**

	HISTORY	**IDEAS**	**LITERATURE**
1450	**Francesco Sforza** becomes Duke of Milan (1450) Fall of Constantinople (1453) **Callixtus III** elected pope (1455) Death of **Doge Francesco Foscari** (1457) **Matthias Corvinus** becomes King of Hungary (1458) **Pius II** elected pope (1458)	Birth of **Lefèvre d'Etaples** (1450) Death of **Gemistus Plethon** (1452) Birth of **Ermolao Barbaro** (1453) Birth of **Poliziano** (1454) Freiburg University founded (1455) Copy of **Suetonius'** *De grammaticis* discovered (1455) **John Argyropoulos** appointed Professor of Greek at Florence (1456) Death of **Lorenzo Valla** (1457) Death of **Poggio Braccolini** (1459)	First printed book, **Gutenberg's** *Bible,* in Gothic type (1455)
1460	**Edward IV** becomes King of England (1461). The Wars of the Roses begin **Louis XI** becomes King of France (1461) **Cosimo de' Medici 'Pater Patriae'** dies (1464) **Paul II** elected pope (1464) Marriage of **Ferdinand** and **Isabella** (1469) **Lorenzo de' Medici the Magnificent** assumes power in Florence (1469)	Death of **Flavio Biondo** (1463) Birth of **Pico della Mirandola** (1463) Birth of **Erasmus** (1466) Birth of **Budé** (1467) **Cardinal Bessarion** presents his collection of Greek books to Venice (1468) Birth of **Machiavelli** (1469)	**Adolph Rusch** uses Roman type (1464) **Sweynheym** and **Pannartz** set up first printing press in Italy (1465) First printing press in Switzerland (1468)
1470	**Sixtus IV** elected pope (1471) Pazzi Conspiracy in Florence (1478) Spanish Inquisition established (1478)	**Chrysoloras'** *Epitome*, first Greek grammar (1471) *Hermes Trismegistus* translated by **Ficino** (1471) **Valla's** *Elegantiae* (1471) Death of **Cardinal Bessarion** (1472) Ingolstadt University founded (1472) Trier University founded (1473) Mainz University founded (1476) Tübingen University founded (1477)	First printing press in France (1470) First printed edition of **Dante's** *Divine Comedy* (1472) Birth of **Ariosto** (1474) First printing press in Spain (1474) First printing press in England, **Caxton** (1476) Birth of **Castiglione** (1478)
1480	Death of **Federigo da Montefeltro** (1482). **Guidobaldo** assumes power in Urbino **Charles VIII** becomes King of France (1483) **Richard III** becomes King of England (1483) **Innocent VIII** elected pope (1484) Battle of Bosworth. **Henry VII** becomes King of England (1485)	Death of **Filelfo** (1481) **Ficino's** translation of Plato (1485) **Guarino da Verona's** *Grammar* printed (1488)	Birth of **Luigi Pulci** (1484)
1490	**Savonarola** Prior of S. Marco (1491) **Alexander VI** elected pope (1492) **Columbus'** first voyage (1492) Conquest of Granada (1492) Death of **Lorenzo de' Medici the Magnificent** (1492) **Maximilian I** elected emperor (1493) **Cabot's** first voyage (1497) **Louis XII** becomes King of France (1498) **Savonarola** executed (1498)	Birth of **Juan Luis Vivès** (1492) Death of **Ermalao Barbaro** (1493) Birth of **Paracelsus** (1493) Deaths of **Poliziano** and **Pico della Mirandola** (1494) Death of **Ficino** (1499)	Birth of **Aretino** (1492) **Diego de San Pedro's** *Carcel d'Amor* published (1492) **Sebastian Brandt's** *Ship of Fools* (1494). Birth of **Rabelais** (*c.* 1494) **Aldus Manutius** sets up Aldine Press in Venice (1495) Birth of **Clement Marot** (1496) First edition of Aristophanes (1498) *Calisto and Melibea* (1499) *Hypnerotomachia Poliphili* (1499)

ART	ARCHITECTURE	
Birth of **Leonardo da Vinci** (1452) **Piero della Francesca** begins work on Arezzo frescoes (1452) Birth of **Pinturicchio** (1454) Deaths of **Ghiberti**, **Pisanello** and **Fra Angelico** (1455) Birth of **Filippino Lippi** (1457) **Gozzoli** paints frescoes in the Medici Chapel (1459)	**Alberti's** Tempio Malatestiano, Rimini (1450) Palazzo Pitti, Florence (1451) **Alberti's** *De re aedificatoria* written (1452) Birth of **Antonio da Sangallo the Elder** (1453) **Alberti's** Façade of S. Maria Novella, Florence, begun (1456)	**1450**
Birth of **Tilman Riemenschneider** (1460) Birth of **Piero di Cosimo** (1462) Death of **Desiderio da Settignano** (1464) Death of **Donatello** (1466) Death of **Fra Filippo Lippi** (1469)	**Alberti's** S. Sebastiano, Mantua (1460) **Codussi's** S. Michele in Isola, Venice (1468) Death of **Filarete** (1469)	**1460**
Birth of **Dürer** (1471) Birth of **Lucas Cranach the Elder** (1472) **Mantegna** paints the Camera degli Sposi, Mantua (completed 1474) **Hugo van der Goes'** *Portinari Altarpiece* (1475) Birth of **Michelangelo** (1475) Deaths of **Uccello** and **Dieric Bouts** (1475) Birth of **Sodoma** (1477) **Botticelli** paints *Primavera* (1478) Birth of **Giorgione** (1478) Death of **Antonello da Messina** (1479)	**Alberti's** S. Andrea, Mantua, begun (1470) Deaths of **Alberti** and **Michelozzo** (1472) **Bramante's** S. Maria presso S. Satiro, Milan, begun (1478)	**1470**
Births of **Titian, Palma Vecchio** and **Lotto** (1480) Death of **Fouquet** (1481) Fresco cycle on walls of Sistine Chapel (1481) Death of **Luca della Robbia** (1482) Birth of **Raphael** (1483) Births of **Hans Baldung Grien** and **Sebastiano del Piombo** (1485) **Botticelli** paints *The Birth of Venus* (1485) Birth of **Andrea del Sarto** (1486) Birth of **Beccafumi** (1486) Death of **Verrocchio** (1488)	Birth of **Peruzzi** (1481) Birth of **Sanmicheli** (1484) **Alberti's** *De re aedificatoria* published (1485) **Giuliano da Sangallo's** S. Maria delle Carceri, Prato, and Villa Medici, Poggio a Caiano, begun (1485) Birth of **Sansovino** (1486) First edition of **Vitruvius** (1486) **Giuliano da Sangallo and Cronaca's** Palazzo Strozzi, Florence (1489)	**1480**
Death of **Piero della Francesca** (1492) **Pinturicchio** paints the Borgia Apartments (1492) Death of **Crivelli** (1494) Death of **Memlinc** (1494) Births of **Pontormo** and **Correggio** (1494) Death of **Gozzoli** (1497) Birth of **Holbein** (1497) **Leonardo** paints *The Last Supper* (1497) Deaths of **Antonio Pollaiuolo** and **Pacher** (1498) Birth of **Giulio Romano** (1499)	**Bramante's** S. Maria delle Grazie, Milan, begun (1492) Piazza at Vigevano (1492) Palazzo dei Diamanti, Ferrara (1493)	**1490**

HISTORY	IDEAS	LITERATURE
1500		
Lorenzo Loredan elected Doge of Venice (1501)	**Erasmus'** *Enchiridion* published (1501)	Birth of **Thomas Wyatt** (1503)
Expulsion of Jews from Spain (1502)	Greek editions of Sophocles, Euripides, Herodotus, Thucydides and Demosthenes published by **Aldus Manutius** (1502–04)	
	Birth of **George Buchanan** (1506)	
	First Greek book printed in France (1507). **Budé's** *Annotationes* (1508)	*Amadis de Gaula* (1508)
League of Cambrai (1508)	Birth of **Calvin** (1509)	**Erasmus'** *Adagia* (1508) and *Praise of Folly* (1509)
Henry VIII becomes King of England (1509)	**Erasmus** lectures at Cambridge (1509)	
	Luca Pacioli's *De divina proportione* (1509)	
1510		
Leo X elected pope (1513)	First edition of **Plato** in Greek (1513)	
	Budé's *De Asse* (1514)	
François I becomes King of France (1515)	**Erasmus** publishes first edition of Greek New Testament (1516)	Death of **Aldus Manutius** (1515)
		Ariosto's *Orlando furioso* (1516)
Charles V becomes King of Spain (1516) and emperor (1519)	**Luther** posts his 95 theses on the door of Wittenberg Castle church (1517)	**More's** *Utopia* (1516)
	Reuchlin's *De arte cabbalistica* (1517)	
	Melanchthon appointed Professor of Greek at Wittenberg University (1518)	**Machiavelli's** *Mandragola* (1518)
Cortez lands in Mexico (1519)	**Zwingli** begins preaching Reformation in Zurich (1519)	
1520		
Diet of Worms (1521)	**Peutinger's** *Inscriptiones vetustae* published (1520)	
Magellan's ships circumnavigate the world (1521)	Complutensian Polyglot Bible published (1522)	**Erasmus'** *Colloquies* (1522)
Adrian VI elected pope (1522)	Deaths of **Reuchlin** and **Nebrija** (1522)	
Clement VII elected pope (1523)		
Peasants' Revolt in Germany (1524–25)	**Tyndale's** English New Testament (1525)	**Bembo's** *Prose della vulgar lingua* (1525)
Battle of Pavia (1525)	Birth of **Luis de León** (1527)	Death of **Machiavelli** (1527)
Sack of Rome (1527)		**Castiglione's** *The Courtier* published (1528)
Andrea Doria establishes republic in Genoa (1528)		**Geoffrey Tory's** *Champfleury* (1529)
1530		
Confession of Augsburg (1530)	Death of **Zwingli** (1531)	**Marot's** *Adolescence Clémentine* (1531)
Death of **Cardinal Wolsey** (1530)	**Machiavelli's** *The Prince* published posthumously (1532)	**Rabelais'** *Pantagruel*, Part 1 (1532)
Pizarro leads expedition to Peru (1532)	First edition of Greek Ptolemy (1533)	Death of **Ariosto** (1533)
Cranmer appointed Archbishop of Canterbury (1533)	Jesuit Order founded (1534)	Birth of **Montaigne** (1533)
Birth of **Queen Elizabeth** (1533)	**Luther's** Bible published (1534)	
Henry VIII's Act of Supremacy (1534)	Dissolution of English monasteries (1535)	
Paul III elected pope (1534)	**Calvin's** *Institutes* published (1536)	
Suppression of the Anabaptists of Münster (1535)	Death of **Erasmus** (1536)	
Execution of **Thomas More** (1535)	**Henry VIII's** 'Great Bible' published (1539)	
1540		
Execution of **Thomas Cromwell** (1540)	Deaths of **Budé** and **Vivès** (1540)	
	Copernicus' *De revolutionibus* (1543)	
	Vesalius' *De humani corporis fabrica* (1543)	
War of the Schmalkaldic League (1546)	First edition of Josephus and Archimedes published in Paris (1544)	Death of **Marot** (1544)
Edward VI becomes King of England (1547)		Birth of **Tasso** (1544)
Henri II becomes King of France (1547)	Council of Trent (1545–63)	
	Death of **Luther** (1546)	Birth of **Cervantes** (1547)
Battle of Mühlberg (1547)		
	Birth of **Giordano Bruno** (1548)	**Du Bellay's** *Défense* (1549)

ART	ARCHITECTURE	
Hieronymus Bosch's *Garden of Earthly Delights* (*c.* 1500) Birth of **Cellini** (1500) **Michelangelo's** *Pietà* (*c.* 1500), *David* (1502–04) and Sistine Ceiling (1508 onwards) **Leonardo's** *Mona Lisa* (*c.* 1502) **Dürer's** *Adam and Eve* (1504) **Dürer's** second visit to Venice (1505) *Laocoön* discovered in Rome (1506) Death of **Mantegna** (1506) Death of **Gentile Bellini** (1507) **Raphael's** Vatican Stanze (1508)	**Bramante's** Tempietto at S. Pietro in Montorio (1502) Henry VII's Chapel, Westminster (1503–19) Death of **Mauro Coducci** (1504) **Bramante's** new St Peter's begun (1506) Birth of **Vignola** (1507) Birth of **Palladio** (1508)	**1500**
Deaths of **Botticelli** and **Giorgione** (1510) **Grünewald's** *Isenheim Altarpiece* (1511–15) Birth of **Vasari** (1511) **Torrigiano** works on tomb of Henry VII (1512) **Michelangelo's** *Moses* (1513–16) **Dürer's** *Melancholia* (1514) Death of **Giovanni Bellini** (1516) **Leonardo da Vinci** invited to France (1516) **Raphael's** *Sistine Madonna* (1516). **Titian's** *Assunta* (1516) Death of **Fra Bartolommeo** (1517) Birth of **Tintoretto** (1518) Death of **Leonardo** (1519)	Birth of **Pirro Ligorio** (1510) **Fra Giocondo's** edition of Vitruvius (1511) Death of **Bramante** (1514) Château of Chenonceau (1515) Hampton Court Palace (1515–30) Château of Chambord (1519)	**1510**
Death of **Raphael** (1520) Deaths of **Perugino** and **Signorelli** (1523) **Giovanni da Bologna** born (1524) Birth of **Pieter Bruegel the Elder** (*c.* 1525) Death of **Carpaccio** (1525) Birth of **Paolo Veronese** (1528) **Altdorfer's** *Battle of the Issus* (1529) Death of **Sansovino** (1529)	**Michelangelo's** Medici Chapel (1520) **Michelangelo's** Laurentian Library begun (1523) Segovia Cathedral begun (1523) Palace of Charles V, Granada (1526) Château of Azay-le-Rideau (1527) Château de Madrid, Paris (1528) Granada Cathedral remodelled (1528)	**1520**
Deaths of **Andrea del Sarto** and **Tilman Riemenschneider** (1531) **Holbein** settles in England (1532) **Holbein's** *The Ambassadors* (1533) **Rosso** and **Pontormo** employed by François I at Fontainebleau (1533) Death of **Viet Stoss** (1533) Death of **Correggio** (1534) **Michelangelo's** *The Last Judgment* (1536–41) Death of **Altdorfer** (1538)	St Eustache, Paris (1530) Death of **Peruzzi** (1536) Publication of the first of Serlio's *Six Books of Architecture* (1537) Nonsuch Palace (1538)	**1530**
Cellini's salt-cellar for François I (1540) Birth of **El Greco** (1541) Death of **Holbein** (1543) **Cellini's** *Perseus* (1545–54) **Goujon's** Fontaine des Innocents (1547–49) Death of **Sebastiano del Piombo** (1547) **Titian's** portrait of Charles V on horseback (1548) Death of **Sodoma** (1549)	**Sansovino's** Library of St Mark's, Venice, begun (1540) **Lescot's** wing of the Louvre begun (1546) **Michelangelo** takes over St Peter's (1546) **Palladio's** Basilica, Vicenza (1546–50) Death of **Antonio da Sangallo the Younger** (1546) **Ligorio's** Villa d'Este, Tivoli (1549)	**1540**

	HISTORY	IDEAS	LITERATURE
1550	**Mary I** becomes Queen of England (1553) Marriage of **Mary I** and **Philip II** of Spain (1554) Peace of Augsburg (1555) **Charles V** abdicates (1556). **Philip II** becomes King of Spain Death of **Charles V** (1558) **Elizabeth I** becomes Queen of England (1558) **Ferdinand I** elected emperor (1558)	First editon of **Longinus'** *On the Sublime* (1552) Death of **St Ignatius Loyola** (1556) Birth of **Isaac Casaubon** (1559)	**Ronsard's** *Odes* (1550) Death of **Rabelais** (1553) **Bandello's** *Novelle* (1554) *Lazarillo de Tormes* (1554) Death of **Aretino** (1556) **Marguerite of Navarre's** *Heptameron* published posthumously (1558)
1560	**Charles IX** becomes King of France with **Catherine de Médicis** as regent (1560) **Maximilian II** elected emperor (1564) **Pius V** elected pope (1566) Execution of Counts **Egmont** and **Hoorn** (1568) **Cosimo de' Medici** created Grand Duke of Tuscany (1569)	Death of **Melanchthon** (1560) Birth of **Francis Bacon** (1561) **Falloppio's** *Observationes anatomicae* (1561) **Foxe's** *Book of Martyrs* (1563) Death of **Calvin** (1564) Birth of **Galileo** (1564) Oratorians founded by **Filippo Neri** (1564) **Plantin** begins printing Polyglot Bible (1568)	Death of **Du Bellay** (1560) **Guicciardini's** *History of Italy* published posthumously (1561) **Hoby** translates *The Courtier* (1561) **Sackville** and **Norton's** *Gorboduc*, first English play in blank verse (1561) Birth of **Lope de Vega** (1562) Births of **Shakespeare** and **Marlowe** (1564)
1570	Battle of Lepanto (1571) **Gregory XIII** elected pope (1572) Massacre of St Bartholomew (1572) Revolt of the Netherlands begins (1572) **Henri III** becomes King of France (1574) **Rudolf II** elected emperor (1576)	Death of **John Knox** (1572) Birth of **Jakob Böhme** (1575) **North's** translation of Plutarch's *Lives* (1579) **St John of the Cross'** *Dark Night of the Soul* (1579)	**Ascham's** *The Schoolmaster* published posthumously (1570) Birth of **Tirso de Molina** (1571) **Camoens'** *Lusiads* (1572) Births of **Donne** and **Jonson** (1572) **Tasso's** *Gerusalemme liberata* (1575) First public theatre opened in London (1577) **Lyly's** *Euphues: The Anatomy of Wit* (1578)
1580	**William of Orange** assassinated (1584) **Sixtus V** elected pope (1585) **Christian IV** becomes King of Denmark and Norway (1588) Spanish Armada (1588) **Henri IV** becomes King of France and converts to Catholicism (1589) Death of **Catherine de Médicis** (1589)	**Edmund Campion** executed (1581) Death of **George Buchanan** (1582) **Knox's** *History of the Reformation in Scotland* published posthumously (1587)	**Montaigne's** *Essais* (1580) Birth of **Webster** (1580) **Luis de León's** *La perfecta casada* (1583) **Marlowe's** *Dr Faustus* (1585) Death of **Ronsard** (1585) Teatro Olimpico, Vicenza, opens (1585) Birth of **Sydney** (1586)
1590	**Innocent IX** elected pope (1591) **Clement VIII** elected pope (1592) Edict of Nantes (1598) **Philip III** becomes King of Spain (1598)	Death of **St John of the Cross** (1591) **Louis Elzevir** begins publishing classical texts (1592) **Justus Lipsius** becomes Professor at Louvain (1592) Remains of Pompeii discovered (1592) **Hooker's** *Laws of Ecclesiastical Polity* (1594)	Book I of **Spenser's** *Faery Queen* (1590) **Kyd's** *The Spanish Tragedy* (1592) Death of **Montaigne** (1592) **Marlowe** killed (1593) Death of **Tasso** (1595) **Shakespeare's** *Henry V, Twelfth Night* and *As You Like It* (1598–1600) Globe Theatre, London, built (1599) Death of **Spenser** (1599)

ART

ARCHITECTURE

Vasari's *Lives*, first edition (1550) Death of **Beccafumi** (1551) Death of **Lucas Cranach the Elder** (1553) **Titian's** *Danaë* (1553) Deaths of **Lotto** and **Pontormo** (1556)	**De l'Orme's** Château of Anet (*c.* 1550) **Palladio's** Palazzo Chiericati and Villa Rotonda, Vicenza, begun (1550) Birth of **Maderno** (1556) Ottheinrichsbau, Heidelberg Castle, begun (1556) Death of **Sanmicheli** (1559)
Birth of **Annibale Carracci** (1560) **Tintoretto's** *Susanna and the Elders* (1560s) **Veronese's** *The Marriage at Cana* (*c.* 1562–63) Death of **Michelangelo** (1564) **Tintoretto's** paintings in the Scuola di S. Rocco, Venice, begun (1564) Death of **Pieter Bruegel the Elder** (1569)	**Herrera's** Escorial begun (1563) **Shute's** *First and Chief Grounds of Architecture* (1563) Tuileries begun (1564) **Palladio's** S. Giorgio Maggiore, Venice (1565) Longleat, Wiltshire, begun (1568) **Vignola's** Gesù, Rome, begun (1568)
Death of **Sansovino** (1570) Birth of **Caravaggio** (1571) Death of **Cellini** (1571) Death of **François Clouet** (1572) Deaths of **Corneille de Lyon** and **Vasari** (1574) Death of **Titian** (1576) **Tintoretto's** *Paradiso* (1577) Birth of **Elsheimer** (1578)	**Palladio's** *Quattro libri* (1570) Birth of **Inigo Jones** (1573) Death of **Vignola** (1573) **Palladio's** Il Redentore, Venice (1576) **Palladio's** Teatro Olimpico, Vicenza (1579)
    El Greco's *Burial of Count Orgaz* (1586) Death of **Paolo Veronese** (1588)	Death of **Palladio** (1580) **Smythson's** Wollaton Hall, Nottinghamshire (1580) Death of **Pirro Ligorio** (1583) Birth of **Jean Le Mercier** (1584)
Giovanni da Bologna's *Mercury* (1590) Deaths of **Palissy** and **Pilon** (1590) Birth of **Guercino** (1591) **Tintoretto's** *The Last Supper* (1592–94) Birth of **Poussin** (1593) Death of **Tintoretto** (1594) Births of **Algardi** and **Bernini** (1598) Births of **Van Dyke** and **Velázquez** (1599)	 Death of **Herrera** (1597) Birth of **François Mansart** (1598)

1550

1560

1570

1580

1590

	HISTORY	IDEAS	LITERATURE
1600	**Henri IV** marries Marie de Médicis (1600) **James I** becomes King of England (1603) Gunpowder Plot (1605) **Paul V** elected pope (1605)	Execution of **Giordano Bruno** (1600) Death of **Tycho Brahe** (1601) Bodleian Library, Oxford, opens (1602) Death of **Theodore de Bèze** (1605) Death of **J. J. Scaliger** (1609)	Birth of **Calderón** (1600) **Shakespeare's** *Hamlet, Othello, Macbeth, King Lear* (1602–08) First part of **Cervantes'** *Don Quixote* published (1605) Birth of **Corneille** (1606) **Jonson's** *Volpone* (1606) Death of **Lyly** (1606) Birth of **Milton** (1608)
1610	**Louis XIII** becomes King of France (1610) **Gustavus Adolphus** becomes King of Sweden (1611) Death of **Henry**, Prince of Wales (1612) **Matthias** elected emperor (1612) **Michael Romanov** becomes Tsar, founding the Romanov dynasty (1613) Revolt of Bohemia; Defenestration of Prague; beginning of Thirty Years War (1618)	King James Authorized Version of the Bible published (1611) Death of **Isaac Casaubon** (1614)	**Jonson's** *The Alchemist* (1610) **Webster's** *Duchess of Malfi* (1614) Death of **Cervantes** (1616) Death of **Shakespeare** (1616)
1620	Battle of the White Mountain (1620) **Gregory XV** elected pope (1621) **Philip IV** becomes King of Spain (1621) **Olivares** becomes chief minister of Spain (1622) **Urban VIII** elected pope (1623) **Charles I** becomes King of England (1625) Duchy of Urbino bequeathed to the pope (1626)	Birth of **Pascal** (1623) Death of **Jakob Böhme** (1624) **Vincent de Paul** founds Sisters of Mercy (1625) Death of **Francis Bacon** (1626)	Birth of **Molière** (1622) First Folio of **Shakespeare** published (1623) Death of **Webster** (1625) Birth of **Bunyan** (1628)
1630	**Gustavus Adolphus** invades Germany (1630) **Gustavus Adolphus** killed (1632) **Ferdinand III** elected emperor (1637)	Académie Française founded (1630) Death of **Kepler** (1630) **Galileo** forced to recant (1633)	Death of **Donne** (1631) Birth of **Dryden** (1631) **Calderón's** *Life is a Dream* (1634) **Milton's** *Comus* (1634) and *Lycidas* (1637) Oberammergan Passion Play first performed (1634) **Corneille's** *Le Cid* (1636) Death of **Jonson** (1637) Birth of **Racine** (1639)
1640	Beginning of English Civil War (1642) **Louis XIV** becomes King of France (1643) **Innocent X** elected pope (1644) Treaty of Westphalia ends Thirty Years War (1648) Execution of **Charles I** (1649)	Death of **Galileo** (1642) **Descartes'** *Principis philosphicae* (1644) Quakers founded by **George Fox** (1648)	English theatres closed by Puritans (1642) Death of **Tirso de Molina** (1648)

ART	ARCHITECTURE	
	Birth of **Alonso Cano** (1601)	**1600**
Carracci brothers complete frescoes in Palazzo Farnese, Rome (1604)	**Maderno's** Nave of St Peter's begun (1603)	
Birth of **Rembrandt** (1606)	Place des Vosges, Paris (1605)	
Death of **Giovanni Bologna** (1608)	Place Dauphine, Paris (1607)	
Death of **Annibale Carracci** (1609)		
Deaths of **Elsheimer** and **Caravaggio** (1610)	Birth of **John Webb** (1610) Birth of **Louis le Vau** (1612) **De Brosse's** Palais du Luxembourg, Paris (1614)	**1610**
Death of **El Greco** (1614)	**Holl's** Augsburg Town Hall begun (1614) Death of **Robert Smythson** (1614) **Scamozzi's** *L'Idea dell'architettura universale* (1615)	
Death of **Isaac Oliver** (1617)	**Jones'** Queen's House, Greenwich (1616)	
Death of **Hilliard** (1619)	**Jones'** Banqueting House, Whitehall, begun (1619)	
Rubens' Marie de Médicis Cycle (1622)	Ste Marie de la Visitation, Paris (1623)	**1620**
Hals' *Laughing Cavalier* (1624)	The Sorbonne, Paris (1626)	
Callot's *Miseries of War* (1633)	Birth of **Wren** (1632) Mauritshuis, The Hague (1633)	**1630**
Van Dyke's *Charles I on Horseback* (1636)		
Rembrandt's *The Night Watch* (1642)	Birth of **Jules Hardouin-Mansart** (1640)	**1640**
Bernini's *Ecstasy of St Theresa* (1644)		
	Van Campen's Amsterdam Town Hall (1648)	

1290	1300	1310	1320	1330	1340	1350	1360	1370	1380	1390	1400	1410	1420	1430	1440

Italy

* Lovato Lovati of Padua discovers, edits and comments on classical texts

* Petrarch begins assembling his collection of Latin mss.

* Boccaccio collects and copies classical mss.

* Chrysoloras comes to Florence to teach Greek

* Poggio Bracciolini discovers many unknown classical texts

* Leonzio Pilato translates Homer and Euripides and teaches Greek in Florence

* Boccaccio's *Genealogia deorum*, on the pagan gods

* Biondo's *De verb Romanae locutionis,* on Latin and Italian

* Filelfo visits Constantinople and brings back Greek mss.

* Giovanni Aurispa brings 23 Greek books to Italy

Valla exposes the Donation of Constantine as a forgery *

Gemistus Pletho, Platonist, in Florence *

Pope Nicholas V commissions translations of Greek texts *

France

Eastern Europe, Germany and the Netherlands

* Nicolas Cusa's *De docta ignoratia*

* Sbignew Olesnicky, Bishop of Cracow, corresponds with Italian humanists

---

The spread of humanism

This chronological chart illustrates graphically the degree of Italian priority in humanist studies, and the extent to which the rest of Europe followed and depended upon Italian precedents. It took roughly a hundred years before France, Spain and Germany began to make their own independent contributions, even longer for Britain to do so. One aspect that still comes as something of a surprise is how early humanist studies began in eastern Europe, particularly Hungary and Poland.

Spain

* The *Aeneid* translated in Spanish, the first translation into a modern language

Britain

* Humphrey, Duke of Gloucester presents his library of 300 classical texts to Oxford University

1290	1300	1310	1320	1330	1340	1350	1360	1370	1380	1390	1400	1410	1420	1430	1440

* Valla's *Elegantiae limgnae Latinae*, a treatise on Latin style
* Politian becomes professor of Greek and Latin at Florence
* Ficino translates Plato
* Chrysoloras' *Epitome, the first Greek gramma*
* Ficino translates *Hermes Trismegistus*
* Aldus Manutius prints nearly all major Greek texts
* First edition of Vitruvius
* Politian's *Miscellanea*, a handbook of scholarly method
* First illustrated edition of Vitruvius (Fra Giocondo)
* John Argyropoulos appointed Professor of Greek at Florence
* First translation of Vitruvius (Cesariano)
* Sweynheym and Pannartz set up first printing press in Italy
* Cardinal Bessarion presents 500 Greek books to Venice
* Homer's *Iliad* translated into Latin by Valla
* Lorenzo de' Medici sends Janus Lascaris to Greece to collect mss.
* First printed edition of Plato in Greek

* Gregorio Tifernate teaches Greek in Paris
* Janus Lascaris comes to Paris and teaches Greek
* Robert and Henri Etienne, *Thesaurus linguae Latinae*
* First printing press set up in the Sorbonne, Paris; Latin classics printed
* Oronce Finé's *Euclid*
* Guillaume Fichet's *Rhetorica*
* Budé visits Italy and learns Greek
* Robert Gaguin lectures in Latin composition
* Budé's *De Asse*, a treatise on Roman coins
* Buchanan's *De sphaera*
* Gaguin's *Ars versificaria*
* Press at Lyon issues many Latin classics
* Virgil's *Aeneid* translated into French
* Salmon Marin's *Carminum libellis*, poems modelled on Horace
* Isaac Casaubon begins his career as editor and commentator
* Lefèvre d'Etaples begins his scholarly career
* The *Iliad* translated into French
* Badius sets up publishing house in Paris and prints Latin classics
* First Greek book printed in France
* J. C. Scaliger, *De causis linguae Latinae*
* Budé's annotations to the *Pandects*, a treatise on Roman law
* Denys Lambin publishes Latin classics
* J. C. Scaliger, *Thesaurus temporum*
* Vitruvius translated into French

* Erasmus publishes *Adagia* and begins learning Greek
* Christophe Plantin sets up printing press in Antwerp
* Gutenberg's *Bible*, the first printed book
* The *Aeneid* translated into German
* Rudolf Agricola travels in Italy and learns Greek
* Erasmus begins long career as editor of classical texts
* Plantin's Polyglot Bible
* Hartmann Schedel's *Opus de Antiquitatibus cum epitaphis*, a collection of Latin inscriptions
* Erasmus' *Praise of Folly*
* Justus Lipsius publishes scholarly editions of Latin classics
* Johannes Vitéz, secretary to Matthias Corvinus, founds classical studies in Hungary
* Conrad Celtis appointed professor of rhetoric at Vienna
* Vitruvius translated into German
* Thierry Martens begins publishing Greek texts at Louvain
* Gregor of Sanok lectures on classics at Cracow
* Erasmus' Greek *New Testament*
* The *Aeneid* translated into Dutch
* Janus Pannonius studies in Italy with Guarino, brings large collection of mss. to Hungary and translates the *Iliad*
* Reuchlin's *De arte cabbalistica*
* Melanchthon professor of Greek at Wittenberg
* Peutinger's *Inscriptiones vetustae*, a collection of Roman inscriptions
* Louis Elzevir begins printing classical texts

* Juan de Mal Lara's *La filosofía vulgár*, a Spanish imitation of the *Adagia*
* First printing press in Spain
* Nebrija publishes the first Spanish grammar
* Complutensian Polyglot Bible printed, but not published till 1520
* Luis Vives, *De ratione studii puerilis*, a treatise on education
* Arias Barbosa publishes Greek grammar
* Pedro Mexia's *Silva de varia lección*, a miscellany of information
* Luis de León professor at Salamanca, translates Greek and Latin classics
* First translation of Vitruvius into Spanish

* English scholars (Robert Flemmyng, John Free, John Tiptoft, William Sellyng) travel in Italy and learn Greek
* Caxton sets up printing press at Westminster
* Terence's *Andria* translated into English
* John Anwykyll's *Compendium totius grammaticae* printed at Oxford
* The *Aeneid* translated into Scottish verse by Gavin Douglas
* Thomas Linacre goes to Italy, studies at Florence and Padua
* William Grocyn returns from Italy and teaches Greek
* The *Aeneid* translated into English by T. Twyne
* John Colet studies in France and Italy
* Erasmus teaches at Cambridge
* Thomas More's *Utopia*
* Two plays by Plautus acted at St Paul's School, London

Europe in the Age
of the Renaissance

NORWAY

Christiania

SWEDEN

SCOTLAND

N O R T H
S E A

DENMARK

BALTIC SEA

Copenhagen

Danzig

IRELAND

ENGLAND

WALES

HESSE

BRANDENBURG

Wittenberg

Vistula

Cambridge
Oxford

Amsterdam
The Hague NETHERLANDS
Utrecht

POLAND

London

Bruges Antwerp
Calais   Ghent FLANDERS Cologne
Brussels

GERMANY

SAXONY

Elbe

ENGLISH CHANNEL

Seine

Rhine

Mainz

Prague

Worms

Nuremberg

A T L A N T I C
O C E A N

Paris

Heidelberg
Strasbourg BAVARIA

Regensburg

BOHEMIA

Vienna

Chambord
Fontainebleau

Augsburg
Munich

F R A N C E

Basle

Zurich

AUSTRIA

Buda

Bordeaux

BURGUNDY

Innsbruck

S W I T Z E R L A N D
Geneva

A L P S

Lyon

Po

Rhône

Avignon

Marseille

I T A L Y

ADRIATIC SEA

P Y R E N E E S

CORSICA

CASTILE

ARAGON

PORTUGAL

Madrid

CATALONIA

Toledo

Lisbon

SPAIN

Rome

Seville

SARDINIA

SEE
INSET

Granada

M E D I T E R R A N E A N   S E A

SICILY

MALTA

PIEDMONT

SAVOY Milan ●

Pavia ● Mantua ● Verona ● LOMBARDY Maser
Po   Vicenza ●
                                    Padua ● Venice ●
                        Parma ● Ferrara ●
GENOA   Modena ●
Genoa ●   Bologna ●
                                    Rimini ●
        Lucca ● Prato ●
Pisa ●   Florence ●
        TUSCANY   Urbino ●
        Siena ● Arezzo ●
        Pienza ● Perugia ●
CORSICA Montepulciano ● UMBRIA
        Orvieto ● Todi ●

                PAPAL STATES
                        Tivoli ●
                Rome ●

SARDINIA   KINGDOM OF NAPLES
                            Naples ●

Moscow ●

RUSSIA

Warsaw ●

Zamosc ●

racow ●

                Palermo ●

                SICILY
                        Syracuse ●

BLACK SEA

Danube

OTTOMAN   Constantinople ●

EMPIRE

GREECE

Athens ●

The main towns and regions mentioned in the book.
Precise political boundaries are not shown,
as they fluctuated during this period.

CRETE

CYPRUS

GLOSSARY

The east end of a **basilica**, showing clerestory windows.

Corinthian and Composite **capitals** *from Vignola's version of the five orders, 1513.*

Caryatids *from Fra Giocondo's illustrated edition of Vitruvius, 1511.*

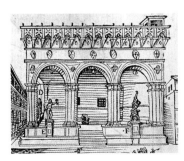

The **loggia** *dei Lanzi, Florence, from a woodcut of 1583.*

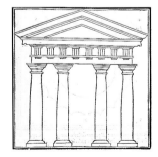

A **pediment**, *supported by four columns, from Fra Giocondo's 1511 edition of Vitruvius.*

An asterisk * refers to another entry

all'antico – after the Antique manner; i.e., in imitation of Greek or Roman precedent

altarpiece – a painting standing on an altar and forming its back

Annunciation – the announcement by Gabriel to the Virgin Mary that she was to become the mother of Jesus

Anti-Pope – from 1378 to 1417 (the so-called Great Schism) two rival factions within the Catholic Church each elected a pope who claimed to be the only authentic one. Seven of the claimants were declared unauthorized and are known as 'Anti-Popes'

Assumption – the miracle by which the Virgin was 'assumed' or taken up into heaven

baptistery – part of a church, or a separate building, containing the font, where baptisms are carried out

base – moulding at the foot of a column

basilica – (1) a church with a certain ecclesiastical status; (2) architecturally, a building with arcade, aisles and *clerestory

campo – literally 'field'; an open space, or (as an abbreviation of *campo santo*) a cemetery

capital – the carved feature forming the top of a column, in classical architecture one of the main distinguishing elements of the orders

caryatid – carved figure supporting a bracket or *cornice

casino – literally 'little house'; a garden building or miniature *villa

cella – the central room of a classical temple

certosa – a Carthusian monastery

chancel – the part of the church, normally the east end, containing the altar and choir-stalls; the most sacred space of a church

chiaroscuro – 'bright-dark', a painting technique that conveys forms by soft shadows

ciborium – a canopied shrine for a relic or the *Eucharist

Cinquecento – the 16th century, the 1500s

clerestory – row of windows above the arcade of a *basilican church

colonnade – line of columns supporting a flat *entablature rather than arches

condottiere – a mercenary military leader

cornice – the top projecting part of a classical *entablature

Corpus Christi – literally, 'Christ's body'; a festival instituted in 1264 to celebrate the Real Presence of Christ in the *Eucharist, according to the doctrine of *transubstantiation. By the 15th century this had become a major Church festival, involving a procession carrying the *host through the streets

cupola – a small dome

disegno – drawing

entablature – horizontal element running across the top of a row of columns or the top of a wall

Eucharist – Holy Communion

ex voto – literally 'from a vow'; an offering, usually an image dedicated to a saint or holy person in gratitude for the answering of a prayer, or salvation from death or disaster

façade – the front of a building

foreshortening – a technique for representing three-dimensional objects on a flat surface

fresco – literally 'fresh'; a painting applied to a wall while the plaster is still wet, so that it becomes part of the surface

frieze – a continuous line of ornament or figural composition above a row of columns or across the upper part of a wall

Gospels – literally 'good news'; the four accounts of the life and teaching of Christ accepted as canonical in the New Testament

host – consecrated bread or wafer in the communion service

icon – a picture or image credited with miraculous powers

International Gothic – a style of painting that became popular in 15th-century Europe, characterized by attention to detail (clothes, jewelry, etc.), elegance of design and attractive subject-matter, but lack of weight and drama

keystone – the central element of an arch

linear perspective – geometrical *perspective, worked out by logical rules

liturgy – the order, wording, actions and accessories of church services

loggia (plural **logge**) – an arcaded gallery open to the air on one side

Mannerist – a name given by 20th-century art-historians to the style that succeeded the Renaissance. Conventionally described as abandoning the sanity, balance and repose of such artists as Raphael and indulging in bizarre juxtapositions of scale, wilful obscurity and strange dramatic and psychological effects; in architecture as contradicting the classical rules and introducing apparently irrational features (reversed pediments, downward-tapering columns, etc.). The motivation behind these innovations is now challenged

morbidezza – softness

nave – the main body of a church, west of the *chancel, holding the congregation

Neoplatonism – a philosophical system, deriving ultimately from Plato and his later disciples, which attempted to reconcile the Platonic doctrine of Forms (the Good, the Beautiful), the immortality of the soul and the immanence of the divine in all things with Christian revelation. Unsystematic and often obscure as it was, it proved an inspiration to artists and poets, encouraging the use of symbols standing for abstract and mystical entities

palazzo – a large town house with an impressive frontage to the street

parapet – a low wall round the roof or upper storey of a building

patristic – relating to the Fathers of the Church

pediment – triangular gable-end of a classical building

peristyle – a *colonnade surrounding a classical temple

perspective – a technique for applying the principles of *foreshortening to the whole space of a composition

piano nobile – literally 'noble storey'; the first floor (or in American usage second) of a palace or aristocratic residence where the state rooms are

piazza – a formal open space in a town

pietà – the Virgin Mary with the dead Christ lying on her lap

polyptych – a painting, usually an *altarpiece, in several sections, often hinged so that they can be opened and closed

portico – large porch consisting of columns surmounted by a *pediment

putti – winged cherubs or babies, symbols of divine love

quadri riportati – framed self-contained pictures set into a ceiling

quatrefoil – a shape with four lobes or cusps

Quattrocento – 15th century, the 1400s

relief – sculpture which projects from the surface but is not fully three dimensional

reliquary – a container, usually of some precious metal, for the display of the relic of a saint or of Christ

Resurrection – Christ's return to life on the third day after his crucifixion

rotunda – a round building

rustication – masonry left rough, as if straight from the quarry

sacra conversazione – a picture that shows several saints together

sacraments – ceremonies requiring the presence of a priest, seven in the Catholic Church, two in the Lutheran

sacristy – room in a church for keeping vestments, vessels, etc.

salone – main room of an Italian house or palace, generally on the first floor

sarcophagus – stone coffin functioning as a tomb

schiacciata – literally 'flattened'. A type of relief sculpture even shallower than conventional low-relief, in which the subject is almost 'drawn' on the stone

scroll-buttress – buttress given the form of an S or double-curve

sfumato – misty, indistinct

sotto in sù – specialized form of *perspective, as if seen from below

stanze – literally 'rooms'; conventionally used for rooms in the Vatican decorated by Raphael

star-bastion – a projecting element in a fortification roughly in the shape of a star

stucco – plaster

studiolo – small room used as a study

tabernacle – an ornamented casket to hold the *host

tempera – paint mixed with egg-white as a binding medium

tempietto – literally 'little temple'. A small building, usually a shrine, usually with columns

tondo – a round painting or sculpture

Transfiguration – on the top of a mountain Jesus appeared to his disciples with shining face and garments and with the prophets Moses and Elias at his side

transubstantiation – the doctrine that the bread and wine of the *Eucharist become the body and blood of Christ

triglyph – part of the *entablature of the Doric order; a stone with three grooves

triptych – painting, generally an *altarpiece, in three parts

triumphal arch – in ancient Rome, an arch erected to celebrate the victory of an emperor. In the Renaissance it was adapted to various architectural contexts

trompe-l'oeil – an artistic effect so realistic that it deceives the eye into thinking the object depicted is real

vault – a stone roof; either continuous (tunnel vault) or divided into bays or sections (groined or ribbed vault)

villa – small country house on a gentleman's estate, often the centre of a farm, but used mainly for relaxation

A group of **putti**, *by Agostino di Duccio, from the Tempio Malatestiano at Rimini, 1450–57.*

A gilt bronze **quatrefoil** *by Lorenzo Ghiberti, showing the Sacrifice of Isaac, 1401–02.*

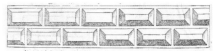

An example of **rustication** *from Serlio, 1554.*

A **scroll-buttress** *from the façade of S. Maria Novella, Florence, by Alberti, 1456–70.*

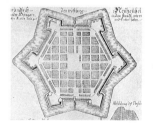

A **star-bastion** *designed by Ottavio Baldigara for the town of Nové Zámky, 1562.*

A preliminary drawing by Bramante for the **tempietto** *in Rome, 1502.*

GAZETTEER OF MUSEUMS AND GALLERIES WITH COLLECTIONS OF RENAISSANCE ART

Today the great works of Renaissance art are dispersed throughout the whole world. The process of diffusion began early. Art-loving monarchs took Italian paintings abroad almost as soon as they were painted. Philip II of Spain laid the foundations for what is now the Prado collection; Louis XIV of France for the Louvre; Catherine the Great of Russia for the Hermitage; Augustus of Saxony for the Dresden Gallery. In the 19th and 20th centuries those countries with the largest resources – supplemented by the generosity of private donors – were able to build up the most outstanding collections, notably in the United States, making the galleries of Washington, D.C., New York and Chicago among the richest in the world. The most recent such enterprise is the Getty Museum in Los Angeles, which seems destined to acquire most of the great art works that come onto the market for the foreseeable future.

These are all great international collections, with works of Renaissance art from all over Europe. Nevertheless, it remains generally true that the highest proportion of any Renaissance artist's work remains in his or her native region. To see Florentine art one has still to go to the Uffizi and the Pitti; to see Venetian to the Accademia; to see Roman to the Vatican; to see Spanish to the Prado. Ideally (though perhaps not for the tourist in a hurry) works are still in the church or palace for which they were originally intended. No museum or gallery holds Michelangelo's Moses (S. Pietro in Vincoli, Rome, p. 262), Piero della Francesca's Legend of the True Cross (S. Francesco, Arezzo, pp. 16, 84) or Van Eyck's Ghent Altarpiece (St Bavon, Ghent, p. 128). The Sistine Chapel and Raphael's Stanze are only in a museum because the Vatican is now in effect one vast museum.

The list that follows is necessarily selective, but provides a rough guide to the main sources of the works illustrated in this book.

AUSTRALIA

The National Gallery of Victoria, Melbourne.
Probably the best collection in Australia, with prints and drawings as well as paintings.

The Art Gallery of New South Wales, Sydney.
A representative collection of painting and sculpture, including Renaissance works.

AUSTRIA

Albertina, Vienna.
One of the world's great collections of drawings, including Dürer's *The Great Piece of Turf* (p. 229) and *Study of a Hare* (p. 183).

Kunsthistorisches Museum, Vienna.
Rivalling the Louvre in the breadth of its holdings, this is the collection of the Habsburgs, built up over many centuries. It is particularly rich in German works, including Pieter Bruegel the Elder's *The Tower of Babel* (p. 279), but also holds such important Italian items as Cellini's salt-cellar (p. 237).

BELGIUM

Musées Royaux des Beaux-Arts, Brussels.
Especially strong in Netherlandish and Flemish works, including Pieter Bruegel the Elder's *The Census at Bethlehem* (p. 185).

CZECH REPUBLIC

National (Národní) Gallery, Prague.
Part of the Habsburg collection from the time of Rudolf II, the gallery is rich in works of the northern Renaissance, including paintings by Pieter Bruegel the Elder and Mabuse, e.g., *St Luke Drawing the Virgin* (p. 272).

FRANCE

Musée Condé, Chantilly.
Housed in the castle of the Prince de Condé, the collection excels in manuscript illuminations, including the *Book of Hours of Etienne Chevalier* (p. 272).

Musée du Louvre, Paris.
Possibly the richest collection of art and archaeology in the world, built up by the French kings and by Napoleon by purchase and plunder. All national schools are represented, often by outstanding masterpieces. The Louvre holds, among other works, Leonardo's *Mona Lisa* (p. 195), Veronese's *The Marriage at Cana* (p. 221), Raphael's portrait of Baldassare Castiglione (p. 38), Ghirlandaio's *Old Man and Boy* (p. 177) and Van Eyck's *Madonna with Chancellor Rolin* (p. 167).

GERMANY

Gemäldegalerie, Dresden.
Assembled by the princes of Saxony from the 17th century onwards, this is one of the most outstanding collections in the world, especially for German and Italian painting. Its most famous possession is Raphael's *Sistine Madonna* (p. 133).

Alte Pinakothek, Munich.
The collection of the Bavarian royal family, especially strong in German Renaissance works, such as Altdorfer's *Battle of the Issus* (p. 84).

Germanisches Nationalmuseum, Nuremberg.
Largely confined to German art, e.g., Spranger's *Venus, Mercury and Cupid* (p. 53), Lucas Cranach the Elder's portraits of Christian II of Denmark (p. 70).

GREAT BRITAIN

The British Museum, London.
Holds an outstanding collection of prints and drawings, including examples of all the great Renaissance masters, such as Michelangelo's *Crucifixion* (p. 141), as well as medals – Niccolò Fiorentino's Poliziano (p. 44).

Hampton Court Palace, near London.
Part of the Royal Collection, includes Mantegna's *Triumphs of Caesar* (p. 57).

The National Gallery, London.
An extremely balanced collection, with fine examples of every school, particularly strong on the early Renaissance – Piero della Francesca's *The Baptism of Christ* (p. 134), Masaccio's *Madonna and Child* (p. 132) and Botticelli's *The Mystical Nativity* (p. 131) – since the English were among the first to appreciate the art of the Quattrocento.

The Victoria & Albert Museum, London.
Focused mainly on the decorative arts, this museum holds many notable works of Renaissance sculpture – Veit Stoss' *Virgin and Child* (p. 263), Adrian de Vries' bust of Rudolf II (p. 68) and Torrigiano's bust of Henry VII (p. 71) – as well as paintings: Hilliard's *Young Man amid Roses* (p. 92) and Denis van Alsloot's *Triumph of Isabella* (pp. 90–91).

The Royal Library, Windsor Castle.
Mostly formed under Prince Albert, this contains the world's largest collection of drawings by Leonardo (pp. 226–28).

ITALY

Accademia di Belle Arti, Florence.
The home of Michelangelo's *David* (p. 250).

Gabinetto dei Disegni e delle Stampe, Florence.
An extremely rich collection of drawings, manuscripts and prints, mostly by Florentine artists, including Antonio Pollaiuolo's *Battle of the Nude Gods* (p. 251), Dürer's *Hercules* (p. 51), Heemskerck's new St Peter's (p. 156) and Uccello's chalice (p. 247).

Galleria degli Uffizi, Florence.
The nucleus of the Uffizi collection is the pictures that belonged to the Medici family. Unrivalled in its representation of Florentine art – e.g., Botticelli's *The Birth of Venus* (p. 53) and *Primavera* (p. 228), Andrea del Sarto's *Madonna of the Harpies* (p. 132) – it also has important works from other schools, e.g., Hugo van der Goes' *Portinari Altarpiece* (p. 130), Jean Clouet's *François I on Horseback* (p. 86), Dürer's *Adoration of the Magi* (p. 199) and Titian's *Venus of Urbino* (p. 52).

Museo Nazionale del Bargello, Florence.
Seat of the chief magistrate of Florence in medieval times and now notable for its collection of sculpture which includes Donatello's *St George* and *David* (p. 250).

Palazzo Pitti (Galleria Palatina), Florence.
Another part of the former Medici collection, containing such masterpieces as Titian's portrait of Pietro Aretino (p. 39), Raphael's *Madonna of the Baldacchino* (p. 137) and *La Gravida* (p. 176).

Palazzo Vecchio, Florence.
The old centre of Florentine government, containing rooms decorated by Vasari and his school (pp. 35, 155).

Pinacoteca di Brera, Milan.
A representative collection of paintings from all over Italy, including Gentile Bellini's *St Mark Preaching in Alexandria* (p. 59), Tintoretto's *Discovery of the Body of St Mark* (p. 247) and Mantegna's *Dead Christ* (p. 247).

Museo di Capodimonte, Naples.
The collection of the kings of Naples, with many notable paintings, such as Titian's *Pope Paul III Farnese with his Nephews* (p. 67) and Giovanni Bellini's *The Transfiguration* (p. 145).

Galleria Borghese, Rome.
Begun by Cardinal Borghese (early 17th century), this contains a notable collection of Renaissance and later works, including Titian's *Sacred and Profane Love* (p. 47).

I Musei Vaticani, Rome.
It was the Renaissance popes themselves who began building up their collection of works of art and making it accessible to the public. Today the Vatican contains several museums, incorporating not only art, but also classical antiquities, e.g., Sleeping Ariadne (p. 54), Egyptology, manuscripts and cartography. Among the works *in situ* but part of the museum are the Sistine Chapel (pp. 147, 256–57), the Stanze of Raphael (pp. 40–41) and the Borgia Apartments (p. 44). The picture gallery holds an unrivalled collection of works painted in Rome, mostly for ecclesiastical patrons, including Raphael's *The Transfiguration* (p. 145) and Melozzo da Forlì's *Pope Sixtus IV Della Rovere appointing Platina as Papal Librarian* (p. 66).

Gallerie dell'Accademia di Belle Arti, Venice.
The main repository of Venetian art, with works by Bellini (p. 88), Carpaccio (p. 178), Titian (p. 143), Giorgione (p. 176) and many others, but weak in anything outside Venice.

NETHERLANDS

Rijksmuseum, Amsterdam.
A great international collection with the major representation of Dutch art in the world.

Museum Boymans-van Beuningen, Rotterdam.
An excellent collection of early Netherlandish works, including Pirckheimer's copy of Aristotle illustrated by Dürer (p. 58).

PORTUGAL

Museu Nacional de Arte Antiga, Lisbon.
There is virtually no Portuguese art in galleries outside the country. Her greatest artist was Nuno Gonçalves, painter of the *St Vincent Altarpiece* (p. 71).

RUSSIA

The Pushkin Museum, Moscow.
A representative collection with fine examples of Renaissance painting.

The Hermitage, St Petersburg.
The collection of the Tsars, begun by Catherine the Great in the late 18th century and continued until 1917. The collection is strong in works of the Italian High Renaissance, as well as in German and French pictures.

SPAIN

Museo Nacional del Prado, Madrid.
There are fine works by Italian and other foreign artists collected by Philip II, notably Titian (pp. 53, 249), but the main strength of the Prado is in Spanish art, which is under-represented in foreign galleries. To appreciate El Greco it is essential to visit Spain (pp. 135, 141). Its early Netherlandish paintings include Van der Weyden's *The Descent from the Cross* (p. 142) and Bosch's *The Garden of Earthly Delights* (p. 259).

USA

The Isabella Stewart Gardner Museum, Boston, Massachusetts.
The collection of a single wealthy connoisseur. Advised by Bernard Berenson, Mrs Gardner was able to acquire an amazing number of works by Renaissance masters, including Piero della Francesca's *Hercules* (p. 50).

The Art Institute of Chicago.
A notable collection, though the Renaissance is not its strongest area.

The J. Paul Getty Museum, Malibu, Los Angeles.
The last of the great collections founded by an oil millionaire and still in the process of formation. Its Renaissance holdings are not large, but already contain several major works.

The Metropolitan Museum of Art, New York.
Founded by private collectors in 1870, this is now the largest art museum in America. It holds a vast collection of works of all periods, including notable Renaissance paintings from Italy, France, Spain, Germany and England. They include Lucas Cranach the Younger's *Judith with the Head of Holofernes* (p. 196).

The National Gallery of Art, Washington, D.C.
Although founded only in 1937 and supplied mainly by private donors, this is now one of the leading art galleries of the world, with works by Castagno (p. 251), Leonardo, Raphael, Titian and El Greco.

BIBLIOGRAPHY

For biographies of individuals, see Biographical Dictionary

General

Braudel, Fernand, *The Mediterranean and the Mediterranean World in the Age of Philip II*, trans. by Siân Reynolds, London and New York, 1972–73

Brown, Alison, *The Renaissance*, London, 1988

Burckhardt, Jacob, *The Civilization of the Renaissance in Italy*, London, 1st ed. 1860 (many editions)

Burke, Peter, *The Renaissance*, London, 1987

Chastel, André, *The Renaissance: Essays in Interpretation*, London, 1982

Da Costa Kaufmann, Thomas, *Court, Cloister and City: The Art and Culture of Central Europe, 1450–1800*, London and Chicago, Ill., 1995

Dickens, A. G. (ed.), *The Courts of Europe: Politics, Patronage and Royalty, 1400–1800*, London, 1977

Hale, J. R., *Renaissance Europe, 1480–1520*, London and New York, 1971

———, *The Civilization of Europe in the Renaissance*, London, 1993

Hay, D., *The Age of the Renaissance*, London and New York, 1967

———, *Europe in the Fourteenth and Fifteenth Centuries*, London, 1971

Huizinga, J., *The Waning of the Middle Ages*, London, 1924, reissued Harmondsworth, 1976

Kamen, Henry, *The Iron Century: Social Change in Europe 1550–1660*, London, 1971

Koenigsberger, H. G., and Mosse, G. C., *Europe in the Sixteenth Century*, London and New York, 1968

Kristeller, P. O., *Cultural Aspects of the Italian Renaissance*, Manchester, 1976

Levey, Michael, *Early Renaissance*, Harmondsworth, 1967, reprinted 1991

———, *High Renaissance*, Harmondsworth, 1975, reprinted 1991

Parker, G., *Europe in Crisis, 1598–1648*, London, 1980

Plumb, J. H. (ed.), *The Penguin Book of the Renaissance*, London, 1964; American edition entitled *The Horizon Book of the Renaissance*, New York

Singleton, Charles S., *Art, Science and History in the Renaissance*, Baltimore, Md., 1967

Yates, Frances A., *Renaissance and Reform: the Italian Contribution*, London, Boston, Mass., and Melbourne, 1983

———, *Ideas and Ideals in the North European Renaissance*, London, Boston, Mass., and Melbourne, 1984

Scholarship, Education and Humanism

D'Amico, John F. D., *Renaissance Humanism in Papal Rome: Humanists and Churchmen on the Eve of the Reformation*, London and Baltimore, Md., 1983

Caspari, F., *Humanism and the Social Order in Tudor England*, Chicago, Ill., 1954

Chastel, André, *The Age of Humanism: Europe 1480–1530*, London and New York, 1963

Gilmore, Myron P., *The World of Humanism, 1453–1517*, New York, 1952

Goodman, Anthony, and Mackay, Angus (eds), *The Impact of Humanism on Western Europe*, London, 1990

Grafton, Anthony, and Jardine, Lisa (eds), *From Humanism to the Humanities: Education and Liberal Arts in Fifteenth- and Sixteenth-Century Europe*, Cambridge, Mass., 1986

Greenblatt, Stephen, *Renaissance Self-Fashioning from More to Shakespeare*, Chicago, Ill., 1980

Grendler, Paul F., *Schooling in Renaissance Italy: Literacy and Learning, 1300–1600*, Baltimore, Md., 1989

Gundersheimer, Werner L. (ed.), *French Humanism, 1470–1600*, New York, 1970

Levi, A. H. T. (ed.), *Humanism in France*, Manchester, 1970

Martines, L., *The Social World of the Florentine Humanists*, London, 1963

Nugent, E. M. (ed.), *The Thought and Culture of the English Renaissance*, Cambridge, 1956

Phillips, M. M., *Erasmus and the Northern Renaissance*, rev. ed., London, 1981

Rabil, Albert (ed.), *Renaissance Humanism: Foundations, Forms and Legacy*, 3 vols, Philadelphia, Pa., 1988

Reynolds, L. D., and Wilson, N. G., *Scribes and Scholars*, Oxford, 1968

Rice, E. F., *The Renaissance Idea of Wisdom*, Cambridge, Mass., 1958

Screech, M. A., *Erasmus: Ecstasy and the Praise of Folly*, London, 1980

Simon, J., *Education and Society in Tudor England*, Cambridge, 1969

Spitz, Lewis W., *The Religious Renaissance of the German Humanists*, Cambridge, Mass., 1963

Tilley, A. A., *The Dawn of the French Renaissance*, Cambridge, 1918

Weiss, R., *The Dawn of Humanism in Italy*, London, 1947

———, *Humanism in England during the Fifteenth Century*, 3rd ed., Oxford, 1967

———, *The Renaissance Discovery of Classical Antiquity*, Oxford, 1969

Philosophy, Neoplatonism and the Hermetic Tradition

Baumer, F. L. (ed.), *Intellectual Movements in Modern European History*, New York, 1965

Cassirer, E., Kristeller, P. O., and Randall, J. H. (eds) *The Renaissance Philosophy of Man*, Chicago, Ill., 1956

Garin, Eugenio, *Italian Humanism: Philosophy and Civic Life in the Renaissance*, trans. by Peter Munz, Oxford, 1965

Kristeller, P. O., *The Classics and Renaissance Thought*, Cambridge, Mass., 1955

———, *Eight Renaissance Philosophers of the Italian Renaissance*, London, 1965

———, *Renaissance Thought and its Sources*, New York, 1979

———, *Renaissance Thought and the Arts*, Oxford and Princeton, N.J., 1990

Overfield, J. H., *Humanism and Scholasticism in Late Medieval Germany*, Princeton, N.J., 1984

Yates, F., *Giordano Bruno and the Hermetic Tradition*, London and New York, 1964

Classical Mythology

Gombrich, E. H., *Symbolic Images*, 3rd ed., Oxford, 1985

Saxl, F., *A Heritage of Images*, Harmondsworth, 1970

Seznec, J., *The Survival of the Pagan Gods*, Princeton, N.J., 1953

Wind, E., *Pagan Mysteries in the Renaissance*, London and New Haven, Conn., 1958

Antique Prototypes in Art

Bober, P. R., and Rubinstein, R., *Renaissance Artists and Antique Sculpture: A Handbook of Sources*, London and New York, 1986

Gombrich, E. H., *Norm and Form*, Oxford and New York, 1971

———, *The Heritage of Apelles*, Oxford and New York, 1976

Haskell, F., and Penny, N., *Taste and the Antique*, London and New Haven, Conn., 1981

Pogany-Balas, E., *The Influence of Rome's Antique Monumental Sculptures on the Great Masters of the Renaissance*, Budapest, 1980

Patronage, Collectors and Collecting

Chambers, D. S., *Patrons and Artists in the Italian Renaissance*, London, 1970

Impey, O., and Macgregor, A. (eds), *The*

Origins of Museums: The Cabinet of Curiosities in Sixteenth- and Seventeenth-Century Europe, Oxford, 1985

Kent, F. W., and Simons, Patricia, *Patronage, Art and Society in Renaissance Italy*, Oxford, 1987

Lytle, G. F., and Orgel, S. (eds), *Patronage in the Renaissance*, Princeton, N.J., 1981

Trevor-Roper, H., *Princes and Artists: Patronage and Ideology at Four Habsburg Courts, 1517–1633*, London and New York, 1976, reprinted 1991

The Papacy

Creighton, M., *A History of the Papacy during the Period of the Reformation*, London, 1897

Hendrix, Scott H., *Luther and the Papacy, Stages in a Reformation Conflict*, Philadelphia, Pa., 1981

Thomson, J. A. F., *Popes and Princes 1417–1517*, London, 1980

The Holy Roman Empire

Bryce, James, *The Holy Roman Empire*, 8th ed., London and New York, 1968

Heer, Friedrich, *The Holy Roman Empire*, trans. by Janet Sondheimer, London and New York, 1968

European Political History

Bonney, R., *The European Dynastic States, 1494–1660*, Oxford, 1991

Cameron, Keith (ed.), *From Valois to Bourbon, Dynasty, State and Society in Early Modern France*, Exeter, 1989

Elliott, J. H., *Imperial Spain, 1469–1716*, London and New York, 1963

Hay, D., *The Italian Renaissance in its Historical Setting*, Cambridge, 1961

Highfield, J. R. L. (ed.), *Spain in the Fifteenth Century*, London, 1972

Hillgarth, J., *The Spanish Kingdoms, The Fifteenth Century*, 2 vols, Oxford, 1978

Lynch, John, *Spain under the Habsburgs*, Oxford, 1964

Mattingly, G., *Renaissance Diplomacy*, London, 1955, reissued Baltimore, Md., 1964

Stone, L., *The Crisis of the Aristocracy, 1558–1641*, Oxford, 1965

Vaughan, Dorothy M., *Europe and the Turk*, 2nd ed., Liverpool, 1967

Feasts and Festivals

Mulryne, J. R., and Shewring, Margaret (ed.), *Italian Renaissance Festivals and their European Influence*, Lewiston, 1992

Russell, J. G., *The Field of Cloth of Gold: Men and Manners in 1520*, London, 1969

Strong, R., *Art and Power: Renaissance Festivals, 1450–1650*, 2nd ed., Woodbridge, 1984

The Italian City States

Ady, C. M., *History of Milan under the Sforzas*, London, 1907

Brucker, G., *Renaissance Florence*, New York, 1969

Burke, Peter, *The Italian Renaissance: Culture and Society in Italy*, Oxford, 1986

Chambers, D. S., *The Imperial Age of Venice 1350–1580*, London and New York, 1970

Coffin, D. R., *The Villa in the Life of Renaissance Rome*, Princeton, N.J., 1979

Edgerton, Samuel Y., *Pictures and Punishment: Art and Criminal Prosecution during the Florentine Renaissance*, London and Ithaca, N.Y., 1985

Goldthwaite, R. A., *The Building of Renaissance Florence*, Baltimore, Md., 1980

Hale, J. R., *Florence and the Medici: the Pattern of Control*, London and New York, 1977

Holmes, George, *The Florentine Enlightenment 1400–1450*, Oxford, 1992

——— (ed.), *Art and Politics in Renaissance Italy*, Oxford, 1993

Lane, F. C., *Venice: A Maritime Republic*, Baltimore, Md., 1973

Ramsay, P. A. (ed.), *Rome in the Renaissance: The City and the Myth*, New York, 1982

Rubinstein, Nicolai, *The Government of Florence under the Medici*, Oxford, 1966

Ryder, A., *The Kingdom of Naples under Alfonso the Magnanimous*, Oxford, 1976

Sismondi, J. C. L. de, *A History of the Italian Republics*, London, 1907

Stinger, C., *The Renaissance in Rome*, Bloomington, Ind., 1985

Trexler, R. C., *Public Life in Renaissance Florence*, London and New York, 1980

The Reformation

Allen, P. S., *The Age of Erasmus*, Oxford, 1914

Aston, M., *England's Iconoclasts, Laws against Images*, vol. 1, Oxford, 1988

Cameron, Euan, *The European Reformation*, Oxford, 1991

Dickens, A. G., *Reformation and Society in Sixteenth-Century Europe*, London and New York, 1966

———, *Martin Luther and the German Nation*, London and New York, 1974

Elliott, J. H., *Europe Divided, 1559–1598*, London and New York, 1968

Elton, G. R., *Reformation Europe, 1517–1559*, London and New York, 1963, reissued 1967

Hyma, A., *The Christian Renaissance*, London and New York, 1965

Jedin, H., *A History of the Council of Trent*, London and New York, 1957

Monter, G. W., *Calvin's Geneva*, New York, 1967

Ozment, Steven, *The Reformation in the Cities*, New Haven, Conn., 1975

Scribner, R. W., *The German Reformation*, London, 1986

Spitz, L. W., *The Religious Renaissance of the German Humanists*, Cambridge, Mass., 1963

Trevor-Roper, H. R., *Religion, the Reformation and Social Change*, 2nd ed., London, 1972

Van Gelder, H. A. Enno, *The Two Reformations of the Sixteenth Century. A Study of the Religious Aspects and Consequences of the Renaissance and Humanism*, The Hague, 1961

Williams, G. H., *The Radical Reformation*, Philadelphia, Pa., 1962

The Bible

The Cambridge History of the Bible, vol. 2, *The West from the Fathers to the Reformation*, G. W. H. Lampe (ed.), Cambridge, 1969

———, vol. 3, *The West from the Reformation to the Present Day*, S. L. Greenslade (ed.), Cambridge, 1970

Stephens, W. P. (ed.), *The Bible, the Reformation and the Church*, Sheffield, 1995

Sunger, Debora Kuller, *The Renaissance Bible, Scholarship, Sacrifice and Subjectivity*, Berkeley, Calif., 1994

Religious Iconography

Hall, J., *History of Ideas and Images in Italian Art*, London, 1983

Maps

Bagrow, L., *History of Cartography*, rev. ed., London, 1964

Tyacke, Sarah (ed.), *English Map-Making 1500–1650*, London, 1983

Whitfield, Peter, *The Image of the World: 20 Centuries of World Maps*, London, 1994

Landscape

Cosgrove, D., and Daniels, S. (eds), *The Iconography of Landscape*, Cambridge, 1988

Turner, R., *The Vision of Landscape in Renaissance Italy*, Princeton, N.J., 1974

Gardens

Lazzaro, Claudia, *The Italian Renaissance Garden*, Cambridge, Mass., 1990

Shepherd, J. C., and Jellicoe, G. A., *Italian Gardens in the Renaissance*, London, 1994

Strong, Roy, *A Celebration of Gardens*, London, 1991

Women, Marriage, the Family

Alberti, Leon Battista, *The Family in Renaissance Florence*, trans. by Renée Neu Watkins, Columbia, S.C., 1969

Klapisch-Zuber, C., *Women, Family and Ritual in Renaissance Italy*, London and Chicago, Ill., 1985

Labalme, P. H. (ed.), *Beyond their Sex: Learned Women of the European Past*, London and New York, 1980

Ozment, S., *When Fathers Ruled: Family Life in Reformation Europe*, Cambridge, Mass., 1983

Sex and Gender

Ferguson, M. W., et al. (eds), *Rewriting the Renaissance, the Discourses of Sexual Difference in Early Modern Europe*, London and Chicago, Ill., 1986

Hays, H. R., *The Dangerous Sex: the Myth of Feminine Evil*, London, 1966

Jordan, Constance, *Renaissance Feminism: Literary Texts and Political Models*, Ithaca, N.Y., 1990

Kelso, R., *Doctrine for the Lady of the Renaissance*, London and Urbana, Ill., 1978

King, Margaret L., *Women of the Renaissance*, London and Chicago, Ill., 1991

MacLean, Ian, *The Renaissance Notion of Woman: A Study in the Fortunes of Scholasticism and Medical Science in European Intellectual Life*, Cambridge, 1980

Muir, Edward, and Ruggiero, Guido (eds), *Sex and Gender in Historical Perspective*, Baltimore, Md., 1990

Printing and Books

Bennett, H. S., *English Books and Readers, 1475–1557*, 2nd ed., Cambridge, 1969

———, *English Books and Readers, 1558–1603*, Cambridge, 1965

Chartier, Roger, *The Cultural Uses of Print in Early Modern France*, Princeton, N.J., 1987

Eisenstein, Elizabeth L., *The Printing Press as an Agent of Change*, 2 vols, Cambridge, 1980

———, *The Printing Revolution in Early Modern Europe*, Cambridge, 1993

Febvre, Lucien, and Martin, Henri-Jean, *The Coming of the Book: The Impact of Printing, 1450–1800*, London, 1976

Painter, George D., *Studies in Fifteenth-Century Printing*, London, 1984

Exploration

Boxer, C. R., *The Portuguese Seaborne Empire*, London, 1969

Brebner, J. B., *The Explorers of North America, 1492–1806*, London, 1964

Cipolla, Carlo, *European Culture and Overseas Expansion*, Harmondsworth, 1970

Elliott, J. H., *The Old World and the New, 1492–1650*, Cambridge, 1970

Hakluyt, R., *Voyages*, 1st ed. 1582 (many editions)

Hoffman, B. G., *Cabot to Cartier*, Toronto, 1961

Parry, J. H., *The Age of Reconnaissance*, London, 1973

Penrose, B., *Travel and Discovery in the Renaissance*, Cambridge, Mass., 1955

Prestage, E., *The Portuguese Pioneers*, London, 1933

Scammell, G. V., *The World Encompassed*, London, 1981

Trevor-Roper, Hugh (ed.), *The Age of Expansion: Europe and the World 1559–1660*, London and New York, 1968

Astronomy

Armitage, Angus, *Copernicus and the Reformation of Astrology*, London, 1950

Crowther, James Gerald, *Six Great Astronomers*, London, 1961

Koyre, A., *The Astronomical Revolution*, London, 1973

Kuhn, T. S., *The Copernican Revolution, Planetary Astronomy in the Development of Western Thought*, Cambridge, Mass., 1957

Morphet, Clive, *Galileo and Copernican Astronomy, a Scientific World View Defined*, London, 1977

Alchemy

Debus, Allen G., *Chemistry, Alchemy and the New Philosophy, 1550–1700*, London, 1987

Smith, Pamela H., *The Business of Alchemy, Science and Culture in the Holy Roman Empire*, Princeton, N.J., 1994

Science

Boas, M., *The Scientific Renaissance, 1450–1630*, London and New York, 1962

Butterfield, H., *The Origins of Modern Science*, London, 1957

Cipolla, C., *Public Health and the Medical Profession in the Renaissance*, Cambridge, 1976

Dijksterhuis, E. J., *The Mechanization of the World Picture*, trans. by C. Dikshoorn, Oxford, 1961

Edgerton, Samuel Y., *The Heritage of Giotto's Geometry: Art and Science on the Eve of the Scientific Revolution*, London and Ithaca, N.Y., 1991

Hall, A. R., *The Scientific Reformation*, London, 1954

Kearney, Hugh F., *Origins of the Scientific Revolution*, London, 1964

Rose, P. L., *The Italian Renaissance of Mathematics*, Geneva, 1975

Sarton, G., *Six Wings: Men of Science in the Renaissance*, London, 1957

Singer, Charles, *A Short History of Medicine*, Oxford, 1928

Smith, Alan G. R., *Science and Society in the Sixteenth and Seventeenth Centuries*, London and New York, 1970

Thorndike, L., *Science and Thought in the Fifteenth Century*, London and New York, 1963

Wightman, W. P. D., *Science in a Renaissance Society*, London, 1976

Warfare

Hale, J. R., *Renaissance Fortification, Art or Engineering?*, London, 1977

———, *Renaissance War Studies*, London, 1983

———, *The Military Organization of a Renaissance State: Venice, c. 1400 to 1617*, Cambridge, 1984

———, *War and Society in Renaissance Europe, 1450–1620*, London and New York, 1985

———, *Artists and Warfare in the Renaissance*, London and New Haven, Conn., 1990

Mallett, M., *Mercenaries and their Masters*, London, 1974

Parker, G., *The Army of Flanders and the Spanish Road*, Cambridge, 1975

———, *The Military Revolution: Military Innovation and the Rise of the West, 1500–1800*, Cambridge, 1988

Finance and Business

Bullard, Melissa M., *Filippo Strozzi and the Medici: Favour and Finance in Sixteenth-Century Florence and Rome*, Cambridge, 1980

Origo, I., *The Merchant of Prato*, Harmondsworth and New York, 1957

Rover, Raymond de, *The Rise and Decline of the Medici Bank*, Cambridge, Mass., 1963

Architecture

Ackerman, J. S., *Palladio's Villas*, New York, 1967

Bialostocki, Jan, *The Art of the Renaissance in Eastern Europe: Hungary, Bohemia, Poland*, London and Ithaca, N.Y., 1976

Burckhardt, J., *The Architecture of the Italian Renaissance*, 1st ed. 1867; trans. by Peter Murray, Harmondsworth, 1987

Gotch, J. A., *Early Renaissance Architecture in England*, 2nd ed., London, 1914

Harvey, J. H., *The Cathedrals of Spain*, London, 1957

Hersey, G. L., *Pythagorean Palaces, Magic and Architecture in the Italian Renaissance*, London and Ithaca, N.Y., 1976

Heydenreich, W., and Lotz, H., *Architecture in Italy 1400–1600*, Harmondsworth and Baltimore, Md., 1974

Hitchcock, H.-R., *German Renaissance Architecture*, Princeton, N.J., 1981

Howard, D., *Architectural History of Venice*, London, 1987

Kubler, G., and Soria, M., *Art and Architecture in Spain and Portugal and their*

American Dominions, Harmondsworth and Baltimore, Md., 1959

Millon, H. A. (ed.), *The Renaissance from Brunelleschi to Michelangelo*, London, 1994

Murray, P., *The Architecture of the Italian Renaissance*, rev. ed., London and New York, 1986

Onions, J., *Bearers of Meaning*, Cambridge, 1989

Summerson, J., *Architecture in Britain, 1530–1830*, 4th ed., Harmondsworth and Baltimore, Md., 1963

Thurley, S., *The Royal Palaces of Tudor England*, London and New Haven, Conn., 1993

Ward, W. H., *French Renaissance Architecture, 1495–1830*, London, 1911

Painting and Sculpture

Baxandall, Michael, *Painting and Experience in Fifteenth Century Italy*, Oxford, 1972

————, *The Limewood Sculptors of Renaissance Germany*, London and New Haven, Conn., 1980

Benesch, Otto, *The Art of the Renaissance in Northern Europe*, London, 1945, rev. ed. 1965

Blunt, Anthony, *Art and Architecture in France, 1400–1500*, London and Baltimore, Md., 1953

————, *Art and Architecture in France 1500–1700*, Harmondsworth and Baltimore, Md., 1953, rev. ed. 1982

Brown, J., *The Golden Age of Painting in Spain*, New Haven, Conn., 1991

Campbell, Lorne, *Renaissance Portraits: European Portrait Painting in the 14th, 15th and 16th Centuries*, New Haven, Conn., 1990

Gilbert, C. E., *Italian Art 1400–1500, Sources and Documents*, London, 1980

Harbison, Craig, *The Art of the Northern Renaissance*, New York, 1995

Hartt, F., *History of Italian Renaissance Art*, 4th rev. ed., London and New York, 1994

Humfrey, Peter, *Painting in Renaissance Venice*, London and New Haven, Conn., 1995

———— and Kemp, Martin (eds), *The Altarpiece in the Renaissance*, Cambridge, 1990

Jestaz, Bertrand, *The Art of the Renaissance*, New York, 1995

Lassaigne, J., *Spanish Painting, From the Catalan Frescoes to El Greco*, vol. 1, New York, 1952

Levey, M., *The Painter Depicted*, London, 1981

Martindale, A., *The Rise of the Artist*, London and New York, 1972

Miller, T., *Sculpture in the Netherlands, Germany, France and Spain, 1400–1500*, Harmondsworth and Baltimore, Md., 1966

Olson, Roberta J. M., *Italian Renaissance Sculpture*, London, 1992

Panofsky, E., *Early Netherlandish Painting*, Cambridge, Mass., 1953

————, *Studies in Iconology, Humanistic Themes in the Art of the Renaissance*, London and New York, 1972

Pope-Hennessy, J., *The Portrait in the Renaissance*, London and Washington, D.C., 1966

————, *Italian Renaissance Sculpture*, 3rd ed., Oxford, 1986

Post, C. R., *A History of Spanish Painting*, vols IX–XII, Cambridge, Mass., 1947–58

Ring, G. A., *A Century of French Painting, 1400–1500*, London, 1949

Seymour, C., *Sculpture in Italy, 1400–1500*, Harmondsworth and Baltimore, Md., 1966

Shearman, John, *Only Connect ... Art and the Spectator in the Italian Renaissance*, Washington, D.C., 1992

Smart, A., *The Renaissance and Mannerism in Italy*, London and New York, 1971

————, *The Renaissance and Mannerism outside Italy*, London, 1972, American edition entitled *The Renaissance and Mannerism in Northern Europe and Spain*, New York

Snyder, J., *Northern Renaissance Art*, New York, 1985

Stechow, W., *Northern Renaissance Art 1400–1600: Sources and Documents*, Englewood Cliffs, N.J., 1966

Vasari, G., *Lives of the Most Excellent Painters, Sculptors and Architects*, 1st ed. 1550 (many editions)

Waterhouse, E., *Painting in Britain, 1530–1830*, Harmondsworth and Baltimore, Md., 1953

Wölfflin, H., *Classic Art*, London, 1952, reissued New York, 1959

————, *Renaissance and Baroque*, London, 1964, reissued New York, 1966

The Theatre

Kernodle, G. R., *From Art to Theatre: Form and Convention in the Renaissance*, Chicago, Ill., 1944

Mulryne, J. R., and Shewring, Margaret, *Theatre of the English and Italian Renaissance*, Basingstoke, 1991

Orrell, John, *The Theatres of Inigo Jones and John Webb*, Cambridge, 1985

Stevens, David, *English Renaissance Theatre History*, Boston, Mass., 1982

Literature

Armstrong, E., *Ronsard and the Age of Gold*, Cambridge, 1968

Braunmuller, A. R., and Hattaway, M., *The Cambridge Companion to English Renaissance Drama*, Cambridge, 1991

Lewis, C. S., *English Literature in the Sixteenth Century*, Oxford, 1954

McFarlane, I. D., *A Literary History of France: Renaissance France, 1470–1589*, London, 1974

Symonds, J. A., *Renaissance in Italy*, 2nd ed., London, 1880

Music

Lockwood, Lewis, *Music in Renaissance Ferrara, 1400–1505*, Oxford, 1984

Lowinsky, Edward E., *Music in the Culture of the Renaissance*, London and Chicago, Ill., 1989

Mayer Brown, Howard, *Music in the Renaissance*, London, 1976

Reese, Gustave, *Music in the Renaissance*, rev. ed., New York, 1959

SOURCES OF ILLUSTRATIONS

Introduction

Abbreviations: a above; c centre; b below;
l left; r right

Where the image shown is a detail this is
noted in the caption

8 Copyright British Museum, London.
9 Vasari, *Le vite de piu eccelente architeti,
pittori, et scultori Italiani*, Florence, 1550.
10 Crowe & Cavacaselle, *A History of
Painting in North Italy*, London, 1871.
11a Photo: Roger Viollet, Paris. **11b** Photo:
Emily Lane.
13 By permission of The British Library,
London.
14a Ospedale di S. Spirito, Rome. Photo:
Alinari. **14b** Ashmolean Museum, Oxford.
15a I Musei Vaticani.
16 S. Francesco, Arezzo. Photo: Alinari.
17 Gabinetto dei Disegni e delle Stampe,
Florence.
18a *Index auctorum et librorum...*, Rome, 1557.
19a Photo: Jakob August Lorent. **19b**
Städtische Kunstsammlungen, Augsburg.
20a Sebalduskirche, Nuremberg. Photo: Lala
Aufsberg. **20b** Château de Versailles.
21a Photo: Mário Novais. **21c** Photo:
Georgina Masson. **21b** Copyright British
Museum, London.
22a Bayerische Verwaltung der Staatliche
Schlosser, Munich. **22b** Philibert de l'Orme,
Le Premier tome de l'architecture, Paris, 1568.
23a S. Maria del Carmine, Florence. Photo:
Alinari.
24a Polska Akademie Nauk Instytut Sstuki,
Warsaw. **24b** Photo: Karel Pliska.
25 Tempio Malatestiano, Rimini. Photo:
Alinari.
26a Pietro Bembo, *Prose della volgar lingua*,
Venice, 1538. **26b** Fernando de Rojas, *Tragi-
comedia de Calisto y Melibea*, Toledo, 1526.
27a Musée du Louvre, Paris. **27b** Alte
Pinakothek, Munich.

1 Rediscovering Antiquity

32a S. Croce, Florence. Photo: Scala.
32b Biblioteca Apostolica, Vatican.
33a Photo: Scala. **33b** F. Imperato, *Historia
naturale*, 1672.
34–35 Humanist beginnings
1 By permission of The British Library,
London. **2** Szépmüvészeti Múzeum,
Budapest. Photo: Bridgeman Art Library,
London. **3** Galleria Palatina, Florence.
Photo: Scala. **4** Biblioteca Trivulziano,
Milan. Photo: Scala. **5** S. Giovanni in
Laterano, Rome. Photo: Mansell Collection.
6 Biblioteca Apostolica, Vatican. **7** Biblioteca
Ambrosiana, Milan. Photo: Scala. **8** Palazzo
Vecchio, Florence. Photo: Scala. **9** Biblioteca
Laurenziana, Florence.

36–37 The northern humanists
1 Erasmus, *Adagia*, Basle, 1523. **2** Copyright
The Frick Collection, New York. **3** Royal
Collection © 1995 Her Majesty Queen
Elizabeth II. **4** Musée Condé, Chantilly.
5 Musée du Louvre, Paris. Photo: Scala.
6 Galleria degli Uffizi, Florence. Photo:
Scala. **7** Öffentliche Kunstsammlung, Basle.
8 Private Collection. Photograph Courtauld
Institute of Art, London.
38–39 Classical models and new literature
1 Reproduced by courtesy of the Trustees,
The National Gallery, London. **2** Palazzo
Vecchio, Florence. Photo: Scala. **3** Musée
du Louvre, Paris. Photo: Scala. **5** William
Shakespeare, *Comedies, Histories, and
Tragedies*, London, 1623. **6** Instituto Valencia
de Don Juan, Madrid. **7** Galleria Palatina,
Florence. Photo: Scala. **8** Thomas More,
Utopia, Basle, 1518. **9** Rabelais, *Le Second
Livre de Pantagruel*, 1547. **10** *Amadis
de Gaula*, Seville, 1531. **11** By permission of
The British Library, London. **12** Museo
Nacional del Prado, Madrid. Photo: Scala.
13 Torquato Tasso *La Gerusalemme liberata*,
Genoa, 1590. **14** Ariosto, *Orlando furioso*,
Venice, 1542.
40–41 The world of humanism
I Musei Vaticani. Photo: Scala.
42–43 Old and new learning
1 Musée Condé, Chantilly. Photo: Giraudon.
2 Photo: Jamusz Kozina. **3** Photo: Scala.
4 Museo dell'Opera del Duomo, Florence.
Photo: Scala. **5** Universidad de Salamanca.
6 By permission of The British Library,
London. **7** S. Agostino, San Gimignano.
Photo: Scala. **8** Photo: Scala.
44–45 Plato and Hermes
1 S. Ambrogio, Florence. Photo: Scala.
2 S. Maria Novella, Florence. Photo: Scala.
3 I Musei Vaticani. Photo: Scala.
4 Copyright British Museum, London.
5 Copyright British Museum, London.
6 Museo Nazionale del Bargello, Florence.
Photo: Scala. **7** I Musei Vaticani. **8** Duomo,
Siena. Photo: Scala.
46–47 Allegory
1 Galleria degli Uffizi, Florence. Photo: Scala.
2 Royal Collection © 1995 Her Majesty
Queen Elizabeth II. **3** Kunsthistorisches
Museum, Vienna. **4** Reproduced by courtesy
of the Trustees, The National Gallery,
London. **5** Galleria degli Uffizi, Florence.
Photo: Scala. **6** Galleria Borghese, Rome.
Photo: Scala. **8** Courtauld Institute Galleries,
University of London. Photo: Bridgeman Art
Library, London. **9** Galleria degli Uffizi,
Florence. Photo: Scala. **10** Accademia,
Venice. Photo: Scala.
48–49 The uses of myth
1 Villa Farnesina, Rome. Photo: Scala.
2 Pinacoteca di Brera, Milan. **3** Musée du
Louvre, Paris. Photo: Giraudon/Bridgeman

Art Library, London. **4** © Bibliothèque
Nationale de France, Paris. **5** Musée
du Louvre, Paris. Photo: Scala.
6 Kupferstichkabinett, Berlin. Photo:
© bpk. **7** Royal Collection © 1995 Her
Majesty Queen Elizabeth II.
50–51 Hercules
1 Isabella Stewart Gardner Museum, Boston.
Photo: Scala. **2** Sebalduskirche, Nuremberg.
Photo: Lala Aufsberg. **3** Piazza della Signoria,
Florence. Photo: Scala. **4** Galleria degli Uffizi,
Florence. Photo: Scala. **5** Gabinetto dei
Disegni e delle Stampe, Florence. Photo:
Scala. **6** Museo Nazionale del Bargello,
Florence. Photo: Scala. **7** Kunsthistorisches
Museum, Vienna. Photo: Bridgeman Art
Library, London.
52–53 Venus
1 Palazzo Schifanoia, Ferrara. Photo: Scala.
2 Galleria degli Uffizi, Florence. Photo: Scala.
3 Palazzo Farnese, Rome. Photo: Scala.
4 Museo Nacional del Prado, Madrid. Photo:
Scala. **5** Museo Nacional del Prado, Madrid.
Photo: Scala. **6** Galleria degli Uffizi, Florence.
Photo: Scala. **7** Galleria Borghese,
Rome. Photo: Scala. **8** Palazzo del Tè,
Mantua. Photo: Scala. **9** Germanisches
Nationalmuseum, Nuremberg. Photo:
Scala.
54–55 The spell of the Antique
1 Museo del'Opera Metropolitana, Siena.
Photo: Scala. **2** Palazzo di Schifanoia, Ferrara.
Photo: Scala. **3** I Musei Vaticani. Photo:
Scala. **4** Museo Nacional del Prado, Madrid.
Photo: Scala. **5** National Gallery of Art,
Washington, D.C., Samuel H. Kress
Collection. **6** Galleria degli Uffizi, Florence.
Photo: Scala. **7** Musée du Louvre, Paris.
56–57 The ruins of Rome
1 Palazzo Ducale, Mantua. Photo: Scala.
2 Colecciones del Real Monastario, El
Escorial, Madrid. **3** Royal Collection © 1995
Her Majesty Queen Elizabeth II. **4** Copyright
British Museum, London. **5** L'Erimitani,
Padua. Photo: Scala. **6** C. Hülsen & H. Egger
*Das Römischen Skizzenbuch von Maerten van
Heemskerck*, Berlin, 1913. **7** Royal Collection
© 1995 Her Majesty Queen Elizabeth II.
8 Biblioteca Apostolica, Vatican.
58–59 Constantinople and Greek learning
1 Royal Collection © 1995 Her Majesty
Queen Elizabeth II. **2** Kunsthistorisches
Museum, Vienna. **3** © Bibliothèque
Nationale de France, Paris. **4** Museum
Boymans-van Beuningen, Rotterdam.
5 Musée du Louvre, Paris. **6** Pinacoteca
di Brera, Milan. Photo: Scala. **7** Reproduced
by courtesy of the Trustees, The National
Gallery, London.
60–61 Collectors and collections
1 Kunsthistorisches Museum, Vienna. Photo:
Bridgeman Art Library, London. **2** Kunsthistorisches Museum, Vienna. **3** Royal

Collection © 1995 Her Majesty Queen Elizabeth II. 4 Arundel Castle, Sussex. Photo: Bridgeman Art Library, London. 6 Photo: A. F. Kersting. 7 Kunsthistorisches Museum, Vienna.

2 Rulers of the World

62 Museo Nacional del Prado, Madrid. Photo: Scala.
64b Galleria degli Uffizi, Florence.
65a Musée Bonnat, Bayonne.
65b Ashmolean Museum, Oxford.

66–67 The Papacy
1 Libreria Piccolomini, Duomo, Siena. Photo: Scala. 2 I Musei Vaticani. 3 I Musei Vaticani. Photo: Scala. 4, 5 Galleria degli Uffizi, Florence. Photo: Scala. 6 Palazzo Vecchio, Florence. Photo: Scala. 7 Museo di Capodimonte, Naples. Photo: Scala

68–69 The Holy Roman Empire
1 Schatzkammer der Residenz, Munich. 2 Kunsthistorisches Museum, Vienna. 3 By courtesy of the Board of Trustees of the Victoria & Albert Museum, London. 5 Alte Pinakothek, Munich. Photo: Scala. 6 Palazzo Vecchio, Florence. Photo: Scala. 7 Copyright British Museum, London.

70–71 The northern monarchies
1 Musée du Louvre, Paris. Photo: Scala. 2 Germanisches Nationalmuseum, Nuremberg. Photo: Scala. 3 Palazzo Pitti, Florence. Photo: Scala. 4 Staatliche Schlosser und Garten, Berlin. 5 By courtesy of the Board of Trustees of the Victoria & Albert Museum, London. 6 Yale Center for British Art, Paul Mellon Collection, New Haven. 7 Museu Nacional de Arte Antiga, Lisbon. 8 Museo Nacional del Prado, Madrid. Photo: Scala.

72–73 The rulers of Italy
1 Galleria degli Uffizi, Florence. Photo: Scala. 2 Palazzo Vecchio, Florence. Photo: Scala. 3 © Bibliothèque Nationale de France, Paris. 4 Accademia Carrara, Bergamo. Photo: Scala. 5 Galleria degli Uffizi, Florence. Photo: Scala. 6 Palazzo Ducale, Mantua. Photo: Scala. 7 Tempio Malatestiano, Rimini. Photo: Scala.

74–75 Government
1 Archivio di Stato, Siena. Photo: Scala. 2 A. Guagninus, *Sarmatiae descriptio,* Cracow, 1590. 3 Royal Collection © 1995 Her Majesty Queen Elizabeth II.

76–77 Law and punishment
1 Palazzo Pitti, Florence. 2 S. Anastasia, Verona. Photo: Scala. 3 Bayerische Staatsbibliothek, Munich. 4, 5, 6 *Bamberger Halsgerichtsordnung,* 1508. 7 Biblioteca Estense, Modena. 8 M. Eytinger, *De leone belgico,* Brussels, 1588.

78–79 Palaces and palazzi
1, 2, 3, 4, 5, 6 Photo: Scala. 7 British Museum, London. Photo: Bridgeman Art Library, London. 8 Photo: Stanislaw Michta. 9 Photo: Scala. 10 Photo: Jean Roubier. 11 Royal Geographic Society, London. Photo: Bridgeman Art Library, London.

80–81 Inside the palace
1, 2, 3, 4 Photo: Scala. 5 Det National-historiske Museum på Frederiksborg, Hillerød. 6 Château de Fontainebleau, Seine-et-Marne. Photo: Giraudon/Bridgeman Art Library, London. 7 Photo: A. F. Kersting.

82–83 Renaissance diplomacy
1 Archivio di Stato, Siena. Photo: Scala. 2 Libreria Piccolomini, Duomo, Siena. Photo: Scala. 3 Hans Burgkmair, *Der Weisskunig,* Vienna, 1775. 4 Galleria degli Uffizi, Florence. Photo: Scala. 5 By courtesy of the Board of Trustees of the Victoria & Albert Museum, London. 6 Royal Collection © 1995 Her Majesty Queen Elizabeth II. 7 Staatliche Museen, Kassel. 8 Courtesy of the National Portrait Gallery, London.

84–85 Faces of battle
1 S. Francesco, Arezzo. Photo: Scala. 2 Musée du Louvre, Paris. Photo: Scala. 3 By Kind Permisssion of the Earl of Leicester and the Trustees of the Holkham Estate. 4 Alte Pinakothek, Munich. Photo: Scala. 5 Reproduced by courtesy of the Trustees, The National Gallery, London. 6 Alte Pinakothek, Munich. Photo: Scala. 7 Narodowe Museum, Warsaw. 8 National Maritime Museum, Greenwich.

86–87 Equestrian monuments
1 Piazza del Campidoglio, Rome. Photo: Scala. 2 Galleria degli Uffizi, Florence. Photo: Scala. 3 Duomo, Florence. Photo: Scala. 4 All rights reserved, The Metropolitan Museum of Art, New York. The Robert Lehman Collection. 5 Royal Collection © 1995 Her Majesty Queen Elizabeth II. 6 Musée du Louvre, Paris. 7 Campo SS. Giovanni e Paolo, Venice. Photo: Scala. 8 Piazza del Santo, Padua. Photo: Scala.

88–89 Religious processions
1 Palazzo Vecchio, Florence. Photo: Scala. 2 Accademia, Venice. Photo: Scala. 3 Pierpont Morgan Library, New York. M.69.

90–91 Civic processions
1 Österreichische Nationalbibliothek, Vienna. 2 By courtesy of the Board of Trustees of the Victoria & Albert Museum, London. 3 Society of Antiquaries, London.

92–93 The secret code of dress
1 Gemäldegalerie, Dresden. Photo: AKG, London. 2 Galleria Nazionale d'Arte Antica, Rome. Photo: Scala. 3 By Courtesy of the Trustees of the Victoria & Albert Museum, London. 4 Ospedale di S. Maria delle Scala, Siena. Photo: Scala. 5 Reproduced by courtesy of the Trustees, The National Gallery, London. 6 Musée Condé, Chantilly. Photo: Giraudon/Bridgeman Art Library, London. 7 Museo Nacional del Prado, Madrid. Photo: Scala.

94–95 The glass of fashion
1 Museo Nacional del Prado, Madrid. Photo: Scala. 2 Galleria degli Uffizi, Florence. Photo: Scala. 3 Reproduced by courtesy of the Trustees, The National Gallery, London. 4 Alte Pinakothek, Munich. Photo: Scala. 5 Musée du Louvre, Paris. Photo: Scala. 6 Hardwick Hall, Derbyshire.

96–97 The gentry at play
1 Palazzo Ducale, Mantua. Photo: Scala. 2 Kunsthistorisches Museum, Vienna. 3 Mauritshuis, The Hague. Photo: Scala. 4 Kunsthistorisches Museum, Vienna. 5 Galleria degli Uffizi, Florence. Photo: Scala. 6, 7 Palazzo Vecchio, Florence. Photo: Scala. 8 Collezione Monte dei Paschi, Siena. Photo: Scala. 9 Museo di Roma, Rome. Photo: Scala.

98–99 Court entertainment
1 Niedersächsisches Landesmuseum, Hanover. 2 Gabinetto dei Disegni e delle Stampe, Florence. Photo: Scala. 3 Copyright British Museum, London. 4 Baldassare de Balgiojoso, *Ballet comique de la Royne,* Paris, 1582. 5 Devonshire Collection, Chatsworth. Reproduced by permission of the Chatsworth Settlement Trustees. Photograph Courtauld Institute of Art, London. 6 Palazzo Poggi, Bologna. Photo: Scala. 7 Courtesy of the National Portrait Gallery, London.

100–01 Italian funerary monuments
1 S. Pietro, Vatican. Photo: Scala. 2 S. Trinita, Florence. Photo: Scala. 3 Battistero, Florence. Photo: Scala. 4 S. Miniato, Florence. Photo: Scala. 5, 6 S. Lorenzo, Florence. Photo: Scala. 7 SS. Giovanni e Paolo, Venice. Photo: Scala. 8 Duomo, Lucca. Photo: Scala. 9 Galleria dell'Accademia, Ravenna. Photo: Scala.

102–03 Funerary monuments of the north
1 Avila Cathedral. 2 El Escorial, Madrid. Photo: Scala. 3 Abbey Church, Brou. Photo: Jean Roubier. 4 Westminster Abbey, London. Photo: A. F. Kersting. 5 Parish Church, Bisham, Berkshire. Photograph Courtauld Institute of Art, London. 6 Hofkirche, Innsbruck. Photo: Bridgeman Art Library, London. 7 The Oude Kerk, Delft. Photo: Rijksdienst v.d. Monumentenzorg, The Hague. 8 Westminster Abbey, London. Photo: A. F. Kersting. 9 Musée de Dijon. Photo: Scala. 10 St Denis, Paris. Photo: Giraudon/Bridgeman Art Library, London.

3 God and Man

104 Kunsthistorisches Museum, Vienna.
106a Palazzo Communale, Borgo Sansepolcro. 106b By permission of the British Library, London.
107a S. Maria della Salute, Venice.

108–09 Christian classicism: Renaissance church design
1, 2, 3, 4 Photo: Scala. 5 Photo: Stanislaw Michta. 6 Photo: Scala. 7 Photo: Giraudon. 8 Photo: Scala. 9 Architekturmuseum der Technischen Universität, Munich.

110–11 Inside the churches
1, 2, 3, 4, 5, 6 Photo: Scala. 7 Galleria Nazionale d'Arte Antica, Rome. Photo: Scala. 8 Photo: Giraudon. 9 Photo: A. F. Kersting. 10 Photo: Stanislaw Michta.

112–13 The sacraments
1, 2 Musée Royaux des Beaux-Arts, Antwerp. Photo: Scala. 3 National Museum, Denmark. 4 Musée Royaux des Beaux-Arts, Antwerp. Photo: Scala.

114–15 Reformation history
1 Photo: Bildarchiv Foto Marburg. 2 Luther, *On Aplas von Rom*, 1520. 4 Germanisches Nationalmuseum, Nuremberg. Photo: Scala. 5 Kunstmuseum, Winterthur. 8 Musée du Louvre, Paris. Photo: Scala.

116–17 Preaching the word
1 Duomo, Siena. Photo: Scala. 2 Photo: Scala. 3 Johannes Geiler von Keysersperg, *Das Buch Granatapfel*, Strasbourg, 1516. 4 Kunsthistorisches Museum, Vienna. 5 Society of Antiquaries, London. Photo: Bridgeman Art Library, London. 6 Lutherhalle, Wittenberg.

118–19 The Bible
1 Complutensian *Polyglot Bible*, 1514. 2 French *Bible*, Lyon, 1521. 3 Luther's *Bible*, 1534. 4 The British Library, London. 5 Danish *Bible*, 1550. 6 Hertford College, Oxford. 7 The British Library, London. Photo: Bridgeman Art Library, London. 8 Coverdale's *Bible*, 1535. 9 *Great Bible*, 1539.

120–21 The Reformation: a battle of images
1 Schlosskirche, Dessau. 2 Jean Calvin, *Der Heylig Brotkorb*, Strasbourg, 1584. 3 Foxe, *Book of Martyrs*, 1563. 4 Staatliche Museen, Berlin. Photo: AKG London. 6 Germanisches Nationalmuseum, Nuremberg.

122–23 Iconoclasm: the Puritan backlash
1 Bibliothèque Publique et Universitaire, Geneva. 2 Zentralbibliothek, Zurich. 3 *Bible*, Cologne, 1565. 4 *Bishop's Bible*, London, 1568. 5 J. Strümpf, *Swiss Chronicle*, 1548. 6 Zentralbibliothek, Zurich. 7 Eytzinger, *De leone belgico*, Cologne, 1583.

124–25 Counter-Reformation
1 Burghley House, Lincolnshire. Photo: Bridgeman Art Library, London. 2 Museo Provincial de Belles Artes, Seville. 3 Descalzas Reales, Madrid. 4 Museo Nacional del Prado, Madrid. 5 Reproduced by courtesy of the Trustees, The National Gallery, London. 6 S. Maria Gloriosa dei Frari, Venice. Photo: Scala.

126–27 The relief of poverty
1 I Musei Vaticani. Photo: Scala. 2, 3 Ospedale del Ceppo, Pistoia. Photo: Scala. 4 Ospedale di S. Maria della Scala, Siena. Photo: Scala. 5 Phillips, the International Fine Arts Auctioneers. Photo: Bridgeman Art Library, London. 6 Städtische Kunstsammlungen, Augsburg. 7 Ospedale del Ceppo, Pistoia. Photo: Scala.

128–29 God the Father
1 SS. Annunziata, Florence. Photo: Scala. 2 Alte Pinakothek, Munich. Photo: Scala. 3 St Bavon, Ghent. Photo: Scala. 4 I Musei Vaticani. Photo: Scala. 5 Accademia, Venice. Photo: Scala.

130–31 The Nativity
1 The National Gallery, London. Photo: Bridgeman Art Library, London. 2 Alte Pinakothek, Munich. Photo: Scala. 3 Galleria degli Uffizi, Florence. Photo: Scala. 4 Alte Pinakothek, Munich. Photo: Scala. 5 Reproduced by courtesy of the Trustees, The National Gallery, London. 6 S. Trinita, Florence. Photo: Scala.

132–33 Virgin and Child
1 The National Gallery, London. Photo: Bridgeman Art Library, London. 2 Galleria degli Uffizi, Florence. Photo: Scala. 3 Galleria Sabauda, Turin. Photo: Scala. 4 Reproduced by courtesy of the Trustees, The National Gallery, London. 5 Galleria degli Uffizi, Florence. Photo: Scala. 6 Gemäldegalerie, Dresden. Photo: AKG London. 7 Museo Nacional del Prado, Madrid. Photo: Scala.

134–35 The baptism of Christ
1 The National Gallery, London. Photo: Bridgeman Art Library, London. 2 Musée du Commune, Bruges. Photo: Scala. 3 Battistero, Florence. Photo: Scala. 4 Santa Corona, Vicenza. 5 Museo Nacional del Prado, Madrid. Photo: Scala.

136–37 Conversing saints
1 Pieve di S. Maria, Arezzo. Photo: Scala. 2 Städelsches Kunstinstitut, Frankfurt-am-Main. Photo: Artothek/Bridgeman Art Library, London. 3 S. Zeno, Verona. Photo: Scala. 4 Accademia, Venice. Photo: Scala. 5 Museo di S. Marco, Florence. Photo: Scala. 6 Galleria Palatina, Florence. Photo: Scala.

138–39 The Last Supper
1 St Pierre, Louvain. Photo: Scala. 2 Museo di S. Marco, Florence. Photo: Scala. 3 S. Maria delle Grazie, Milan. Photo: Scala. 4 S. Giorgio Maggiore, Venice. Photo: Scala.

140–41 The Crucifixion
1 S. Maria Maddalena dei Pazzi, Florence. Photo: Scala. 2 Museo di Capodimonte, Naples. Photo: Scala. 3 Copyright British Museum, London. 4 Musée Unterlinden, Colmar. Photo: Scala. 5 Scuola Grande di S. Rocco, Venice. Photo: Scala. 6 Museo Nacional del Prado, Madrid. Photo: Scala.

142–43 Lamentation
1 Museo Nacional del Prado, Madrid. Photo: Scala. 2 Öffentliche Kunstsammlung, Basle. 3 Alte Pinakothek, Munich. Photo: Scala. 4 Kunsthistorisches Museum, Vienna. 5 Walker Art Gallery, Liverpool. Photo: Board of Trustees of the National Museums & Galleries on Merseyside. 6 S. Pietro, Vatican. Photo: Scala. 7 Accademia, Venice. Photo: Scala. 8 Museo Civico, Viterbo. Photo: K & B News Foto, Florence/Bridgeman Art Library, London.

144–45 The Resurrection
1 Bayerische Staatsgemäldesammlungen, Munich. Photo: Artothek. 2 Musée Unterlinden, Colmar. Photo: Scala. 3 S. Marco, Florence. Photo: Scala. 4 Palazzo Communale, Borgo S. Sepolcro. Photo: Scala. 5 I Musei Vaticani. Photo: Scala. 6 Museo di Capodimonte, Naples. Photo: Scala.

146–47 The Last Judgment
1 Hôtel Dieu, Beaune. Photo: Bridgeman Art Library, London. 2 Duomo, Orvieto. Photo: Scala. 3 I Musei Vaticani. Photo: Scala.

4 The Image of the World
148 I Musei Vaticani. Photo: Scala. 150a Fischer & Wieser, *Die Älteste Karte mit dem Namen America*, 1903. 150b Braun & Hogenberg, *Civitas orbis terrarum*, 1574. 151a Museo Correr, Venice. 151b Národní Galerie, Prague.

152–53 Mapping the world
1 Biblioteca Estense, Modena. Photo: Scala. 2 Biblioteca Marciana, Venezia. Photo: Scala. 3 Biblioteca Estense, Modena. Photo: Scala.

154–55 Florence
1 Museo di Firenze com'era, Florence. Photo: Scala. 2 S. Trinita, Florence. Photo: Scala. 3 Museo di Firenze com'era, Florence. Photo: Scala. 4 Photo: Scala. 5 Museo di S. Marco, Florence. Photo: Scala. 6 Palazzo Vecchio, Florence. Photo: Scala.

156–57 Rome
3 Gabinetto dei Disegno e delle Stampe, Florence. Photo: Scala. 4 Biblioteca Apostolica, Vatican. 5 Photo: Scala. 6 Photo: Georgina Masson. 7 Photo: Scala.

158–59 Venice
1 Museo Correr, Venice. Photo: Scala. 2, 3 Photo: Scala. 4 Palazzo Ducale, Venice. Photo: Scala. 5 Photo: Archivio Fotografico Veneziano. 6 Photo: Alinari. 7 Museo Correr, Venice. Photo: Scala.

160–61 Cities of central Europe
1 Photo: Bildarchiv Foto Marburg. 2 Maximilian Museum, Augsburg. 3 Museum voor Schone Kunsten, Antwerp. 5 Germanisches Nationalmuseum, Nuremberg. 6 Photo: John Wright. 7, 8 Photo: V. Hyhlik. 9 Umeleckoprůmyslové Muzeum, Prague. 10 Sotheby's, London.

162 London
3 William Dugdale, *The History of St Paul's Cathedral*, London, 1658.

163 Paris
2 Claude Châtillon, *Topographie française*, Paris, 1641. 3 Musée Carnavalet, Paris. 4 Claude Châtillon, *Topographie française*, Paris, 1641.

164–65 Defensible spaces
1 Collection Chigi Saracini, Siena. Photo: Scala. 2 Archivio di Stato, Siena. Photo: Scala. 3 Biblioteca Ambrosiana, Milan. 4 Casa Buonarroti, Florence. 5 Photo: Guido Alberto Rossi, courtesy Image Bank. 6 Braun & Hohenberg, *Civitas orbis terrarum*, Cologne, 1597. 7 Photo: Aerofilms Ltd. 8 Royal Institute of British Architects, British Architectural Drawings Collection. 9, 10 Braun & Hohenberg, *Civitas orbis terrarum*, Cologne, 1597.

166–67 The landscape of reality
1 Libreria Piccolomini, Duomo, Siena. Photo: Scala. 2 Accademia, Venice. Photo: Scala. 3 Museo Nacional del Prado, Madrid. Photo: Scala. 4 The National Gallery, London. Photo: Bridgeman Art Library, London. 5 Reproduced by courtesy of the Trustees, The National Gallery, London. 6 Museo Nacional del Prado, Madrid. Photo: Scala.

7 Musée d'Art et d'histoire, Geneva.
8 Musée du Louvre, Paris. Photo: Scala.
9 Alte Pinakothek, Munich. Photo: Scala.
10 Musée du Louvre, Paris. Photo: Scala.
168–69 Landscapes of fantasy
1 Reproduced by courtesy of the
Trustees, The National Gallery, London.
2 Reproduced by courtesy of the Trustees,
The National Gallery, London. 3 Musée
du Louvre, Paris. Photo: Scala. 4 Alte
Pinakothek, Munich. Photo: Scala. 5 Alte
Pinakothek, Munich. Photo: Scala. 6 Museo
Nacional del Prado, Madrid. Photo: Scala.
170–71 The art of the garden
1 Museo di Firenze com'era, Florence. Photo:
Scala. 2 Kurpfalzisches Museum, Heidelberg.
3 Francesco Colonna, *Hypnerotomachia
Poliphili*, Venice, 1499. 5 Royal Institute
of British Architects, British Architectural
Drawings Collection. 6 Royal Collection
© 1995 Her Majesty Queen Elizabeth II.
7, 8 Photo: Hugh Palmer.

5 Living and Dying

172 Biblioteca Estense, Modena.
174a Photo: Alinari. **174b** Duke of
Sutherland Collection, on loan to the
National Gallery of Scotland, Edinburgh.
175a Kunstsammlungen, Basle. **175b** De Bry,
Historia Americas, 1599.
176–77 The Ages of Man
1 Galleria Palatina, Florence. Photo: Scala.
2 By permission of The British Library,
London. 3 Accademia, Venice. Photo: Scala.
4 Galleria Palatina, Florence. Photo: Scala.
5 Kupferstichkabinett, Staatliche Museen,
Berlin. Photo: © bpk. 8 Musée du Louvre,
Paris. Photo: Scala.
178–79 Travel and transport
1 Accademia, Venice. Photo: Scala.
2 Copyright British Museum, London.
3 Braun & Hohenberg, *Civitas orbis terrarum*,
Cologne, 1597. 4 Giacomo Franco, *Habiti
d'uomeni et donne Venetiane*, 1609. 5 Braun &
Hohenberg, *Civitas orbis terrarum*, Cologne,
1597. 7 Alte Pinakothek, Munich. Photo:
Scala. 8 Tesoro di S. Giovanni in Laterano,
Rome. 9 Reproduced by permission of the
Trustees of the Science Museum, London.
180–81 Pleasures and pastimes
1 Ashmolean Museum, Oxford. 2 Museo
Civico, Cremona. Photo: Scala. 3 Ghent
Museum. Photo: Scala. 4 University Library,
Edinburgh. 5 Amsterdams Historisch
Museum.
182–83 The animal kingdom
1 Biblioteca Civica, Bergamo. Photo: Scala.
2 Czartorysky Museum, Cracow. Photo:
Scala. 3 Galleria Doria Pamphili, Rome.
Photo: Scala. 4 Galleria Doria Pamphili,
Rome. Photo: Scala. 5 Albertina, Vienna.
6 Palazzo del Tè, Mantua. Photo: Scala.
7 Copyright British Museum, London.
8 Tempio Malatestiano, Rimini. Photo:
Scala.
184–85 In the countryside
1 Fonte Maggiore, Perugia. Photo: Ilario
Bessi. 2 Castello del Buonconsiglio,

Trento. Photo: Scala. 3 Gallerie Palatina,
Florence. Photo: Scala. 4 Bayerische
Staatsbibliothek, Munich. 5, 6 Germanisches
Nationalmuseum, Nuremberg. Photo: Scala.
7 Biblioteca de la Universidad Valencia.
9 Musées royaux des beaux-arts de Belgique,
Brussels. Photo: Scala.
186–87 Work and trade
1 Castello, Issogne. Photo: Scala. 2 The
Metropolitan Museum of Art, New York.
Photo: The Bridgeman Art Library, London.
3 H. Schopperus, *Panoplia*, 1568. 6 Musées
royaux des beaux-arts de Belgique, Brussels.
7 Biblioteca Estense, Modena. Photo: Scala.
8 Palazzo Vecchio, Florence. Photo: Scala.
188–89 The domestic setting
1 Gabinetto dei Disegni e delle Stampe,
Florence. Photo: Scala. 2 Palazzo Vecchio,
Florence. Photo: Scala. 3, 4, 5 Photo: Emily
Lane. 6 Photo: Klaus G. Beyer, Weimar.
7 Photo: R. Wessendorf, Schaffhausen.
190–91 Marriage and the family
1 Devonshire Collection, Chatsworth.
Reproduced by permission of the Chatsworth
Settlement Trustees. Photograph Courtauld
Institute of Art, London. 2 Museo
Real Academia de Belles Artes, Madrid.
Photo: Bridgeman Art Library, London.
3 Reproduced by courtesy of the Trustees,
The National Gallery, London. 4 Museo
Nacional del Prado, Madrid. Photo: Scala.
5 Öffentliche Kunstsammlung, Basle.
6 Reproduced by courtesy of the Trustees,
The National Gallery, London. 7 Alte
Pinakothek, Munich. Photo: Scala.
192–93 A new eroticism
1 By permission of The British Library,
London. 2, 3 Reproduced by courtesy of
the Trustees, the National Gallery, London.
4 Museum der Stadt, Regensburg.
5 © Bibliothèque Nationale de France,
Paris. 6 Kunsthistorisches Museum, Vienna.
194–95 Renaissance women
1 Galleria Borghese, Rome. Photo: Scala.
2 Pinacoteca Nazionale, Siena. 3 Palazzo
Vecchio, Florence. Photo: Scala. 4 By
permission of The British Library, London.
5 Musée du Louvre, Paris. Photo: Scala.
6 Galleria degli Uffizi, Florence. Photo: Scala.
7 Národní Galerie, Prague. Photo: Scala.
8 Musée Condé, Chantilly. 9 Museo Correr,
Venice. Photo: Scala.
196–97 Sex and gender
1 Fitzwilliam Museum, University of
Cambridge. 2 Copyright © 1995 The
Metropolitan Museum of Art, New York.
Rogers Fund, 1911. 3 Museo di San Petranio,
Bologna. 4 Galleria degli Uffizi, Florence.
Photo: Scala. 5 Royal Collection © 1995
Her Majesty Queen Elizabeth II. 6 Kunsthistorisches Museum, Vienna.
198–99 Race and colour
1 Accademia de Belles Artes, Puebla.
2 Accademia, Venice. Photo: Scala.
3 Reproduced by permission of the Marquess
of Bath, Longleat House, Warminster,
Wiltshire. 4 By permission of The British
Library, London. 5 Museo di S. Marco.

Photo: Scala. 6 Accademia, Venice. Photo:
Scala. 7 Galleria degli Uffizi, Florence. Photo:
Scala.
200–01 Illness and death
2 By courtesy of the National Portrait
Gallery, London. 4 Pinacoteca Communale,
Sansepolcro. Photo: Scala. 5 S. Martino
dei Bounomini, Florence. Photo: Scala.
6 Biblioteca Laurenziana, Florence.
Photo: Scala. 7, 8 Musée du Louvre, Paris.
Photo: Scala.

6 Science, Invention and Discovery

202 Reproduced by courtesy of the Trustees,
The National Gallery, London.
204b © Bibliothèque Nationale de France,
Paris.
205a Leopold of Austria, *De astronum scienta*,
1489. **205b** Copyright British Museum,
London.
206–07 The printing revolution
1 Christie's, London. Photo: Bridgeman Art
Library, London. 2 Xenophon, *Hellenica*,
Venice, 1503. 3 Chaucer, *The Canterbury
Tales*, c. 1487. 5, 6, 7 H. Schoppe, *Book of
Trades*, 1568. 8 P. Schrijer, *Laurens Coster
van Haarlem*, 1628. 9, 10 H. Schoppe, *Book
of Trades*, 1568.
208–09 The printed page
1 Cicero, *De oratore*, Subiaco, c. 1465.
2 Chaucer, *The Canterbury Tales*, c. 1478.
3 Landesbibliothek, Gotha. 4 Constantine
Lascaris, *Epitome*, Venice, 1494. 5 Colonna,
Hypnerotomachia Poliphili, Venice, 1499.
6 Colonna, *Hypnerotomachia Poliphili*,
Paris, 1546. 7 *Heures de la Vierge*, Paris, 1525.
8 Budespostmuseum, Frankfurt-am-Main.
210–11 Exploration and discovery
1 Pedro de Medina, *Regimiento de
Navagacion*, Seville, 1563. 2 André Thevet,
Cosmographie, 1575. 3 Pedro de Medina,
Regimiento de Navagacion, Seville, 1563.
4 Museum of the History of Science, Oxford.
5 National Maritime Museum, Greenwich.
6 Antonio Bocarro, *Luiro do Estado da India
Oriental*, 1646. 9 Museo Navale di Pegli,
Genoa. Photo: Scala. 10 Frans Halsmuseum,
Haarlem. 11 Copyright British Museum,
London.
212–13 Ships and shipbuilding
1 Giovanni Villani, *Cronica di Partenope*,
1481. 2 John Dee, *General & Rare Memorials
pertaining to the Perfect Art of Navigation*,
1577. 3 Courtesy of the Master and
Fellows, Magdalene College, Cambridge.
4 Städelsches Kunstinstitut, Frankfurt-am-
Main. 5 Museo di Storia Veneziana. Photo:
Scala. 6 Courtesy of the Master and Fellows,
Magdalene College, Cambridge.
214–15 Astronomy
1 Johannes Stöffler, *Calender*, 1518.
2 Johannes de Montregis, *Epitoma...*,
Venice, 1496. 3 Musée du Louvre, Paris.
Photo: Scala. 4 By courtesy of the Board of
Trustees of the Victoria & Albert Museum,
London. 5 Horloge Astronomique de la

Cathedral, Strasbourg. 6 Tycho Brahe, *Astronomical instauratae mechanica*, 1602. 7 Museo delle Scienza, Florence. Photo: Scala. 8. Biblioteca Nazionale, Florence.

216–17 Alchemy and astrology
1 Palazzo Vecchio, Florence. Photo: Scala. 2, 3 Biblioteca Aspotolica, Vatican. 4 Biblioteca Estense, Modena. 6. L. Thurneysser, *Quinta Essentia*, Leipzig, 1574. 8 Tempio Malatestiano, Rimini. Photo: Scala.

218–19 Mathematics: the power of number
1 Euclid trans. H. Billingsley, *Elementa*, London, 1570. 2 I Musei Vaticani. Photo: Scala. 3 Euclid, *Elementa*, Venice, 1482. 4 Gregorius Riesch, *Margarita Philisophica*, 1515. 5 T. Hood, *Making and Use of ... the Sector*, 1598. 6 Stevin, *Disme: The Art of Tenths*, London, 1608. 7 I Musei Vaticani. Photo: Scala. 8 Museo di Capodimonte, Naples. Photo: Scala.

220–21 The measure of music
2 Copyright the British Museum, London. 3 Museo Nacional del Prado, Madrid. Photo: Scala. 4 Musée du Louvre, Paris. Photo: Scala. 5 Franchino Gaffurio, *Practica musica*, Venice, 1512. 6 Archivio di S. Giovanni in Laterano, Rome. 7 William Byrd et al, *Parthenia*, London, 1611. 8 Orlando Lassus, *The First Book of Madrigals*, 1557. 9 Franchino Gaffurio, *De harmonia musicorum*, Milan, 1512.

222–23 The art of war
1 Christie's, London. 2 Galleria degli Uffizi, Florence. Photo: Scala. 3 Reproduced by permission of the Trustees of the Science Museum, London. 4 Copyright British Museum, London. 5 Kunsthistorisches Museum, Vienna. 6 Palazzo Ducale, Urbino. Photo: Scala. 7 National Maritime Museum, Greenwich. 8 Lodovico Melzo, *Regale militari della cavalleria*, Antwerp, 1611.

224–25 Medicine: theory and practice
1 By permission of The British Library, London. 2, 3 Biblioteca Laurenziano, Florence. Photo: Scala. 4 Johannes di Kethan, *Fasciculus medicinae*, 1495. 5 *Hortus Sanitatis* (German version), Augsburg, 1496. 6 *Hortus sanitatis* (Latin Version), Mainz, 1491. 8 Della Croce, *Chinirgiae libri septem*, 1573. 9 Johannes de Capua, *Directorium humanae vitae*, Strasbourg, c. 1488–93.

226–27 Anatomy: the body's structure
1 Wellcome Historical Medical Museum & Library, London. 2 The Royal Collection © 1995 Her Majesty Queen Elizabeth II. 3 Wellcome Historical Medical Museum & Library, London. 4 The Royal Collection © 1995 Her Majesty Queen Elizabeth II. 5 Vesalius, *De humani corporis fabrica*, 1543. 6 Vesalius, *De humani corporis fabrica*, 1547. 7 Realdus Columbus, *De re anatomica*, Venice, 1559.

228–29 Botany: medicine and art
1, 2 The Royal Collection © 1995 Her Majesty Queen Elizabeth II. 3 Musée du Louvre, Paris. Photo: Scala. 4 Galleria degli Uffizi, Florence. Photo: Scala. 5 L. Fuchs, *De historia stirpium*, Basle, 1547. 6 Albertina,

Vienna. 7 Hernandes, *Rerum medicarum novae hispaniae...*, 1649. 8 Basil Besler, *Hortus eystettensis*, Augsburg/Nuremberg, 1613. 9 Gerard, *The Herball*, 1636.

230–31 Time and the hour
1 Schatzkammer Residenz, Munich. 2 Copyright British Museum, London. 3 Photo: Royal Commission on the Historical Monuments of England, Swindon. 4 Photo: Scala. 5 Kunsthistorisches Museum, Vienna. 6 Photo: John Wright. 7 By courtesy of the Board of Trustees of the Victoria & Albert Museum, London.

232–33 A new world of finance
1 By permission of The British Library, London. 3 Archivio di Stato, Siena. Photo: Scala. 4 Herzog Anton Ulrich Museum, Brunswick. 5 Alte Pinakothek, Munich. Photo: Scala. 7, 8 Ashmolean Museum, Oxford. 9 Archivio di Stato, Siena. Photo: Scala.

234–35 Water for recreation and work
1 Photo: John Wright. 2 Villa d'Este, Tivoli. Photo: Scala. 3 Trustees of the Earl of Scarbrough's Children's Settlement. 5 Reproduced by permission of the Trustees of the Science Museum, London. 7 Museo di Firenze com'era, Florence. Photo: Scala.

236–37 Treasures in metalwork
1, 2 Agricola, *De re metallica*, 1556. 3 Galleria Doria Pamphili, Rome. Photo: Scala. 4 Palazzo del Tè, Mantua. Photo: Scala. 5 Trésor de la Cathédral, Liège. 6 Basilica del Santo, Padua. Photo: Scala. 7 Germanisches Nationalmuseum, Nuremberg. 8 Museo Nazionale del Bargello, Florence. Photo: Scala. 9 Kunsthistorisches Museum, Vienna.

7 The Power of Art

238 Casa del Vasari, Florence. Photo: Scala.

240a Orsanmichele, Florence. Photo: Soprintendenza, Florence. 240b By courtesy of the Trustees of the Victoria & Albert Museum, London.

241a Photo: R. Kozlowski. 241b S. Pietro in Vincoli, Rome. Photo: Alinari.

242–43 The artist's image
1 Museo Nacional del Prado, Madrid. Photo: Scala. 2 S. Giovanni Battista, Florence. Photo: Scala. 3 Kunsthistorisches Museum, Vienna. Photo: Bridgeman Art Library, London. 4 St Lorenz, Nuremberg. Photo: Bridgeman Art Library, London. 5, 6 Galleria degli Uffizi, Florence. Photo: Scala. 7 Museo Nacional del Prado, Madrid. Photo: Scala. 8 Biblioteca Reale, Turin. 9 I Musei Vaticani.

244–45 The Renaissance medal
1 Museo Nazionale del Bargello, Florence. Photo: Scala. 2 Musée du Louvre, Paris. 3, 4, 5, 6, 7 Museo Nazionale del Bargello, Florence. Photo: Scala. 8 The British Museum, London. Photo: Bridgeman Art Library, London. 9 Fitzwilliam Museum, University of Cambridge. Photo: Bridgeman Art Library, London. 10, 11, 12, 13, 14, 15 Copyright British Museum, London.

246–47 The mastery of space
1, 2 Jean Cousin, *Livre de Perspective*, Paris, 1560. 4 S. Maria Novella, Florence. Photo: Scala. 5 Gabinetto dei Designi e delle Stampe, Florence. 6 Palazzo Ducale, Urbino. Photo: Scala. 7 St Wolfgang Altar, Salzkammergut. 8 Pinacoteca di Brera, Milan. Photo: Scala. 9 Pinacoteca di Brera, Milan. Photo: Scala.

248–49 The human form
1 Accademia, Venice. 2 Museo Nacional del Prado, Madrid. Photo: Scala. 3 Chiesa del Carmine, Florence. Photo: Scala. 4 Musée du Louvre. Photo: Scala. 5 Kunsthistorisches Museum, Vienna. 6 Museo Nacional del Prado, Madrid. Photo: Scala. 7 Musée du Louvre, Paris. Photo: © RMN.

250–51 The heroic
1, 2 Museo Nazionale del Bargello, Florence. Photo: Scala. 3 Accademia, Florence. Photo: Scala. 4 Loggia dei Lanzi, Florence. Photo: Scala. 5 National Gallery of Art, Washington, D.C., Widener Collection, 1942. 6 Gabinetto dei Disegni e delle Stampe, Florence. Photo: Scala. 7 *The Roman Heroes*, c. 1586.

252–53 Italy: the language of decoration
1, 2 I Musei Vaticani. Photo: Scala. 3 Palazzo Farnese, Rome. Photo: Scala. 4 Palazzo Vecchio, Florence. Photo: Scala. 5 Villa Farnesina, Rome. Photo: Scala. 6 Château de Fontainebleau. Photo: Scala. 7 Palazzo Ducale, Venice. Photo: Scala.

254–55 The interior as work of art
1 Castello Sforza, Milan. Foto Saporetti. 2 Palazzo Ducale, Mantua. Photo: Scala. 3 Villa Farnesina, Rome. Photo: Scala. 4 Palazzo Ducale, Mantua. Photo: Scala. 5 Palazzo Medici-Riccardi, Florence. Photo: Scala. 6 Duomo, Parma. Photo: Scala. 7 Villa Barbaro, Maser. Photo: Scala.

256–57 The Sistine ceiling
I Musei Vaticani. Photo: Scala.

258–59 The grotesque
1 Accademia, Venice. Photo: Scala. 2 National Gallery, London. Photo: Bridgeman Art Library, London. 3 Villa Demidoff, Partolino. Photo: Scala. 4 Photo: Hubert Josse. 5 Sebastian Münster, *Cosmographia universalis*, 1544. 6 Museo Civico, Cremona. Photo: Scala. 7 Museo Nacional del Prado, Madrid. Photo: Scala.

260–61 Sculpture in relief
1 Basilica del Santo, Padua. Photo: Scala. 2, 3 Battistero, Florence. Photo: Scala. 4 S. Petronio, Bologna. Photo: Scala. 5 Tempio Malatestiano, Rimini. 6 Château Montrottier. Photo: Helga Schmidt-Glassner. 7 Musée du Louvre, Paris. 8 S. Lorenzo, Florence. Photo: Scala.

262–63 Sculpture: a new dimension
1 Museo dell'Opera del Duomo, Florence. Photo: Scala. 2 Loggia dei Lanzi, Florence. Photo: Scala. 3 S. Pietro in Vincoli, Rome. Photo: Scala. 4 Piazza della Signoria, Florence. Photo: Scala. 5 Palazzo Ducale, Venice. Photo: P. Cannon Brookes, Abingdon. 6 The Well of Moses, Dijon.

7 Manfränkisches Museum, Würzburg. Photo: Helga Schmidt-Glassner. 8 By Courtesy of the Board of Trustess of the Victoria & Albert Museum, London. 9 Staatliche Museen, Berlin. © bpk.

8 Rebuilding Antiquity

264 Musée du Louvre, Paris. Photo: Giraudon/Bridgeman Art Library, London.
266a Real Monasterio del El Escorial, Madrid. 266b Alberti, *L'Archittetura*, Florence, 1550.
267a Walters Art Gallery, Baltimore.
267b Palazzo Ducale, Mantua.
268–69 **The classical orders**
1, 2 Photo: Scala. 3, 4 John Shute *First and Chief Groundes of Architecture*, 1563. 5 Serlio, *Il libro primo d'architettura*, 1554. 6 Photo: Scala. 7 Ecole nationale supérieure des beaux-arts, Paris. Photo: Giraudon. 8 Photo: A. F. Kersting. 9 Palladio, *Quattro libri dell'architettura*, Venice, 1570. 10 Philibert de l'Orme, *Le Premier tome de l'architecture*, Paris, 1568. 11 Albertina, Vienna. 12 Photo: Alinari.
270–71 **Planned urban space**
1 Palazzo Ducale, Urbino. Photo: Scala. 2. Photo: Scala. 4 Photo: Scala. 5 Biblioteca Nazionale, Florence. 6 Photo: Aerofilms Ltd. 7 Photo: Scala. 8 Claude Châtillon, *Topographie française*, 1641. 9 Polska Akademia Nauk Instytut Sztuki, Warsaw.
272–73 **Gothic survival**
1 Národní Galerie, Prague. 2 Musée Condé, Chantilly. 3 Ospedale Maggiore, Milan. Photo: K & B News Foto, Florence/ Bridgeman Art Library, London. 4 Photo: A. F. Kersting. 5 Photo: Helga Schmidt-Glassner. 6 Photo: Scala. 7 Photo: Emily Lane.
274–75 **The central-space church**
1, 2 Photo: Scala. 3 Institut de France, Paris. 4 I Musei Vaticani. Photo: Scala. 5 Copyright British Museum, London. 7, 8, 9 Photo: Scala.
276–77 **The rise of the dome**
1 Photo: Scala. 2 Museo dell'Opera del Duomo, Florence. 3, 4, 5 Photo: Scala. 6 Serlio, *Tutti l'opera d'architettura et prospettica*, 1584. 7 Photo: H. Boucher. 8 Photo: Giraudon.
278–79 **The Colosseum**
1 Photo: Scala. 2 Lipsius *De amphiteatro liber*, Antwerp, 1584. 3 Gabinetto dei Disegni e delle Stampe, Florence. 4 Photo: Scala. 5 Palazzo Ducale, Mantua. Photo: Scala. 6 Fitzwilliam Museum, University of Cambridge. Photo: Bridgeman Art Library. 7 Kunsthistorisches Museum, Vienna.
280–81 **Triumphal arches**
1 I Musei Vaticani. Photo: Scala. 2, 3, 4 Photo: Scala. 5 Stephen Harrison, *Arches of Triumph*, 1604. 6 Ecole nationale supérieure des beaux-arts, Paris. 7 Photo: Scala. 8 Ecole nationale des beaux-arts, Paris. Photo: Giraudon.

282–83 **The theatre**
1 Photo: Scala. 2 Vitruvius, *De architectura*, Como, 1521. 3 Daniele Barbaro, *Vitruvius I dieci libri dell'architectura*, 1556.
4 Universiteitsbibliotheek, Utrecht.
6 *Terentius cum tribus commentis*, 1497.
7 By permission of the Provost and Fellows, Worcester College Library, Oxford.
9 Sebastiano Serlio, *Architettura*, Venice, 1569. 10 Devonshire Collection, Chatsworth. Reproduced by permission of the Chatsworth Settlement Trustees. Photograph Courtauld Institute of Art, London.
284–85 **Villa life**
1, 2, 3 Photo: Scala. 4 Photo: Alexander Zielcke. 5 Museo del Firenze com'era, Florence. Photo: Scala. 6, 7, 8 Photo: Scala. 9 Photo: A. F. Kersting.
286–87 **Obelisks: 'star-y-pointing pyramids'**
1 Domenico Fontana, *Della trasportazione dell'obelisco Vaticano...*, Rome, 1590.
2 Melchior Jamnitzer, *Perspectiva coporum regularium*, Nuremberg, 1568. 3 Domenico Fontana, *Della trasportazione dell'obelisco Vaticano...*, Rome, 1590. 5 Szépmüvészeti Múzeum, Budapest. 6 Photo: Royal Commission on the Historical Monuments of England, Swindon. 7 Musée du Louvre, Paris. Photo: Scala.
288 **Mannerism: an end or a beginning?**
1 Pinacoteca Nazionale, Siena. Photo: Scala. 2, 3 Photo: Scala.

Biographical Dictionary

290 National Gallery of Art, Washington, D.C., Samuel H. Kress Collection.
291l By courtesy of Earl Spencer, Althorp, Northampton.
293r Paolo Giovio, *Elogia virorum bellica virtute illustrium*, Basle, 1577.
295l Staatliche Kunsthalle, Karlsruhe.
295r Dominicus Lampsonius, *Pictorium aliquot celebrium Germaniae miferioris effigies*, Antwerp, 1572.
298 © Bibliothèque Nationale de France, Paris.
299l Museo di Capodimonte, Naples. Photo: Scala.
300 By courtesy of the National Portrait Gallery, London.
302b © Bibliothèque Nationale de France, Paris.
303 By courtesy of the Marquess of Salisbury.
305l By courtesy of the Board of Trustees of the Victoria & Albert Museum, London.
305c Bodleian Library, Oxford. 305r The Royal Society, London.
306 Vasari, *Le vite de piu eccelente architeti, pittori, et scultori Italiani*, 1568.
308 Museo Nacional del Prado, Madrid. Photo: Scala.
309 Copyright British Museum, London.
310a © Bibliothèque Nationale de France, Paris.
311l Private Collection. 311c By courtesy of the National Portrait Gallery, London.

311r Devonshire Collection, Chatsworth. Reproduced by permission of the Chatsworth Settlement Trustees. Photograph Courtauld Institute of Art, London.
312 Devonshire Collection, Chatsworth. Reproduced by permission of the Chatsworth Settlement Trustees. Photograph Courtauld Institute of Art, London.
313 Vasari, *Le vite de piu eccelente architeti, pittori, et scultori Italiani*, 1568.
315 Museo Correr, Venice.
316l Museo Nacional del Prado, Madrid.
316r Szépmüvészeti Múzeum, Budapest.
318al Staatliche Museen, Berlin. © bpk.
318bl National Gallery of Art, Washington, D.C., Samuel H. Kress Collection.
318r © Bibliothèque Nationale de France, Paris.
319l Palazzo della Cancelleria, Rome.
319r By courtesy of the Board of Trustees of the Victoria & Albert Museum, London.
320 Centro Internazionale di Studi de Architettura 'Andrea Palladio', Vicenza.
321 Museo di Capodimonte, Naples.
322l Copyright British Museum, London.
322r S. Maria Maggiore, Spello. Photo: Villani, Bologna.
324l By courtesy of the National Portrait Gallery, London. 324c Vasari, *Le vite de piu eccelente architeti, pittori, et scultori Italiani*, 1568. 324r © Bibliothèque Nationale de France, Paris.
325r Vasari, *Le vite de piu eccelente architeti, pittori, et scultori Italiani*, 1568
326l Kunsthistorisches Museum, Vienna. Photo: Bridgeman Art Library, London.
326r Vasari, *Le vite de piu eccelente architeti, pittori, et scultori Italiani*, 1568.
327l Galleria degli Uffizi, Florence. Photo: Bridgeman Art Library. 327c © Bibliothèque Nationale de France, Paris. 327r © Bibliothèque Nationale de France, Paris.
328l By courtesy of the National Portrait Gallery, London. 328r I Musei Vaticani.
329l Peter Clayton.
330c Galleria Palatina, Florence. Photo: Scala.
330r Musée du Louvre, Paris. Photo: Bridgeman Art Library.
332r Tate Gallery, London.
333 Galleria degli Uffizi, Florence.
334l Museo di Capodimonte, Naples.
334r Copyright the British Museum, London.

350–51 **Glossary**
Vignola, *Regola delli cinque ordini d'architettura*, 1513; Vitruvius, *De architectura*, ed. Fra Giocondo, Venice, 1511; Tempio Malatestiano, Rimini; Museo Nazionale del Bargello, Florence; Serlio, *Il libro quinti d'architettura*, 1554; By courtesy of the Trustees of Sir John Soane's Museum, London.

INDEX

Page numbers in **bold** indicate entries in the Biographical Dictionary, where references to illustrations are given more fully.

365

Any copy of this book issued by the publisher as a paperback is sold subject to the condition that it shall not by way of trade or otherwise be lent, resold, hired out or otherwise circulated without the publisher's prior consent in any form of binding or cover other than that in which it is published and without a similar condition including these words being imposed on a subsequent purchaser.

© 1996 Thames and Hudson Ltd, London

Introduction and Chapter Introductions:
Text © 1996 Margaret Aston
Biographical Dictionary: Mary Peskett Smith
Texts on picture-spreads: Ian Sutton
Design: Ian Mackenzie-Kerr
Jacket design: Shalom Schotten
Picture Research: Sally Nicholls
Editorial: Ilona de Nemethy
Production: Margaret Hickson

All Rights Reserved. No part of this publication may be reproduced or transmitted in any form or by any means, electronic or mechanical, including photocopy, recording or any other information storage and retrieval system, without prior permission in writing from the publisher.

British Library Cataloguing-in-Publication Data
A catalogue record for this book is available
from the British Library

ISBN 0-500-01727-1

Origination in Hong Kong by HK Scanner Arts Int'l

Printed and bound in Singapore
by C. S. Graphics